THE
TRANSFORMATION
OF WORK?

THE TRANSFORMATION OF WORK?

Skill, flexibility and the labour process

Edited by
Stephen Wood

London
UNWIN HYMAN
Boston   Sydney   Wellington

Published by the Academic Division of
Unwin Hyman Ltd
15/17 Broadwick Street, London W1V 1FP, UK

Unwin Hyman Inc.,
8 Winchester Place, Winchester, Mass. 01890, USA

Allen & Unwin (Australia) Ltd,
8 Napier Street, North Sydney, NSW 2060, Australia

Allen & Unwin (New Zealand) Ltd in association with the Port Nicholson
Press Ltd,
Compusales Building, 75 Ghuznee Street, Wellington 1, New Zealand.

First published in 1989

British Library Cataloguing in Publication Data
The transformation of work? : skill,
   flexibility and the labour process.
   1. Work. Organisation
   I. Wood, Stephen, 1948–
306'.36

   ISBN 0-04-445356-6
        0-04-445357-4 PBK

Library of Congress Cataloging in Publication Data
The Transformation of Work?
   Bibliography: p.
   Includes index.
   1. Labor supply – Effect of technical innovations
on.   2. Machinery in industry.   3. Division of labor.
4. Quality of work life.   5. Work. I. Wood, Stephen G.
HD6331.T73   1989   331.25   89-5649
ISBN 0-04-445356-6
ISBN 0-04-445357-4 (pbk.)

Typeset in 10 on 11 point Bembo by Saxon Printing Ltd, Derby, and
printed in Great Britain by Billing and Sons, London and Worcester

Contents

List of Figures

List of Tables

List of Contributors

Stephen Wood is Senior Lecturer in Industrial Relations at the London School of Economics, England, and was a Research Associate at the Center for European Studies, at Harvard University, 1984–5 and Visiting Professor, University Rio Grande du Sul, Brazil, Autumn, 1985, and University of Pernambuco, Brazil, Summer, 1988. He was a member of the British team on the MIT Future of the Automobile Industry Project, and has carried out other comparative projects, including an Anglo–German project on employers' hiring practices. He is a member of the Editorial Boards of the *British Journal of Industrial Relations,* and *Work, Employment and Society.* He has written or edited several books including *The Degradation of Work?* (Hutchinson, 1982); (with D. Marsden, T. Morris and P. Willman) *The Car Industry* (Tavistock, 1985); (with S. Allen, K. Purcell and A. Waton) *The Changing Experience of Employment* (Macmillan, 1986); (with P. Windolf) *ecruitment and Selection in the Labour Market* (Gower, 1988). Currently he is completing a project on productivity change in the British coal mining industry since the 1984–5 strike.

Peter Albin is Professor of Economics at the City University of New York where he is also Director of the Center for Study of System Structure and Industrial Complexity. His publications include *Analysis of Complex Socioeconomic Systems* (Lexington: D.C. Heath, 1975), *Progress Without Poverty* (New York: Basic Books, 1978) and numerous articles.

Eileen Appelbaum is Professor of Economics at Temple University and holds a concurrent appointment at the Wissenschaftszentrum Berlin. She writes on issues related to the employment of women and on technology and work; and has served as a consultant to the US Congress, Office of Technology Assessment, on several volumes including *Programmable Automation Technologies in Manufacturing* (1984) and *Automation of America's Offices* (1985).

Christian Berggren gained his BA in sociology at the University of Stockholm in 1979 after working in the engineering industry for several years. Since 1982 he has been a researcher at the Work Science Department of the Royal Institute of Technology in Sweden. During the 1980s the major part of his research has been devoted to studies of the automative industry, new rationalization strategies and changes in technology, organization and work conditions.

Michael Burawoy teaches at the University of California, Berkeley and is the author of *Manufacturing Consent* (University of Chicago Press, 1979) and *The Politics of Production* (Verso, 1985).

William Cavestro gained his Ph.D in economics from Grenoble University, France. He is co-author of a book *Technologies nouvelles, nouveau travail* (Fédération de l'Education Nationale Ed, 1987). He is currently a Senior Lecturer in Economics at the University of Grenoble.

Rod Coombs is a Senior Lecturer at the Manchester School of Management, the University of Manchester Institute of Science and Technology. His research interests are centred on the economic and sociological analysis of technological change. He is co-author of *Technology, Economic Growth and the Labour Process* (Macmillan, 1985).

Ken Green is a Lecturer at the Manchester School of Management, the University of Manchester Institute of Science and Technology. He lectured in technology policy at Manchester University from 1973-88. He is co-author of *Research and Technology as Economic Activities* (Butterworth, 1977), *The Effects of Micro-electronic Technologies on Employment Prospects* (Gower, 1980) and, most recently, *Technology, Economic Growth and the Labour Process* (Macmillan, 1985). He is currently researching into medical technology policy.

Jane Jenson is a Professor of Political Science at Carleton University in Ottawa, Canada and a Research Associate of the Center for European Studies, Harvard University. She has written extensively on French politics, with particular attention to the parties of the Left and to social movements. A current research interest is the gendering process in welfare state societies. In addition to numerous articles in journals and edited books, she is the author of *The View from Inside: A French Communist Cell in Crisis* (University of California, 1984) with G. Ross, and *Crisis, Challenge and Change: Party and Class in Canada Revisited* (Carleton University Press, 1988) with J. Brodie. She is also co-editor of *Behind the Lines: Gender and the Two World Wars* (Yale University Press, 1987) and *Feminization of the Labour Force: Paradoxes and Promises* (Polity, 1988).

Bryn Jones is an LSE sociology graduate and a University of Liverpool Ph.D. While lecturing in industrial sociology at Bath University since 1979, he has also been a visiting researcher at the University of Wisconsin, MIT and the University of Bologna. He is the author of articles on industrial relations, work organization and technological change and a forthcoming book to be published by Basil Blackwell, on flexible automation in Europe, Japan and the USA.

Ulrich Jürgens studied economics and political science at the Free University in Berlin and is presently employed as a full-time researcher at the Wissenschaftszentrum Berlin für Sozialforschung (Science Centre Berlin, Research Unit: Technology – Labour – Environment). His main publications are in the fields of state theory, social policy, industrial relations and new organizational and production concepts in manufacturing, especially in the auto industry.

Maryellen R. Kelley is an Assistant Professor of Management in the School of Urban and Public Affairs at Carnegie Mellon University and a Research Associate of the Program on Technology, Public Policy and Human Development at Harvard University where she is co-principal investigator of a major ongoing study of the state of computerized automation in U.S. manufacturing. She received her Ph.D in Management from the Sloan School at MIT and a Masters degree in City and Regional Planning from Harvard. Professor Kelley has published in *Industrial Relations, Industrial and Labor Relations Review* and *Human Systems Management*.

Sarah Kuhn gained her BA in Philosophy and Social Relations from Harvard University in 1974 and her Ph.D in Employment and Organization Studies in 1987 from the Massachusetts Institute of Technology. Her research has focused on work organization, new technology, industry structure, and public policy. She has taught at MIT and with the Women's Economic Literacy Project. Currently she is at the Stone Center at Wellesley College, managing a project on women in engineering at Digital Equipment Corporation.

Makoto Kumazawa is a Professor in the Department of Economics, Konan University, and gained his BA in 1961, his Ph.D in 1969, both from the Department of Economics of Kyoto University. He began his scholastic career as a lecturer at the Department of Economics of Konan University in 1966, and has remained there ever since. He has written many books in the field of industrial relations, including *Workers' Resistance from Within Labouring – Enterprise as a Community and Labour Union* (1972); *A State Within the State – Trade Unions under the Labour Government, 1964-1970 (1976)* and *Enduring Workers on Rationalized Shop-Floors – Working People in Recent Japan* (1986).

David Lee is Senior Lecturer in Sociology at the University of Essex. He has written numerous articles on education, training and occupational stratification and is the author (with Howard Newby) of *The Problem of Sociology*, Hutchinson, 1983.

János Lukács is a researcher at the Hungarian Academy of Science in the Institute of Sociology. He is currently researching into the impact of numerically-controlled machinery in Hungary.

Erica Schoenberger teaches in the Department of Geography and Environmental Engineering at The Johns Hopkins University and has degrees from Stanford University (BA, History) and the University of California at Berkeley (Masters and Ph.D, City and Regional Planning). She does research on the investment strategies of multinational corporations, especially regarding cross-investments among advanced industrial countries. She has also written on the electronics and automobile industries.

Sylvia Walby gained her BA from the University of Reading and her MA and Ph.D from the University of Essex. She has been Lecturer in Sociology at the University of Lancaster since 1979 and founding Director of the Women's Studies Research Centre there since 1984. She is author of *Patriarchy at Work* (Polity, 1986), joint author of *Localities, Class and Gender* (with the Lancaster Regionalism Group, 1985), *Contemporary British Society* (with N. Abercrombie, A. Warde, K. Soothill and J. Urry, Polity, 1988) and the forthcoming *Restructuring Class and Gender* (with the Lancaster Regionalism Group), author of the forthcoming *Theorising Patriarchy*, and editor of the forthcoming *Gender Segregation at Work*.

Richard Walker is Associate Professor of Geography, University of California, Berkeley. He received his doctorate from The Johns Hopkins University, under the direction of David Harvey, in 1977. He has written on diverse topics in geography, including urban history, environmental policy and philosophy, and has just completed a book on industrial location and regional growth with Michael Storper, *The Capitalist Imperative: Territory, Technology and Industrial Growth* (Basil Blackwell, 1989). He is co-coordinator of the Faculty for Human Rights in El Salvador and Central America.

Jun Yamada is a teacher in the Department of Evening Classes, Imamiya Technical Senior High School of Osaka. He gained his BA from the Department of Literature of Kyoto University in 1971, and majored in the history of German industrialization. After graduation, he took a one-year course of vocational training for sheet-metal processing, then joined a small sheet-metal workshop which specialized in prototype making of mainly electrical appliances. He passed the national skill test for sheet-metal craftsman in 1975 and continued to work for the workshop until he got the certificate of high-school teacher of English from Osaka City University in 1977. Published papers include: 'What is Workers' Control?' (included in *Workers' Autonomy on the Shopfloor*, ed. Makoto Kumazawa, 1982), 'Technology, Skill, Occupation – on the Debate over Braverman's *Labour and Monopoly Capital*' (1986). He also translated, in collaboration with Makoto Kumazawa, Paul E. Willis' *Learning to Labour*, and the Japanese version was published in 1985.

Acknowledgements

I would like to thank the following for their help and encouragement in the development of this book: Peter Albin, Eileen Appelbaum, Christian Berggren, Michael Burawoy, William Cavestro, Rod Coombs, Rosemary Crompton, Tony Elger, François Eyraud, Ken Green, Masaki Hayashi, Jane Jenson, Bryn Jones, Gareth Jones, Uli Jürgens, Maryellen Kelley, John Kelly, Sarah Kuhn, Jolanta Kulpinska, Makoto Kumazawa, David Lee, Kari Lilja, János Lukács, David Marsden, Marc Maurice, Ruth Milkman, Sylvia Roesch, Erica Schoenberger, Karen Thomsen, Sylvia Walby, Richard Walker and Jan Yamada. I am especially indebted to the following for their valuable comments on drafts of my chapter: John Atkinson, Stephen Dunn, Paul Edwards, Ken Green, Ben Harrison, Eddie Heery, Jane Jenson, Bryn Jones, Maryellen Kelley, John Kelly, David Lee, Kari Lilja, David Metcalf, Sylvia Roesch, Mari Sako, Erica Schoenberger, Agnes Simonyi, and Sylvia Walby.

I also owe a special thanks to Anne Morris for her typing and administrative assistance throughout this project, and Claire L'Enfant of Unwin Hyman for her considerable editorial assistance.

Stephen J. Wood

July 1988

1 The transformation of work?

STEPHEN WOOD

A fundamental transformation of work commenced in the 1980s: this is the memory which many commentators expect, or at least hope, to share as the end of the decade approaches. Businessmen, trade unionists, politicians and journalists have all joined in a debate about the changes in employment and labour practices thought to be necessary for advanced capitalist economies to overcome the economic crisis which characterized the early 1980s. This has also been an element of the reformist thrust in the Socialist countries, particularly in the Soviet Union.

In most industrialized countries the 'flexibility debate' (National Economic Development Office (NEDO), 1986: 4), concerned with changing rigidities in labour and employment patterns, has been an important element in industrial policy-making and industrial relations throughout most of the 1980s (see e.g. Metcalf, 1986; Organisation for Economic Co-operation and Development, 1986; Shackleton, 1985). Governments have debated ways of reducing labour market (including pay) rigidity as well as overall organizational flexibility; managements have been concerned with job flexibility, multi-skilling and increasing their ability to hire and fire; while trade unionists and socialist parties have debated their stance towards the new production concepts and employee involvement. Attention has particularly been given to two types of flexibility. First, what Atkinson and Meager (Atkinson, 1985, 1988; National Economic Development Office (NEDO) 1986: 3) call numerical flexibility or Streeck (987: 290) terms external flexibility which is concerned with enhancing the firm's ability to adjust labour inputs to fluctuations in output. Second, functional (or internal) flexibility – which is about what workers 'do and consists of a firm's ability to adjust and deploy the skills of its employees to match the tasks required by its changing workload, production methods and/ or technology' (NEDO, 1986:4). Allied to both is pay flexibility, which is concerned with a firm's ability to adjust labour costs, particularly pay, to changing market (both product and labour) conditions.

The precise form of the flexibility debate has varied among countries, depending on the prevailing types of flexibility. In Japan, for example, it began after the 1973 oil shock with the *genryō-keiei* (the slimming management debate) and because of the ease of mobility within plants (internal flexibility) has recently concentrated on how to handle reductions in labour demand, whereas in the USA attention has especially centred on changing work rules which are thought to inhibit intra-organizational job mobility. In Britain, while both emphases have been present, because of the relative ease with which employers can make redundancies, aided by the distinctive 'voluntary' redundancy system, much of the concern has been with the balance between non-standard and regular contracts.

In Britain also considerable attention has been given to the notion of the flexible firm developed at the Institute of Manpower Studies, principally by Atkinson (hereafter the Atkinson model). This outlines the combination of practices which would enable organizations to adjust to market and technological changes 'more quickly, smoothly and cheaply' (NEDO, 1986: 83). Apart from numerical and functional flexibility, the flexible firm will aim for pay flexibility, and use 'distancing strategies' which involve 'the displacement of employment contracts by commercial ones, as exemplified by subcontracting' (ibid.: 9). The flexible firm has many similarities with the primary Japanese firms, with functional flexibility being provided by core workers and numerical flexibility through the use of both temporary workers and subcontractors. Nevertheless in the Western version lifetime employment guarantees for core workers or close long-term relationships between suppliers and customers are not given prominence. Atkinson's model has particularly attracted attention as a possible analytical framework for 'the main parameters of change' (ibid.: 3) in employment practices *and* as a normative tool to help managements plan new strategies, as well as trade unionists to react to them.

Much academic discussion has mirrored the flexibility vogue. Some prominent writers have argued that we have been witnessing in the 1980s the beginnings of a major change of the economic, or at least the production, regime as organizations face a much 'more unstable and uncertain' environment (Piore, 1986.: 162). The old system which many characterize as a mass production regime is giving way to a new basis of production rooted in the more flexible new technologies and working methods (Adler, 1985b; Beaumont, 1987; Brodner, 1985; Katz, 1985; Kern and Schumann, 1984, 1987, 1989; Kochan et al., 1986; Piore and Sabel, 1984; Sabel, 1982; Streeck, 1987; Tolliday and Zeitlin, 1986). The outcome of firms'. responding to more fragmented consumer tastes and the opportunities provided by new technology will be increased product differentiation and a proliferation of specialist production, with even assembly-line methods being modified or abandoned in favour of more integrated and fulfilling workplaces.

In such discussion, Taylorism – that management strategy which aimed to have tight pre-set specifications of tasks embedded in a high division of labour – is treated as the benchmark against which change is judged. Present concerns with flexibility herald a rupture with the assumed past domination of Taylorist and Fordist methods, themselves often automatically associated with mass production. According to the Americans Piore and Sabel (1984) the result will be what they call flexible specialization, or Kern and Schumann (1984) from West Germany label the end of the division of labour, Tolliday and Zeitlin (1986) in Britain the end of Fordism. Although there are differences in emphasis between such writers they can be treated as having developed a new perspective around the new technology (hereafter called flexible specialization theory in accordance with the usage of Piore and Sabel). It offers a new basis for upgrading earlier theories of post-industrialism predicted, as it stresses the potential of the new technology to increase flexibility and skill levels and offer more rewarding work.

In the 1970s, by contrast, Braverman's (1974) deskilling thesis argued that there could be no end to Taylorism without an end of capitalism. Deskilled workforces inevitably result from management's compulsion to assert direct control over workers. The implication of this deskilling thesis – also known as orthodox labour process theory – is that the main transformation of work under capitalism took place with the advent of mass production and Taylorist methods. In manufacturing the key period in many countries was the inter-war period. The contemporary relevance of such theories lay in the post-war rise of the service and tertiary sector. For in the 1970s we were witnessing the Taylorization of office and other service work. In manufacturing, further gains for capitalists could only come about through automation or relocation to the newly developing countries. The rise of such new technologies as numerically controlled machines in manufacturing were designed to arrest any remaining autonomy and control skilled workers may have had. Given that Taylorism is effectively treated as *the* central strategy for managerial control in capitalism, no further developments of an anti-Taylorist character are possible (Wood and Kelly, 1982: 87); no possible transformation of work is conceivable within this historical form outside of the dispersion of Taylorism throughout the economy.

Between the two extremes of labour process theory and Piore and Sabel's flexible specialization theory[1] lies the possibility of transformations *within* Fordism and Taylorism. The term neo-Fordism has been coined by some to refer to this. Fordist production methods have reached their limits in that no further productivity gains are possible without fundamental changes in production practices. Neo-Fordism refers to various processes by which this 'crisis of Fordism' may be overcome, principally by changing fundamentally one or other of the level of automation, task structures of firms, or the spatial division of labour.

The flexibility issue can be debated within the social sciences in a number of ways. First, such a debate could critically evaluate the 'flexibility debate' of the practioners. Thus far this has centred on the extent to which changes are occurring and has increasingly crystallized around core-periphery models such as Atkinson's. Second, it can be treated as a debate between labour process and flexible specialization theories, or – put in substantive terms – about the continuity of Fordism versus the emergence of flexible specialization. Third, it could be concerned to explore more fully the space between Fordism and flexible specialization and particularly the models of neo-Fordism. Fourth, the debate might be taken further and ask questions about the conceptions underlying the social scientific theories to which we have already referred and which dominate discussion. The 'flexibility debate' can then be incorporated into a wider remapping of the terrain of industrial sociology in the light of some of the current changes, such as computerized technologies, advanced telecommunications, new managerial conceptions, and the intensified internationalization of the economy.

What follows involves all the four possible dimensions of the debate. The structure of this opening chapter mirrors these; it opens with a discussion of the flexible firm model, continues with the flexibility versus Fordism issue, follows with a consideration of neo-Fordism and finally it concludes by sketching some of the issues involved in a remapping of the debate. The prime aim of this introductory chapter is to discuss some of the main parameters and terms of the debate and to introduce some of the issues to which the book is directed. It concludes with a brief outline of the structure of the remainder of the book. The book is based on the view that the academic flexibility debate should not simply mirror that of practitioners. Its starting point is the debate between the two (deskilling and upgrading) scenarios. But, it attempts to avoid the stereotypical positions to which polarized debate all too often gravitates. First, it critically evaluates some of the underlying issues of both theses and the empirical support for them. Second, it seeks to encourage debate between the poles and about the fundamental concepts which have thus far constituted the terrain of debate. Third, it presents research on many of the issues underlying the study of work organizations, skill and flexibility. The fundamental objective of the book is to contribute to these more telling versions of the flexibility debate. Overall it will reinforce the view that the quest for general trends about the development of skills levels, or general conclusions about the impact of technologies, is likely to be in vain and misleading (Wood, 1982:18). It is not likely to do justice to all the various developments that are under way or to the possible range of scenarios for the future.

Debating the flexible firm model

Atkinsons's approach is distinctive because he is particularly concerned with the extent to which there is an explicit strategy on the part of employers to become more flexible and develop more of a Japanese approach to labour utilization and subcontracting. If firms are flexible, they will extend subcontracting and other forms of distancing, as Atkinson calls it. Accordingly, they will also segment their workforces more, having a core workforce which is multi-skilled and functionally flexible, and a peripheral workforce which is more disposable, with fewer employment rights, facilitated through such practices as temporary employment, short-term contracts and part-time working.

Atkinson's model may be linked to the issue of skill levels by assuming that high-skilled jobs are in the core and low-skilled Taylorist jobs at the periphery. We might even link Atkinson's model to the debate about labour process and flexible specialization theory and suggest that there is a general and clear tendency towards an intensified dualism, as Goldthorpe (1984, 1985) and others (Harrison and Bluestone, 1988; Harris, 1987; Pfeffer and Baron, 1988; Christopherson and Storper, 1989) have suggested: flexible work situations characterize the core and Fordism remains and is being intensified at the periphery. We might also be tempted to introduce gender into the picture and suggest that while restructuring may mean more flexible and demanding work for men it may imply something quite different for women – more intensification, deskilling and control. In this way dualistic models may be seen as an attempt to combine both flexibility specialization and labour process theories.

Nevertheless, this may be too neat and misleading: what if flexible specialization is not happening to any significant extent, even in the core? What of the many men with 'casual' contracts in, for example, construction and catering? What of the skills utilized by women (Cockburn, 1983; Dex, 1985: 100–1; Wood, 1987; see also Chapter 7 below)? We must acknowledge also a number of potential pitfalls in the Atkinson model. Several have been raised. First, the identification of the core can, so it is argued (Pollert 1987:17), easily become circular: core workers have secure employment, and the fact of such employment is used as evidence for the presence of a core. If the core is more clearly defined by both its employment status (and especially its security and legal rights) and its tasks, there is a problem because some groups may have relatively secure employment but not be treated as part of the core of the business; whilst such 'peripheral' workers as part-time women workers in retailing, may be central to the functioning and profitability of the business. Part-time work should not necessarily be treated in all cases as peripheral, and certainly not by definition, although Atkinson may be right to imply that most employers do treat their part-time workers exactly in this manner.

Atkinson puts stress on functional flexibility as the defining criteria of the core. But this itself creates problems, as it implies that part-time workers, subcontracted labour and distance working are all subject to tight and narrow job specifications, which may be far from the case. Many such jobs have highly diffuse specifications and obligations which enable considerable flexibility (see for example Cunnison's [1986] excellent account of wardens of shelter homes). Such criticisms may not be devastating for the model. It does mean, however, we must be absolutely clear about the referent of the terms core and periphery when we use them. For a worker in a subcontractor, for example, may be providing part of the numerical flexibility (through distancing) for the large flexible firm, but still be employed as a core worker by his or her employer (as for example in a systems house), although he or she may equally be employed on a peripheral basis (as in an office cleaning firm).

Second, there is the benchmark problem. If, for example, Friedman (1977) is right and the core–periphery model is useful for analysing past practices in at least some British firms in the post-war period, what is new? Pollert (1987:33) has asked if it is simply a continuation of the labour market segmentation by gender, race and age, and of a wide repertoire of management strategies, including lowering labour costs and rationalization. This is perhaps to go too far: for Atkinson's speculation is that the extent to which firms are pursuing functional and numerical flexibility is new; the exploitation of weakened trade unions to bring about such changes is new; and the intention of designing firms in the image of the flexible firm model is new.

So – thirdly – the main empirical question is indeed the extent to which firms are moving towards the flexible firm model. This itself has a number of dimensions: how many firms are attempting to increase their flexibility? To what degree are individual firms increasing their flexibility? And, finally, are firms consciously pursuing a core–periphery model? There is no denying that managements in key manufacturing sectors in most economies have given considerable attention in the 1980s to increased functional flexibility, especially amongst their skilled workforces, as well as to enhancing numerical flexibility. In certain sectors firms may be changing their practices to explicitly increase functional flexibility and multi-skilling (as is clear in the car industry (Katz, 1985; Wood, 1988a) or from the several reported cases, e.g. Hendry and Pettigrew, 1988). This was, for example, a major source of a dispute at Ford in the UK in 1987–8, and inspiration for their world-wide 'employee involvement' strategy.

Whilst the numbers of temporary workers and others in forms of non-standard working such as homeworking are small there is evidence of some increase in the 1980s in most industrialized countries (see e.g. Appelbaum, 1989; Dale and Bamford, 1988; Marginson *et al.*, 1988:215). In some sectors, at least in Britain, there was some increased use of subcontracting in the early 1980s, either for peripheral functions such as security and catering as in British Leyland (as it was then) or for maintenance and other 'service' roles (Fevre, 1986; Rajan 1987). In retailing, again at least in Britain, there has been a trend towards the substitution of part-time for full-time workers, as some major retailers have had a quite explicit policy of replacing all full-time leavers with part-time equivalents. In certain 'greenfield sites' temporary workers have been used and more functional flexibility has been achieved than existed in existing sites in the same industry (or even firm). The great difference between Nissan's practices in its car plant in Tennessee in the United States and in the North-East of England and its existing rivals is a classic example of this. The ability of one UK chocolate manufacturer, Cadbury, to innovate even before we entered the 1980s, in a fresh site away from its traditional (Bournville) Birmingham base, has been well described, for example, by Whitaker (1986). Such examples are strongly influencing other firms, as is again illustrated by the attempts of all the major car companies throughout the world to bridge the gap between themselves and their Japanese rivals (Wood, 1988a, 1988c).

Atkinson is himself cautious about concluding any widespread adoption of the core–periphery model from his own empirical work in a sample of eighty British manufacturing and service firms. It would appear that for Atkinson the number of firms attempting some form of increased flexibility is large, the degree to which particular firms are pursuing all forms is not so great, whilst those explicitly replicating the model even less. He concludes that the focus of the increased flexibility will vary depending on the sector. Increasing numerical flexibility is more important than functional flexibility in services, whilst in manufacturing the emphasis is on functional flexibility. The extent of change within most firms remains limited. So for example all engineering firms may be pursuing some integration of mechanical and electrical maintenance roles but this may mean little more than an overlap of responsibilities and a partial broadening of training, and there has been no significant change in vertical job structures or development of fully–fledged, multi-skilled and trained craftsmen. The overall conclusion as of the mid-1980s is that 'flexibility has become an important theme in emerging corporate thinking' (Atkinson, 1985:26). In practice 'relatively few UK firms have explicitly and comprehensively reorganized their labour force on this basis' (Ibid.:28). Assuming this to be an accurate judgement there are at least two, not necessarily mutually exclusive, implications: that firms' practices do not follow in any smooth or direct way their strategies, or that, whilst the 'desire to increase flexibility' has been an important aspect of firms' evolving labour strategies in the 1980s, they have not necessarily embraced the 'core–periphery model', or even developed any coherent strategy for increasing flexibility. So it is important to ask whether the developments to which Atkinson refers could ever be part of a widespread explicit managerial strategy.

The problem of the strong version of the flexible firm model may well be that it over-emphasizes management's co-ordinated pursuit of flexibility, almost as if were an end in itself. Flexibility is only one managerial concern and cannot be abstracted from its other goals and areas of interest (MacInnes, 1987: 114; Pollert, 1987). Firms may be exploring ways of increasing functional flexibility or alternatively the use of part-time workers, without this meaning that they are pursuing all forms of flexibility.

Also, there may be certain sectors of the economy, for example, construction, in which the core–periphery model is most appropriate and in which it always existed to some extent. It may be precisely in these sectors that we have seen in the 1980s the most rigorous pursuit of the core–periphery model. My observations of the firms (twenty-four leading British firms) used as part of the LSE link programme suggest those firms who have sharpened their divide between core and peripheral employment in the mid-1980s and increased the latter (cf. Casey, 1988), as well as their distancing, were already operating on a somewhat similar basis before the 1980s. Atkinson is working with a model which assumes that firms will transform their strategies when faced with increasingly competitive markets and complex technology. If, however, there are sectors of the economy in which the model is deemed more appropriate, then any significant move towards it could be explained less by the switching of managerial strategies as by changes in the structure of the economy.

Structural change in the economy does seem important. For a large part of the growth of part-time workers, dominated by women, reflects the expansion of the service sector and is, as Walby says in Chapter 6, the continuation of the post-war trend for the female participation rate to increase. We should not neglect the sexual division of labour on which this practice is predicated. Why is it, for example, that banks and retailers, as they begin to set employment levels to meet fluctuations in the demand throughout the day and not orientated to the peak periods, can formulate new part-time shifts or plan to replace any full-timers who leave with part-timers on the certain expectation that a ready supply of such workers is available?

As Pollert says (1987), and Harrison and Bluestone (1988) confirm for the US, government policies may also be of considerable importance. Atkinson, at least in his reports, neglects the public sector and the impact of government policies – for example of privatization and deregulation. It may well be, as Pollert again (1987) suggests, that it is precisely in the public sector (past and present presumably, for the British case at least) that we have seen the emergence of new strategies along the core–periphery model. For example, in the British National Health Service a great deal of work has been subcontracted, although any increased functional flexibility could be very limited (Ascher, 1987; Cousins, 1988). Lee in Chapter 8 of this book shows the importance of the government's youth training and unemployment policies in the development of marginal workforces. In so far as the conceptual edifices utilized suppress such questions they underplay the significance of such policies, as well as of occupational segregation by gender (and race), which forms one of the basic continuities between the pre- and post-1980 eras (see Walby, Chapter 6 below). This suggests that debate about flexibility must go beyond the emphasis on managerial strategy perhaps inevitably implicit in frameworks designed to both help description and influence policy developments. The flexible firm is too descriptive and neglectful of what underpins changing employment practices to provide anything more than a reference point for social scientists. Essentially the model serves the function of an ideal type. Consequently debating it will never get much beyond the question of its utility and an assessment of the extent to which firms approximate to it, with all the usual provisos and uncertainties surrounding such ideal-type models.

Flexibility versus Fordism

Labour process theory

When flexible specialization theses with their emphasis on rupture bloomed in the mid-1980s, debate tended to polarize around their scenarios of reskilling and Braverman's deskilling model which implied an underlying continuity. This polarization was encouraged as much by the proponents of flexible specialization as it was by their opponents. There have subsequently appeared some pretty fundamental defences of labour process theory (Armstrong, 1988; S. Cohen, 1987; Shaiken, 1984; Thompson, 1989), which try to indicate, by, for example, reasserting that the control of labour will always be a basic motive of capitalist managements, how Braverman's thesis may still be the most pertinent. Consequently for Braverman's supporters any restructuring and managerial initiatives will always involve labour intensification and the enhancement of managerial control. The great growth of service work in the post-war era represents no fundamental change, as is for example assumed in post-industrialization theories (see e.g. Bell, 1974). Indeed, one of Braverman's major motivations for his book was indeed to argue against them. He did this principally by attempting to show that white-collar work is subject to the same process of Taylorism as manual work.

Furthermore, for labour process theory, technology has no influence on work organization independently of management's need to control. The new technology is significant in so far as control is built into its very nuts and bolts, or to be more accurate wires and chips (Noble, 1977, 1979). Moreover, according to Braverman's argument, the impression given by the new forms of management such as quality of work life initiatives and quality circles that Taylorism is being abandoned is deceptive. They are essentially managerial responses to new problems of control or attempts to destroy remaining areas of worker control. Labour process writers also tend to contest the extent to which significant managerial reorganizations are really under way. They may at times appear to be arguing that the new initiatives do not represent breaks away from the basic Fordist model and/or that there are not really many taking place anyway. The debate then becomes polarized on empirical grounds, as well as theoretically.

Proponents of labour process theory are rightly cautious about over-reacting to any seemingly new organizational and technological initiatives and not getting caught in the trap of managerial hype. But there is a danger of over-reacting to this, and denying that there is anything much at all in the flexibility vogue, or at best reducing it to a simple matter of yet another control mechanism. Polarized debate can at certain times be very useful, especially when there is a large body of conflicting and messy empirical research in an area. In this case there is, however, a risk of underplaying the various criticisms of the two positions, with the associated danger of assuming that the criticisms of one mirror the strengths of the other, and any criticism of one amounts to an acceptance of the other.

Criticisms of labour process theory

Criticisms of Braverman's labour process theory are well rehearsed[2]: his neglect of worker resistance, the element of active partiipation required in most production systems, and the possibility of alternatives to Taylorism even in capitalism. His excessive focus on management's labour problem and the structures of control in the labour process is of crucial importance to all these and Braverman's over-reliance on Taylorism as his central concept has been a core preoccupation of many critics. First, several authors urge that we distinguish Taylorism from Fordism. The former is a more limited concept than the latter and is principally concerned with shop-floor labour management through the techniques of work study used to assure economy in performing specific tasks. It is, as indeed Braverman assumes, an approach 'by which management seeks a monopoly of knowledge over how production processes should be organised' (Blackburn *et al.*, 1985: 43). Fordism is a more wide-ranging strategy of organizing production which involves linear work sequencing, the moving assembly line, the use and refinement of dedicated machinery, and the design of parts to ease assembly and minimize fitting. Fordism may involve highly Taylorized fragmented jobs, but, as Walker says in Chapter 3 below (p72), it is more than Taylorism writ large. Taylorism may be and has been applied in small – and medium – batch production, but Fordism is a strategy of work organization and mechanization orientated to mass production and mass marketing. Fordism was aimed at the cheap mass production of technically complex products by utilizing economies of scale and innovations in product design and assembly techniques: a straight deskilling strategy would hardly have been adequate for this.

Second, it is argued that Taylorism was not as uniformly applied as Braverman implied. Its precise form varied between countries, sectors and firms (Wood and Kelly, 1982: 80), and it has been implemented within a number of quite different strategic frameworks and industrial relations contexts. It is thus a mistake to assume that the only framework in which it has been adapted is Fordism, or that this itself has not taken on different forms (cf. Tolliday and Zeitlin, 1986).

Third, there is the whole issue of 'new' forms of work organization and Braverman's inflation of Taylorism so that he rules out non-Taylorist developments within capitalism. A major aspect of the labour process debate has concerned the extent and nature of so-called alternatives to Taylorism (Wood, 1987). For some, Braverman is broadly right in that management's prime aim is control and it will only resort to tactics which enhance workers' autonomy – what Friedman (1977) calls responsible autonomy strategies – when workers' resistance and power is high, as when labour is relatively scarce. For others, the non-Taylorist forms of management reflect developments in technology and products, and are less concerned with management's so-called labour problem (Blackburn, *et al* ., 1985; Kelly, 1982; Littler, 1985).

Flexible specialization

Flexible specialization theory took the various arguments about alternatives to Taylorism and packaged them in a new extreme approach.[3] According to flexible specialization theory the market and technological conditions for Taylorism no longer exist. In contrast to labour process theory its advocates detect in the new managerial initiatives a break with managements' past orientation to control and intensification. Functional flexibility, teamworking, quality of work life programmes and Japanese-style quality circles (groups of workers who meet to discuss improvements in the work system and their jobs) all herald a new regime of production rooted in the new technology. We are witnessing the new flexibly specialized firm which can quickly respond to sudden changes in costs, market opportunities and/or new technologies, through adopting flexible, multi-purpose equipment and creating a flexible, re-integrated and co-operative workforce free of the shackles of rigid job specifications, narrow job-centred orientations and excessive regulation and control.

Accordingly initiatives to increase involvement and invert the division of labour reflect managements' attempts to react particularly to changing market and technological factors. In a nutshell, the argument is that there is a need for managements in designing work organization to mirror the increased differentiation of consumer demand and the flexibility of the technology. In effect it is saying that the job redesign and increased participation that the normative organizational theorists had long been campaigning for are becoming a reality (cf. Hirschhorn, 1984; Kochan, *et al* ., 1986; Walton, 1985). They have though 'less to do with concern for the workers' contentedness than with the need to reduce the rigidity of existing assembly procedures' (Sabel, 1982:213).

Mass production is the benchmark of the past. So the flexible specialization theory shares a common starting point with the labour process theory: the importance in the twentieth century of mass production and automation within management concerns. The starting point is the extreme Taylorist division of labour. Moreover the model of it is similar to that offered by Braverman. It is as if Braverman got it right for the past, but his analysis is now – like his central object of study, Taylorism – obsolete. Kern and Schumann (1987: 154–5), in a similar vein to Braverman, write that throughout much of this century 'the concept of mass production was promoted as the generally accepted model of capitalist rationality', and managements were inspired 'by the conviction that workers are an obstacle to production which should be removed by technical means as much as possible'. The labour problem was defined as one of labour control and substituting workers by machinery. Work was viewed 'only from the perspective of control and regulation' and the solution was 'the most restrictive organization ...one can imagine' (ibid.: 155). Such ideas became so deeply embedded in the minds of managers, accountants and engineers, so the argument goes, that they took them to their logical extremes and began seeking a fully automatized, worker-less factory. Now, so Kern and Schumann (1984, 1987, 1989), Piore and Sabel (1984) and others argue, a redefinition by management of their labour problem is taking place: labour is no longer seen as so expendable. There is an increasing realization of the 'qualitative significance of human work performance' (Kern and Schumann, 1987: 160); a growing recognition of the problems created by highly restrictive work organizations and the limits they may place on productivity growth; as well as an acknowledgement of the demands the new technologies make for more skilled and integrated workforces.

Whilst Piore and Sabel reject iron laws of historical necessity and technological determinism, they give a strong impression that once a firm has gone down a particular technological route, the work organization and skill profile are relatively settled, or at least their optimum forms. The crucial choice, when there is an industrial divide (to use the terms of their title), concerns technology. Moreover, this choice is conceived by Piore and Sabel at the societal level – and this may well differentiate them from other writers (e.g. Sorge and Streeck, 1988) in the same broad genre – and concerns what they call the technological paradigm. This then becomes the dominant form of production. At certain moments, which by implication are rare, 'the path of technological development is at issue' (Piore and Sabel, 1984: 5). Piore and Sabel operate, as Williams, Cutler *et al.* (1987) amplify so well, with a simple dichotomous choice between craft and mass production. Sometime in the early part of this century, the choice was made in favour of mass production. But now with what Piore and Sabel see as the saturation of demand, fragmentation of markets, and fresh technological opportunities, the technological paradigm is again at issue, with the distinct possibility of a revival of craft production.

Economies of scale, so central to the Fordist conception, no longer need be such a determining force in competitive advantage. The new technology offers the possibility of reducing break-even points, so small- and medium-batch production become more viable even in what were once exclusively mass-production industries. Also it offers economies of scope, as they have become known, which refer to the flexible organization of production and use of equipment so that the firm can, regardless of its size, switch production from one batch of products to another relatively costlessly and hence serve relatively small markets, regardless of their size (see Mahon, 1987: 54). The emerging flexible specialization can then reverse the previous pattern of increased concentration and the dominance of large firms in the economy. There will be a re-emergence of what Sabel (1989) calls 'regional economies' built around a network of flexible firms in which no one firm is dominant, or by implication, especially large. At this point the argument often becomes normative and indeed the flexible specialization thesis is very much an intellectual manifesto, or what the French term a *traité* [which aims to provide both 'comprehensive information...(and) to offer a kind of normative scaffolding of knowledge' (Monjardet, 1987: 119)]. Its normative dimension itself has two elements. It is concerned, as such *traités* are, to foster a reorientation of academic thought, so that more prominence is given to small firms and networks amongst firms, as well as flexibility rather than control. It also aims to encourage the development of flexible specialization as an alternative to the existing strategies of large enterprises, with their assumed emphasis on the standardization and internationalization of production, and centralization of finance, design and administration. Flexible specialization is seen as stimulating both a revival of the small-scale craft sector and a restructuring of the large oligopolies which dominated the mass production era.

A recurring example of what flexible specialization can replace is the 'world car strategy'[4] of the major car producers according to which cars will be designed in a small number of firms and in only one or two centres, and the increasing outsourcing and use of newly industrialized countries will result in a division between the type of work done in these countries and the traditional primary countries. Not only, so Piore and Sabel (1984) claim, will flexible specialization be more efficient and viable than such strategies, but it can provide for a more decentralized and hence democratic solution to the enduring economic crisis, what they (ibid: 303-6) call yeoman democracy.

Political forces and specific societal conditions are assumed to intervene in the processes by which firms adapt to the new 'imperatives'. First conditions in some countries are assumed to make it easier for them to adopt the new 'manufacturing policy' (Lane, 1988). Second, in some discussions it is hypothesized that the outcomes of flexible specialization may sometimes differ between societies and political regimes, so in some cases a polarization of income and skills may follow, whilst not in others (Mahon, 1987). There are two possible adaptations: a kind of neo-liberal version and a more socialist one – the former will not necessarily have a democratizing effect and may well lead to an increased polarization of incomes, skill and working conditions. It cannot, even in Piore and Sabel's terms, be ruled out that the political forces do not 'opt' for the new technological paradigm. Although this is a possibility, the flexible specialization argument is stacked against this eventuality. There is a new basis for a mutuality of interest between managements and workers rooted in the upgrading assumed to follow from the functional flexibility inherent to the new paradigm.

Moreover, at least to Sabel (1984), the alternatives such as the world car strategy are not viable, and have already shown themselves to have failed. Using rather dramatic terminology he claims the world car 'strategy .. collapsed under its own weight' (ibid: 348) and has effectively been abandoned by the mass producers. It is at this point that the argument no longer appears to rest on political forces for it is simply a matter of economics: what the market will or will not validate. Political or societal conditions then are treated as constraints on the adoption of the rationality of flexible specialization. The task then is a comparative study of the kind of conditions that favour adoption, much as Lane (1988), Sorge and Warner (1986), and Streeck and Hoff (1983) have done. Emphasis thus far has been especially given to industrial relations and training systems, though the question of managerial traditions clearly lurks behind these.

Critical evaluation of flexible specialization

Because of its normative orientation, as well as the contingent nature of many of the arguments, it is not easy to devise conclusive tests of the flexible specialization thesis which will enable refutation or verification. Is, for example, the argument about the potential or the real effects of new technology, or is it more fundamentally about the need to transform social relations and develop networks of firms to take advantage of the new technology? As Block (1985: 500) notes, the notion of flexible specialization is not very well specified. What should be the appropriate referent, the firm or the industry? If it is the firm, the extreme version, as Hyman (1988: 49) characterizes it, would imply a move to a world of quasi-bespoke production concerned with gratifying fleeting market whims as basic needs are assumed to be increasingly saturated and others are constantly changing. If the central unit of analysis is the industry or locality, the emphasis would be more on the specialized nature of each firm's production, and the network between firms as the source of flexibility, although it is assumed that such firms have considerable functional, if not external, flexibility. According to this emphasis flexible specialization is interpreted (see for example, Christopherson and Storper, 1989) as the development of vertically disintegrated industries in which individual firms are specialized but the complex as a whole is flexible – its mix of output can be changed by altering the group of firms participating in the production of any particular output.

There can, however, be taken to be a core argument that, in so far as firms and countries are facing up to the increased fragmentation in consumer markets and do adopt the new technology, flexible specialization will prevail and upgraded flexible workforces will follow. The danger then is that a whole set of associations are assumed and not explored, as increasing fragmentation and complexity in the product market are assumed to 'demand' flexible technology which in turn 'demands' the 'flexible' worker, assumed to be a kind of multi-skilled craftsman. The flexible specialization thesis can be questioned at each stage of this chain of argument.

First, are consumer tastes really becoming more differentiated, or is it largely a matter of the availability of more diversified products? Are the changes in markets demand- or supply-led? Are we not seeing firms simply creating a more 'defined' variety (Galjaard, 1982), albeit perhaps at an increasing rate? Are all markets necessarily becoming more fragmented and is product differentiation substantially increasing? Niche marketing may be on the increase but is it necessarily increasing the demand for the 'industry' as whole, or reducing the elasticity of substitution for given 'products'? Doubts have in fact been cast upon the idea of the maturity of mass-consumption products as it appears that the production of such consumer products as cars and televisions has not peaked (Williams, Cutler, *et al.*, 1987). Moreover, exactly how much flexibility or specialization are we talking about? The lack of specificity of the central concept is a particular problem in the case of conventional manufacturing sectors. For example, in the case of car plants – one of the central examples used by proponents of flexible specialization – is flexibility simply the ability to alternate styles, product models in the same size range, models of significantly different size ranges, cars and trucks, or cars one day or week, another product the next?

Second, is computer technology and the latest round of micro-electronics necessarily being used to increase product-mix flexibility? Does it necessarily reduce the break-even point and make economies of scale less important? How widespread are flexible manufacturing systems? Have not improved quality, cost-reduction and integration been the major motivations for firms' introducing new technology? Has there not been an over-reaction to the new technology within social science, as it has concentrated on what Hirschhorn (1984) terms its cybernetic qualities, namely its abilities to bring self-correction and speedy adjustment to what were in the past relatively rigid manufacturing systems? Flexible specialization theory is in danger of assuming that all the new technology is inherently flexible and that this flexible potential is being fully used. It may also neglect the problems of implementation and the gradual way in which the new technology has been introduced – one obvious reason being that capital is lumpy and in limited supply. The emphasis in much manufacture is on increasing routing, production, volume and programming flexibility within given capital installations and not primarily on product flexibility.[5] In Japan (and probably elsewhere) some engineering firms, for example, have used dedicated machines more effectively by improving the linkages between them (routing flexibility), whilst potentially flexible machinery is being used non-flexibly to reap certain other benefits such as improved quality. The evidence thus far is that flexible manufacturing systems, however defined, are not, even in Japan, being used to the extent that flexible specialization theorists imply (Adler, n.d; Jones 1987; Kelley, 1986). Managements have, as Williams, Cutler, *et al.* (1987) stress, some choice about the degree and type of flexibility they desire when purchasing capital equipment. Furthermore, both managers and researchers stress features of the new technology other than its flexibility: its ability to considerably improve quality, reduce waste, and enhance integration, co-ordination and control of production.

Also the overemphasis on the flexible quality of the new technology reflects an over-concentration on the computer at the expense of other factors such as factory layouts, disposable tools and product design. We must certainly be clear about what 'new technology' we are talking about. The *kanban* (just-in-time) system – whilst increasingly reliant on the computer – illustrates this well as it led to new ideas about factory design so, for example, delivery lorries can arrive at the exact place in the production process where their cargoes are needed. The differentiation among technological, product and material changes is important. It may well be, for example, that the greater use of steel alloy metals and ceramic tools will have more impact on production processes, the quality of work and skill levels than any computer-controlled machinery. Many of the significant developments in established industries are indeed related to changes in materials and products. So, whilst the tacit skills of previous technological regimes may be required to successfully adapt the new technology in certain circumstances (cf. Jones and Wood, 1984), completely new materials and processes may equally render them redundant. Technological developments also have implications for the design of products and parts. For example, the design of the second Volkswagen Golf car was influenced by the fact that it was going to be produced in a more automated setting. Developments in the service sector also illustrate the varying potential effects of new technology – increased integration, self-servicing, the creation of new products and quality standards – are all present here. Coombs and Green in Chapter 15 of this book show how new technologies have the potential to transform the health 'products' and means of administering health care. Their examples do not necessarily imply any greater flexibility or even less standardization. Service products are conspicuously absent in the flexible specialization literature thus far[6] (Block, 1985; Wood, 1988b). Yet in the service sector the new technology is perhaps having a greater effect than in manufacturing. In many services, for example, keying-in by customers, sales representatives and others may well totally do away with vast numbers of intermediate workers. Administrative work in particular may be transformed by information technology (Miles, 1988). Nevertheless, it is also in the service sector where we have probably seen the most dramatic growth of new types of monotonous and routinized labour, as well as labour intensification. The fast-food chains such as McDonald's provide an excellent example of this, as they tend to operate with a small administrative core and a large predominantly unskilled workforce.

Third, are the new patterns of work organization and the latest idiom of flexibility as big a rupture from Fordism as flexible specialization assumes? And, again, how pervasive are these innovations and are all jobs equally affected? Do they definitely increase the skill levels of all jobs? Are not many of the calls for functional flexibility largely directed either at those whose jobs are already relatively skilled or at simply increasing mobility between relatively unskilled jobs? Flexible technology, even if it is being adopted, may not necessarily, or in all instances, require a much greater degree of flexibility on the part of workers (Shaiken, *et al*, 1986; Wood, 1988a). Many of the jobs may still remain short-cycle tasks, and adding extra maintenance and inspection functions to semi-skilled jobs may not substantially alter them. There is certainly no guarantee that the transformation of jobs so they are less physical will in turn involve more mental work. For example, in steel-rolling mills the advent of new technologies and statistical process control has indirectly increased the range of products produced, but this does not appear, from my observations of two British plants, to have significantly increased the demands made upon workers or the level of intrinsic satisfaction offered to them. Moreover, technological developments are uneven and within many of these either new or old unskilled jobs remain which are often highly physical and routine, what some have called residual jobs. For example, in a highly automated ice cream plant, I observed, as the ice creams came down a conveyor there was a tendency for some of them to get stuck and two men were permanently required to move those that did, significantly using a rather primitive broom-like tool.

As part of the over-concentration on upgrading in the flexible specialization theory, some arguments imply that a new basis for a mutuality of interest between workers and managements exists, as both have a shared interest in flexible specialization. It is indeed 'predicated on collaboration' (Piore and Sabel, 1984: 278). The assumption appears to be that the new technology reverses the zero-sum situation assumed by labour process theory to be at the heart of the antagonism between managers and workers. The new technology can achieve both parties' objectives:

> the literature on new technologies and new production concepts is arguing that it is management itself that should be interested in diminishing the division of labour, in reintegrating tasks and functions and in improving the quality of work. In other words, it is suggested that, concerning the quality of work, the interests of management and workers are no longer necessarily antagonistic. (Dankbaar, 1988: 26)

The fact that managements introduce work restructuring for their own more conventional economic objectives may not, of course, rule out gains for workers and increased job satisfaction and autonomy. There is a potential overlapping of interests between managers and workers which the whole battery of co-operative schemes aimed at increasing commitment can build upon and indeed foster, especially in times of generalized economic crisis (Manwaring and Wood, 1985). There are, however, several reasons for doubting that a new mutuality of interests is emerging – not least that mutual dependency is not the same as common interests (Hyman, 1988: 54). Indeed we have to be cautious when using such terms as mutuality of interest, co-operation, consent, and consensus, and particularly sensitive to differences between them, as well as the precise referent of each – which interests, co-operation over what, for example? Nor is it so clear that any fresh managerial initiatives will produce a 'new' consensus, even if they do enhance co-operation.

For example, there may be cases where new production methods and increased managerially inspired acts of involvement may increase workers' leverage over management. For example, the increased mobility desired by management may give a basis for the workers concerned to restrict or bargain about mobility. Similarly having workers' 'participation' when introducing change and new technology may foster commitment as Littek (1986) suggests, but equally it might lead to a questioning of managements' legitimacy especially if they for whatever reason appear incompetent or uncertain. We also know that managements may increase information and involvement but *still* withhold vital, more telling, information about contradictory and damaging (for workers) developments which may lead to friction. For example, firms may increase the level of information and involvement offered to workers without, however, putting this in the context of other developments such as their joint ventures an increased foreign sourcing.

There is also the problem that functional flexibility may enhance the skill levels of some workers (though this cannot be taken for granted), whilst for many there remains only low-skilled and marginal employment. In Atkinson's model the numerical flexibility is, as we have seen, almost a condition for sustaining the functional flexibiliy of the core. Whilst not totally neglectful of the diversity in workforces, Piore and Sabel do appear to underplay its importance (cf. Pollert, 1988), especially when judged against the significance they have accorded it in their previous work (Doeringer and Piore, 1971; Sabel, 1982). In contrast Kern and Schumann have been explicit about the possibility of heightened segmentation following the new production concepts. They indeed talk of there being winners and losers resulting from the new flexible regime (Kern and Schumann, 1987).[7]

Part of the debate within flexible specialization theory, that is amongst writers who are broadly supportive of it, is, as I implied earlier, about the distribution of the benefits of flexible specialization. Polarization of income and new forms of deskilled work as a possible result of flexible specialization are acknowledged by some (Storper and Christopherson, 1988; Mahon, 1987; Streeck and Hoff, 1983), as they note that more work may become non-standard and peripheral. Within such a debate there still remains the underlying assumption that economies are adapting flexible specialization, and the issue is its effects and what mediates these. The tendency also remains for discussion to pivot around the new core workforce, the 'winners', in a potentially misleading way.

Piore and Sabel nevertheless are extreme, so their over-concentration on the potentialities of new technology in the 1980s means that there is a neglect of the job losses, unemployment, tightening of performance standards, labour intensification, changing employment contracts and reduction of the power of trade unions and workers' representatives which have characterized the decade – except in so far as their advocacy of flexible specialization is offering solutions to such problems. Piore and Sabel's break with Marxism is most pronounced and it is this perhaps as much as anything that led to the apparent polarization of debate. Yet, the two theories, as we have already noted, share Fordism as a common starting point. This makes the debate between flexible specialization and labour process theory easier, if not more profound. So, for example, questions about the Japanese management model which has attracted increasing attention in the 1980s are reduced to a simple matter of whether it is a continuation and perfection of Fordism or, alternatively, a complete rupture with it (cf Tolliday and Zeitlin, 1986: 20). From the flexible specialization perspective, given the success of Japan in the 1970s and 1980s, this then easily slides into an assumption that Japan had a head start in the flexibility game.[8] This illustrates perfectly the costs of constraining debate to such dichotomous choices. In this case some fairly obvious points about the Japanese management model are in danger of being side-stepped, in particular the way just-in-time and Japanese-style employee involvement represent basic innovations, without necessarily reversing all aspects of Taylorism or negating the central principles of mass production (Dohse *et al.*, 1985; Monden, 1981, 1983; Sayer, 1986b; Schonberger, 1982; Wood, 1989). There seem to be two ways of developing beyond the polarized debate. First, we can explore more fully the space between the two theories; second we can delve more deeply into some of the conceptual issues entailed in any debate about work organization. These are not, however, necessarily mutually exclusive. But if we take the former we need not question the adequacy of the common ground between labour process and flexible specialization theories, namely Fordism's domination of modern industrial production thus far. In contrast, taking the latter course involves confronting this assumption.

Neo–Fordism: between Fordism and flexibility

Neo–Fordism is a term used to describe recent attempts to go beyond Fordism, presumably without negating its fundamental principles. It attempts to overcome the problems of Taylor in a variety of ways: the restructuring of tasks, a quantum leap in automation, and increased internationalization of production. Adopting any one is often taken to be adopting a neo-Fordist strategy. There are different versions of neo–Fordism depending on which of the above paths is given most weight, and also whether it is seen as a transitional form unable to solve contemporary crises or more of an end-state (albeit within capitalism) which is potentially able to arrest what some see as a global crisis of capitalist accumulation. Above all else different explorations of neo-Fordism reflect theoretical departures. We can in fact detect a flexible specialization and labour process version. There is, nonetheless, a broad agreement on the essential dimensions of neo-Fordism.

At the job level, neo-Fordism involves reversing the existing division of labour, through the adoption, for example, of job enrichment and other schemes which may enhance productivity (Palloix, 1976). For Aglietta (1979), Blackburn, *et al.* (1985) and others the restructuring of tasks must go beyond a simple enrichment or combining of two previously separate tasks and hence involves organizing work around semi-autonomous or flexible work groups or teams. In neo-Fordist discussions of technology the emphasis is on the way increased automation enhances integration and overall co-ordination and control, and in so doing may profitably increase the product range of a given installation. The intensified internationalization is assumed to be along the lines of what Froebel *et al.* (1980) call the new international division of labour. This involves the major multinationals increasingly relocating production to what was previously the periphery, the southern hemisphere or southern Europe (Lipietz, 1982, 1985). For it is assumed that where production remained labour-intensive managements would switch production to low wage economies, such as Portugal and Greece. A prototypical example is the world car concept, as mentioned earlier.

Neo-Fordism in the hands of writers such as Aglietta (1979) forms part of what has become known as the French regulation school.[9] It is broader than a simple application of Braverman to the era of high-level automation and increased internationalism (Shaiken, 1984). The regulation school's concept of Fordism involved much more than the labour process. It was also applied at the societal level, to a specific regime of accumulation, and referred to both a paradigm of production and a pattern of consumption. The former is again characterized by the use of assembly-line methods being used to make standardized commodities. The latter is taken beyond the increasing homogeneity of consumption implied by mass marketing, as it concerns 'a way of life' (de Vroey, 1984: 52). Fordism both generated and requires the maintenance of sufficient aggregate demand to sustain the consumption of the mass-production goods through productivity-related pay increases. This in turn is often treated as requiring a particular form of 'Keynesian' politics. The crisis of Fordism is then more than simply a crisis of production; it has both an economic – a problem of aggregate demand resulting from stagnating mass production and a failure of the service sector to generate productivity improvements – and political dimension. Nevertheless at least in the early formulations of Aglietta (1979) changes in the production sphere are accorded a central role in solving the crisis, and more specifically rearrangements along neo-Fordist lines. The importance of managements' monopolizing conception *à la* Braverman remains central. Automation offers increased precision, flexibility and integration. But it further eliminates 'the need for skilled personnel' (Aglietta, 1979: 125) and deskilling of production work is further achieved as it literally, so the argument goes, only involves minding machines, that is simply testing their current functioning. The key for management is to have total domination of the programming of the computerized technology as well as of research and development and information processing and dissemination. At the end of the day managements must separate conception from execution for the 'regime of intensive accumulation to survive' (Aglietta, 1979: 126).

For regulation theorists neo–Fordism arises not so much directly from changes in demand or technology, as flexible specialization theory would have it, but from a crisis within production. Developments in work reflect a deeper problem within Fordism which must be addressed. The crisis of Taylorism or Fordism has arisen not because it has failed, but rather because it has been too successful. Although in some accounts allowance is made for one of Fordism's problems, workers' resistance, the emphasis is placed on the limits to further productivity under existing Fordist arrangements. In effect the argument is that assembly lines are perfectly balanced, jobs have been 'work studied' to perfection, and the cycle times given workers have been set at their optimum levels. Furthermore, Taylorism is assumed not to be easily, if at all, applicable to the fast growing provision of services, or this is at least likely to be characterized by sluggish productivity (Aglietta, 1984). Neo-Fordism offers a solution to this crisis through a transformation of the production sphere which may, as in flexible specialization theory, involve the increasing diversification of products and a 'new flexibility', for 'it is adaptable both to mass production and to production in short and medium batches' (Aglietta, 1979: 125). The extreme of this argument is that the vision of the capitalist factory of the future remains worker-less.

Kaplinsky (1984), for example, has argued that technology may well have the potential of upgrading work. But, he argues this is not likely to be realized given present power relations, embodied in what he calls the modern 'industrial-military complex'. For him, like Braverman, technology can never have any influence independent of the pattern of domination in society. Kaplinsky recognizes that the development of technology may have some autonomy from the dictates of managerial control, but he is equally convinced that within capitalism it will be used to reduce the worker input, both qualitatively and quantitatively. The implication is that whilst technology may develop independently of capitalist goals, only in a non-capitalist society can flexible techniques develop and the enriching potential of computerized technologies be unearthed.[10]

In contrast, Sabel uses the term neo-Fordism to convey a move away from the rigid control model of management. When he first used it in *Work and Politics* (Sabel, 1982) he was mainly referring to changes in car plants, and indeed he overconcentrates on the quality of work life initiatives in the US car industry. Because they did not represent a full movement away from Fordism he labelled these neo-Fordism. As Sabel's ideas about flexible specialization developed the implication was that neo-Fordism was a kind of step on the way to flexible specialization, or even that it was a pathological and temporary response to the assumed crisis of mass production. Exploring the space between Fordism and flexible specialization is then an exploration of managements' adaptation to the problems of the former without their fully embracing the latter. The restructuring of tasks under neo-Fordism for Sabel would be the adoption of 'quality of work' schemes, that is increased functional flexibility, but no genuine teamworking which he sees as a hallmark of flexible specialization. Managements had in effect failed to read correctly the implications for work organization of the changing market situation. Neo-Fordism describes for Sabel what he saw as management's timidity towards the wholesale changes in work organization commensurable with the emerging flexible specialization regime.

In his later writings Sabel put more weight on technology and internationalism in his (albeit brief) discussions of the neo-Fordist strategy. Automation in neo-Fordism would be used to substitute for labour and improve quality and integration, but not to increase flexibility as it would in the flexible specialization regime. The emphasis would be on standardization: moreover 'global' standardization as under the world car concept. Sabel saw a competition between neo-Fordism and flexible specialization – the former being associated primarily with internationalization. In such a formulation a contrast is often made between the world car strategy which exemplifies neo-Fordism and that of what Sabel and others call the Third Italy region, assumed to be prototypical of flexible specialization, and describable as an emerging 'high-technology cottage industry' (Sabel, 1982: 220). The Third Italy (Bagnasco, 1977; Brusco, 1982; Piore and Sabel, 1984: 226–9; Sabel, 1982: 220–31) – the northern part of Italy which experienced very high growth rates relative to the rest of the country in the 1970s – is seen as prototypical of this development, as its network of small and medium firms is assumed to lie behind this economic success. Having made this contrast Sabel (Katz and Sabel 1985: 297; Piore and Sabel, 1984; Sabel 1984) attempted to gain credence for the flexible specialization scenario by asserting that the world car strategy had failed, and by emphasizing the success of the assumed alternative. Neither example may, however, be as clear-cut as Sabel implies.

First, the explicit world car strategy as exemplified in Ford's Escort and GM's Cavalier in the late 1970s appeared less prominent in the 1980s, but it is a mistake to equate this with a move away from internationalization or even from the world car scenario, or with a failure to reap profits from the attempts thus far (Dankbaar, 1984; Wood, 1988a). Ford, for example, has explicitly revived interest in the world car, aiming to orient the generation of European cars in the

1990s to the concept (Beavis, 1988). It is already enhancing the worldwide integration of its design function and planning to supply the total worldwide demand for particular parts in one specific plant. Since the late 1970s, global competition and the global integration of many industries, not just the car industry, have been developing. Internationalization in manufacturing, as well as in financial services, involves the co-ordination of production, marketing and product design across national boundaries.

Second, there are a number of problems of using the Third Italy as a prototypical case or model for the development of a new 'network' economy. For crucial to the region's success were the long-established vocational training system within firms, and the round of technological transfer in the late nineteenth century which fostered the development of an entrepreneurial class. There is little to suggest that it can be easily developed in areas without such a history, in for example Southern Italy, or in areas or industries previously dominated by large firms. Furthermore, it is not so clear that the networks of firms in the Third Italy can provide fundamental innovation – their flexibility may be limited. To be flexible to meet changes in fashion, as in one of its main industries, textiles, is not the same as being able to make major innovations independently of the large firms' dominance in research and development.

A much used example is the clothing firm, Benetton, as it is involved in a network of small-scale artisan-based firms, the most dramatic example of its use being in Murray's (1985) Benetton Britain. It should be said at the outset that it should not be treated as a typical example of the whole area of the Third Italy, not least because of its great growth in size in the past decade. Nevertheless it continues to be used as a major example of a firm continually adapting its stocks and products to an assumed highly volatile fashion market. It seems to illustrate the point which Sabel and others stress that the widespread development of flexible specialization will depend on co-ordination and long-term links between firms, each of which will be specialized in one part of the total production process (including design and distribution). Flexibility is thus provided as much by this overall arrangement as by anything one firm does.

But the 'Benetton' case does not match up to the image of a nexus of firms all flexibly specialized and employing highly committed, skilled workforces. It appears if anything more like a network dominated by the large firm modelled along the lines of Atkinson's flexible firm. Distancing is a, or even the, major element of Benetton's labour and commercial policies; the retail outlets for the products operate on a franchise basis; and it has a highly dualistic structure – the skilled parts of the process are handled in-house, including the dyeing, cutting and final ironing, as well as the design, and the unskilled weaving and making up is done outside in the seemingly artisan firms, employing a large percentage of women.[11] As Luciano Benetton himself is reported as saying (Mitter, 1986: 48), he has raised fashion from the artisanal to the industrial level. The 'artisan' stage of the process is more standardized than the 'industrial'. The firm makes its basic products in a highly standard form – for example jumpers are made undyed, so they are all a 'neutral colour' and the responsiveness to the immediate market demand is largely a matter of being able to dye the garments in varying colours. Moreover, it is at this industrial stage that its major competitive advantage enters: the firm has developed a technology which can make subtle differences in what have previously been difficult-to-achieve colours. Finally, the most important feature of Benetton's development in the 1980s has been its internationalization. Through extending its retail operations, with shops as far apart as Scotland and São Paulo selling basically the same products, Benetton has become a huge multinational operation. Its opening of production facilities outside Italy has been very much along the world car model with the various locations specializing in the production of one or more types of product.

What then are we to make of the contrasts between the Third Italy and conventional mass production or attempts to adapt it through such concepts as the world car? Ought we not to be emphasizing the similarities between the strategies of Benetton and the leading car companies: the globalization, increased automation, adaption of just-in-time procedures and the intensified use of the computer for design, production and stock control. Benetton's development and dominance of a network of suppliers seems little different from that used by Japanese car firms, and its competitors have been considering ways of emulating it in the 1980s. Is the Benetton Economy Murray (1985) alludes to a world of flexible specialization or of Japanese-led revitalized Fordism? Even in his own account it is not clear. The major contrast within the normal models of Japan and the Third Italy is between a network of firms built around the large oligopolies (as in Japan), and the assumed more egalitarian relations of the Third Italy. But perhaps even this is not helpful: Japan has its Third Italy and Benetton and other firms of Northern Italy are increasingly forming assymetrical power relations with their suppliers.

All this highlights the need for more conceptual clarity and the danger of building edifices on the basis of selective and empirical examples. Since Piore and Sabel coined the term flexible specialization, there has been a tendency for some writers (e.g. Murray, 1987) to slip into using the terms neo-Fordism, flexible specialization, as well as the more recent term post-Fordism, almost interchangeably. This is not, as we have seen, consistent with Sabel's own formulation, or especially useful. Post-Fordism has crept into discussion it seems because some writers detect a reskilling and fusing of vertical relations, rather than the deskilling and concentration of programming in the hands of a technocratic elite *à la* Aglietta. It is acknowledged that under the most technologically advanced production systems, the notion of job cycles and individualized jobs may be rendered redundant, but far from this reducing skills or making workers more disposable, as Aglietta (1979: 126) predicted, it puts a premium on initiative, quick reactions and diagnostic skills (Papadimitriou, 1986: 47). From the little that those such as Jessop *et al.* (1988) who use the term post-Fordism say, it appears that at least at the task level it goes beyond the simple injection of teams. Some see it as a merging of direct and indirect work, while others as the devolvement of certain supervisory functions to previously non-supervisory grades, or as the end of the division between production and white-collar work (Jessop *et al.*, 1988). Although none of these developments is incompatible with team working their distinctiveness seems to be the collapsing of hierarchy and not just fusing of lateral relations. All such developments represent some pretty fundamental moves away from the original Fordist conception with its emphasis on a clear specification of individualized jobs and separation of supervisory and managerial roles from operational duties. Many writers do though appear to be using the term post-Fordism to convey more than possible changes in the labour process, but rather broader changes in either the forms of regulation or accumulation or the politics associated with these. As such, post-Fordism is an era when the neo-Fordist transformation of work is less relevant as a solution to the crisis of Fordism, than as a means of adjusting to a new (post-Fordist) regime of accumulation, which itself may require going beyond neo-Fordist redesigns and involve more restructuring of hierarchical relations.

How the various terms such as neo-Fordism are used, as we have seen, depends on one's theory. Despite this it ought to be possible to tidy up the nomenclature in order to bring more clarity to the discussion. Though this need not be seen as prejudging its precise utility for understanding contemporary changes in work organizations, it may well help us to identify, for example, the different ways in which flexible manufacturing systems are being used. For there are examples of their use with conventional Taylorist work patterns, and cases where they have entailed radical changes in organization. A major problem with the various usages of such terms as neo-Fordism is that when applying them to labour processes writers continue to seek one path towards which firms and sectors will develop. There do not, however, appear to be powerful homogenizing forces to push work organizations and market strategies down one channel. Even if we are to use the terms neo-Fordism and the like, they are best seen as different paths down which firms may be going. This formulation does not have to assume they all have total freedom of choice. As Coombs and Jones (1988) say, 'the identification of a single and well defined successor to Fordism can now be seen to be premature...The new forms of production which are emerging contain the seeds of a number of alternative new [production] paradigms.' Unless we acknowledge this, it is likely that underlying the discussion of transformations in work will remain an assumption that all roads lead to post-Fordism or flexible specialization. Neo-Fordism need not be seen as a transitional state or a pathological response to an assumed crisis of Fordism. It may though be a major aspect of the strategies of some core firms in the economy and indeed only viable for certain firms.

Coombs and Jones (1988) have suggested we distinguish between neo-Fordism and post-Fordism, at least in flexible manufacturing cases, prinicipally on the basis of how the new technology is being used. In the former, technology is being used primarily to save labour and improve quality. So task structures and modes of labour management may differ from conventional Taylorism. But they are not significantly different in terms of either the horizontal or vertical division of labour. In contrast, under post-Fordism there are genuine breaks in the degree of product variability and division of labour. We could go on to demarcate post-Fordism from flexible specialization on the basis that the latter will be concerned with much more bespoke manufacturing and have highly fragmented labour processes. In post-Fordism, the emphasis is on increased product innovation and improving design capability, relations with suppliers, and responsiveness to the market. But the conception of products and production processes remains ahead of sales and production, and involves prototypes and experimentation. In flexible specialization the organization is aiming to be highly responsive to the market, and this means that conception and execution collapse, becoming almost one and the same thing (Sabel, 1982: 224, 1988: 24). Put this way the conditions for flexible specialization to exist seem rather limited. How many people can afford to have their bespoke clothes with several try-ons during the production process? What proportion of the cars of even the British royal family or president of the USA are custom-built?

We might also think about differentiating concepts on the basis of territorial developments.[12] Neo-Fordism may be associated with a more fully fledged internationalization, with spatial divisions of labour within firms and the supply of uniform products in all markets. In post-Fordism, products are more geared to local markets. This may involve the greater use of local suppliers, locally based information systems, with design and marketing functions being more dispersed. Finally, under flexible specialization internationalism is primarily limited to trading, perhaps supplemented with some joint ventures and international networks for marketing and sales. The emphasis will be on the customer or his/her agent coming to the production location, much as ten years ago one of the motivations for Europeans for visiting Singapore was to get comparatively cheap bespoke suits made.

Even though such conceptual exercises may improve greatly the clarity of argument, the danger remains that built into the neo-Fordist exploration of the space 'between Fordism and flexibility' are assumptions about a neat and tidy relationship between spatial divisions of labour, technological developments and labour processes. We should not, however, expect to be able to read off precisely changes in the spatial divisions of labour from technological or labour process changes. And certainly we should not prejudge any geographical developments which would follow from any such changes. Just-in-time systems may imply a given spatial pattern *à la* Toyota City but this does not mean that a recentralization and dispersal to small production units *will* take place. Similarly we need not assume that intensified automation will extend the standardization of production methods throughout the world, for the lower costs of labour in newly industrialized and Third World countries may limit the extent of automation in these countries.

Whilst it is tempting to associate neo-Fordism with internationalization and flexibility with a technology-led strategy and recentralization, the mistake is to present internationalization and flexibility as necessary alternatives (c.f. Abernathy, 1978; R. Cohen, 1987; and Chapter 4, below). Big multinationals can follow more than one course, with domestic reconcentration being associated with increasing decentralization worldwide, particularly for example, in cars, in parts or engine production where economies of scale still matter. However, in recognizing the importance of the internationalization process we must break the association of it with product standardization and the transfer of all low-skilled jobs to the newly industrialized countries, except in so far as component manufacture accounts for a disproportionate number of such jobs. We must also, as Schoenberger argues in Chapter 4 below, bring technology into the geographical picture. 'Neo-Fordist' developments in production technology (robotics for example), as well as changes in organizational methods and the products themselves, may well mitigate against the development of neo-Fordism, constituted geographically. If advanced automation is associated with lower employment levels and higher skill profiles the attraction of lower cost labour will diminish in importance.

Reconstructing the terrain of debate: beyond Fordism and flexibility

Much of the above implies the debate needs recasting. Control and flexibility are not two ends of a single unidimensional continuum. There was considerable flexibility in Fordism – indeed central to Taylorism was the idea of workers being disposable and hence the association of routinization and low training times with numerical flexibility. Moreover, it was never applied as rigidly as the stereotype suggests. The seemingly easy option of switching the axis of debate from control to another umbrella-term, flexibility, is then not only of doubtful utility but also of dubious validity. The danger is then of a potentially fruitless or at best misleading polarization of debate, and more seriously of a skating over of the many issues which still surround analysis of the transformation of work.

Developing the many strands of argument which lie between the two extremes may be fruitful. Yet this may result in an exclusion of questions which should be addressed, the answers to which may bear considerable fruit for theories of work. In the previous section we have explored some of the possible arguments between the two extremes. But even here the argument seems to be too orientated to broad sweeps of history. Neologisms such as neo-Fordism are too often used with insufficient specification and whilst conceptual clarification is feasible, as I have illustrated, its utility may be limited and give the impression of a significant breakthrough which is misleading. The problem also remains that built into such concepts may be particular models of history, implied trajectories of the future and given ways of explaining transformations of work. The basic methodological problem – namely whether they are falsifiable – of both labour process and flexible specialization theory persists. This arises partly from the problem of the very broad and not always well specified concepts[13] on which the theories are anchored, and partly because they imply contrasts between current (and past) developments with an imperfectly specified and – more importantly – known past.

The starting point for any reappraisal of the terrain of debate must be both a clearer specification and differentation of concepts, and a questioning of the use by both labour process and flexible specialization theories of Fordism as a benchmark of the past. We can illustrate the former with a number of examples from our discussion so far. An obvious example is the way in which the concept of new technology is too often bandied about as if its referent is unmistakably obvious, thus encouraging a glossing over of the nature of the ongoing changes. Another example is the differentiation between Fordism and Taylorism. Whilst useful, we must go well beyond this, differentiating between the assembly line and Taylorism, scientific management and Taylorism, and specialization and Taylorism, for example.

The historical issue includes two basic questions: was there really ever a choice for the production of mass consumer products between craft-type and industrial engineering methods, and 'was Fordism ever dominant' (cf. Williams, Cutler *et al.*, 1987)? The continued importance of small- and medium-batch production in manufacturing, particularly in engineering has often been noted (Bell, 1972; Kaplinsky, 1984; Kelley, 1986; More, 1982). Also as Linn 1987: 130 notes, 'an assembly line can only be *one* part of a productive enterprise: even in the most line-focused industries there are probably as many people off the line as on it'.[14] Finally it should be stressed not all mass production is the assembly of complex products as is all too often implied. Until the differences between work organizations have been systematically compared, Williams, Cutler *et al.* (1987: 423) are right to question Fordism as the model of the past and caution against its use as a central organizing concept, as it 'elides too many differences and establishes an uninformative stereotype'.

How are we then to proceed? Given the range of problems surrounding both the flexible specialization and deskilling theses, it is tempting to eschew the quest for general theories. It is, however, one thing to question the utility of historical trajectories, it is another thing to abandon the pursuit of general overarching theories. We need not retreat into empiricism or middle-range theory. But we do need to make sure we specify clearly both the level of abstraction and the level of aggregation with which we are working. Whilst the different levels – the international, the country, the region, the firm, the plant, and the shop- or office-floor – are related, they should be clearly demarcated. At this stage it may be fruitful in developing research problems and designs to keep them separate. The value of overarching approaches is that they guide the identification of research problems and the integration of disparate empirical studies through suggesting themes which have a relevance over and beyond the narrow confines of the observations and the single research project. The danger is, however, that analysis slips almost unknowingly from one level of aggregation to another. This was highlighted earlier in the discussion of the problem of the precise referent of flexible specialization – the firm, the industry or the locality? Too many theories predicting a major transformation of work seem to jump too readily from the production system to the basic structure of economies, or even capitalism, or vice versa. It ought to be possible to admit of the importance of flexibility without assuming that this involves a fundamental change in the mode of regulation, or alternatively of changes in the economy or political institutions without assuming a transformation of labour processes or consumption patterns such as an end of mass production.

The terrain of debate need not discard some of the central elements of the labour process and flexible specialization theses. Indeed whole slabs of both may be highly significant. Whilst the idea of an absolute level of deskilling may have been undermined, this does not mean that the distinction between conception and the execution and the notion of relative deskilling defined in these terms may not remain central (cf. Armstrong, 1988: 150). Increasing internationalization, computerization and telecommunications mean conception is becoming even more removed from the shop-floor or plant level: technical advances 'facilitate the concentration of "conception" (research, planning, directive and strategic management) at corporate headquarters, while "execution" is dispersed around the globe in often low-cost installations which may be abandoned with market alterations' (Hyman, 1988:

57). There is also the increasing application of science to the productive forces, which as Armstrong (*op.cit.*) notes, 'if wholly incorporated within the structures of capitalist management, could be said to result in a relative deskilling of (for example) ... machine–shop crafts'. This highlights the question raised by Adler (n.d.) of how useful the concepts of (craft) autonomy and control are in the context of advanced science.[15] It also makes the claim of Sabel (1988: 29) that the division between conception and execution no longer makes sense – as mass production is declining and 'firms learned to expect the unexpected from the market' – seem even more extreme. This should not, however, be interpreted to mean that the degree and nature of the divorce between conception and execution is unchanging. Indeed, an initial starting point might be that firms are becoming more centralized on a number of dimensions, particularly their strategy formulation, whilst on others – more specifically the operational level of decision-making – they are becoming more decentralized. This may well mean that there has been some increase in the involvement of workers in conception. Although the development of 'functional flexibility', teamworking, and quality circles may be limited and certainly should not be automatically associated with multi–skilling or upgrading, they may be important parts of such processes.

Questioning the concept of flexible specialization need not entail a rejection of the significance of the 'flexibility debate' or its desire to link the new technology to the upgrading of skills. Advanced automation certainly does appear to call into question the whole notion of 'job cycles' and routinized performance, as diagnostic skills, coping with uncertainty, and mutual interdependence become more important, and low error–rates and high capital utilization become prime objectives. Yet, much of the increased effort and flexibility has been subtle and unrelated to technological change. It has, for example, depended heavily on people taking over the jobs of leavers who have not been replaced, and has been based on the exploitation of longstanding notions of service and welfare, especially in the service sector (Cunnison, 1986).

There are, of course, limits to the amount and kind of flexibility firms need. Complete job flexibility with constant toing and froing would, for example, conflict with the principle of teambuilding inherent in both the Japanese and Swedish models. Furthermore, much of the flexibility sought in the 1980s has simply involved people accepting more responsibilities, being more prepared to cover for people and taking more care over their quality, timekeeping and general behaviour. Through natural wastage or redundancies, firms attempt to reduce the number of jobs, as well as perhaps improve their quality. So, whilst the various changes coming under the flexibility rubric may appear on the surface rather limited, they may in practice have considerable importance in explaining productivity changes.

They may have considerable impact over and beyond the productivity increase resulting from job loss and individuals working more hours and more consistently. Changes in work systems may genuinely foster and increase knowledge, through (a) increasing the number of jobs to which an individual is exposed; (b) increasing workers' involvement in problem situations calling for diagnosis and considered judgement; and (c) increasing workers' awareness of aspects of the production system beyond their immediate and narrowly defined role.

We must also acknowledge the continuation or even creation of rigidities. The most obvious one is the continued segregation of men's and women's jobs (Hakim, 1981; Killeen with Robertson, 1988; Martin and Roberts, 1984; Milkman, 1976, 1983), as Walby highlights in her chapter below. If firms do move towards a more rigid version of the flexible firm, this will involve them in the creation of a new kind of rigidity: job tenure for the core workforce. It is necessary to examine all the types of flexibility in relation to each other, as well as to rigidities, as is implied by Dore's (1986) term *flexible rigidities*, and by Kumazawa and Yamada in Chapter 5 below.

Moreover, that mass production may never have been dominant does not imply anything about its current development and certainly not that it is ending. Nor does a rejection of much of the labour process theory prejudge questions about the extent of mass production or Taylorism in some form or another.[16] Most of the products associated with the ascendency of Japan in world trade are classic mass-produced goods, such as cameras, transistors, televisions and cars, and Japan more than any other country has opened up the markets for such new mass products as videos and cassette players. The role of scientific management and conventional methods of management in the restructuring and productivity improvements of the 1980s has certainly been overshadowed by the emphasis on flexibility and structural change. In many cases, for example in Britain, the calls for management to manage, to set and stick to work standards, however, all echo Taylor's words. It is probably not just in Third World, socialist or Southern European countries that, what the Hungarian Simonyi *et al.* (1985) have rightly (to avoid any associations with stage theory) called quasi-Taylorism, existed. Aspects of scientific management are finding further applications in some service industries and much of the productivity improvements in key industries seem to be due to improved use of scientific methods and intensified motivation through changed payments systems as well as new investment. Evidence from the author's own research in the British car and coal industries would bear this out (Marsden *et al.* 1985; Richardson and Wood, 1989). Moreover, much new technology is introduced with none of the genuine participation socio-technical theorists prescribe. That this has gone on in tandem with attempts to increase the flexibility of workers, or at increasing employee involvement or to use quality circles supports

Kelly's (1985) view that what is crucial is to study Taylorism in relation to other managerial practices and approaches.

All too often changes in work organization are automatically assumed to be a move towards non-Taylorist and innovative forms of management. Any transformation of work is approached in terms of whether it reverses Taylorism or represents an abandonment of Fordism, and a move towards autonomous working arrangements, as exemplified by craft working. New forms of work organization may co-exist with many of the elements of Taylorism, as they reflect managements' need for co-operation and developments within their product markets. The fact that they co-exist with Taylorist practices, of course, further questions whether Taylorism ever dominated the world of production (Kelly, 1985), and certainly in the way Braverman suggests. The relationship between Taylorist and other past methods and new forms of organization, as well as industrial relations strategies, should then be treated as contingent. In some circumstances the alternatives may amount to genuine reversals of some features, but not all (Berggren, 1980; Dull, 1985); in some situations they may only represent modifications of it, and finally they may simply represent a gloss on the underlying Taylorist approach which Braverman implies is universally the case. It is here that the Japanese example is significant, as it illustrates the complexity of the problem.

The over-riding significance of the Japanese management model appears to be that it has sought to overcome some of the nagging problems of Fordist-type production systems such as of quality and balancing the line. The 'problems' of Taylorism, assumed to be endemic in the 'crisis of Taylorism' thesis and insurmountable by Sabel, have been tackled partly through new management methods and partly through involving workers. This has turned 'on their head' (Altshuler *et al.*, 1984) many of the features of Taylorism as conventionally practised, but not necessarily the fundamental principles of Fordism. Much of the Japanese management model is a hybrid of existing theories of organization, allied to important new discoveries, particularly the just-in-time production method, new forms of quality control and the value placed on close relations between suppliers and final users (Sayer, 1986b; Wood, 1988b, 1989). But nothing in these innovations necessarily implies an end of mass production.

The quality circle is an important innovation and a distinctive element of the Japanese model precisely because it is the explicit involvement of workers in industrial engineering. These and other *kaizen* (Wickens, 1987: 46) techniques are concerned to make every worker realize she/he is an industrial engineer, to develop an awareness of the need for continuous improvement, and to forsake, as one manager in a Japanese plant in the North of England described it, 'plateau thinking'. Clearly, though, some of the conditions for the successful implementation of these 'new' methods do not contradict

Taylorism.[17] The 'weak' trade unionism, the intensive and highly sophisticated selection processes, for example, all echo Taylor's own words. What is not so obviously Taylorist is the greater use of assessment systems and the increase in training for future needs and perhaps even the segmentation of the internal labour market which results from this. Enhanced training opportunities, training for the future, and use of training as a screening device for promotion, all are distinctive from the Fordist emphasis on training for immediate needs and for narrowly-defined task performance.

The Japanese example illustrates the point that it is important to have more nuanced categorizations of forms of work organization. Not only are the simple dichotomous classifications such as Friedman's popular direct control versus responsible autonomy inadequately specified (Wood and Kelly, 1982), but the categories may also be too broad. The Japanese management model, for example, should not be lumped together with the Swedish model of semi-autonomous working groups. For one of the former's distinguishing characteristics is the centrality accorded to the supervisor, who is awarded equal status with the industrial engineer and responsible for setting standard operating times (Wood, 1988c; Wickens, 1987). In contrast, the idea behind the Swedish 'model', at least in theory, is to reduce the role of supervision. Also Swedish innovations in work organization have tended to rely on breaking up the assembly line and increasing the levels of buffer stocks between elements in this, which again, as Berggren suggests in Chapter 10 below, contrasts with Japanese-style just-in-time production.

Organizational conceptions such as Taylorism and *kanban* must then, *contra* Braverman, be treated as distinct from technological changes. This opens up the possibility that the former will have more influence than any technological changes on skill levels and divisions of labour, as Kelley suggests in Chapter 12. The precise developments which emerge will depend very much, as Applebaum and Alben argue in Chapter 13 of this book, on the kind of markets firms pursue, as well as the existing extent of bureaucracy and state of industrial relations.

Finally, one of the major problems of debate which I have refrained from mentioning so far is the lack of a good empirical base. Both Braverman and Piore and Sabel over-rely on managerial theorists' accounts of what ought to happen or pundits' forecasts of the capabilities of technologies. Kern and Schuman have more direct observations, but the precise nature of their fieldwork is, however, not clearly relayed, though it appears to be primarily based on interviews with works council officials and their own direct observation. There was of course an important empirical dimension to the labour process debate, as a considerable volume of historical material, case studies, and aggregate data analysis has been directed at assessing developments in skill levels, the emergence of Taylorism and its possible alternatives, and the impact of technology on work organization and job require-ments.[18] It is this, perhaps more than some of the more general and theoretical work, which has made the most lasting contribution.

Yet, too many of the thorny problems of empirical work have been side-stepped in the flexibility debate up till now. What, for example, are we to make of the fact that, according to one measure, sex segregation is on the increase whilst according to another it is decreasing (Bagguley and Walby, 1988)?[19] What of the difference between survey results and case studies, the former, if industrial relations research is anything to go by, stressing continuity, the latter change? Can we conclude anything much about change on the basis of one-off cases, or cross-sectional analysis, without more longitudinal analysis?[20] All the contributions to this book have a strong basis in empirical research. Much of it shows how wide of the mark the judgements made on the basis of limited data, technological pos-sibilities, or conjectures of managerial strategies can be. Walby's chapter, for example, shows how with additional data the same basic commonly accepted data, the rise of part-time work, can be interpreted very differently from conventional, 'flexibility' accounts. Part of the difficulty of debate, as Hyman (1988: 54) says, is that detailed research has 'as yet covered a very limited range of contexts'. We need then to extend the range of cases studied and particularly give far more attention to the service sector.

The structure of the book

This book presents original material on the theoretical, methodological and empirical questions surrounding the debate on flexibility, skill and work organization. Whilst they do not all directly contribute to or confront the flexibility debate, they all make a substantial input to the reconstruction of the terrain of debate. They deal with major themes and issues which have been broached or raised in this chapter. These include technological development and the limits of automation; internationalization and the geography of production; Japanese man-agement and developments in concepts of management; gender relations and occupational segregation; developments in skill require-ments and forms of work organization; the service sector and new service products; conception and execution as the defining characteris-tics of capitalist labour processes.

Jones opens in Chapter 2 by analysing the appeal of the mythology of the worker-less factory. Drawing on studies of advanced auto-mated factories in Japan, the USA and Britain, he stresses how the expectations of managers and pundits have not so far been met: for example, manning levels and costs are higher than anticipated. Part of the explanation is that the implemention and operation of these systems require considerable levels of worker input – the tacit skills acquired in old regimes coupled with new diagnostic ones. (Cavestro also highlights this in Chapter 11.) Moreover, assumptions about labour and work organization strongly influenced by preconceptions of a worker-less factory and its Taylorist underpinnings exaggerate the problem, since generally work organizations are not designed to harness workers' knowledge. It seems, therefore, highly premature to anticipate that the present generation of 'new' technologies heralds a world of total managerial control, worker-less factories, or a monopolization of industrial jobs held by a technocratic elite.

Chapter 3, by Walker, contains one of the most thorough attempts to break down technology into a number of constituent elements. To overcome Braverman's neglect of technology, Walker suggests ways in which we might capture the various dimensions of the labour process to help understand the development of mechanized production. He also seeks to come to terms with the variety of the raw materials being converted in labour processes, and with product, as well as process change. It is the multi-dimensional and diverse nature, as well as irregular course, of automation that our concepts must capture. The implications for analysing both workers' skills and the geography of production are drawn out by the author. Walker's argument reaffirms the need, highlighted by Elger (1982) and others in the earlier labour process debate, for highly detailed and specific examinations of both historical and contemporary changes in the labour process that avoid an over-concentration on engineering and assembly work.

Schoenberger in Chapter 4 continues to explore the locational dimension of the transformation of work. She questions the new international division of labour (NIDL) thesis along lines similar to Walker by noting the limited conception of technology in such models. They assume that certain products and processes have reached maturity and no significant technological developments are likely to emerge that may make the continuation of investment in the developed economies worthwhile, when compared with low wage economies. On the contrary, for Schoenberger improved technology and product quality provide renewed bases for competitive advantage, closer producer–buyer relations in space and time, and some reduction of standardization. Some multinationals behave as the NIDL model predicts but this, Schoenberger argues, is not the dominant mode if only because its successful exploitation by some firms precludes it as a viable competitive strategy for others.

In Chapter 5 Kumazawa and Yamada discuss some of the key features of the Japanese system. They highlight both the competition between workers entailed in it and the historical context in which it has developed. They also remind us that Japanese management should itself not be treated statically. Japan, despite its seemingly greater flexibility, has not itself been immune from the pressures to increase flexibility in the 1980s, in response partly to intensified world competition and technological developments. Kumazawa and Yamada note the way in which in the past the Japanese answer to the numerical flexibility problem, the explicit segregation of the workforce into various types of core and peripheral workers facilitated its high degree of functional flexibility. Now, with pressure to reduce numbers of employees, the lever of the system has turned to its functional flexibility. This is enabling employers to transfer employees to jobs which bear little or no resemblance to their previous ones, often in workplaces belonging to a different firm or in a subcontractor for example. As such the Japanese *nenko* system with its life-time employment for certain core workers is being changed but is unlikely to be fundamentally transformed as some have predicted. But the relative size of the core workforce may be reduced and the merit element in the pay packet may increase in importance relative to the seniority element which has under the *nenko* system long been the dominant determinant of an individual's pay (and promotion).

Chapters 6 and 7 focus on the importance of the sexual division of labour for understanding contemporary changes in employment. Both criticize flexibility theses for their insufficient treatment of gender relations. Walby's chapter focuses on Atkinson's model; Jenson's on that of Piore and Sabel. Walby asks whether Atkinson's distinction between 'core' and 'peripheral' workers can be mapped onto male and female workers. While part-time workers, who are largely female, apparently belong in the second of Atkinson's categories, in other respects such a mapping exercise is shown to fail. In contrast to Atkinson, Walby suggests that changes in the structure of the workforce are significantly the result of changes in the form of gender relations. Reductions in forms of patriarchal closure are more important to an understanding of the massive increase in post-war part-time work than is Atkinson's flexibility thesis. Walby's work is also a further challenge to the Marxist notion of women as a reserve army of labour as utilized by Braverman. For women's paid work – both full-time and part-time – is still growing, despite the 1980s recession.

Jenson concentrates on the flexible specialization thesis, arguing that it is gender-blind. At worst it completely disregards occupational segregation by gender or at best it treats the workforce as uni-sex. If moves towards more flexible working (whether along the lines envisaged by Piore and Sabel or not) do take place (or are taking place) and employers continue to use male and female labour in different ways, then the world will be very different from that implied by Piore, Sabel, Streeck and others. For technology and other factors implicated in any transformation of work do not appear to be breaking down conventional gender stereotypes and segregation at work. The restructuring of labour processes and 'quality of work life' initiatives continue to privilege male workers and the processes by which skills are defined and constructed continue to be gender-biased. The implication is that no matter what changes in work are under way, the basic gender segregation would appear to be an unchanging element, and indeed it may well be underpinning these transformations.

Lee in Chapter 8 shows, through a study of the youth training policies of British governments of the 1980s, how the transformation of training has been an important element in the increased flexibility in the labour market and workplace. He argues that training systems and other allocative mechanisms of the labour market, both affected by state policies, are vital determinants of the way various jobs are defined and structured, as well as who gets them. The growth of young jobless trainees on government-training programmes has, in particular, enabled firms with flexible employment systems and low training costs to reduce their wages bill and obligations to employees. Noting that gender is an important basis for the traditional divisions within the adult labour market, Lee confirms that the youth training schemes have done nothing to erode traditional gender segmentation.

Berggren and Jürgens in Chapters 9 and 10 concentrate on developments in the car industry, the birthplace of Fordism. Both deal with attempts to apply new concepts of management. Berggren examines the development of new types of production systems in the final assembly lines of Swedish car producers. He shows that the experimentation at the now famous Kalmar plant in southern Sweden was only the beginning of change. Kalmar itself was far from the radical break that some portrayed it. The basic overall structure of the organization remained the same and the pacing of the flow of work was just as centralized in Kalmar as elsewhere. Subsequent developments have given more rein to teamworking and the need for flexible working, but most of them still remain within the overall scientific management concept. As such Berggren coins the term flexible Taylorism to describe the current state of the art in car plants, at least within Sweden. Attempts to radically break with the past, and abandon the line, are still in embryonic form, or limited to truck and bus production (albeit a very significant part of the Swedish auto industry). But they are gaining momentum. On the one hand, pressed by strongly increasing demands for flexibility, by a tight labour market resulting in very high levels of labour turnover, and by articulated union demands for work reform, production management in the Swedish auto industry increasingly realizes that it is no longer possible to build new factories on the traditional lines. On the other hand, there is a noticeable influence of Japanese methods, which according to Berggren mean flexible personnel usage based on a largely Taylorist production structure. If taken further this may retard the development of the Swedish model – at least in its original concept of reducing supervision and building buffers into the production system – towards its logical conclusion, that is, the end of the line and the reskilling of a classical type of degraded work.

Jürgens, in Chapter 10, looks at the transference of the Japanese model. He outlines the principal elements of it which may be attractive to managers wishing to emulate Japanese success, or what he calls transfer rails. Then he examines the extent to which car manufacturers in Germany, Britain and the USA have thus far attempted to use or adapt Japanese concepts. He shows that there is an enduring quality about the experimentation, but that thus far it has been rather limited and selective. Principally it has been confined to the development of problem-solving/quality circle-type groups and improvements in production and stock control procedures in the direction of the just-in-time model. It has also been modified to dovetail with existing industrial relations and training arrangements, as well as with the other developing modern western concepts of management, such as organizational development, with their similar emphasis on teamworking and collective decision-making.

Cavestro in Chapter 11 takes the discussion beyond the car sector and new organizational theories towards a broader range of industries and new technologies. He focuses on the effects of micro-electronics in both the process and engineering industries. Drawing on his research in France, he argues that increased automation, far from deskilling jobs, brings a new diversity of tasks and particularly involves increased skills of a diagnostic kind required to handle the unpredictable problems which arise in increasingly complex automated and programmable machinery. With automation the job of the operator involves anticipating and resolving problems. This reinforces and may enhance the intellectual aspects of the job, as well as involve the existing tacit knowledge and craft skills of operators. This means that changes in responsibilities and jobs follow automation, with some jobs and skills even disappearing, but it creates a widening of the knowledge base of the majority of workers. Certainly the simple notion of a transference to management, through computer programmes, of any remaining know-how workers have, and their increasing control by machines, as in a Bravermanesque world, seems unwarranted.

Kelley in Chapter 12 concentrates on the use of computerized technology – CNC machines and Flexible Manufacturing Systems – in US manufacturing. She particularly focuses on the division of labour surrounding programming, so central to the arguments of Aglietta, Braverman, Noble, Shaiken, Piore and Sabel. In her previous research and secondary analysis of the other studies in the area, Kelley (1986) detected no one dominant trend. Her study is the first systematic investigation of the patterns of programmable automation (PA) among a wide spectrum of industries. She finds three forms prevailed, with neither the Taylorist mode of organizing programming tasks *à la* Braverman or the worker-centred mode implied by Piore and Sabel predominating. In the survey she reports here she finds that the modal type of work organization with micro–PA is the mixed case; she labels it the shared–control model. There is limited support for an element of the flexible specialization thesis since 31 per cent of workplaces do use a worker–centred approach to programming. Although she does not measure skill levels directly, Kelley's survey suggests that under worker–centred arrangements most workers who operated PA machines appear to have had new skill demands placed upon them, and also the less Taylorist approaches are more likely to be found in workplaces concerned with small–batch production. But, the use of Taylorism is not necessarily related to batch size or mass production, the latter in fact applying to very few firms. Batch size is independent of the size of establishment, and Taylorist approaches to programming responsibilities reflect a more general bureaucratic orientation and structure within the enterprise as a whole. Thus, there is no technological imperative shaping the division of labour. Rather, a combination of institutional, organizational, and technological factors is at play.

In a somewhat similar vein to Kelley, Appelbaum and Albin in Chapter 13 address the effects of computerization in insurance, also in the USA. Using strategically selected cases they point to the diversity of forms of work organization adopted by the insurance companies. The choices in insurance lie between two extremes: using the computer to further routinize work and to reduce decision–making to a possible set of algorithms or using it to give more discretion to lower–level participants, particularly sales, claims and service representatives. But there is a considerable space between these two for different divisions of labour and computer systems. The type and scale of the operation is seen to be important for explaining the diversity, with the implication that large–scale standardized insurance production tends to favour Taylorist routinized organizations. Even here, however, the cases studied indicate that increased skill and responsibility are not only possible but yield substantial labour savings as well. The choices made inevitably reflect managers' evaluations of the potential cumulative effects of productivity gains achieved through training or attracting already qualified workers versus the immediate savings in training and wage costs achieved by reducing the need for skilled workers through routinization. The terms of this trade–off will, in turn, be influenced by managers' underlying objectives, corporate strategies, worker resistance and trade union power.

Kuhn in Chapter 14 examines the extent to which there has been a deskilling of the new computer–based occupations, as the technology has developed and they have increasingly been incorporated into the bureaucracy of large–scale organizations, as Kraft (1977) and other followers of Braverman predicted. Her research amongst software specialists in a large commercial bank in the USA reveals no such tendency. Rigorously assessing their jobs on the dimensions of Braverman's definition of skill, she finds no consistent separation of conception from execution, in this case, separation of systems analysis from coding. The division of labour is rarely fixed, undergoing modifications from one project to another, and although there has been a decline in the technical demands of some aspects of work, the demands of other skills have increased. There is increasing emphasis being placed on systems analysis, developing software to suit local conditions and specific users, as well as on the diagnostic, organizational and social skills implied by this.

Coombs and Green in Chapter 15 continue the focus on service and administrative work. They, like previous authors, place a good deal of emphasis on the changes in products, as opposed to production processes, consequent upon technological developments and changes in management conceptions. For them the interesting question from the point of view of analysing work organization is how the changing structures of service industries and of employment are linked to changes in the mode of satisfaction of various human service funtions. They, in effect, apply part of Walker's argument to the service sector and emphasize how new technologies which, for example, permit new forms of patient self-diagnosis change the 'service products', to use Gershuny and Miles' terms (1983). This, more than any direct change in the process of health production, is effecting changes in the divisions of labour and work organization within the health-care industry. They draw on research in the British National Health Service into changes in two aspects of the delivery of health care: management information systems and diagnostic testing. The impact of technological developments in these areas are being mediated by organizational innovations which are not directly derived from them. In Britain and elsewhere state agencies are major actors in these developments. The combination of technical and organizational change is permitting a more strategic approach to the determination of health-care delivery, the definition of what will be treated, by whom and how it will be treated. The implication Coombs and Green draw from this is that studies of work organization cannot simply focus on the changing nature of the work of particular occupational groups.

In the final chapter Burawoy and Lukács take the debate into socialist countries. They report detailed research in a Hungarian steel mill. The increasing policy of Hungarian politicians and businessmen of developing competitive strategies aimed at penetrating export markets lies at the heart of the case. The firm purchased advanced technology, but somewhat like Jones' capitalist cases, it was not easily able to utilize the equipment economically and to its full potential. Workers' participation was vital for overcoming problems of production and, unlike Jones' cases, the *de facto* autonomy of shop-floor workers and corresponding weakness of middle managers provided a work organization conducive to progress with the new technology and towards realizing the top managements' production targets. Burawoy and

Lukács bring us back, full turn, to Braverman, suggesting that any significant fusion of conception and execution, at least at the shop-floor level, is perhaps more likely to happen outside capitalist relations.

The chapters of this book were largely commissioned in 1985, and therefore reflect the debate then and some of the main research under way at that time. As the debate progresses new areas take on greater significance. It is to be hoped that this book contributes to defining topics for future research. We can, however, already detect some neglected areas of importance on which, regretfully, we do not have material in this book. Especially important is the impact of the various developments on administrative and managerial work. It is ultimately here, as suggested earlier, that the next generation of new technology, rooted in telecommunications, may have its largest impact. We should also not neglect the effect that new organizational methods have on management, for the Japanese method may increase workers' involvement in conception; it may also increase managements' involvement on the shop- or office-floor, that is in execution. Other important areas not covered in this volume include changing design methods (for example computer-aided design) and their impact on the horizontal division of labour; temporary employment and homeworking; subcontracting and the changing nature of relations between firms. To get things into some kind of proportion we also urgently need some more surveys of the kind conducted by Kelley and reported in this volume, so we know, for example, the extent and nature of just-in-time and flexible arrangements.

Overall, this collection extends the debate well beyond the confines of technology and flexible forms of work organization. Taken together, the contributions to this book suggest though that overcoming the problems of current theories involves more than extending one's analysis; it amounts to a theoretical reconsideration which must begin with an unpacking of key concepts. If labour process theory is in danger of being too one-dimensional, and reducing everything to labour control, then flexible specialization theory runs the risk of over-packing a whole set of elements which are all assumed to be marching to the same drummer – technology, scale of production, labour skills, job flexibility, market strategies, internalization and product differentiation – and also of neglecting the multi-dimensionality of these.

What follows points to the difficulty of establishing where the balance lies between change and continuity or upgrading and deskilling. Yet, the book highlights certain changes, including the increased demands made upon some workers by increased automation, and new forms of organizing work in both manufacturing and services. It also points to some fundamental continuities, particularly in the extent of low-skilled work, the sexual division of labour, and the limited nature of new initiatives which offer at best highly controlled autonomy.

Enhancing flexibility in one place does not necessarily ramify throughout organizations and entire economies, or preclude the development of increased standardization or fresh rigidities. Some element of flexibility in work organizations has always existed, and it is doubtful if a rigid assembly-style mass-production system was ever dominant enough to warrant its being the central organizing principle of models of industrialism. The nature of current impact technology and new managerial concepts will vary depending on the starting point, the sector, and even the firm. The overall message of the book though is that there is no reason to suppose that changes in work organization are all headed in the same direction. Various forms of work organization will remain, and flexibility will continue to co-exist with standardization.

2 When certainty fails: inside the factory of the future

BRYN JONES

Introduction

Kurt Vonnegut's *Player Piano* is a futuristic account of industrial automation, written at the start of the premature automation scare of the 1950s and 1960s.[1] Computerized worker-less factories are dramatized as the means by which a technocratic elite plans and controls all industrial production. Though written in 1952, this fictional account captures many current views of the social impact of automation.[2] For the last few years the business and technical press have been acclaiming the advent of the crucial element in the plot – the automatic, worker-less factory. A poll of members of the (British) Institute of Production Engineers confidently predicted in 1980 that similar automatic production systems to the ones described by Vonnegut – made up of individual machine tools with linked operations all control ed from a central computer – would be widespread by the late 1990s. Another estimate of computerized manufacturing suggests an associated reduction in employment of up to 80 per cent of current jobs by the year 1994 (Hartley, 1984). On many accounts the conventional factory appears to be at the brink of the greatest technological and organizational change since Henry Ford popularized the principle of standardized production.

The aim of this chapter is to explain why it is that, despite the advanced levels of automation involved, some skilled workers always remain in any flexible manufacturing system (hereinafter FMS) and related systems. Their continuing presence seems to challenge both the presumptions of technologists, that labour can simply be replaced by computerized machines, and the predictions of academics (e.g. Lund and Hansen, 1983) of an occupational segregation between technical groups of computer-aided experts and peripheral unskilled labourers.

Existing theoretical perspectives do not fully explain the survival of skilled work. Standard economic analysis would suggest that relative cost advantages determine the technological substitution of labour. Such theories assume a universal capital-investment logic aimed at minimizing the ratio of costs to output.[3] However the most advanced production technology, for example, that of FMS, is neither best suited to increasing volumes of standard products, nor to major savings in labour and other direct costs. The alternative logic for automation, suggested by Marxist-inspired critiques of managerial strategies, attributes the introduction of the technology to the capitalist imperatives to exploit and control labour. These explanations, however, do not satisfactorily show why managers should be trying to eliminate labour and, simultaneously, still be relying upon skilled workers to run the new systems.

The seeming discrepancy – between technological panaceas and visions such as Vonnegut's, and the contemporary realities of a considerable human presence – can be resolved by analysing automation as a social process with its own internal dynamic, and its ideological underpinnings. The belief systems of mature capitalist societies seemingly need a faith in technological certainty. Because scientific reasoning can be embodied in machines and operating methods the belief has spread that its apparent logical certainty also guarantees an empirical certainty. Shock and surprise result when certainty fails. When automobiles cease to function, when securely designed ships sink, when buildings collapse or, more horrifically, when nuclear power stations run amok, invariably the finger of blame points to human error as the guilty party. Since the widespread availability of electric power and self-correcting control mechanisms the search for certainty has been progressively applied to the historical stronghold of human ingenuity in the workplace. If the latest icon of technical certainty is the re-programmable computer its credo is the myth of certainty. Machines can replace human actions and humans err. Machines, it is believed, do not.

This fantasy is so powerful that it has partly been accepted by some of the otherwise most radical critics of the technological solution to the crises of factory production.[4] This technicist myth, of the power of technological change, entails two major fallacies. Because human efforts are associated with fallibility it presumes, as a consequence, a mythical identification of technology with certainty. Second, it sees only the manager and engineer as the authors of these innovations and over-estimates the importance of design stages as compared to the subsequent phases of implementation and normal running.

Complete automation seems now to be almost within the practical grasp of factory engineers and managers. Just because the tasks and skills of conventional production workers can be eliminated *in principle*, does not mean that this will happen in practice. However to sustain their aspirations managers and technologists must believe in their own capability to convert logical truths and formal models into fully operational processes. Implementation is regarded as a subsidiary and inevitable consequence of innovation and adoption. But design and planning operations are only the beginning of a chain of continuous modification and innovation to make computer-integrated manufacturing (CIM) systems work. At each stage of this automation process various levels of working knowledge, often rooted in manual skills, will be necessary.

My own studies of computerized systems in Britain, the USA, and Japan, together with the findings of other relevant investigations, suggest a need to break with dominant analytical distinctions between a pioneering innovation stage and mundane implementation phase of technological reorganization. If the commercial implementation and day-to-day running-in of these new technologies is itself an 'innovative' process, comprising various stages of completion and 'normalization', then production workers must themselves be regarded as continuous innovators. Far from replacing, or absolutely deskilling, craft-trained machinists the continuation of innovative and problem-solving activity into the operating phase of factory automation makes their presence indispensable.

The role of worker resistance in shaping the final forms in which new systems are used has already been established by case studies (cf. Wilkinson, 1983). But such accounts rarely explicate the shared understandings and collective knowledge (we might call these cognitive relationships) upon which opposition is based. Indeed one view is that specialist skills are artificially defined, or 'socially constructed' by the relevant interest groups in order to legitimize their positions and wage levels. By contrast, the view developed in this chapter is that factory work depends upon objective skills and knowledge which exist independently of their labelling and organization into the jurisdiction of particular occupational groups (cf. Jones and Wood, 1984). Think of it this way. If the working knowledge, which supplements and underlies the computerization of manufacturing processes, were equally distributed through the organization competing interests would lack any practical function of their own and the implementation of automation would be unproblematic. In reality there are gaps in the working knowledge of different work groups and specialists. As a result, those who manage and control the overall process do not have the detailed understanding of those who keep it running. Such 'cognitive disjunctions' become critical in the implementation and early operational stages of the automation of production and they guarantee a continuing need for craft-trained and experienced manual workers.

This thesis will be developed in three parts. First of all by describing the relevant technical properties of automated systems such as FMS. Then, second, the alternative ways of conceptualizing the process of technical innovation in production automation will be outlined and linked to the issues of occupational skills and cognitive disjunctions. The final section provides illustrations, from my cross-national study of FMS, of the indispensability of workers' skills and craft knowledge in the normal operation of computer-controlled production systems.

Computer-integrated manufacturing

The Fordist refinement of mechanized production gave only a temporary boost to the factory's reputation as the paragon of labour productivity. It failed to decide between two opposite solutions to the perennial human and social conflicts and complexities of the factory system. On the one hand, as far back as *The Communist Manifesto* socialists, and later sociologists, have attributed the problems to imperfect *social* organization; to the underlying contradiction between interdependent work roles and technical co-operation, and the despotic system of authority over this co-operation.

For the manager and engineer, however, amelioration of such conflicts has been seen in terms of technical perfection that will also eliminate the social problems. From this perspective the logic of the factory system culminates in combining the various machine units which make up the production process into one integral machine system. This system, in turn, is to be supplied and co-ordinated by computer systems specifying designs, methods, parts, materials, quantities and sequences. Limited forms of such computer-integrated operations (CIM), chiefly in the form of FMS, have recently been introduced, often as solutions to local operational objectives.[5]

Hastened by the enormous potential of the micro processor, CIM has been adopted as the generic term for automatic co-ordination of both the production and ancillary processes of manufacturing industry. In its optimal form CIM would link together the production stages of metal forming, fabrication and assembly of components into a final product; while pre-production and ancillary functions such as design, material supply, production methods and stock transfer would be programmed and co-ordinated with each of the constituent processes. There is, as yet, no proven commercial version of such a total system but the constituent processes and functions have all been computerized and made available in some form or another over the past ten years.

Computer-aided design and computer-aided manufacturing (process planning), which drastically alter the lead times for specifying component characteristics and processing requirements, are now generally available. Computer numerical control (CNC) machine tools which can be programmed to perform a variety of metal-removal operations are increasingly replacing conventional human-operated machine tools; and the programming of cells of CNC can in turn be prompted and allocated by mainframe computers within so-called direct numerical control (DNC) systems. The closest approximation yet to the CIM model are FMSs. These systems (of which there were by the mid-1980s several hundred throughout the world) have been limited in the range of manufacturing functions which they have brought together and the extent of vertical integration of design, planning and stock control. They do, however, represent CIM in miniature. Moreover they appear to have cracked the toughest nut for manufacturing automation: the machining of small batches (that are less than one or two hundred), which is the predominant size range for metal components (Kochan, 1984:153). This is where aggregate changes may be most marked, for the machining of small batches is (contrary to dominant images of mass production) the principal activity for most machine shops. One estimate is that up to 70 per cent of the work of machine tools is concerned with batches of 50 or fewer components (Stute, 1981).

The typical FMS now in operation consists of between six and a dozen CNC machine tools, or a proportionately smaller number of multi-functional 'machining centres'. There are automatic tool-changing devices, robotic handling of components onto the machines and an automatic system, normally of remotely guided carts, to transfer the parts through various stages of machining. In addition to instructing the CNC machines which programme is to be executed, and when (as in the DNC mode), a central computer also controls the movement of components around the machining units. The principal claim to the 'flexible' label is that, in theory at least, the system can switch automatically from production of one item to another, dimensionally different one, or even work simultaneously on several different products.

DNC and, more completely, FMS are credited with revolutionizing small batch manufacture because such operations had previously required intensive contributions from shopfloor workers. The latter usually reset the machine tools and other workers co-ordinated the supply and transfer of components into and within the machine shop. Even simply with automation of the machining operation itself, in CNC and DNC, it proved impractical (despite determined efforts and erroneous reports to the contrary) to eliminate human machine operators and setter-operators. There remained a need to take remedial actions when a machine encountered unforeseen difficulties and a need to re-set tools and workpieces for new jobs. Technologists and vendors claim however that FMS programmes incorporate data processing which can pre-empt machining problems by means of automatic renewal of tools before their wear has become critical. Some automatic sensors, and also automatic call-up and re-setting of tools and blanks for new jobs are also available.

In the past eight to ten years FMS activity and publicity has moved from the level of a novelty to that of the commercially commonplace. Most of the main international machine tool suppliers now have FMS systems or elements on offer (the list includes Cincinatti-Milacron, Comau, Cross and Trecker, GEC, Giddings and Lewis, Ingersoll, Fanuc, Mandelli, White-Sundstrand and Yamazaki) while large manu-facturing conglomerates such as General Electric of the USA have developed 'in-house' systems to supply their own metalworking divisions. A signal of the FMS market's level of development was the announcements in 1986/7 that the world computer manufacturing leader, IBM, was also to develop and supply factory automation systems.

Yet important gaps remain between the potential of these systems and their operational reality. So far FMS has stood mainly for flexible *machining* systems rather than the broader span of fabrication and assembly, and second, within the machining sphere, FMS has been mainly confined to a small and well-defined section of the total size range of metal components (Sackett, 1983). More significantly for the commercial acceptability of the systems is the admission that the physical economies in shop-floor labour, reduced stocks and enhanced changeover times are not reflected in 'the actual financial performance predicted for them', while the financially positive instances of FMS 'were special cases where the commercial environment was somewhat artificial in that they served a guaranteed and steady workload for a defence contract or were very restricted in the flexibility needed' (Dempsey, 1983).

Also, there are conflicting assessments about the operational merits of FMS. The early and influential feasibility study of the (British) National Engineering Laboratory into (what was then termed) Automated Small-Batch Production gave the main justification as the direct cost savings to be secured from lower stocks of work-in-progress, reduced labour costs per unit of output and higher machine utilization rates. Such a perspective is guided by the traditional measures of productivity per item of equipment, that is with labour costs as the accounting yardstick. These kinds of accounting conventions make dedicated automation of mass production by single purpose transfer lines (as with, for example, the machining of engine blocks for volume producers of motor cars) appear more cost effective. They are not, however, so easy to apply to batch production where flexibility between short runs of different products is a more important gain.

FMSs do offer some savings of direct labour costs compared to more conventional methods of small-batch production. The higher fixed capital outlays, longer running-in periods and higher 'backroom costs' of planning and programming may, however, outweigh these savings. This inconsistency has led several champions of FMS (cf. R.Jones, 1983; Sackett and Rathmill, 1982) to argue for alternative accounting protocols which assess cost-savings on the basis of system flexibility and market/customer responsiveness. Especially in the USA, the analyses of management specialists such as Jaikumar (1984), and fieldwork evidence on approaches to utilization (B. Jones, 1985b), suggests that company accountants are unimpressed by the fact that the FMS might be able to switch from producing 500 items of one type to 5 of another in order to meet a specific order, unless this is reflected in lower long-run average costs. As a result higher levels of automation which will reduce 'scope costs' (of flexible switching between products at lower levels of output) still appear to be less likely than the use of the new technologies to reduce 'scale costs' in larger volume operations.

System design and process innovation: iron cage or seamless web?

Production workers and their unions are rarely consulted about the design and specification of new process technologies (Williams, 1986). For critics of such decisions there is a consequent temptation to assume that this lack of influence in the crucial early stages condemns workers to the most restrictive, and often menial, work roles associated with task automation. Some observers have recognized that there is sufficient imprecision between plans and working practices to constitute an organizational 'design space' within which new demands about job content can be promoted (Bessant, Lamming and Senker, 1985). On the whole, however, there is a widespread assumption that the considerable scope for organizational choice and workers' influence in the early stages of the design and implementation of new systems narrows to virtually nothing once operations begin. It is assumed that once choices are made a continuous logic, a consistent and immutable rationality, flows from investment decisions. This, it is further assumed, dominates the implementation and operational stages of automation projects and determines all their aspects.

Such an 'iron cage' view of process innovation prevails both in the formalistic theories of neo-classsical economics, and Marxist labour process theory.[6] There are three related but empirically independent influences on the choice of technique and the role of the worker in the automation process: workplace politics, rival managerial views on goals and methods of automation, and the problem of harnessing together specialized sets of occupational knowledge.

Consistent with some labour process accounts such as those of Wilkinson (1983) or Noble (1979, 1984), the influence of employees, whether unionized or manual, technical or managerial, gives managerial decisions a 'political' as well as a strictly economic character. A second influence is the pre-existence of conflicting definitions of preferred operating methods and the organization of occupations within the management and engineering personnel (Kelly and Wood, 1984; Rose and Jones, 1985). Third there is the largely unexplored dimension of the organization of the knowledge process. Each of these influences has been discussed in some detail elsewhere (Jones and Scott, 1987). The most important for present purposes is the organization of occupational knowledge because it has the most relevance for the analysis of the innovation process, and hence the role of production workers in flexible automation systems.

The problem of co-ordinating the knowledge of specialized occupational roles was highlighted in Burns and Stalker's classic study of design staff in the product innovation process (Burns and Stalker, 1961). But it has also been confirmed for seemingly routine manual work by more recent research (Jones 1983, 1984b; Kusterer 1978; Libetta, 1988; Manwaring and Wood, 1985). What appear to be routinized and unskilled tasks, in reality, involve the possession and practice of highly detailed, often tacit, skills. Such skills are difficult for managers to formalize and predetermine; for they rest upon stocks of knowledge that are equally difficult to communicate. When these tacit occupational specialisms are applied to the process of operationalizing a new automated production system they take on the character of piecemeal modifications of which senior managers and engineers remain partly or totally ignorant. But, cumulatively, they diverge sufficiently from the procedures and capacities set by the original design to be considered innovations in their own right. This suggests the need for a redefinition of the innovation process.

The classical definition of innovation is that a technical or scientific breakthrough gains the status of an innovation when the relevant product or process clearly demonstrates greater practical or financial efficiencies (Langrish, *et al.*, 1972). But as investigators of this topic are only too aware the precise differences and boundaries between fundamental and localized, incremental innovations are difficult to establish *a priori* (Rothwell and Zegveld, 1982: 105–6, 165).

The initial system design is linked by a chain of related cognitive inputs to the problem-solving which takes place on a day-to-day basis (once a process is effectively operational). A useful analytical distinction may therefore be made between *primary, secondary* and *iterative* (or incremental) stages of innovation. In the primary stage, technologists and system designers (from the supplying firm or department) work out blue-prints and simulations to establish the capacity and constraints of the design. In the secondary stage, which British engineering managers refer to as 'productionization' (Wilkinson, 1983), the system is adapted to the real world conditions of the shop-floor. This stage, so crucial for the later operational success of the system (and, therefore, later diffusion by imitators), is often overlooked by commentators whose attention is drawn to the initial design success.

This, seemingly obvious, 'debugging' phase is crucial to the continuing capability of the equipment. Even more important, however, is the later continual process of minor adaptions, improvizations and unacknowledged tinkerings through which foremen, operators and maintenance workers attempt to achieve what the firm requires of the system. The men in white coats, the project engineers and head-office boffins, assuming that the system is now fully operational, formally hand over the system to the production staff. Designers and project engineers conceive of system flexibility as the flexibility that they programme into the system and its receptiveness to receive and execute the 'part-programmes' of particular machining jobs that may subsequently be required. But long after this the production staff will be engaged in continual contests to meet order deadlines to match their most workable methods to the demands of quality controllers and cost accountants, as well as to reduce the stresses and pressures on their own work lives. To succeed, the work crews – sometimes in alliance with technicians, maintenance workers or their immediate superiors – implement a variety of minute essential departures from the original specifications. It may be that a particular sequence of parts takes longer to load onto pallets or it takes longer to change the appropriate tools than is allowed for in the computer schedule; or that the programmed checks on the accuracy of part dimensions are at points in their circuit between the different machines that need to be modified for certain parts. More exceptionally, technicians and work crews may rewrite some of the software parameters in order to accomodate parts that are theoretically marginal to the original specifications of the system. In one US case study production and maintenance staff were even modifying computer components instead of relying upon the delivery times and costly supplies from vendors.[7]

Whatever precise changes are made, it can thus be seen that progression between these 'secondary' and 'iterative' forms of innovation in particular workplaces hinges upon success in co-ordinating the cognitive disjunctions between the specialisms of the conventional factory's division of labour. The most obvious are those : (a) between suppliers/designers and operating managers of new production systems; (b) between project managers and the immediate production staff and (c), *within* the last group, the immediate process workers and the controllers of the process. These disjunctions can be just as important in the implementation and 'normal running' stages as in the design and planning stages. At this point continuing or 'iterative' inputs of skills are required of workers whose tasks new systems may be intended to replace: for they provide the opportunity for small-scale 'innovations' that will affect day-to-day operations. Rather than automation being subject to any single over-riding logic or agency it is more accurate to picture a particular automated installation as determined by a welter of different interests and cognitive perspectives. It somehow needs to be a compromise operation if everyone's requirements are to be met. In this respect related departures from plan, so often reported in the literature, can be seen as normal rather than unusual. Aspects of the phenomenon have already been noted in other types of major re-equipment exercises; when pay rates, manning levels and skill requirements end up way above the levels originally specified for a new system, primarily because managers become dependent upon the most skilled workers to make them operational (Piore, 1968; Wilkinson, 1983).

In the case of the implementation of production technologies, such as FMS, there are particular problems in balancing the need to get very costly systems into production quickly and the politics of co-ordinating the occupational and organizational disjunctures between their skills and knowledge. The design and procurement staff in both the supplying and acquiring organizations provide knowledge of general systems properties, limitations and prerequisites. Through contract bidding and feasibility exercises this information can be matched with the knowledge of project engineers in the user firm. Rivalries and disagreements of approach can arise at this level of expertise. But then, in addition, there are the more particularistic views and expertise of the production managers, technicians and operators. The latter are interested in the system's capacity to make the products to specific quality requirements, within their day-to-day available resources and time constraints.

For example, in one British FMS studied the discrepancies between the parts to be made and the capacity of the machining processes led the firm's production managers to prevail upon their own engineers to rewrite most of the original software supplied by the vendor company (Jones and Scott, 1985). The way such firms' attempt to counter such confusion confirms the scope for divergence of views and information during this stage of implementation. Frequently an overall project co-ordinator is appointed, or the temporary authority of a 'project champion' figure from their management complement is established.

During the phase of iterative innovation, when the system is 'up and running', the very nature of the conventional division of labour causes more profound disjunctures and precarious overlaps of knowledge and expertise. Particularly noticeable is the political delicacy between the aims of the managerial designers and planners to automate and control previous areas of production workers' discretion and the need to draw upon the same workers' know-how in order to make the systems operational. For the shop-floor staff pick up by trial and error the idiosyncracies and detailed problems of the system. On the other hand, the knowledge of the system's characteristics held by technicians and production managers (the 'controllers' of the system) is based on various formal and quantitative records of its capability, routines and requirements. For example, the CNC programmer who works out the machining routines for the milling or turning of a particular part may work from standardized data on cutting tools and on assumptions about depths of cut and machine speeds. The shop-floor worker, on the other hand, would want to vary these to take account of the unreliability of a particular machine or the uneven quality of the metals to be machined.

What if the process of introducing production automation is less of an iron cage of predetermined cost calculations and operating requirements and more of a seamless web? If it is not dictated by transcendent economic or organizational logics, a single decision-making stage or a single type of actor then the nature of lower-level workers' involvement has to be re-thought. With innovative activity persisting throughout the process of introducing, implementing and operating a new system and its success depending upon actors with different interests, perceptions and knowledge, the role of the worker in the factory of the future begins to look much less cut and dried.

Work in the 'worker-less' factory

It has been argued elsewhere (Collins, 1985: Jones, 1985b; Jones and Wood, 1984; Libetta, 1988) that there are inherent limits to the extent to which computerization of work processes can do without human initiative and support. Such processes are only effective to the limited extent that they can draw from the tacit knowledge and skills of human agents. Computer systems cannot reproduce these tacit elements. Consequently the occurrence of the unexpected, the deviations from programmed standards and measurements and the need to develop *ad hoc* solutions must continue to depend upon human knowledge and inventiveness.

Advanced FMSs, however, are often reported as not needing any human presence, apart from maintenance and initial and minor remedial re-programming by technicians (Marsh, 1980). The much publicized paragon being Fujitsu-Fanuc's Tokyo factory which, reportedly, runs on unattended throughout the night. Here, at least in microcosm, is that worker-less factory of the future which Vonnegut imagined during and after his spell as a technical writer for General Electric – one of the pioneers in automated machining. Closer examinations however have shown that production staff are still necessary and present for the running of formally 'unmanned' shifts (Jones, 1989; Senker and Beesley, 1986). The claims of publicists, managerial pundits and technologists that FMSs run without human intervention are true only in a limited sense. More critical social science perspectives, such as those of Noble (1979) and Shaiken (1984) admit that the technology still requires the involvement of manual workers; although they characterize these jobs in terms of marginal and deskilled tasks. Yet in crucial respects such accounts distract attention from the more fundamental question of *why* even the most technologically advanced of the new computerized production processes are unable to do without conventional or new skills.

The principal software elements of FMSs are the system programme, for the routing of parts between machines and the individual part-programmes for metal cutting. Once these have been tested, or – in shop language – 'proved out', no major human modifications to these programmes are required. Even with the less complex 'stand alone' CNC machines shop managers soon learnt, however, that they needed experienced machinists to monitor the running of the programmes and to take corrective action when, for example, a tool tip broke or wore down unexpectedly. FMS users now have much more computer surveillance and automatic monitoring at their disposal and the ability to switch work from an inoperative machine to another of the same type. However the interdependence of all elements in the system means that the remaining staff have to be alert to rectify mechanical and electro-mechanical errors and failures in order to prevent knock-on effects throughout the system.

For example the guided vehicles (carts) which shuttle parts between the machines in some FMSs may sometimes stop *en route* because the trip mechanisms attached to the under-floor guidance system have been activated accidentally. The computer holds up the work station and signals the human operator to check and rectify any fault. Or again, maybe a part is not correctly aligned in its pallet; or, because of changing atmospheric conditions, a tool holding is too loose or too tight. In such cases, unless an operative can intervene in good time, parts from that work station go on through the system accumulating more and more errors: precisely because the system is designed to operate automatically. For these and other socio-organizational reasons a team of FMS manual workers is still crucial to the operation of an 'automatic' operation. Gerwin, who has studied several FMS installations over the last decade, goes further. He and Blumberg argue that:

> as machinery becomes more complex it also becomes less reliable...it may well be a nightmare of uncontrollable problems requiring unanticipated human intervention at critical points and unexpected upheavals in the workflow structure. (Blumberg and Gerwin, 1981: 23)

There are, however, cross-national variations in the explicit work roles and levels of discretion and responsibility of FMS work crews, which affect the underlying dependence upon their non-mechanical skills. American managers attempt to maintain highly specialized job classifications and a prohibition upon the operating staff having any involvement in the computer programs. In Japan work roles under FMSs are more fluid and the production-level staff are encouraged to take some responsibility for subsidiary program modifications. Britain falls in between the US and Japanese patterns. The differences between British firms constitute an eclectic mixture ranging from narrow occupational specialization to flexible working between technical and manual functions. The importance of an integral and sometimes expanded role for craft-type skills in advanced FMSs may be denied by managerial ideologies and practices. In the USA, especially, highly detailed and, in some respects, contractually regulated work roles are aimed at policing and circumscribing these skilled contributions. The temptation for Anglo-American writers is, therefore, to deduce that skills and responsibilities have actually been superseded or degraded, as Shaiken (1984) suggests. The analysis offered here would suggest, on the contrary, that a distinction should be made between, on the one hand, the formal organization of work roles and 'official' duties – which may well deny that production staff make any significant contribution to automated processes and, on the other hand, the tasks and skills actually performed.

The American evidence provides a stringent test of the thesis of inherent limits to the automation of manual expertise. For US managers have pursued labour and skill displacement more systematically than the British and Japanese. Both the technological sophistication of the systems and the occupational and organizational deskilling of shopfloor staff are greater. In principle the reorganization of tasks and expertise should provide the human complement to these computer controls, without the need to involve the production crews. US managements thus frequently staff managerial and technician-grade posts with employees who can supply shop-floor know-how 'from above', because they have had previous training or experience of machine-tool setting and operating. So in a typical FMS occupational structure the technical responsibility for changes to programmes and for interventions into machining techniques and work scheduling is formally in the hands of one or two system programmers (sometimes called systems supervisors) who normally work from an adjacent control room. The typical work crew for FMS in the USA is composed of one or two loaders who insert work pieces onto pallets, a couple of operators who monitor between three and six machines each, a tool setter who deals with tooling problems and adjustments, sometimes a separate mechanical maintenance worker to carry out more fundamental repairs *in situ*, and a foreman/supervisor who may or may not have charge of some other part of the plant in addition to the FMS.

Now in most cases, it is true, the crews are formally excluded from participation in the controllers' tasks. The adherence, in the USA, to a strict division between managerial and production grades is justified by reference to legal and contractual provisions (Jones 1985a,b). There are, however, occasions when setters or operators may stand in for the programmer. More importantly, even where work rules forbid such involvement, the production workers informally learn the logic of the computer programs in order to rectify errors or respond to problems. There is therefore even more dependence on the interventionist abilities of the remaining workers. These abilities are, in turn, based on acquired skills, particularly the workers' craft capacity to 'see' or imagine the physical characteristics of the problem.

In some cases attempts had been made towards harnessing the *ad hoc* and voluntary practices of informal flexibility into an officially organized flexible pattern. Yet the few recorded moves that have been made in this direction have tended to founder on the underlying social constraints against more autonomous work roles: low trust labour relations, managerial control systems and departmental rivalries. Jones and Scott (1987) report on a British case of this kind. In an American example management engendered a labour dispute and a breakdown of co-operation with the FMS workforce in order to retreat from a work organization scheme which involved considerable autonomy and responsibility for the work crew. The reversal to a more conventional grading arrangement achieved total weekly savings of only a few thousand dollars. Yet the system had cost, in total, several million dollars. So inoperative machinery, because of occupational rigidities or operators' lack of co-operation, could result in equally substantial costs.

Conclusion

There is then an important paradox in the organizational devices that are applied in order to pursue the objectives of near-total FMS automation, especially in the USA. The rigid and highly specialized divisions of labour that aim, in part, to exclude or marginalize the skilled contributions of the manual workers actually contribute to disjunctions between the necessary elements of working knowledge; especially between the operators and technicians and managers. Communication difficulties – inherent in the transmission of tacit knowledge – status resentments, resistance to hierarchical authority and logistical difficulties (having the right specialist in the right place at the right time) are all obstacles to the necessary sharing of information and knowledge about processes and problems.

There are limits to the computerization of human competence, and the march to computer-integrated automation is now beginning to confront them. To embody experiential and manual skills into computer software requires a transformation of the tacit knowledge on which they are based. Even the most advanced artificial intelligence projects have yet to come up with cost-effective methods of converting the unexplicated, subconscious and complex data of practical skills into sufficiently comprehensive software to provide automated substitutes (Collins, 1985). Grudgingly, and often unconsciously managers incorporate the exercise of these skills into the roles to which they assign workers in FMSs. But their ideologies and preoccupations with the politics of labour management lead them to sub-optimal divisions of labour which do not correspond to the required distribution of the relevant knowledge. Officially recognized responsibilities may not correspond to the actual competences that workers apply.

The principal manifestation is that those who know the cause of a fault or a better response to an operating problem do not have the technical training or the organizational entitlement to adapt the controlling software. The result is that the practical day-to-day operation of the systems only works as the summation of the expertise of all of the relevant agents involved. It is therefore highly premature to assume that future refinements of anything like the existing technology will lead to Vonnegut's scenario nor, especially, to the monopolization of industrial jobs by an information-processing technical elite, as some contemporary commentators have predicted (Lund and Hansen, 1983)

If we remove the assumption that a universal logic underlies the decision-making and implementation phases of automation then the subsequent operation of the new systems ceases to have the character of an iron cage predetermined by economic rationality or imperatives of control. Innovation ceases to be the heroic or villainous preserve of technical and managerial elites. It is, instead, an extended process which continues on a day-to-day and incremental basis well into the maturity of the production process. The lack of social recognition for the worker-as-innovator should not be allowed to conceal her or his practical importance.

Especially in the USA managers' persistence with specialized and sub-divided work roles on Tayloristic lines precludes a more optimal harmonization of skills with technology, such as polyvalent and autonomous work groups. Unlike Japan, and without some major revision to social attitudes and relations in the workplace, this particular trajectory is likely to continue to lead managers and engineers to try to solve operating difficulties by the application of yet more sophisticated technology. Yet the fundamental cognitive limitations to the certainty principle only make even more crucial the skilled interventions of the workers whose jobs are supposedly automated. Under present social and technological regimes we may be heading for the paradox that the more extensive the automation of functions the more dependent on human actions it will become.

3   *Machinery, labour and location*

RICHARD WALKER

Mechanization lies at the heart of industrialization and the wholesale transformation of work and life under capitalism.[1] That is no less true in the last decades of the twentieth century, with the dramatic improvements in machinery made possible by computers, micro-electronics, lasers and others of the new technologies. These innovations have led to new optimism about the ability of machines to transform work for the better, as in Piore and Sabel's vision of 'flexible specialization' or Hirschhorn's 'creative interaction' between humans and machine, or even to eliminate human labour altogether, as in the industrialists' pipe dream of the 'fully automated factory' (Hirschhorn, 1984; Mehler, 1985; Piore and Sabel, 1984). These have a family resemblance to the post-industrial and automation enthusiasms of Daniel Bell and others during the post-war heyday of Fordist mass production (Bell, 1974; cf. Bright, 1958; Coombs, 1985). Against the latter, Harry Braverman (1974) revived Marx's scathing critique of the capitalist factory, and was widely followed in his belief that capitalist management systematically degraded work through the application of Taylorist principles of division of labour, followed by the adoption of machinery to take the place of the diminished worker.

Marx and Braverman are surely right in large measure about the oppressive nature of capitalist class relations, but this must be weighed against three other powerful general Marxian tenets about the labour process: that human labour is the irreplaceable centrepiece of social production, with its own peculiar nature; that human beings must confront the physical laws of nature in order to bring nature under their sway; and that in developing the forces of production, people transform themselves and develop their slumbering powers (Marx, 1967: 177). I take these to mean that human labour sets the basic terms of production, on which mechanization develops; that the physical characteristics of materials, products and machines affect the course of mechanization; and that labour develops as well as loses skills over time, and that despite the best efforts of capitalists, workers cannot be altogether eliminated from production, as Jones also argues in Chapter 2.

My disagreement with Braverman's version of Marxism is that it gives unduly short shift to the technological. While Braverman has been criticized by those who protest his objectification of capital and labour, and who seek to develop the social relations *in* production more richly (Burawoy, 1985; Wood, 1982), he actually fails to be objective enough in dealing with the technological side of production. We have to take the study of mechanization very seriously, as did Marx; and we must do so to discover its true rather than imagined effects, and to strike the proper balance in the explanatory powers of the social relations and forces of production in the development of the labour process.

This chapter advances a new framework for the study of mechanization, by marrying the social and technical relations of production more closely. It is organized broadly around the three principles just enunciated. In the first section, I look at the multi-dimensionality of human labour and mechanization, and situate various partial views such as Taylorism, flexible mechanization, and just-in-time. The second section draws conclusions about the irregular course of mechanization over time, and the inability of any set of practices to lay claim to the future of automation. In the third section, the role of materials and products in the diversity and irregularities of industrial paths of automation is considered. The fourth section then takes up the question of labour skills and the counter-tendencies to Braverman's deskilling thesis.

In the final section of the paper, I bring geography into the predominantly 'sociological' discourse on the labour process. Geography has been not altogether forgotten in the Braverman debates, especially as regards the uneven diffusion of Taylorist practices (Littler, 1982) and the differential politics of production under different national variants of Fordism (Burawoy, 1985). But the new technologies and the decline of the Fordist regime of accumulation have drawn renewed attention to this neglected cousin of the social sciences.

The dimensions of the labour process and the application of machinery

The labour process begins with the human beings who conceive and execute their plans on nature. Mechanization must first of all be addressed to the labourer in the labour process; machines must be made to do what people do. Mechanization thus has a common foundation across all industries, and defines a certain progression toward higher human capacities of self-regulation and ultimately creative thought. In all labour processes, workers manipulate things, move them about, observe what they do through the five senses, regulate their actions in light of observation, and think, imagining the end-product of their actions, setting their faculties in motion, solving puzzles along the way, taking pleasure from the work and a job well done. They also, as a group, work together so that their individual, partial labours congeal as a single product. These characteristic facets of the labour process establish the five basic dimensions of production and mechanization: (1) conversion, or the transformation of materials into different forms; (2) assembly, or the combination of parts; (3) transfer, or the movement of materials from one work station to another; (4) integration, or the co-ordination of various subprocesses in complex production systems; (5) regulation, or the self direction and correction of machine performance.

The independence of the five dimensions is not sufficiently appreciated, and hence the problem of mechanization has been considered too narrowly (Bell, 1972). Mechanization is conventionally measured along a unitary scale of 'automation' (Bright, 1958). As a result, new developments in machine production are wrongly imagined to be mere *extensions* of past practices, as when 'Fordism' is treated as the perfection of 'Taylorism' or even of 'the Babbage principle' alone. Recent innovations in production have made it clear that Fordism is being supplanted more than extended. Yet this has led to the converse mistake of treating 'flexible production' as a complete break with past trends (Piore and Sabel, 1984; Storper and Scott, 1988). Because of the multi-dimensionality of labour and mechanization, people are often talking about quite different problems when they compare, say, Taylorist rationalization of hand motions with Japanese just-in-time methods. It is therefore necessary to consider the specificity of each dimension and the developments peculiar to each. While there is a core social logic to automation – the drive to increase the productivity of human labour (Walker, 1988; cf. Brenner, 1977) – the paths to this end are several.

Conversion

Every production process involves many individual acts of conversion, or the transformation of inputs into new forms. Mechanical advance in conversion has consisted principally of the achievement of greater precision, speed and strength in specific human actions: improvements on the hand, above all, but also on the power of the back, legs and eyesight. For example, a turning lathe allows a rapid and uniform cut; a hand-rest steadies the tool, improving the uniformity; attaching the tool to the machine increases precision even more; a cam-driven tool can cut irregular shapes smoothly. For such advances to proceed, it is usually necessary to break down human action into its component parts through the detailed division of labour – in the manner first enunciated by Babbage (1832) and Ure (1858) – to be repeated speedily and endlessly (Rosenberg, 1976). This is the realm in which Taylorism applies with force: creating simple acts of labour for mechanical reproduction. Historically it is a crucial moment in the development of mechanization, and is repeated over and over in new fields of work. But it is not the whole story, because of the other dimensions of production and the further development of machine capabilities.

Specialization of machines themselves is a further step in the application of the Babbage principle. A key breakthrough in Henry Ford's system of mass production – which owed its origins to Thomas Blanchard not Frederick Taylor – was the dedication of specialized machine tools to a single task (Hounshell, 1984). (Ford's moving production lines were not all strictly assembly work, it should be noted.) Dedication of specialized machinery has sharp limits, however, because large fixed costs require high utilization to repay themselves, each machine is locked into a rigid system, and alteration of the system demands expensive retooling.

General purpose machines, on the other hand, can do several different operations: machining stations can do either milling or grinding, depending on which tool is brought into place. Even mill stones can be adjusted for different grinds of flour. Machines that can do several tasks have long been essential for batch production, which still predominates in many if not most industrial processes (Littler, 1985:19). General purpose machines are the basis for a distinct industrial history that has not depended primarily on the principles of Taylorism and Fordism (Hounshell, 1984). Indeed, the very inappropriateness of crude Taylorist rationalization to machining is what has prompted the outcries of Braverman (a machinist) and his followers, such as Shaiken (1984). The methods needed for advancing the efficiency of generalized 'set up' or oversight of such work are not confined to simple principles of division of labour, repetitive motions, and mindless application of rules.

General purpose machines are what advocates of flexible specialization, such as Piore and Sabel (1984), have in mind. As they have pointed out, such machines are applied most efficiently in situations where one has (and is able) to switch rapidly from one output to another. 'Flexibility', in this instance, means several things: more adaptable machines, shorter set-up times, more broadly skilled workers. (There are other aspects of flexibility, such as better product design and integration of parts production, that we shall consider later.) Better automation of batch production thus embraces quite different principles of machine design and usage than automation of repetitive mass conversion systems. Confusion of terms is rampant here as was suggested in Chapter 1, with Piore now seemingly backing off from 'flexible specialization' and speaking of 'flexible mass production', which may apply either to expanded batch production or reduced runs within Fordist systems. The source of confusion is the misplaced emphasis on scale of output (length of runs) instead of production methods (type of machinery). One may yet get very long runs out of generalized machinery or short runs out of dedicated machinery, with corresponding effects on overall efficiency of labour and machine use, but the principles of mechanical improvement in each case are different.

Assembly

Most products are combinations of component parts which must be brought together for final assembly (or even a series of sub-assemblies). Some products, such as jet engines, consist of thousands of parts. Assembly is often much more difficult to mechanize than conversion, because it requires motions of joining and fitting which are surprisingly complex and subtle. Therefore, assembly lines for many simple products consist of little more than a belt moving past various manned work stations. Assembly work also frequently involves many small operations over the bulk of large products, such as welds on airframes. These are especially unwieldy to mechanize and do not involve the assembly line of Ford at all. Hence automation in the aerospace industry moves in different ways than in the automobile or machining industries.

Flexibility means something different in assembly work than in conversion because of the complex motions required. The current wave of robots consists primarily of mechanical arms, which are undoubtedly a great breakthrough in the imitation of the human hand, wrist and elbow. In a sense, they are the most advanced form of general purpose machine. They markedly reduce the need to break down human actions into flexible component movements before transferring work to the machine. Many observers have become transfixed by robotics, regarding this as the key breakthrough in modern automation. General Motors appears to have thought the Japanese performed miracles with robots and was 'shaken to the core' to discover that its New United Motors joint venture with Toyota in Fremont, California is more productive than other, more highly mechanized GM plants (*Business Week*, 1987a: 104). In fact, robot applications are still quite limited, the majority being found in the automobile industry doing welding and painting.

The most important advances in assembly have had little to do with automation of the work itself but with three other developments. One is the preparation of truly interchangeable parts that require no 'fitting', that is, filing into proper shape; this is an overlooked part of Fordism, with deep roots in US machining practices (Hounshell, 1984). Another is the design of products with fewer components to assemble – due in part to more advanced conversion methods such as laser etching in the fabrication of very large-scale integrated circuits or continuous cutting methods in metals. The third is the rationalization and mechanization of transfer methods, to which we now turn.

Transfer

Because all production involves multiple actions on the same materials, partly formed components and products must be moved from one step to another. There is, in other words, a problem of materials flow through production to which attention must be given. Transfer begins as the labour process of carrying things around. The simplest aids to human labour in effecting transfer are animals or some form of wheeled cart; today most heavy loads are moved with the aid of power vehicles. A surprising amount of transfer work still proceeds in this manner, despite the imagery of the assembly line (see e.g. Pfeffer, 1979). An important advance is the continuity of flow achieved with the help of fixed conveyors from one point to another, by dead-line (rollers, slides), steered line (cranes, locomotives), and live-line (over-head conveyors, belts, chains).

Ford's revolution in assembly is most widely associated with the moving line. This was, indeed, a great breakthrough in transfer methods, although it had been anticipated by the overhead, hand-pushed 'disassembly' lines of slaughterhouses. Ford reduced the labour of hand transfer, but the transfer element in Fordism was subordinate to achievements in work organization and integration, which we shall consider below.

The limits of Fordist moving lines have rekindled interest in the flow of materials through the production process. Improvements here have been labelled 'flexible production', but the meaning of the term in this context has little to do with the flexibility engendered by either generalized machinery or robotics. One concern is adapting to variable product demand. This may be achieved, however, without fancy machinery by simply breaking up assembly lines into smaller units so they can be working on different parts or products (Kelly, 1985: 38–40). Another concern lies in effectively transferring materials to generalized work stations without sequentially linked lines; this can be done with hand carts or aided by more sophisticated machines, such as computer-guided carts with programmable routing. Still another means of improving the transfer function is by more effective co-ordination of work between stations without the rigidity of the moving line or even sequential ordering on the shop-floor; this, however, takes us into a new realm of the labour process – integration – which will be considered below.

There are other elements of the overall transfer function than the movement between work stations in a factory. The first is the feeding and discharge of machines and on-loading and off-loading of movers.

In the beginning, each piece has to be individually fed and positioned, and each one removed and placed in a bin or on a cart. Machine feeding and discharge are often difficult to mechanize because of the need to position pieces for processing or to avoid harm to delicate materials. 'Pick-and-feed' robot arms can mechanize individual feeding, while in more advanced systems one machine feeds the next as it completes its task. The mechanization of transfer is closely allied to the automaticity of machine function, however; the more automatic become feeding, loading and movement, the more the rhythms of the machines must be unified. Putting together such systems requires close attention to the meshing of different actions, often at different speeds; for example the lathe turns the piece at one speed and moves the tool at another. For this purpose, electric motors are a great help (Hirschhorn, 1984: 21). The transfer function may ultimately be absorbed into the innards of machine systems (Marx, 1967: 381).

Another aspect of transfer is movement in and out of the factory (or department) as a whole, or what is called shipping and receiving, with its attendant functions of stock maintenance and inventory control. Shipping and receiving have languished in lack of attention from management and from mechanization, as compared to core production activities. Most factories are hand-fed by labourers unloading trucks on the receiving dock. Fully automatic processes may be initiated by discontinuous entry of a mass of materials, as when harvested wine grapes are dumped into the crusher. Management's inattention to material flows in and out of the factory and to departments turns out to be very costly, as when finished goods pile up awaiting shipment. Large buffer stocks are expensive to carry: one estimate in 1985 was that 30 per cent of production costs in industry go to warehousing, inventory, carrying and monitoring stocks (*Business Week,* 14 April 1985: 45).

Poor inventory management has often been identified with Fordism but has little to do with the actual achievements of Ford; they are, rather, the loose ends that Ford and his engineers did not attend to carefully. They are now being challenged by Japanese methods of inventory control inside the factory (e.g. *kanban* boards) and just-in-time methods of integrating work between factories (Cusumano, 1985; Sayer, 1986b; Schonberger, 1982). These methods have been equated with 'flexible production' (Scott and Storper, 1988), but this is probably unwise because while the use of just-in-time delivery and *kanban* yield a certain degree of flexibility with regard to changes in final demand, they also link extensive production systems more rigidly due to lack of buffer stocks and requirements for fully integrated production design and scheduling. What is striking about these methods is the low level of mechanization involved, although computerized records and information transfer can be applied once a determinate method is in place (rather like Ford's need to reorganize the factory floor before applying the moving line). We see, therefore, that the transfer function and its mechanization are accessory to the integration of production, which we can now take up.

Integration

Under the modern division of labour, production systems are parcelled among many workers and work units, thereby creating the problem of integration. Under this heading should be included all the co-ordinative functions that go beyond mere physical linkage and material flows (transfer and inventory control), such as making parts that fit together, equalization of work loads, and even effective organization for technical innovation. Labour productivity depends not only on the minimization of direct work time – which it was estimated constituted as little as 15 per cent of the cost of goods in the US in 1986 *Business Week*, 1986: 101) – but on the allocation of labour, time of circulation of capital in materials, machines and products, and production of quality products which sell effectively.

The integration problem is easily overlooked where machines link together several operations in one continuous whole – by rigidly tied mechanisms, by moving line or through continuous feed and discharge. Yet behind these mechanically integrated systems lies a long history of the rationalization of work flow and machine performance to achieve a sequence of operations that mesh properly. Ford's moving assembly line presupposes careful organization of work and machine functioning, the roots of which go back primarily to the genesis of the 'American system' of manufacture in New England armouries in the early nineteenth century (Hounshell, 1984: 25–46), but also to Oliver Evans' continuous grain mill in the eighteenth century, the disassembly lines of meat-packers, and the layout of canneries (Hounshell, 1984: 241). Ford's breakthrough depended on careful dissection and ordering of the work, close machining of parts, and dedicated machine tools and, in addition, the careful positioning of work stations to minimize distance and ease work flow (Hounshell, 1984: 217–61). It also eliminated the waste of excess parts lying around work stations (he was, like the Japanese today, attentive to problems of material flow in the factory, as they then existed).

However, mechanical lines created a new set of problems with flow co-ordination, work pace equalization and fixed work sequencing (Kelly, 1985: 35–6). Once the machine or line is running, it becomes a rigid system that can only vary in speed, and to which workers must adjust their rhythms (Edwards, 1979). Fordist systems of 'rigid integration' are now under assault for poor performance in terms of machine downtime, worker deadtime, bottlenecks, inventory build-up and shoddy workmanship (*Business Week*, 1987b: 132). Japanese innovations in work organization have reawakened interest in what had long been the forgotten dimension of production (for instance, neither Bright (1958) nor Bell (1972) theorized the problem of integration).

It is necessary to step back from the mechanical integration of the assembly line to reconsider the integration function afresh as a labour process. Most production systems actually consist of 'islands of automation' with substantial breaks between them, labour-intensive bits involving simple tools or operator-directed machines (Mehler, 1985). As a consequence, 'workers still link different parts of the manufacturing cycle' in otherwise highly automated systems (*Business Week*, 27 May 1985: 44). Such 'simple co-operation', as Marx (1967: 322–35) called it, may be achieved by organizing workers in groups with team leaders as in die-making or by formal meetings and consultations; but a great deal of it is still carried out informally through personal contact, mutual stimulation, the exercise of collective judgement and joint problem-solving.

Capitalists have proceeded to divide, simplify and take command of the labour of integration, in the Taylorist fashion. On the one hand, they hand the work of co-ordination and direction over to a special group called 'managers'. Managerial bureaucracy has been refined to a high degree, with company rule books, collective bargaining procedures, and organization charts. On the other hand, management must also begin to record information about the flow of work and materials on routing slips or in ledgers. Information handling, like direction, becomes separated from the rest of productive labour. Both of these new divisions of labour may subsequently become mechanized.

Mechanization of information flow begins with devices such as typewriters and adding machines that help to clarify and organize manual records of inventories, machine repair, work performance, and other data-tracking production. With early computers, data can be electronically stored and processed, but only after tedious hand entry, occupying armies of clericals. A big jump is achieved with on-line monitoring for continuous data collection on the various dimensions of production, directed automatically by computers with sophisticated programming. Major barriers to such integrated information processing are poor monitoring techniques, lack of data standards, incompatibility between computers, inadequate local area networks and the failure to develop powerful enough integrative software. Nonetheless, mechanization of information flows may be more important for overall productivity than mechanization of individual tasks. For example, retailing is being greatly aided by electronic point of sale systems and bar codes on labels, which provide instant information to the stock room on the flow of purchases (*Business Week*, 8 Nov. 1986: 64–5). Neither the labour of stocking shelves, unloading trucks nor moving produce from the stockroom to the floor has changed much, but overall productivity is elevated by eliminating the time spent on surveying shelf stock, ordering stockboys to fill gaps, and preparing orders to suppliers, as well as by reducing inventories of, and space devoted to, slow-moving items.

Mechanization of managerial direction has proceeded in several ways. One is the ability to monitor workers at their work stations through the machine rather than the foreman (Nelson, 1984). (One may even be able to reprimand the worker and indicate errors automatically.) Another is the programmed operation of a machine or set of machines, which shifts the managerial function over to technical workers in the engineering or computing department. Both these methods depend heavily on computers. Yet even with computer control, workers are still needed to watch over machines, enter information, and intervene as needed (see Chapters 1, 2, and 11).

Where computerized information and machine direction are combined to co-ordinate disparate machinery across the factory, it is called 'computer integrated manufacturing' (CIM). But progress down the road of fully automated systems is uncertain. A leading industrial automation consulting firm in Britain, Ingersoll Engineers, reports that it could not find a single instance of full CIM (*Computer Weekly*, 23 May 1985: 11; see also *Business Week*, 1986; Mehler, 1985). The biggest barrier to CIM is laying sufficient organizational and informational groundwork; a lot of sophisticated machines cannot overcome a failure to rationalize the integrative functions in production. As the author of the Ingersoll report observed, 'manufacturers should not be thinking of bringing computers in to integrate their systems until they have taken a hard look at the way their factories are run without computers' (*Business Week*, 17 June 1985: 39).

Certain Japanese companies have shown the benefits of rethinking integration before throwing machines at the job (Cusumano, 1985; Sayer, 1986b; Schonberger, 1982). This not only means a redirection from the classic Fordist obsessions with specialized conversion machinery or automated transfer toward the integration function in general. Improved integration also requires that management go back to a new starting-point other than Taylorist division of tasks between workers and management, so that workers are more involved in oversight and managers more in production. This may be achieved through new kinds of work teams, less-structured job assignments, reduced management hierarchy or hands-on managerial participation in work. Closer worker and management participation can provide better error detection and correction at the point of issue. Indeed, it is, as Sayer observes, a way of building in 'learning by doing' in place of pre-engineered factory systems. Additional benefits are reductions of set-up times, buffer stocks and downtime. Less stock and fewer errors are mutually reinforcing, in that errors are detected more quickly and cannot be evaded by turning to other available parts.

Regulation

All workers regulate their labour in three ways: they have a plan in mind beforehand, which can be changed from job to job; they undertake a number of tasks, whose sequence can be altered to fit different jobs or to improve the way a job is done; and they adjust their plans and actions in light of product demands and production results. In craft-type work the regulatory function is subsumed in the continual reflection of the worker. Regulation develops as a problem as machines take over from workers, for no matter how gifted machines may appear at transcending human motions of body and limb, they usually suffer by comparison with such elemental human abilities as versatility, perception and creative reaction. The task of engineers thus becomes one of rying to capture some of the higher capacities of the worker: imagining the result beforehand and observing and reflecting on the results. This is done in two main ways: by *programming*, or the ability to change the sequence of machine operations, and *correction*, or the adjustment of machine performance in light of the outcome. For either programming or correction to be possible, machines must have some general capabilities and degrees of freedom in their operation.

The crudest programming is exemplified by the manual set-up of tools and pieces on a generalized machine tool or the pre-setting of heat on an oven. The machine is told exactly what to do in this simple fashion. With machines capable of variable sequencing of operations, the steps of processing may be predetermined and changed from one run to another. The simplest such programming is mechanical and fixed, as in the rotating drum with movable pins guiding Jacquard's loom or the curved cams directing Blanchard's lathes for making gunstocks. Cams became the standard for more than a century.

The next step is to separate the drive mechanism from the regulation device (a cam is both), allowing the latter to develop on its own (Hirschhorn, 1984: 22–4). The modern history of programmable machines thus commences with numerically controlled (NC) machine tools, where the machine is guided by a program punched into paper tape. Their chief virtue was an improved ability to cut odd shapes to close specifications and reprogramming without changing the parts of the machine itself. But reprogramming was still a slow process of working out sequences by hand and punching tapes or copying the motions of skilled workers (record-playback). NC did not take off until its programmes could be computer-generated (CNC).

CNC is the beginning of computer-aided manufacturing (CAM). Many individually programmed machines can be found in today's factories with an industrial mini-computer by their side or a micro-processor within them to guide them through complex and varied sequences of operations. Flexible robots hold particular promise under computer guidance because of the complexity of their movements, as in making dozens of welds around a car body, and the possibility of varying the programme in response to the object before them, as in reading a tag on an incoming car body indicating the model number and doing the welds called for on that particular make of car. Much has also been made of so-called 'flexible manufacturing stations' (FMS), which are generalized machine tools that can change programmes for different tasks, change their own tools for different tasks, and adjust and change the parts on which they are working. In their full-blown form, FMS are combined into flexible manufacturing systems that integrate machine feeding by pick-and-feed robots and removal by shuttle carriages and transfer by mobile carts (Coriat, 1983: 24). CNC, robotics and FMS have the potential to revolutionize the economics of batch production in machining, but they still suffer from sharp limits in performance: considerable downtime, a limited range of actions, and little ability to detect or anticipate errors (Shaiken, 1984: 8, 75; Hirschhorn, 1984: 49). As a result, the spread of such techniques has not been as rapid as hoped by their promoters (see e.g. Kinnucan, 1983; cf. Jones, Chapter 2).

The second facet of regulation, correction, is needed because of, for example, limits on machine capabilities and variable conditions of materials. People adjust as they work, but machines repeat the same mistakes over and over. This affects product quality, reject rates, downtime, and machine wear and tear. Correction can be broken down into observation, linkage and response, which may be undertaken as separate acts of labour. Observation (measurement, testing) may be done, at first, by such human methods as eyeballing flaws in glass containers against a light or sniffing the soup. Improvements in manual tests can achieve a great deal: standardized gauges made possible interchangeable parts and Fordist assembly methods (Hounshell, 1984). The simplest form of response is to discard the ill-made product, which is still common in silicon wafer production and apricot drying, for example. One can also try to respond to errors by making ongoing adjustments to production methods, rather than wasting large batches of output, as US semiconductor producers have found. Linkage can be as simple as a pilot reading a compass and changing course.

Observation can be mechanized by means of such devices as thermometers, counters or electric eyes. It is best to get inside the process to measure things as they are happening rather than just measuring final results. Accurate sensory devices have proved to be a major bottleneck to automation (Kaplinsky, 1984: 30). For example, the use of robot arms is still sharply limited by the lack of 'sight': the human eye and brain do amazing things when they see, such as visualizing dimensionality of objects, separating mixed images, adjusting to variable lighting, and following objects in motion (*Business Week*, 29 July 1985: 49). Mechanical response has lowly beginnings such as Watts' governor on the steam engine, thermostats for furnaces, and toilet-tank floats. More sophisticated adjustment requires not only measuring devices capable of sensing small differences but mechanical linkages able to transform weak signals into strong adjustments. Electronics provided an epochal breakthrough in feedback systems by allowing electric current to amplify, modulate or rectify itself (Hirschhorn, 1984: 34-40).

Computers have raised automatic adjustment to still higher levels, because they can both run complex programmes and modify those programmes in the middle of processing as new information becomes available. Self-regulation at this level is no longer a mute reaction to sensory input but requires an algorithm to interpret incoming data and make an appropriate response. Thus software is increasingly central to further mechanical advance. The regulators must be regulated. Software is needed to create more sophisticated programmes; to speed up reprogramming; to facilitate machine operation by non-programmers; to evaluate sensory inputs in more sophisticated ways; and to provide 'expert' decision systems. Think of the evaluative process required to use robots to pick fruit – a notorious job for 'unskilled' labour – which has been stymied by the random distribution of fruit in the tree, wind motion, uneven ripening, pest damage, and variable weather conditions (*Business Week*, 8 Sept. 1986: 66-7). This emphasis on advanced programming raises the pressure to automate software production. More intriguingly, it opens up questions about 'artificial intelligence' (AI) as efforts turn toward capturing the abilities of knowledgeable workers on computer (*Business Week*, 7 Oct. 1985: 104-5).

Because labour processes, machine functioning and materials transformation are only imperfectly understood by the engineers who design self-regulating machine systems, all possible contingencies cannot be anticipated and designed into automated systems (Hirschhorn, 1984). In practice, workers' experience may be a better guide than textbook formulae, or even sophisticated computer programmes, so people remain at the site of production to monitor and correct machine performance (Shaiken, 1984). With computer-driven flexibility, regulation and in-built expertise in machinery, however, it becomes possible to design machines that interact creatively with workers rather than taking all operative and regulatory functions unto themselves. Such interactive regulation of both the worker and the machine may open up new horizons in automation (Hirschhorn, 1984).

Irregular paths of automation in a multidimensional labour process

Because the labour process is not a singular entity, mechanization proceeds along several different fronts: conversion, assembly transfer, integration and regulation. Automation cannot, therefore, be measured unambiguously as a sequence of steps on a unitary scale, in the manner of Bright (1958: 45). The multiple dimensions of the problem mean that mechanical progress will trace an irregular path as the leading edge of innovation shifts from one axis to another (cf. Bell, 1972). Furthermore, the path of mechanization does not always trace a steady upward course because progress in one dimension can require dismantling gains in another. Japanese work teams represent a retreat from strict assembly–line principles and a certain demechanization in the transfer dimension to explore the productivity gains possible with an alternative method of work organization. Just-in-time delivery methods mean less inventory to move, hence less need for mechanical storage and retrieval devices and more use of hand carts (*Business Week*, 13 Jan. 1986: 69). Computer-controlled machine tools can produce complex parts from a single piece that once was assembled from several components, rendering previous advances irrelevant. In short, there can be one step back for two steps forward. This phenomenon has been called 'dematuring' of an industry, but it bears no necessary relation to age or product cycles (Abernathy *et al.*, 1983). Rather, industrialization proceeds in ways that are often unexpected, and caution is called for in extrapolating from past experience without attention to the development of the labour process as a whole.

Given the generally unanticipated 'crisis' of Fordist production methods, it is not surprising that various observers, whether critical or optimistic, have seized upon advances in different realms of the labour process as the key to contemporary mechanization. Unfortunately, they are frequently not referring to the same things, and end up talking past each other. A multidimensional approach makes the opposing stances of students of the labour process mutually intelligible. For example, the Braverman school is occupied with the detail division of labour in basic conversion activities and the disintegration of craft-type jobs in the face of Taylorist rationalization. Advocates of flexible specialization, on the other hand, are entranced by the possibilities for sustaining craft traditions due to advances in generalized machinery; but this, too, remains firmly within the sphere of conversion labour by the individual worker or small workshop. Fordism is neither Taylorism writ large, as Braverman implies, nor oblivious to problems of work integration. Nonetheless, it was a strategy of production rationalization that had as its focal point the problems of manual assembly and mechanization of the transfer function. And Fordism still represents a powerful model of transfer, specialization and work integration at the level of the factory, with continuing relevance to certain kinds of mass production.

Students of Japanese work organization today stress innovations largely within the realm of production integration involving better relations between workers and managers, improved feedback between steps in a complex process, closer monitoring of material flows, and tighter co-ordination between factories. These strategies bear surprisingly little relation to the classic concerns of Taylorism for the dissection and rationalization of individual tasks, or Fordism with the sequential ordering and mechanical linkage of steps in the assembly process. Indeed they often involve a measure of retreat from extreme forms of Taylorism, Fordism and other conventional solutions adopted in the Anglo-American world over the last fifty years, and they have often surprised outsiders by their relative lack of mechanization. But Japanese manufacturers have not entirely forsaken Fordist assembly-line principles, as they have pushed forward in other dimensions of labour process improvement (see Chapters 1, 9, and 10). Nor have they ignored discrete or complementary advances in machinery.

The Japanese are also far advanced in the realm of robotics, which combines advances in flexible conversion (chiefly assembly motions) with sophisticated computer regulation of robot arms. Confusion of robotics with work reorganization led General Motors badly astray, as noted above. General Electric (GE), on the other hand, has emphasized FMS and CIM as most appropriate to its needs, giving it a certain kind of flexible mass-production capability. This has led to claims for 'the fully automated factory' (e.g. Kinnucan, 1983) redolent with the same excess of enthusiasm that first greeted the computer in the early 1950s (Bright, 1958). Nonetheless, GE's particular combination of generalized work station and computer-driven programming is not generalizable to production problems in which either large-scale assembly or small-scale customization is the crux.

At the frontiers of machine regulation, exemplified by nuclear power plants or petrochemical facilities, very different considerations arise. The kind of problems and possibilities presented by such machines are worlds apart from those of small machine shops or auto plants. Similarly, discussions of AI and expert systems put one into areas of great uncertainty about the implications of automation, to which the categories derived from the study of manual conversion and transfer processes can be applied only with great care.

Mechanical progress is open-ended, and the level of automation achieved at any point is never the last word. This evolution involves the discovery (and rediscovery in new ways) of dimensions of the labour process and machine capabilities not previously thought possible. For Adam Smith, the pin factory and its division of labour was at the forefront of modern industry. For Marx, it was the textile mill. For Braverman's generation the car assembly plant was the paragon of automation to which machine shops and offices would also eventually conform. Smith, Marx and Braverman each contributed important insights into the process of capitalist industrialization. But capitalist production continues to revolutionize itself in unexpected ways.

Now Fordist production is under fire from several directions, due to both its inadequate treatment of certain problems and to new capabilities of machinery, workers and management. It has been supplemented by robotics, FMS, CIM and other exemplars of a new age of computer-driven, 'flexible mechanization'. Which of several budding machine architectures will become the basic technology of tomorrow? Some (Piore and Sabel, 1984) have seized on a tendency toward a new workshop-scale flexibility as found in Italy's Emilia-Romagna region as the future of automation. Others (Schonberger, 1982) see Japanese methods of work organization as reconstituting the bases of factory production. Still others (*Business Week*, 1986) argue that developments in machine creativity through neural net hardware and AI software make our present computers seem as archaic as the vacuum tube. One simply cannot know either how far or down which branch mechanization will proceed, and we shall forever be pressed to come up with new concepts with which to grasp the course of machine technologies.

Materials and products, or the objects of the labour process

The materials basis of production

Since production involves both people and nature it has two sides: human labour and the material objects of labour. The labour process is therefore also a materials transformation process, and means working on nature in accordance with the physical properties of things. Marx was well aware of this second side of the labour process, yet he and its most modern students have failed to pay sufficient attention to the material differences among labour processes and the implications of materials and product changes for industrial development. Although the human actors are still the starting-point for any dissection of production and enhancing labour productivity is the touchstone for industrialization, mechanization involves more than automating the physical and mental actions of the worker. Technological change cannot proceed without reference to the evolution of materials processing.

One dimension of materials processing is that nature can transform itself without direct human intervention, and this can be improved without otherwise altering the labour process; for example, oxygen-injection to remove impurities in steel making. A second dimension is that improvement in materials is frequently crucial to advances in machine processing; for example, high speed machining depends on better steel alloys and lubricants. A third dimension is that one must grasp the nature of materials in order to transform them; advances in the study of crystal structure in metals permit better types of alloys and stronger-cast pieces. Lastly, machines are physical entities whose technical development is structured by their material form; hence, improvements in the shape of mill wheels or steam engines rest on the principles of flow and condensation of water.

Because materials differ in their properties every labour process has a distinctive cast. The way labour pushes, pulls, cuts or watches the materials depends on whether they are solid or liquid, hot ot cold, living or dead. Polymerization, grinding and growing are so disparate as to defy easy generalization about the way machines might be involved in the process. While harvesting may involve a cutting action similar to metal working, there is nothing in the latter comparable to hybridization. As a first cut, one can distinguish the following general material realms. For the inanimate world, there is the mass level (solids, liquids and gases) to which 'mechanical' action can be applied as in lifting, moving, cutting or squeezing; the molecular level, at which chemical reactions take place, especially operative in liquids and gases, less so with solids; and the atomic level, a catch-all that includes electromagnetic radiation, heat and nuclear reactions. For the animate world, there are organic systems, in which biological processes are at work; human beings, as the object of managerial labour; and the immaterial substance, knowledge ('information'), which must be applied in every labour process.

In most discussions of mechanization there is an implicit assumption that one is treating of essentially 'mechanical' processes, and that the machine tool industry is the exemplar of the process (see e.g. Braverman, 1974; Noble, 1979; Shaiken, 1984). Ordinary language is confusing here, because 'mechanization' connotes the mechanical world that predominated in nineteenth-century industrialization. But with twentieth-century developments in petrochemicals, electricity and electronics, agriculture, office work and telecommunications, the fixation on mechanical industry seems rather outdated. It is also odd to see Piore and Sabel (1984) herald the arrival of a 'second industrial divide' on the basis chiefly of improvements in mechanical processing when there have already been major revolutions in chemicals, electricity and agriculture that have utterly changed the face of industrialization in this century. Similarly, the current love affair with electronics-based 'high tech' industries (e.g. Hall and Markusen, 1985) ought not to blind us to the differences among all the supposedly 'low tech' sectors.

In terms of conversion and assembly the various material realms are quite distinct. Chemical processing deals chiefly with the initiation of molecular reactions. Workers only assemble materials; they do not convert molecules by hand. Early batch-processing involved such actions as mixing, heating and filtering of natural – usually organic – ingredients, which in time could be aided by machinery. But the major advances of the late nineteenth and early twentieth centuries came with the shift in material base toward coal, oil and gas feedstocks, electrolytic processing, and catalytic conversion. Machinery's role was to contain, move and regulate the increasingly intense, rapid and fine-tuned chemical reactions with better pumps, valves and pressure vessels (Freeman, 1982: 28). The key to further advance lay, above all, in grasping and operationalizing the principles of chemistry, hence science and engineering entered the picture very early. Electricity is similar to chemistry in this. There were no 'electrical handicrafts' to mechanize and deskill. Machines entered from the beginning with the generation of power, and mechanical advance consists chiefly of more sophisticated manipulations of electromagnetic signals, beginning with amplification. The biological level is very special indeed, as has been implicitly recognized in the separate treatment always accorded agriculture, despite a history of mechanical advance as old as any industry. Mechanization in agriculture has required, in addition to machinery to help farmers till, plough, milk or harvest, improvements in growing conditions and alteration of the organisms themselves. In short, by moving away from labour processes involving simple solids, the internal physical processes of materials transformation loom much greater in the mechanical calculus.

Transfer in non-mechanical industries also cannot be treated in the same terms as the assembly line. Continuous flow processing is a commonplace in handling liquids and gases in the chemical industries, but a distant hope in the production of furniture or cars. Indeed, for certain flow industries such as water, gas and electrical power supply, storage and distribution are the central tasks, not conversion. The development of the machinery in a power grid is a far cry from the problems met by pick-and-feed robots. Agriculture's transfer problems such as herding animals, irrigating and moving the harvest from the open field have no parallel in other industries. In order to use moving lines, for instance, one has to breed living animals that sit in one place all day, such as the continuously laying hens of the modern automated henhouse.

In the realms of integration and regulation, current advances in the control of mechanical processes are still usually far behind those made long ago in chemistry and electronics. When petroleum refining moved to continuous flow processing in the 1920s, automatic controls for close supervision of processing and rate of transfer became necessary because tighter integration of processes meant a closer meshing of rates of flow and greater potential for failure in one step leading to overall failure (Hirschhorn, 1984: 43-4). The first controls were not electrical (for fear of fire) but mechanical, based on springs, thermometers, thermostats and floats, whose signals were amplified by simple principles of hydraulics and pneumatics. But control was decisively separated from the rest of the machinery where it could be easily modified without other changes in the equipment.

Self-regulation came to the electrical industries with the invention of the vacuum tube, by which one electrical current could be used to modify another. Thus was born electronics. The *differens specifica* of electronics is that electric current can be used to regulate itself. Self-regulation has therefore proceeded by leaps and bounds in electronics in a way unimaginable with strictly mechanical devices. Solid state, microcircuitry and digitized information have subsequently carried the revolution in automation to greater heights. A digitized telephone signal, for instance, has no parallel in solid or liquid flow, because the medium has indeed become the message!

Agriculture is the most resistant to mechanical regulation because it depends on organisms which have their own rhythms of growth and activity (MacLennan and Walker, 1980). Interventions here have followed two courses: greater control of growing conditions through fertilization, irrigation and use of pesticides, and altered the state of the organisms themselves through the use of synthetic hormones, anti-biotics, and selective breeding (and soon genetic engineering). The modern feedlot, dairy or henhouse depends for its success on the changes in the animals as much as on those in the preparation of feed or removal of egg produce.

We can draw some conclusions from the above points for the general course of mechanization. First, industries develop along distinctive pathways owing to their fundamentally different material foundations. Mechanization has a logic based on the way things work, as well as the way people work. The course of mechanization is fundamentally altered by the contours of the product and the nature of the material transformations required to make it. Hence, industries do not all mechanize in the same way. While mechanical progress shares certain features across sectors, owing to the universality of labour, inappropriate generalization collapses profound material differences and does violence to the distinctive histories of industries. The technological breakthroughs that made possible the great eras of steel, home-building, air travel, railroading, textiles, or electronics may be so different as to defy abstractions such as Taylorism, Fordist production or flexible specialization as means of grasping the whole (or perhaps even the main part) of mechanical advance and transformation of the labour process.

Second, all industry does not mechanize equally fast or equally far. It is easy to forget how dilatory mechanical advance has been in so many important industries, from lumbering to house-building. This 'back-wardness' derives not from a lack of capitalist motivation, abundance of cheap labour or absolute rent, but from the fractious nature of particular materials, work tasks and machines. Woodworking, for example, cannot ever hope to attain the liquid flow properties of oil refining. On the other hand, seemingly small mechanical break-throughs in such industries may make a big difference in production capabilities, for example the lathe or the sewing machine. The corollary is that often too much attention is given to highly automated industries in our understanding of industrialization. Textiles and railroads were not the whole of the industrial revolution. There were many workshop industries that do not fit the cyclopean stereotypes of weaving factories or steam engines (Sabel, 1982; Samuel, 1977). Crucial advances in making dyes and other chemicals were also propulsive of nineteenth-century industrialization (Schumpeter, 1939). In the twentieth century, Fordist mass-production practices, for all their importance, were always concentrated in a few industries: autos, appliances, radio/TV, cameras, toys/sporting goods and watches/clocks. Perhaps only 1 in 30 employees in Britain circa 1980 were classic line workers (Littler, 1985: 19). Batch- and custom-production remain extremely important today in industries as disparate as electronics, aeronautics, shipping and garments.

Product shifts

Up to this point we have assumed an unchanging product as the production process has been mechanized. This is frequently invalid. Product change can redefine the problem of process mechanization and mechanization can redefine the nature of the product. Product and process change are deeply wedded. On the one hand, product design modification can alter the need for machines. For example, as more and more circuits are crammed on a single semiconductor, fewer external leads are needed and assembly work diminishes; in some cases, the latter has fallen below 5 per cent of costs. At this point mechanization of assembly ceases to be an important issue. The focus of mechanization shifts to design, in fact, because the immense circuitry of present-day microprocessors exceeds the capabilities of manual engineering and drafting. On the other hand, advances in mechanization can alter the product (cf. Chapter 15). Owing to computer-aided design (CAD) and laser cutting, the semiconductor industry has been branching into a whole new area of specialized and customized chips. While everyone has been waiting for the industry to 'mature' to mechanized mass production – which it has done to a large degree in random access memories – it has just as rapidly sustained its 'youth' by the proliferation of new products. An even more graphic case of product proliferation due to automation is in the petrochemical industry: high-temperature cracking of oil generates a host of exotic organic chemicals, for which uses are subsequently found – or foisted on the public (such as artificial turf). The products only come into being because of the highly advanced state of modern refining (Commoner, 1976: 183–97).

Dramatic instances of the dialectic of product and process can be found throughout the history of industrialization, as the search for improvements in the performance or manufacture of a product leads to the creation of a new one, sometimes quite tangential to the original purpose. Machines themselves can become new products and the basis for whole new industries; textile machinery broke off to become a separate industry around 1840, eventually moving into locomotives and other large devices. The same thing can happen by altering the materials; after a century of incremental improvements in spinning and weaving machines, the textile industry was deeply transformed by the introduction of synthetics and knitted fabrics. Or the product and process can change together as a whole technology is revolutionized: cast iron became steel at the same time it was being made in bigger machines. In the twentieth century, transforming electricity into light images yielded the picture tube, giving rise to oscilloscopes and televisions; storing information electrically in binary form gave birth to the computer.

The dialectics of product and process change make for a path of mechanical advance, which conflicts with organic models of industry growth and maturation. A new product may appear to metamorphose continually, preventing evolution to more standardized machine production; or it may only appear at a high level of automation, completely skipping a craft stage; or it may split off a new product at a lower level of mechanization; or it may be replaced by a better substitute and die out before all the mechanical processing problems are solved. In short, industrial production is not a set problem to which machines are applied with predictable results. The nature of the problem shifts due to the technological capacities unleashed by the machines themselves. This means we can never have a fully closed model of industrial maturation and mechanization that holds for all industry and all times, even under the general guiding hand of capitalism.

Braverman and many others implicitly accept a 'maturation' or 'product cycle' model of the development of industries. In this model, first formalized by Simon Kuznets and Arthur Burns, industries proceed organically from the birth of a new product to a youth of handicraft production to an old age of machine mass production (Burns, 1934; Kuznets, 1930). That is, every industry is expected to mechanize fully, to follow the same general technological path and to eventually exhaust its possibilities for further mechanization. But industrialization does not work that way. It was shown long ago that industry growth paths do not follow the S-shaped pattern expected by the life-cycle model (Gold, 1964). It should now be clear why. Mechanization proceeds along several dimensions not a single line of advance, and can even run backward at times. Mechanization is open-ended, so there is always the possibility of further renewal of an industry. Industries are terribly diverse in their material bases, and either never mature or never have a proper youth. And just when an industry seems over the hill, a new product may burst from within to set down a fresh path of development. Ironically, the originator of the product cycle theory, Raymond Vernon, took as his model the US radio industry (Vernon, 1960), which promptly went through a revolutionary kink in its development path by the introduction of transistors – and moved to Japan. It appears that Kuznets, Burns and Vernon's notion of standardized progress from hand labour to mass production was a mid-century idealization of what happened in automobiles and a few other large consumer durables, as Fordist methods diffused (Coombs, 1985).

The effects of mechanization on workers

The transformation of work which Marx identified – jobs divided into minute, motions rationalized and work transferred to machines (Marx, 1967: 359-68, 418-26) – has happened in many industries with the development of mass production. But the deskilling of work and unemployment due to automation have not been universal tendencies, owing in large part to the technological nature of the labour process. This has been true for three principal reasons which relate to the nature of production and mechanization as just described: the resistance of many labour processes to rationalization, division and mechanization; the ability of machines to enhance, as well as demean, the powers of human labour; and the development of social labour as opposed to individual skills in the transition from craftwork to the machine age.

The supplanting of people by machines has been limited by the simple technical difficulty of mechanizing many labour processes. This has several dimensions, but the essential point is straight-forward: capturing the powers of living labour in the machine is not easy because human beings are incredibly 'skilful' animals by their very nature. Even what is commonly considered 'unskilled' labour – because almost everyone can potentially do it – is still beyond the reach of machines. Therefore, if machines are to do the things that humans do, the tasks must be made very simple or the instructions to the machines made very clever. But how far has the emulation of the human hand gone and how far does this replace human beings with machines? We forget how clumsy machines can be, where human fingers are supple; how blind they are, how sharp the human eye; how oblivious to noises apparent to the human ear; how stupidly the computer follows orders without the slightest glint of imagination! Reality was inverted by Frederick Taylor to make the problem appear to be one of fitting uneducated workers to clever machines, rather than the reverse.

The principles of Taylorism and Fordism just do not apply to many kinds of jobs. Consider basic acts of conversion and transfer to begin with. Garments are difficult to machine produce, for example, because the human body comes in such odd shapes. Clerical work is less amenable to mechanization than office managers hope because, among other things, of the infinite variety of things to be filed. Telephone operators have been hard to displace owing to the unstructured nature of caller requests. Bigger trucks can raise the productivity of labour in transport, but it is impossible to dispense with the driver. All these are, furthermore, quite venerable jobs whose fractiousness cannot be explained away by reference to the youth of the industries involved. Several writers have noted the importance of 'tacit skills', or the concrete know-how accumulated by the worker after ten years on the job, as forming a barrier to worker displacement (Cressey and MacInnes, 1980; Manwaring and Wood, 1985). The persistence of such concrete skills is not, however, a quirk to be easily overcome, for it is grounded in the very diversity of the division of labour itself. In general, too much attention has been given to changes up and down a single scale of abstract skill (as if all work could be directly compared as more or less skilled) and too little to the persistent variations across the division of labour that make skills incommensurable. Furthermore, machinery itself creates concrete skills consisting of the knowledge of particular machines and their quirks.

Assembly labour is even more intractable than most acts of conversion. Despite Ford, the bulk of assembly has never been automated because joining odd-shaped parts is exceptionally difficult for machines, because they can neither see, feel, nor make the subtle adjustments necessary not to jam or damage close-fitting pieces. We forget how difficult it is to fit a square peg in a square hole without jamming it, although it is the merest child's play to most human beings. Robotics finally allow a machine to carry out the extraordinary movements of the hand and arm as a complete, integrated unit.

The more sophisticated dimensions of the labour process are the hardest to rationalize, divide and mechanize. Most mechanization has been confined thus far to such actions as cutting, squeezing and moving, which barely scratch the surface of many production problems. Process regulation, consisting of initiation and response, requires powers of invention, observation (sensation) and reflection that are extraordinarily complex. The art of building machines that 'see', let alone those that 'think' is still in its infancy. Computer-aided product design is making great strides, but the acts of imagination that guide the process are still the province of the fashion designer, engineer or architect. Braverman was wrong to think that where this sort of 'mental labour' is concerned Taylorist principles will work effectively, because human self-regulation and creativity are not amenable to crude strategies of fragmentation and mechanical repetition (Varaiya, 1987).

Even basic acts of work integration also involve the not unsophisticated skills of communication, organization, co-operation, and competition. Marx and others have passed too quickly over the analysis of 'simple co-operation' to the division of labour without appreciating sufficiently that the one must be balanced against the other. In Taylorism work integration is almost completely absent. Fordism did achieve certain advances in work integration, to be sure, but it did so at the expense of ignoring others, such as the inventories on the loading dock, slow response time to errors, and worker interaction – precisely because its main focus was on continuous transfer and specialization in jobs and machines for simple acts of processing and assembly. The Japanese have achieved high levels of productivity by exploiting this 'lost dimension' of production. Japanese innovations in work organization show that Taylorism and Fordist assembly lines can be a barrier to greater productivity in the integrative dimension of work, and that a reconsideration of the basics of the labour process is needed before applying machinery indiscriminately.

Different material bases of industry pose further problems for capitalist rationalization and mechanization. Time and motion studies have had little to offer agriculture, electric power or oil refining. Moreover, the industrialization of everything from steel to pharmaceuticals has been propelled to a significant degree by the mastery of natural materials through metallurgy, chemistry or engineering, using scientific and technical labour that is itself highly unrationalized in Taylorist terms. Even the Taylorization of seemingly ordinary office and sales labour, which presents such a pressing need for twentieth-century capitalists, has proven surprisingly resistant to mechanization, for the reason of the kind of work involved – manipulation of information and personnel.

A second major difficulty with the Braverman thesis is that working with machines creates as well as destroys skills (Adler, 1985a). Machines have made possible many jobs and skills that were hardly imaginable before, whether for pilots, recording engineers or tool and die makers. In more humble fashion, even relatively unskilled machine operatives must intervene in the areas where machines remain helpless, as in set-up, speed and pressure adjustments or reactions to variable materials and wear and tear (Shaiken, 1984: 87–92). At the other end of the spectrum, new levels of creativity, responsibility and flexibility are required for the handling of immense machine systems whose malfunctioning can be terribly costly, even disastrous (Hirschhorn, 1984: 71–86). In between, one finds machines augmenting the capabilities of many workers in more or less traditional jobs, even where some of the previous functions of human labour have been moved into the machines: machinists can cut better parts with more advanced lathes; word processors can help the secretary type, edit, print and store work in ways not possible with typewriters; power tools have made the carpenter's job easier. In some cases, new 'flexible' machinery has greatly enhanced the competitive standing of more craft-like, multi-skilled labour in small workshops (Piore and Sabel, 1984). In general, the 'machine culture' that pervades modern industrial societies creates a certain broad technical literacy of its own (Adler, 1985a). Truck driving is not considered skilled work today, but it would have amazed a citizen of the nineteenth century.

A third and final point is that the analysis of deskilling and reskilling labour cannot proceed on the basis of the individual worker. Both Marxist critics of the Braverman school or technological optimists such as Sabel and Hirschhorn err by generalizing too widely from limited experience. Many people are, of course, grievously hurt by capitalist rationalization, division and mechanization, while others benefit, but neither tells us what has happened to what Marx called the 'collective labourer'. It is increasingly imperative to evaluate the transformation of work at the level of production systems and their complex divisions of labour within and beyond the factory, because of the widening scope of industrialization and social labour.

To begin with, mechanization creates masses of new jobs at the same time as it eliminates old ones. Even within the factory, the introduction of machine processes is usually markedly uneven. Between the 'islands of machinery' may be found large numbers of workers engaged with manual tasks such as sorting, testing or moving. As a result, the most advanced and most primitive kind of labour still go on cheek by jowl. Indeed, machinery may actually create more jobs at the labour-intensive bottlenecks by virtue of its expanded throughput: in the chemical industry, for example, one can still find gangs of common labourers filling, tying, carrying and loading bags of chemicals generated by highly automated processes (Nichols and Beynon, 1977: 11–12). More broadly, machinery creates a host of new labour-intensive jobs in repair, packing, shipping and design. Indeed, this effect is felt far beyond the factory in the legions of sales, advertising or managerial workers (cf. Walker, 1985a). Finally, as entirely new products and materials processes are brought into being because of the advancing front of machine technology, as in the case of plastics or silicon chips, wholly new industries grow up on the basis of new realms of know-how and practical skills.

The matter is more complicated than numbers of jobs and average labour-intensity across the social division of labour, because of the shifting nature of skills involved. Not only have new spheres of work arisen to be perhaps attacked anew by capitalist rationalization, as Braverman notes, but the centre of gravity of collective labour has changed, so that old skills and old capitalist conquests matter less than they once did. The production process has been extended to new spheres, from pre-production design to post-production repair, and the productivity of labour depends on all spheres, not just direct hands-on work (Kaplinsky, 1984; Varaiya, 1987; Walker, 1985a). Industrializ-ation has advanced to successively higher planes of technological competence, a process closely associated with the development of new industries; while this is widely acknowledged in misleading terms such as 'high-tech' or 'science-based' industry, the process goes back at least to the invention of steel, steam engines and coal-tar dyes, and the new industries they spawned (Walker, 1985c). When we look at the whole division of labour the living tissue of production is little diminished. But its look has changed as has its point of entry, its skills, its tools, and its venue – to drafting boards, computer terminals and fixing installed machines on site (cf. Jones, Chapter 2, above).

It is enormously difficult to assess the moving average of skill across the shifting division of labour in single industries, let alone the whole industrial system. Computer processing, for example, can involve a mix of tedious data entry (transfer) work and creative programming (regulation) work, but the average skill level of word or data processing can be quite high. Furthermore, skills will move in several dimensions at once as new machinery is adopted. The overall tendency appears to put greater and greater stress on the higher kinds of labour capacities such as observation, regulation, integration and creativity that are, as argued above, the least susceptible to machine domination at this time (Varaiya, 1987). Braverman gives too much credit to management and too little to the evolving forces of production by posing technological advance as chiefly a matter of 'conception' passing over to the side of capital.

It is easy to fall prey to the illusions created by a carelessly moving division of labour. But one cannot simply read skill off from the state of technology. At the micro-level, jobs are constructed in such a way as to concentrate better and worse tasks, then allocated according to gender, race and other 'background' factors (Edwards *et al.*, 1975). More broadly, the skill content of work is raised or demoted ideologically according to the bearer of the job, so that many of the jobs typically held by women branded unskilled may have a consider-able skill content (Jenson, Chapter 7, below; Phillips and Taylor, 1980). In making the case for a revival of craft skills with the coming of flexible specialization, Piore and Sabel (1984) extract only the better aspects of the overall situation of workers. Despite the admirable strength of the craft workers in today's Emilia Romagna or the Paris of Proudhon's time, the best jobs have been reserved for a select group of men (Harvey, 1985; Vinay, 1987). In fact, production 'flexibility' in such contexts may depend less on new machinery and upgraded skills than on flexible methods of exploiting labour such as the use of temporaries, external subcontracting, and abuse of illegal immigrants (Storper and Christopherson, 1987; Jenson, Chapter 7 and Walby, Chapter 6, below).

Human labour is then still the central force of production, not an afterthought to machines – or science and engineering in general. Mechanical advance can proceed in certain ways without immediate reference to the way human labour functions, as in advances in catalytic cracking. But social production as a whole cannot. The dialectic of labour and machines in the development of the forces of production is an ongoing one. Again and again, living labour reasserts itself as necessary. Not only is the fully automated factory an unattainable pipe dream of some capitalists (cf. Jones, Chapter 2, above), but the notion of full automation is itself an illusion. Industrial production is something that only humans do. While it may change form over time, human labour can never be eliminated. Braverman's model effectively annihilates the subject of labour – and not just the workers' will to resist. Yet production remains entirely humanly conceived, directed and undertaken, no matter how capital may distort that effort or how many machines participate.

To sum up, on the one hand, Braverman exaggerates the purely technical degradation of labour under capitalism, and it is this that leads him to underestimate worker resistance to capitalist offensives. The nature of human action, materials and machinery involved in particular labour processes, as well as the dynamics of product and process development, make work less susceptible to the logic of Taylorism or other existing strategies of capital than he suggests. Some solid foundations of resistance are granted workers by the technical realities of production (Storper and Walker, 1983) – although we know little about the exact relations between technology and politics; for example, the degree of work integration may be significant to worker solidarity (Mills, 1979). On the other hand, the manifest degradation of so much work under capitalism belies the views of technological optimists. The reason is that it has less to do with the division of labour and mechanization than with the relations of production, as Marx, I believe, came to realize by the time he wrote *Capital*. To blame technology for the conditions of work is to fall captive to a certain fetishism of that most impressive of commodities, the machine. While mechanization engenders real dangers and deprivations – nuclear power is not magically rendered safe by socialism, for instance – it still pales by comparison as a source of labour's degradation with the central social fact of having to work for someone else by virtue of the latter's ownership of property, with all that follows from that: demeaning treatment, inequitable assignment of tasks, lack of protection from hazards.

The geography of industrialization

We can now turn to the implications of the approach to mechanization outlined here for understanding the geographical tendencies of capitalist industrialization. The transformation of work is, more often than not, also the transformation of the *place* of work, as well. The geography of industrialization is not just the outcome of changes in production, however, but part and parcel of those changes and how they are brought into being (see also Chapter 13).

The prevailing models linking mechanization to industrial location are of two broad types. The first group includes the product cycle and two variants, the new international division of labour and corporate spatial hierarchy. Under the simple product cycle theory new industries arise in old industrial centres, or seedbeds, where a good supply of skilled labour and specialized markets and suppliers can be found. As they grow up – in this organic metaphor – the product and its production methods become increasingly standardized and mechanized, with consequent expansion of market area and deskilling of labour. These two conditions sever the link to the old industrial cores and make locations in peripheral, cheap labour areas more attractive (Scott, 1983; Vernon, 1960). Mechanization, therefore, leads to deskilling which leads in turn to dispersal of large plants, in a geographic extension of the deskilling thesis.

The new division of labour theory expands the model to allow for a spatial division of labour within industries such that more skilled, less mechanized units such as research or factories specializing in new products remain within the compass of old industrial centres while only standardized factory production disperses to the periphery (Froebel, *et al.*, 1980). The corporate hierarchy model adds that this is all possible due chiefly to the modern multilocational firm, whose headquarters move to the largest metropolitan centres, mid-level functions, such as research and divisional management, reside in medium–size cities or suburbs, and 'branch plants' are banished to the hinterlands in search of cheap and docile labour supplies (R. Cohen, 1981; Hymer, 1972). The two principal implications of these models for industrial geography are the growing separation of specialized bits of production across wider national and international arenas and the long-term stability of the urban, regional and national hierarchy of capitalist development.

These formerly dominant explanations for the spatial order of capitalist industrialization are yielding to two theses drawn from recent inquiries into machine technologies, employment practices and business organization. One involves the 'flexible production complex', defined at a regional or large metropolitan scale, and the other focuses on Japan and the newly industrializing East Asian countries, at an international scale. Within the former, the flexible specialization school has been captivated by the example of the Third Italy. In the approach taken by Sabel (1982; Brusco and Sabel, 1983; Piore and Sabel, 1984) it is the skill base of the new high-tech workshops that is making rapid industrial growth possible and attracting subcontracts from Fiat in Turin and elsewhere (Murray, 1983). A similar argument has been made for Silicon Valley, where engineering skills and technical innovation in microelectronics are said to create a unique centre of growth (Hall and Markusen, 1985). Storper and Scott (1988) have tried to generalize the principle of 'flexible production complexes', but on a broader basis than flexible automation. They argue that the flexible organization (integration) of production possible in such agglomerations of activity is central to their expansion at the expense of more isolated production sites (see also Scott, 1983).

Another group sees the focal point of advances in production and mechanization as Japan, and the competitive advantage it has gained in many industries by means of just-in-time, *kanban*, work teams, product quality and robotics. The background to Japan's breakthrough into world industrial leadership in innovation is explained in various ways, such as a long process of development from older, less sophisticated industries to newer high-tech ones (Cummings, 1984), highly organized state planning (Johnson, 1982), or protectionism and low interest rates (Okimoto *et al.*, 1984). Whatever the causes, however, it is agreed that the Japanese have pushed ahead of the pack in many critical areas of production organization and automation, especially in contrast to American Fordism (Abernathy *et al.*, 1983; Cusumano, 1985).

Common to both the Japanese and 'flexible cluster' models is a view that emerging centres of industry can eclipse the old on the basis of innovations in products and production methods. This is a dramatic reversal from the product cycle and new international division of labour models, in which established urban-industrial core areas remain the centres of innovation and accumulation. The view of hierarchical stability has been shattered by the wholesale geographic restructuring of industry in all advanced capitalist nations, as in the collapse of northern Britain, the rapid growth of the US sunbelt, and the shift of the entire world capitalist economy toward the Pacific. In fact, capitalist industrialization has repeatedly ignited the rapid growth of formerly outlying areas, from eighteenth-century Coalbrookdale to twentieth-century Los Angeles. Once the rapid growth potential of a new product or process is unleashed, a new locus of industry can mushroom, attracting suppliers investors and workers to it and forging them into the new configurations needed to master a new technology. The dynamics of industrialization allow firms to overcome the limitations of outlying areas, which may at first appear unattractive. Yet the very freedom of operation which capitalists find away from the centres of activity can be highly desirable in terms of moulding labour, management and local politics to new ways of producing – which are likely to include new product and process technologies, new ways of working and forms of labour control, and new forms of business organization. Conversely, older core areas can be paralysed by their traditional specializations in the face of continuously altered circumstances: new industries, new production methods, new labour relations, new business practices. This is not to say that it is easy for all peripheral places to forge ahead – as dependency theorists stress there are many ways in which backwardness is reproduced in the international capitalist world – but at least it is possible in this manner to explain what was impossible in the top-down models of spatial hierarchy (Storper and Walker, 1989).

These revised views of spatial clustering and changing locus of industry fit with the model of the labour process and mechanization presented here. First, mechanization does not proceed uniformly across industries, as depicted by the product cycle; instead it follows diverse and irregular paths of automation among different industries. Industries thus find their own particular locales and do not, as they expand over time, necessarily conform to one overarching spatial division of labour, or place hierarchy.

Second, spatial decentralization does not follow from the product cycle of mechanical maturation, deskilling and the search for outlying cheap labour sites. The kind of dispersal of branch plants captured by the prroduct cycle model is only significant in selected industries utilizing Fordist methods and faced with increasing competition, as in General Motors' unsuccessful strategy in the 1970s of moving plants to the southern US to evade the United Auto Workers union. The auto assembly factories involved were not significantly more mechanized or deskilled than their predecessors. Historically, US (and world) car production had earlier become more concentrated in and around Detroit precisely because of Ford's breakthrough into mass production with the assembly line – quite the reverse of the product cycle model. The spread of Ford plants around the country and abroad followed very quickly, as competitors were laid to rest and new markets captured by the Model T.

Third, the formation of territorial production clusters continues to rest heavily on spatial concentration as a way of handling the innumerable problems of interfirm organization of production systems. While not directly tied to mechanization, it follows from what has been said here about the 'lost dimension' of the labour process, integration. Neither the factory nor automated machine systems can alone cope with the manner of co-ordinating work across complex divisions of labour, and in this sense there is no such thing as a self-contained branch plant. Therefore, a theory such as the product cycle that tries to read off location from the level of mechanization in one factory is bound to err.

Fourth, industries periodically lurch in new directions owing to fundamental shifts in product technology or production methods (which usually involve important changes in emphasis among the five dimensions of labour and mechanization). Such restructurings can rejuvenate an industry or create entirely new industries at an experimental, labour-intensive stage of development, thereby rupturing any simple temporal relation between industrial evolution, mechanization and location. For example, gains in standardization or machine assembly of random memory semiconductor chips are overturned with each new generation of very large-scale integration. More dramatically, when electronics broke off from the electrical equipment industry, with the invention of the semiconductor, it also jumped from the northeastern USA to Silicon Valley in California. When Japanese automakers came up with just-in-time and other advances, the world centre of auto production began to shift from Detroit to Nagoya. Mechanization and technological change are inherently revolutionary processes, and so is geographical industrialization.

Fifth, when new centres of industry, such as Hollywood in the 1920s, begin to develop, they do so by creating new skills and new machines (Christopherson and Storper, 1989). Many of the requisite skills have never existed before, owing to the new products, new materials and new machinery needed to explore an uncharted technological terrain. This is what industrialization has always entailed: the creation of a productive power which did not exist before (Walker, 1988). And it does so in particular places, from the earliest experiments in Shropshire and Derbyshire through the miraculous growth of Manchester or Lowell to the explosive expansion of Paris and New York.

In short, the growth of capitalism, and the renewal of its prodigious powers of expansion, is intimately connected to industry localization, territorial clustering and the periodic opening up of new industrial centres. Alas, most social scientists, trained in aspatial ways of thinking, have been blind to the geographic dimension of industrialization. The transformation of work must be taken up in the broadest possible terms, in which changes in the labour process, technology, organization and industry location are seen as so many facets of the same immense process: capitalism's never-ending revolution of the forces of production and of the conditions of life for working people around the world. The transformations of work capitalism brought on by the rationalization, division and automation of labour processes are quite diverse, as we have seen, and can move in unexpected directions. This creates an uneven and unstable terrain on which capital and labour contest the content, performance and rewards of work. It is nonetheless a literal terrain, moreover, a place of cities and regions as well as shop-floors. The global transformation of work rests on the ability of capital to command that larger field of battle by dividing and conquering scattered labour forces, by tactical expansion, retreat and reposition of its industries, and by the build-up of whole new territorial bases of operation (Storper and Walker, 1989). It is, ultimately, this ability that checks the social forces – especially an organized working class – that can bring about a widespread transformation to more humane conditions of work.

4 Multinational corporations and the new international division of labour: a critical appraisal

ERICA SCHOENBERGER

Introduction

The study of multinational corporations came of age during the period of US dominance of an expanding global economy. In this context, explanations of the determinants of foreign direct investment – why firms invest abroad – focused to a great extent on questions of market power.[1] Firms moved abroad to exploit (or defend) their oligopolistic or 'ownership' advantages in foreign markets, including proprietary technology, greater capital resources and product differentiation (Caves, 1971, 1974, 1982; Dunning, 1971, 1974, 1981; Hymer, 1976; Kindleberger, 1970; Kindleberger and Audretsch, 1983; Vernon, 1966, 1974). Alternatively, it was argued that firms invest abroad to maximize efficiency by internalizing trade within the firm (Buckley and Casson, 1976; Teece, 1981). Both lines of analysis implicitly suggest that direct investment will be oriented principally to major market areas, hence, in all likelihood, other developed countries.

As the advanced industrial economies entered a period of stagnation, accompanied by large-scale rationalization and restructuring of industry, a new line of analysis emerged that viewed foreign investment primarily as a defensive reaction to problems of profitability and competitiveness in the core of the world economy arising from the pressures of high labour costs, union militancy and labour-market rigidities (Amin, 1979; Frobel et al., 1980, Susman, 1984; Vuskovic, 1980). In this new international division of labour concept (NIDL), production moves offshore primarily in search of low-cost, relatively docile labour in the periphery.

The NIDL has become very much a part of the working vocabulary of those concerned with questions of industrial restructuring on a global scale. In contrast to the old, broadly sectoral and horizontal division of labour, where the periphery provided food and raw materials in exchange for manufactured goods from the core (Lipietz, 1985), the NIDL highlights the changing spatial distribution of functions in the global economy. In this process of intra-sectoral, vertical de-linking, the core retains high-level knowledge and skill-

intensive activities, while low-skilled, standardized production processes are increasingly decentralized to the periphery. Whether
advanced as a theory (Frobel *et al.*, 1980) or a more descriptive phrase to
encapsulate observed trends (Perrons, 1981), the NIDL model foresees
a continued shift of standardized production processes to less-
developed areas. The geographical outcome, then, is analysed largely
through the optic of production and spatially differentiated factor
supply conditions while questions related to markets for output and
strategies for defending or expanding them are left aside.

This chapter will look specifically at the role of the multinational
corporation which is seen to be a major (though not the only) agent in
the evolution of the NIDL (Frobel, *et al.*, 1980; Lipietz, 1985; Perrons,
1981; Susman, 1984). The context, then, is a partial one as it leaves
aside, for example, the growth of indigenous firms in the periphery or
subcontracting relationships between the latter and firms in the core.
Yet this partial approach may help to elucidate the ways in which the
NIDL model itself reflects only a part of a complex and variegated
reality. While this may be recognized by those who use the phrase as a
kind of conceptual shorthand, it is only rarely acknowledged explicitly
(Lipietz, 1982, 1985, 1986; Taylor and Thrift, 1982).

Two principal arguments will be proposed. First, the NIDL model
takes an overly narrow view of the relationship between technological
and organizational change in production, cost competitiveness and
corporate location strategies. The almost total emphasis on cost
minimization and factor supply conditions contributes to a rather
mechanistic and uni-directional view of the evolution of the geography of production. Second, an accurate assessment of the role of
the multinational corporation (MNC) in the global allocation of
production depends also on an understanding of the nature of output
markets and the competitive strategies of firms within them. In sum,
the analysis of the international division of labour must comprehend
the nature of production *and* competition, strategies for revenue maxi-
mization *and* cost minimization, and the character of factor supply *and*
output markets. These relationships are fraught with tensions and
potential contradictions – the task of analysing the trade-offs involved
is an exceptionally difficult one.

The multinational corporation in the new international division of labour

The role of the MNC in the new international division of labour model
is predicated on several observable tendencies within the corporation
itself and the global economy. First, the intensification of international
competition means that even oligopolistic corporations are under
considerable pressure to seek new competitive advantages in order to

preserve and expand their markets and profits (Bluestone and Harrison, 1982; Bowles *et al.*, 1983; Hymer, 1972). Second, the MNC, by virtue of its size, organizational structure, wide horizons and massive capital resources, is able to physically separate various functions of the firm and locate them differentially to maximize its global profits. Improvements in transportation and communications have reinforced this effect by greatly enhancing the corporation's ability to oversee and co-ordinate the activities of its far-flung empire at a reasonable cost (Frobel *et al.*, 1980; cf. also Herold and Kozlov, 1987; Jenkins, 1984).

The effects of this evolution of corporate structures and capabilities are backed by parallel changes in the technology and organization of production, bearing in particular on the nature of the division of labour within the firm and the assumed deskilling of workers (Braverman, 1974; Frobel *et al.*, 1980; Lipietz, 1982, 1985). The division of labour within the firm becomes schematically a tripartite hierarchy, with knowledge-intensive control, engineering and advanced technical functions at the top, an intermediate level of higher-skilled production activities, and, finally, low-skilled, standardized production operations (Hymer, 1972; Lipietz, 1982, 1985).[2]

These three levels can be de-linked geographically, with each one seeking its appropriate supply of labour in different areas. There has been, consequently, a process of redistribution of these activities in accordance with regional disparities in conditions of labour supply (skills, cost, militancy), first within the core countries themselves, then towards the periphery.

In sum, in so far as the process of standardization proceeds, with its associated fragmentation and simplification of tasks, the corporation's demand for labour in production is increasingly oriented to low-skilled workers (Perrons, 1981; Braverman, 1974; Froebel *et al.*, 1980; Gibson *et al.*, 1984). In the face of intensified competition and threatened profits, the lure of developing country locations becomes very powerful as they offer large supplies of low-skilled and extremely low-cost labour.[3] In addition, lacking a strong industrial tradition, these workers are likely to be less militant (Bluestone and Harrison, 1982; Massey, 1984; Massey and Meegan, 1982; Walker and Storper, 1981), an effect often reinforced by domestic political conditions.

How close a correspondence between corporate functional hierarchies and regional specialization are we to expect? In some cases, this correspondence appears to be very strict indeed. Thus Susman, for example, summarizes his argument about the capital restructuring process in the advanced countries by stating:

> The shape of the world economy is strongly influenced by the relationships of national economies to TNCs (transnational corporations) and by the changing role each national population plays in the new international division of labour. This theoretical

focus provides the basis for understanding why regional change in one country is tied to the operations of TNCs that seek capital accumulation on a world scale. (Susman, 1984: 93)

As an example of the 'shorthand' use of the NIDL model alluded to above, this statement illustrates the way in which the evolution of corporate structures is associated with the assignment of specific regional 'roles'. As Sayer notes, this gives rise to the expectation that 'the general nature of regional or national economies can be "read off" from their place within the corporate divisions of labour' (Sayer, 1985a: 14). Moreover, coupled with the rather unidirectional view of the evolution of production processes toward standardization and deskilling (cf. Storper, 1985), the process assumes an air of inevitability.[4]

It should be stressed that the model is describing tendencies that are not necessarily expected to be equally evident across all industries or across all segments of a production process within an industry. For example, the persistence of skilled-labour demand means that many firms are not in a position to take advantage of the present pattern of global uneven development in quite this way (Lipietz, 1985, 1986; Noyelle, 1983). It seems, however, likely that the deepening industrial experience of many developing countries will enable them to offer increasingly substantial supplies of skilled labour. Thus, continued demand for the latter does not of itself undermine the argument. In the first instance, it merely signals that movement in this direction will be gradual and uneven. Indeed, the logic of the scenario is so persuasive that it is hard to see why firms with the necessary resources and capabilities would not take maximum advantage of this opportunity to reduce costs and thereby restore their competitiveness and profitability. Yet the picture that emerges from a consideration of US-based MNC investments is, to say the least, ambiguous.

The distribution of US manufacturing investments abroad

From 1970 to 1984, the US foreign manufacturing investment position grew from $31 billion to $86 billion. This time span encompasses a period of deepening crisis for the US economy and the intensification of international competition – precisely the circumstances in which one would look for a significant reallocation of resources. Second, a nearly three-fold increase over fourteen years would seem to leave ample room for such a reallocation, even allowing for the lumpiness of investment and extended planning horizons. This is the context in which the geographic redistribution of resources must be evaluated.

A certain amount of resource redirection has occurred. Yet the pace has been rather slower than might be expected. During these years, less developed countries increased their share of the total from 17.6 percent to 22 per cent with nearly three-quarters of that share located in just six countries (Argentina, Brazil, Mexico, Hong Kong, Singapore, and Taiwan). The countries of the European semi-periphery (Greece, Ireland, Portugal, Spain and Turkey) increased their share from 2.6 per cent to 4.4 per cent.

The core developed countries, then, did lose ground (from a 79.7 per cent share to 72.5 per cent), but still remained overwhelmingly dominant as a location for US investment. Indeed, by 1986, they had recovered to a 76.2 per cent share of a total position equal to $107 billion, entirely at the expense of the less developed countries which declined to an 18.8 per cent share. Moreover, the US itself has become a favoured location for foreign manufacturers, their investments having risen from $8.2 billion in 1973 to $50.7 billion in 1984 (US Department of Commerce, 1976, 1982; *Survey of Current Business* various issues).

Clearly, the bulk of foreign manufacturing investment remains oriented to relatively high-cost, major foreign markets despite the theoretical possibility of de-linking production and locating it separately in order to reduce costs. Some factors which may help to explain why many MNCs are not pursuing an NIDL-type of international production strategy as aggressively as may have been expected are discussed in the following sections.

Technical and organizational change in production and spatial strategies

The consideration of technological change in the NIDL model is focused principally on the standardization of products and production processes and the deskilling of labour. The associated decentralization of production is in part a response to a technological opportunity, but is principally motivated by labour cost and control problems in the face of intensified competition.

The first question that arises is to what extent these trends are empirically generalizable. This applies to the issues of deskilling, the spatial de-linking of functions and the hypothesized geographical destination of these functions. One may ask, therefore, if standardization of products is the norm or deskilling the general outcome of the application of automated production processes. The evidence on both points is decidedly mixed. For example, it has been observed that the automobile industry has entered a phase of 'dematurity' with a greatly intensified segmentation of markets and diversification of products (Abernathy *et al.*, 1984; Altshuler *et al.*, 1984).[5] Moreover, despite our preoccupation with mass production in a mass consumption society, small-batch production methods still account for a large proportion of industrial output in the US (Piore and Sabel, 1984; Storper, 1985). At the same time, the application of new automation technologies in many instances appears to lead to an upgrading of the skills mix within the firm, often at the cost of the elimination of large numbers of low-skilled jobs (Baran, 1985; Bonnafos, *et al.*, 1983; Durand, *et al.*, 1984; Piore and Sabel, 1984; Sabel, 1982; Shaiken, 1984).

The question of the extent of de-linking of functions according to skill category must also be examined. First, while it may be true that automation reduces the skill level of the firm's own production process, this is often at the expense of increased reliance on sophisticated machinery and the skilled programmers, service and maintenance workers that keep it running (Durand, *et al.*, 1984; Sabel, 1982; Shaiken, 1984). There is a trade-off between assuring that the firm's fixed capital stock is kept constantly in motion, which may require access to skilled support workers, and opting for reducing direct (production) labour costs by locating in the periphery. Similarly, the need to assure quality control may promote the retention of more skilled workers on the shop-floor. The point here is not to debate whether computer-integrated manufacturing is supplanting more traditional mechanization processes. Rather it is to suggest that different technological options exist, and that an element of indeterminacy in their choice remains.

Also connected with the de-linking issue is the question of the organization of production within and across firms. A key example, particularly evident in the case of the automobile industry, concerns the Japanese *kanban* or 'just-in-time' (JIT) system. Although often viewed simply as a system of inventory control, the JIT approach actually implies a substantially different organization of production within the firm, increasing the flexible utilization of workers and reducing considerably dead time of machinery (Ohno, 1984; Sayer, 1985b; Schoenberger, 1987b; Sugimori *et al.*, 1977). It also transforms relationships within and between firms and their suppliers, increasing the importance of spatial proximity to assure the smooth and flexible flow of parts through the system (Holmes, 1985; Sayer, 1985b; Sheard, 1983).

Two factors should be stressed. First, dramatic cost savings are realized from the reorganization of production itself rather than solely through factor input cost adjustments. It has been estimated that Japanese manufacturers can build an automobile with only 65 per cent of the labour hours required by US firms with roughly equivalent technology and *less* capital employed per unit of output (Abernathy *et al.*, 1984; Altshuler *et al.*, 1984). Second, the increased importance of spatial proximity suggests the reassertion of the role of agglomeration economies that counter the decentralization and dispersal of the manufacturing process.

Finally, even given pressure to reduce costs combined with a tendency toward deskilling and de-linking as suggested in the NIDL model, it is not clear that we should expect a unique spatial outcome. For example, increased automation may or may not imply a new location strategy for the firm. If the direct labour share of total costs is sufficiently reduced by the elimination of workers and the reorganization of work processes, the additional savings that could be achieved by relocating production to the periphery may not significantly strengthen the competitive position of the firm. Further, if automation is combined with deskilling, segmentation of local labour markets can permit firms to reduce wage costs on site through the substitution of unskilled workers for a previously skilled (and high-cost) workforce (Massey, 1978). The growing presence of immigrants and undocumented workers has gone some way to reproducing the labour supply conditions of the periphery at the core (Glickman and Petras, 1981). Finally, the persistence of uneven regional development within the advanced countries means that firms can still achieve significant cost reductions through highly differentiated regional strategies within the core (Hansen, 1979; Moulaert and Salinas, 1983). In this way, transformation of production processes and relocation may be either alternative or complementary strategies, depending on a variety of factors.

Of course, where further automation is not a feasible option, a cost-cutting location strategy may become paramount. This last has been the case in the assembly phase of the electronics industry, the archetype of the NIDL. While automated assembly is not technically impossible, it has historically not been widely implemented due in part to highly compressed product life cycles and insufficiently long production runs to justify the investment in specialized or dedicated equipment (Flamm, 1985). Yet, the development of more flexible automated machinery capable of adapting to changing product configurations or specifications may significantly alter the location patterns of the industry. There are already signs that assembly automation is accompanied by relocation of offshore production to the core in some cases (Castells, 1985; Sayer, 1985a, 1986a; Schoenberger, 1986).

The point is not to dismiss the interest of peripheral locations, which technical change has in many respects made more feasible. But it is the dynamic interaction among geographically-defined factor supply conditions, technical change in production and, as I will seek to show, competitive strategies, that count. The NIDL model consistently discounts the possibility of reorganizing production in the core to reduce factor costs and restore profitability (Herold and Kozlov, 1987; Jenkins, 1984). In stressing a given trajectory of technical change leading to a singular spatial pattern of production, it loses sight of sectoral diversity and the variety of strategic options that exist for firms within and across industries.

Market orientation, competitive strategies and location

The market as place

The NIDL model focuses on factor-supply markets, particularly labour, as the key to understanding the international reallocation of production. Yet there is reason to believe that a significant share of direct investment in the periphery is motivated more by the desire to gain access to developing-country markets (often highly protected) than by a strategy of cost reduction. In 1976, for example, 79 per cent of the sales of US subsidiaries (in all sectors) in Asia and the Pacific were to the local (regional) market. For Latin America, the figure rises to 94 per cent (Herold and Kozlov, 1987). In 1984, the share of total multinational corporate intra-firm manufacturing imports (that is, goods transferred back to the USA) shipped by their offshore affiliates in the Third World was, at 25.6 per cent, only slightly higher than their share of the total position. These data suggest that less developed countries do not function primarily as cost-cutting export platforms supplying core country markets. Their chief importance to MNCs continues to be as markets in their own right.

This is not an original observation (cf. Glickman and Petras, 1981; Hansen, 1979; Harvey, 1977; Jenkins, 1984; Lipietz, 1985) but it is one that is missed by the NIDL model with its cost and supply-side focus. Moreover, the further development of Third World countries will deepen their market potential and expand it to a wider range of sectors unless this process is choked off as a result of the debt crisis. Combined with lagging growth rates and market saturation in the core countries, this suggests that the observed shift in MNC investments will continue to be market oriented to a significant extent.

The market as strategy

Just as alternative production strategies exist for firms facing intensified cost pressures, alternative competitive strategies also offer a means of countering competition from low-cost producers of standardized goods. In particular, the orientation to different types of markets within a given sector has significant implications for the location of production, even where the labour process remains predominantly unskilled and, hence, susceptible in theory to an NIDL-type of allocation.

Consider first the relationship between competitive strategy and location in technology-intensive sectors. There is, of course, good reason to believe that technological change and product innovation or adaptation constitute one of the primary determinants of foreign direct investment (Dunning, 1981; Vernon, 1966, 1974). Under these circumstances, market orientation may be expected to be a significant component of the firm's strategic behaviour, especially in the face of highly differentiated national markets. Yet, this does not necessarily explain why production, as opposed to marketing and information-gathering outposts (to ensure that products are adapted to the specificities of a given market) will be located in the target market. We need to explain why the firm's competitive position in particular kinds of markets may be strengthened by locating production in the market, even when this in not the least-cost solution.

Where technology and product performance (rather than price) are the basis of competition, product technology is subject to considerable renewal and adaptation over time. This means that in contrast to, for example, product cycle theory, there is no presumption that product characteristics are fixed once past the early innovation stage. Continual product development implies strong forward linkages from research and development (R&D) into marketing and backward linkages to production. In rapidly changing markets, firms need to be flexible and prepared to respond quickly to changes in demand and competitive behaviour (Sayer, 1985a; Schoenberger, 1985, 1987a).

This adaptation demands considerable flexibility and responsiveness on the production side. The production process itself has to be readily adaptable to changes in product specifications, to the introduction of new products, or to changes in product mix. This implies close co-ordination with the marketing and R&D functions of the firm. In addition, turnaround times on product orders are frequently of great importance – the ability to supply on demand may outweigh differences in supply price. Cost savings that could be achieved through a more extensive geographic division of labour within the firm must be traded off against the disadvantages this presents in terms of the firm's ability to develop an effective supply response (Schoenberger, 1985).

This is not an argument that concerns solely 'high-tech' industries. First, it is really lack of standardization in the market that draws even low-skilled segments of the production process to relatively high cost locations. Moreover, even in high-technology sectors, a range of competitive strategies is possible. Firms can target higher volume, relatively standardized commodity segments of their 'high-tech' markets (for example, standardized dynamic random access memories in semiconductors) or more specialized, non-standardized segments (custom and semi-custom chips). In the first case, standardization, combined with intense price competition, creates considerable pressure to reduce costs. In the second case, where price competition is less important and the need for flexibility is high, relatively high production costs may be tolerated in an effort to remain responsive to and competitive in a rapidly changing market.

Thus, the distinction between 'high-tech' and 'non-high-tech' is not necessarily the crucial one. The key difference even *within* a generally 'high-tech' sector may instead be that between standardized and non-standardized market segments (Schoenberger, 1986). In this light, even traditional sectors such as textiles appear to offer considerable scope for alternative competitive strategies. What Piore and Sabel call 'flexible specialization' is a response to market instability, leading firms to target smaller, more rapidly changing and more specialized market segments (Piore and Sabel, 1984; Sabel, 1982). The development of more flexible production processes – through, for example, numerical and computer-controlled equipment – greatly enhances the firm's ability to implement this type of strategy. Nor does this apply only to small, 'niche' firms. Aggregate output of the firm may be quite high but, due in part to more flexible manufacturing systems that allow smaller runs of individual product types without sacrificing economies of scale, the firm can still respond to a highly differentiated sectoral market.

In so far as a strategy of non-standardization in traditional sectors gives rise to the same linkages among marketing, product development and production that were described for 'high-tech' industries, the locational dynamics may be similar. Even low-skilled segments of the production process will be drawn to the market despite potentially higher wage costs.

The NIDL model seems implicitly to assume that competitiveness and profitability hinge, in the end, uniquely on price. Pure price competition may be unavoidable in some markets or for some commodity types. For others, this is manifestly not the case. Moreover, firms have every incentive to perpetuate non-price based competition in the markets they target. In these cases, production at the market, even where this entails higher costs, may be an effective strategy for maximizing market share and revenues.

In sum, if the NIDL model has an overly restrictive view of the role in production of technological and organizational change and its relationship to the international allocation of investment, it has completely discounted the role of markets in orienting that investment. Similarly, it has failed to incorporate a sufficiently nuanced analysis of how firms compete with one another in those markets and what this means for the type of products they produce or how and where they produce them.

Conclusion

Undoubtedly, many multinational corporations do behave in the way that the NIDL model suggests. This is not at present, however, the dominant trend. Nor is there strong reason to believe that it will become a general model of international direct investment. Fundamentally, the model has an excessively narrow view of the direction of technological change and its relationship to location and of the nature of competition among firms in different kinds of markets.

To argue for a more restrained and critical usage of the NIDL concept may appear unexceptional. Yet, the model has important political and policy implications, hinging notably on the extent to which relocation of production to the periphery in order to minimize costs accounts for the decline of manufacturing employment in the core.

In particular, the NIDL approach seems to underestimate the extent to which the employment crisis in the advanced regions is also generated internally as the result of labour-saving technological changes in production (Freeman *et al.*, 1983; Harvey, 1982; Jenkins, 1984; Leontief, 1983; Massey, 1984; Massey and Meegan, 1982) combined with problems of aggregate demand growth and the lack of outlets for profitable investment of surplus capital. This reinforces the impression that employment gains in one location are made strictly at the expense of jobs in another, distracting attention from the further question of what forces inhibit the creation of enough jobs to go around. It also encourages workers in the industrial countries to view low cost foreign labour as the primary threat to their well-being. Among policy responses which would seem to follow logically from this view are the acceptance of wage cuts and other concessions, combined with calls for protectionism. While such an approach may preserve some jobs, it may not of itself reverse the decline in manufacturing employment in the advanced regions.

The NIDL model in many respects constitutes progress in our thinking about spatial change. In particular, it ties together the strands of industrial location and regional development which have remained largely separate in the literature. It also recognizes the interaction of corporate structures, technological change and spatial patterns of investment. The principal caution here is against encapsulating many tendencies and strategic options into a single evolutionary path or trajectory of change. In our use of the term, and in our thinking about strategies to combat the decline of manufacturing employment in the industrialized countries, we need to confront the diversity of strategic options and responses that exist at the level of the firm.

5 Jobs and skills under the lifelong nenkō employment practice

MAKOTO KUMAZAWA and JUN YAMADA

Introduction

It is said that the post-war system of Japanese industrial relations is now in a process of profound transformation. Warning is being repeatedly given to Japanese workers that the process should be drastic and demanding because such recent conditions as reduced rate of economic growth, intensified international productivity competition, and rapid technological innovation are all pressing the management-labour relations system to free itself from the custom of lifelong seniority-based (known as *nenkō*) employment practice. Indeed, since the oil crises in the 1970s most of the major Japanese manufacturing establishments have taken and are still taking severe 'downsizing' measures which tend to concentrate redundancy among long-serving employees of middle-age or over. Enterprise unionism is quite powerless to counter the process which is undermining the very basis of its existence.

To grasp the nature of the transformation in progress, we shall in this chapter see how the conventional *nenkō* practice used to work as an apparently stable compromise between both sides of the industry. The lifelong *nenkō* system specifically acting as an employer's paternalistic strategy dates from pre-war years. Labour unions in Japan, fully legitimized only after the Second World War, challenged the paternalism and demanded employment as the principal right of all regular employees. After initial conflicts, the post-war industrial relations system stabilized over a period of two decades of continued high economic growth preceding the oil crises. Our concern is mainly with this stage of the development.

The set of popularly perceived productivity advantages of so-called Japanese-style management largely rest on management's unchallenged power to reorganize the existing production process more efficiently. In other words, greater flexibility in shop-floor labour-force deployment and work effort results from the absence of independent union control over members' day-to-day work. This goes hand-in-hand with the competitive individualism increasingly widespread on the shop-floor. Organized labour has got used to entering into the production process alongside the unorganized mass as though they were themselves unorganized. Although the lifetime employment practice in a large firm secludes its regular employees from the outside labour market, it encourages competition among the organized regulars themselves.

These features of Japanese management practice took shape and established themselves quite effectively under the lifelong *nenkō* system long before the present transformation gained momentum under the recent conditions of a low growth economy. A new development is to be seen, therefore, in the employers' attack on some residual rigidities of the system, as a result of which a more selective meritocratically based system is developing. Undoubtedly the situation poses a great threat to the cohesiveness of workers as regular members of a firm, driving enterprise unionism into a tight corner.

One of the pivotal concepts in the controversy surrounding Braverman has always been 'worker resistance', and a number of studies have attempted to show, contradicting Braverman's thesis of management's unlimited power to deskill labour, how 'worker resistance' affects the actual process of reproduction of the work organization itself (Littler, 1982; Wilkinson, 1983). However, what strikes us most is not Braverman's often-quoted 'self-imposed omission of the subjective', but rather the careless way in which he repeatedly referred to the 'natural resistance' or 'natural revulsion' on the part of workers against what he called the 'dehumanizing effects' of the capitalist labour process (Braverman, 1974: 139, 149 ff). Braverman seems to have assumed human resistance to the dehumanizing process to be so absolutely 'natural' that he could presuppose the omnipresence of worker resistance *a priori*.

Worker resistance, at least of such magnitude as to be able to influence the organization of the production process, presupposes workers' autonomous community which nurtures, and is nurtured by, workers' own notions as to what their jobs should be like. This can take shape only if workers try to restrict competition among themselves, regulating how and how much they should work. After all, what Braverman (1974: 6) called 'craft heritage' is just a typical model of it. Needless to say, it is a historical creation, neither 'natural' nor omnipresent.

As is well known, Japanese labour unions are generally organized on an enterprise-wide basis. In fact, for the last forty years enterprise unionism has been almost the only model of collective representation of workers' interests. The far-reaching effects of that fact cannot be emphasized too much. The dominance of enterprise-wide organization makes it very difficult, if not impossible, for workers to combine themselves on other levels or according to other principles than 'the company as a community of interests'. Virtually excluded from the

Japanese labour-relations system are job- or occupation-oriented models of social combination such as autonomous shop-floor solidarity of workers based on the similarity of the skill requirements of their immediate and prospective jobs; local residentially based communities of the working population beyond company walls as could be organized in a craft or general union; or industry-wide organization regulating basic working conditions for all the workers in a particular industry irrespective of their different employers. Many federal organizations of unions on an industry-wide basis in Japan have no effective power to control the policies or industrial actions of individual enterprise unions. The most important result of this is that the majority of workers working in medium- and small-sized firms are left largely unorganized, for the sheer size of these firms makes an enterprise union unfeasible. And this lack of occupation-oriented models, in turn, tends to reinforce unionized employees' dependence on their large firms.

Unionization concentrates heavily in the large-firm sector, and organized labour has generally acquiesced to its lifelong *nenkō* practice. This chapter is an attempt to make clear what effects this tradition, as the dominant model, has had on the working population in general, organized or unorganized. First we see them in terms of the industrial dualism in Japan, then describe the typical structure of the entire workforce composition of a large manufacturing firm, where various types of unorganized workers are mobilized, directly or indirectly, into its production process. Finally we feature the intra-firm career formation of the regular male employees who are at the core of the segmented labour-force structure.

Dependence on the company

What appears as the strong loyalty of Japanese workers to the company is not self-evident. We know that a worker's self-identification is composed of several different layers as the following comparative characterization shows.

> If you meet a Bradford English Electric foundryman on a train and ask him what he does, the first thing he will probably say is that he is a foundryman, the second thing that he comes from Bradford, and the third that he works for English Electric. His Japanese counterpart would most naturally define himself first as a member of the Hitachi Company, secondly as working at such and such a factory, and thirdly as being a foundryman.
> (Dore, 1973: 115)

We must now examine how and why for the Japanese counterpart the aspect of being an occupant of a specific job tends to be submerged in the aspect of being an employee of a specific company.

Before discussing further the nature of the employment security of regular employees in major firms, we must observe here what reply we will get if another foundryman on the train works for a small firm whose name is, accordingly, unknown. The worker perhaps feels embarrassed at the question. Anyway the probability of his saying 'a foundryman' will, still, nevertheless be low, reflecting the fact 'that consciousness of occupation – job characteristics that are transferable among employers – is rather weakly developed in Japan' (Cole, 1971: 13). Underlying the fragile occupation consciousness is, among other things, the lack of such standardization of working conditions across firms, large or small, as is often concisely summarized in the phrase 'equal pay for equal work'. Indeed, it is not unusual for a highly skilled worker of a smaller firm to have total compensation considerably lower than that of an equally or even less skilled worker who happens to work for a larger firm.

In Japan, differentials of firm-size, age, and sex are far more significant than skill-grade or job-evaluation in determining wage differentials. An approximate profile of the wage differentials determined by these three factors is given in Figure 5.1. The seniority-linked rise in wages for male employees is flatter and reaches its peak earlier as the size of firms reduces. Although the *nenkō*-based payment method in the large-firm sector works as the model for smaller firms to follow, the actual wage level in the latter depends directly on an individual firm's capacity to pay. (By the way, take note of the very sharp decline of the line for the males in the large-scale sector around age fifty. It reveals the effects of severe merit assessment of senior employees.) Furthermore, there is virtually no seniority increase in pay for female workers, especially in the smaller-scale sections.

The differential in general working conditions as well as in wage levels between employees of smaller and of larger companies is usually interpreted in terms of the industrial dualism peculiar to Japan, that is the interdependent co-existence of capital-intensive larger firms achieving high productivity, and labour-intensive smaller firms lagging behind in productivity. Koike (1987: 324) says as regards the dualism, 'the greatest divergence between large firms and small ones is that workers in large firms are of a single type – namely, white-collarized workers with intellectual skills – and that small firms employ a variety of workers'. Koike's concept of 'white-collarization' is pertinent in so far as it points out a Japanese feature comparable with other advanced economies, namely blue-collar workers' general tendency to pursue a lifelong career formation within a firm just like their white-collar counterparts in a large firm. We cannot agree, however, with his interpretation of the gap by firm-size in terms of different skill-grades. That the differential has little to do with the skill level

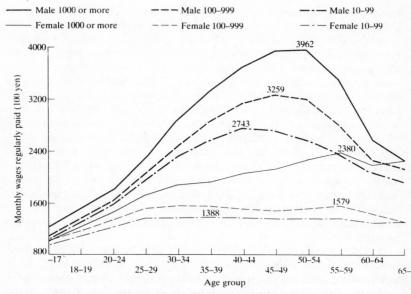

Figure 5.1   Wage differentials

Note: 'Large-scale' means enterprises with 1,000 or more employees, 'medium-scale'; 100–999, 'small-scale' 10–99

Source: Based on the Basic Survey of Wage Structure by the Ministry of Labour, 1985.

of workers is clear from Figure 5.1 where the difference between the age/wage lines for males gets narrower as workers approach their retiring ages. The differential depends, rather, on larger or smaller firms' profitability and thus on their ability to pay wages. In fact, many of those skilled manual workers who, in Western countries, would have been organized in relevant craft or trade unions are found in Japan in the lower part of the dual economy, often unorganized and working harder and longer hours to make up for the lower wage rates. The form of 'worker resistance' by the skilled which has been discussed in terms of 'social construction of skill' (Wood, 1982: 17) is, therefore, hardly to be seen in Japan.

Cole (1971: 63), unlike Dore, studied a medium-sized diecasting firm and reported that the workers:

> were reluctant to permit the company to become involved in their personal affairs. Their desire for independence could also be seen in the high value they placed on securing a skill. Skills that could be transferred to other companies put them in a better bargaining position with their company.

Not all Japanese workers identify themselves with the company. Since smaller firms cannot provide employees with such lifelong security of employment as larger ones do, workers in smaller firms are usually more concerned with their acquired skills than those in larger ones. In fact, workers change employers more frequently in the lower half of the dual economy. On the other hand, once employed as a regular employee in a large firm (usually directly from school), one's probable lifelong career in the same firm tends to weaken one's interests in the working conditions of the local labour market (cf. Dore, 1973: 415). Enterprise unions reflect this lack of interest. Therefore, the possibility of strengthening the collective bargaining position through acquired skills is strictly limited in the small–firm sector because there is no effective machinery to standardize inter-firm working conditions according to job or skill-grade. Skill remains a matter of an individual worker and is subjected to evaluation by an employer on an individual basis. The high value that workers in smaller firms place on skill may rather be explained in terms of their ambition some day to become self-employed craftsmen, an ambition which is sometimes achieved.

It is this part of the labour force which needs an occupation–oriented organization most, and it is this same sector which faces the most difficult situation for unionization. The following observation, also by Cole (1971: 13), illustrates how even in the small-firm sector workers are more often than not divided company by company:

> One of the first things I found remarkable about the diecast workers was that they associated only among themselves during the lunch recess, despite the plant's location in a crowded factory area. They knew none of the workers in the factory across the narrow street although for years they had been having baseball catches side by side at noon.

The loyalty to organization or the 'group-centered pattern of value orientation' (Odaka, 1984: 71) of the Japanese is invariably alluded to when describing Japanese-style management. But what is really important is to grasp how and why the company comes to the fore as the dominant social group for Japanese workers at the cost of other possible forms of grouping. The loyalty to the company is neither spontaneous nor absolute. It is a hierarchical segmentation of the nation's working population which generates the dependence the privileged minority have on the company.

Flexibility in workforce deployment

The most important feature of so-called Japanese-style management rests on the enormous flexibility a large-scale enterprise has in the deployment of its 'manpower'. Major firms in Japan derive superior productivity from their power to control total labour costs by means of flexibility in workforce deployment. There are basically two types of flexibility which enable a large-scale employer to adapt its labour-force composition to changing production goals: labour-market type and internal-career type of flexibility.

Seeking an important feature of the Japanese labour-relations system in flexibility, just as we do, Koike (1987: 308) attributes this feature to the fact that Japanese blue-collar workers in large firms share lifelong career development within a single firm with white-collar workers. And when Koike says 'workers in large firms are of a single type – namely, white-collarized workers with intellectual skills', what is in mind is exclusively the case of the regular, and mostly male, employees. But a large company's labour-force structure, being a mosaic construction and far from a single solid community, is divided sharply into full-time regular employees and non-regular or indirectly employed workers. The latter category of workers serves as an indispensable buffer against production fluctuation, thus providing the labour-market type of flexibility. As Dore (1973: 399) points out, 'temporary workers, not admitted to the enterprise family, enjoying none of the privileges of the permanent workforce and dismissible whenever times are bad, offered the necessary flexibility'.

As for the internal-career type of flexibility which rules 'permanent' employees, Cole (1979: 200), contrasting Japan with the United States, characterizes it as follows;

> In America, the employer benefits from having clearly defined jobs so that job occupants can be more easily treated as replaceable parts. This provides an important kind of flexibility for employers, though it is, so to speak, a flexibility 'between' occupants while the Japanese emphasize a flexibility in using the occupant himself.

The regular male employees are expected to form the 'core' of a large firm's labour-force. And it is often suggested that diffuse or ambiguous job definitions enable them to experience a wide variety of related jobs and to become multi-skilled workers (Littler, 1982: 194), or, in the case of blue-collars, to become 'white-collarized workers'. This sort of lifelong employment security, however, does not necessarily mean job security for the regulars. In extreme cases, though more and more frequent in recent years, the 'flexibility in using the occupant himself' results in the transfer of employees between such different fields as car assembly-line work and sales promotion departments. Possible disturbing effects for the employee of this type of flexibility must not be overlooked, while, in general, Japanese management distinctly benefits from the practice.

The so-called lifelong *nenkō* practice in Japanese large firms has been said to be the cause and the result of the internal career formation within a firm. But recently an increasing number of observers say that this traditional practice has at last begun to dissolve. Most often quoted causes are managements' rationalization efforts to remain competitive in the world market, technological innovation based on micro-electronics, and finally but not the least, the rapidly aging working population in Japan. The observation on the end of the lifelong seniority principle appears plausible, for employment security has markedly deteriorated, as a result of the 'slimming-down' policies now rigorously pursued in many firms, among precisely middle-aged and older workers with long years of service.

What has the lifelong *nenkō* system been, then, and what is really indicated by its supposed demise? Is the change really so radical as is widely claimed to be? To answer these questions, we will look first at the entire labour-force construction of a large firm and examine afterwards how the system used to work, and how it is still working in a much more flexible way.

Hierarchical segmentation of the workforce

Figure 5.2 represents the segmented hierarchy of the entire labour force under the control of a large parent company. Needless to say, the relative size of each section of the pyramid is quite different from industry to industry. The chart should be considered as conceptualizing the typical structure of a large-scale manufacturing enterprise. Although we do not discuss the matter in depth, the hegemonic power of such a parent corporation prevails not only among its employees but also in the rest of the society. The Toyota-style production control based on the 'no-buffer principle' or the 'just-in-time system', for example, would not work efficiently without the parent firm's power also to control the production of parts-suppliers, and the parts-delivery service of forwarding firms. Giant firms distinctly benefit from the large-small industrial gradation of firms. (See also the figure in the appendix to this chapter, which is borrowed and slightly adapted [for the sake of translation into English and to correlate with our Figure 5.2] from Tsuda's recent paper, 'Is the Dual Structure Being Renewed?' [Tsuda, 1987]. Tsuda's and our classification happen to represent the same complex structure, one horizontally and the other vertically. Tsuda's is useful when we see the movements of some sections of the workforce.)

To begin with, even within a large parent company, those employees who can expect to be covered by the lifelong *nenkō* practices are limited to the innermost trapezoid section in Figure 5.2 of the male regular employees [C]. Female employees [D] are also regular members of the company, and are accordingly organized in the enterprise union, which usually enjoys 100 per cent membership amongst the regulars. Women are, however, virtually excluded from the lifelong career ladder. Most of them are assigned clerical or miscellaneous tasks ancillary to those of males in white-collar departments, unskilled or semi-skilled routine jobs on manufacturing shop-floors and are expected to retire when they marry or have their first baby. The fact is clearly reflected in the wage profile given in Figure 5.1, where the age-wage line for women is much flatter than for men. Although the Equal Employment Opportunity Law of 1985 is beginning to have some effects, recently there has also been a tendency to take in fewer women as full-time regular members of the firm. In fact, some aspects of the jobs which have been assigned usually to young female regulars are now either farmed out or performed by female part-time workers.

It is exactly an increasing number of these ex-senior employees [E] which seems to prove the end of seniority-linked employment security. The employees in their forties or fifties are exposed to increasingly severe selection based on the evaluation of their merits and work capability. Some of them are persuaded to accept early retirement, or simply transferred to the subsidiaries or subcontractors under the influence of the parent firm. We will discuss this intensified process of the meritocratic selection later in terms of the contradictions inherent in the lifelong *nenkō* system.

The very bottom of the pyramid, separated sharply from the main body of the regulars, consists of a variety of non-regular employees, namely seasonal or temporary workers on a full-time basis [H], and those who work on a part-time or short-time basis, chiefly housewives [I] and students [J]. They are employed at a firm's local sites explicitly for a fixed period of employment, mostly from a few weeks to several months. But some of them may be re-hired many times for a considerable number of years. They are generally excluded from enterprise-union membership. Needless to say, it is this section of the whole structure which is directly affected by the product market's vicissitudes. And this form of employment suggests that large firms also have highly routinized dead-end jobs with short training periods for the unskilled.

The proportion of the seasonal/temporary workers [H] in the non-regular segment began to decline when labour shortages emerged and intensified in the mid-1960s. It must be remembered in this connection that a great migration from rural agricultural areas to urban industrial centres has occurred right through the post-war economic recovery and its immense expansion. In fact, the percentage of employed workers in the primary sector of the economy (mainly agriculture, fisheries and extraction), including self-employed and family co-workers, decreased from 48.3 per cent in 1950 to 10.9 per cent in 1980. Meanwhile, the percentage of gainfully employed people in the secondary, manufacturing, sector increased from 21.9 to 33.6 per cent in the same period. As a result of the land reforms immediately after

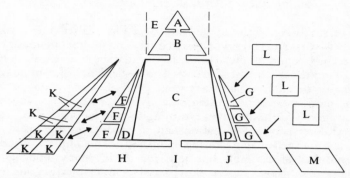

Figure 5.2 Segmented hierarchy of the workforce directly or indirectly employed by a big company

Key: A: top management
   B: middle management
   C: male regular employees
   D: female regular employees
   E: ex-senior-employees screened off from [B] or retired ones
   F: subcontractor's employees working within the parent company
   G: more or less specialized workers dispatched from independent labour-force supplying firms [L]
   H: seasonal or temporary employees
   I, J: part-time workers, mainly housewives and students
   K: subcontractors or suppliers and their employees, the lower half of the so-called dual economic structure
   M: foreign cheap labour employed abroad

the Second World War, most tenant farmers became small land-owning self-employed farmers. But they as well as their families have been pulled incessantly to urban manufacturing industries without any previous real experience of factory work. This ample supply of labour has been absorbed into various segments of the rapidly expanding pyramid. While a great part of it eventually moved out of agriculture, another part has remained in the farm household, working simul-taneously in other industries as seasonal/temporary workers either by commuting daily or by migrating from home. The fairly large proportion of small-scale family enterprises in non–agricultural indus-tries has been another source of temporary workers for the large companies. According to Kamata (1979: 231), the number of seasonal workers employed by the Toyota Automobile Manufacturing Co. in 1961 was 5,127, representing about 52 per cent of the firm's entire labour force. This might have been an extreme case, for the average percentage in the manufacturing firms in general is said to be around 10 per cent throughout the 1960s (Uchiyama, 1982: 104). Though declining in proportion thereafter, this form of labour utilization played an important role when the lifelong *nenkō* system was fairly well established among the regular male employees in the years before the oil crises.

Increasingly significant in the bottom section are part-time workers, mainly housewives and students. An increasing number of housewives has recently begun to return to the labour market mostly on part-time terms, and the trend is still strong. Those standardized routine tasks, clerical or manual, which were once performed by young women before marriage, are now often done by this sector. The two major reasons given for housewives returning to paid labour are to pay for their children's better education and to repay housing loans. The electric appliance manufacturing industry, for example, provides a vast number of assembly-line jobs for them. Many students (the percentage of those proceeding to university education including junior college was 36.3 in 1982, in spite of the heavy financial burden on their families) work part-time for various reasons, and the student labour force is now highly integrated into general business activities. Both housewives and students have their primary interests in fields other than their part-time jobs, which makes it most unlikely that they will raise serious demands about the nature and conditions of their often highly unrewarding jobs.

Lastly come those workers who are other agents' employees, not the parent company's, but who work regularly in the premises of the parent company under its direct or indirect control. There are two types in this category of labour force, conventional and newly created. Some of the subcontractors' employees [F] perform contracted tasks at the main contractor's site usually under the supervision of their own employers, that is, the subcontractors. This is the conventional type. The manpower leasing agency [L] and the agency's employees [G] dispatched to the client company constitute a newly forged employment relationship under the Employee Dispatching Business Law of 1985. In this case, the agency's employees do their work under the supervision of the client company. As Inagami says, however:

> In certain aspects the manpower leasing services and the conventional type of subcontracting to outside or affiliated firms overlap with each other. It is often difficult to clearly distinguish between the two. This is because the conventional type of subcontracting not only takes the form of ordering the subcontractor to produce certain types of parts or components in the specified quality and quantity but in other cases also enables the employer to secure only manpower from the subcontracting firms. Such subcontract workers perform their jobs in the same workshop as regular full-time employees, as is widely seen in construction, ship-building, iron and steel industries, and so on. (Inagami, 1984: 6)

Particularly in these industries there have always been groups of workers such as welders, electricians and plumbers headed by sub-contractors who are themselves experienced and skilled tradesmen. In spite of their constant participation in the client's production process, in legal terms there is no formal labour contract concluded between these workers and their 'parent' company, which enables the latter to evade any statutory obligations arising when it directly employs the former. In the disguise of this type of subcontracting, however, there have rapidly developed various arrangements for intermediary labour utilization since the mid-1970s as a result of the large firms' intensified efforts to reduce or to suppress the growth in the size of the directly employed labour force. The 'downsizing', coupled with recent micro-electronics-based rationalization in offices as well as in factories, has created considerable demand for temporary manpower, particularly in such fields as installation and maintenance of electronic devices, programming and routine tasks related to electronic data-processing. Since the existing labour laws prohibit in principle both intermediary exploitation of labour and fee-charging labour supply business, the new Employee Dispatching Business Law was contrived to follow this trend and to officially recognize it.

As for the conventional type of subcontracted labour, in the iron and steel industry, for example, the largest five companies' eighteen establishments utilized 156,068 such 'outside hands' from 1824 sub-contractors as against a total of 148,067 'inside' regular employees in 1976. And Table 5.1 shows the wage differential between 'outside' and 'inside' in Nippon Steel Corporation in 1975 (Iwao *et al.*, 1979: 90, 91). As we said when we discussed industrial dualism, the financial differential is not always related to the actual difference in skill-grade between 'inside regulars' and 'outside hands'. Some outside hands are, indeed, unskilled labourers such as carriers, security guards or janitors, but others are skilled workers engaged, for instance, in a variety of maintenance work for production machinery. Moreover, it is not unusual that they do virtually the same line of jobs as the inside regulars. If welfare benefits and retirement allowance are included the differential rewards appear to be getting even wider. What determines

Table 5.1 Wage differential between 'outside hands' and regulars in the Nippon Steel Corporation (1975)

	Average earning (yen)	Index number	Average wage rate (yen)[a]	Index number	Average age	Average length of service (years)
Subcontract workers	146.837	100	114.814	100	30.5	3.96
Regular employees	165.086	112.4	144.329	125.7	30.7	10.8

(a) Overtime pay is excluded from the average wage rate; from Iwao *et al.*, 1979

such a differential is the employer's position in the industrial hierarchy of firms rather than the employee's job or skill.

The constitution and proportion of the labour force's peripheral segments have changed in the course of post-war developments and are still changing. But, when major Japanese companies adjust their workforce in response to fluctuations in the product market or to technological changes, they always make the best use of flexibility by increasing and decreasing those various types of workers outside the core trapezoid where there are virtually no independent combinations of workers for the collective representation of their own interests.

Flexibility and worker competition

Having described the whole pyramidal labour-force construction, we can see one crucial issue latent in the large firm's employment practice: the employer's apparent unilateral discretion in distributing jobs among various segments of the pyramid which is sharply divided particularly between regulars and non-regulars and between the directly and indirectly employed. In spite of the seemingly rigid division in employment status, actually a fairly wide range of jobs spreads right across the division. Underneath the dividing lines there exists certainly one closely-knit production process of the parent firm. Indeed, a large part of 'blind alley' jobs, and dangerous, dirty or physically demanding tasks also tend to go outside of the inner trapezoid. In the same way, some skilled jobs which have to be done occasionally or for fixed periods are often assigned to those dispatched workers from subcontractors and manpower agencies. But, generally speaking, who does which job depends on the employer's personnel strategy, the goal of which is the optimum control of the total wage bill as well as skill-mix and age-structure of the workforce. Always underlying such a strategy is the critical issue of determining the optimum proportion of the inner core in the entire labour-force structure, as long as the lifelong *nenkō* practice is to be maintained among the regular employees. Needless to say, the lifelong *nenkō* practice, in the conventional sense of no lay-offs and automatic wage increases according to the length of service, imposes a great rigidity on the wage bill.

The issue of defining the extent of those jobs, hence the extent of those job-occupants, which ought to be organized in the core section is supposed to be of crucial importance also for the enterprise union. Generally, however, the unions have failed to formulate any clear policy as regards the job distribution between unionized regular employees and various sections of peripheral workforce. They tend to comply with management's list of subcontracting and temporary workers on condition that the regular employee status, hence lifelong employment, has been secured for their constituent workers. Thereby little attention is paid to the actual jobs which are subcontracted or allocated to temporary workers. This also reflects the diffuse job definitions which dominate the working life of the regular males. And here arises another potentially crucial issue inherent in the lifelong *nenkō* system, namely the nature of the rewarding by *nenkō* arrangement.

Although the *nenkō* system is often interpreted as something like a seniority system, it is quite different from, in a sense contrary to, the system of seniority among the organized manual workers in the United States. The seniority principle there consists of minute job definitions, wages by job, and length of service as the objectively measurable standard, and as such prevents employers or supervisors from arbitrary selection of workers in case of lay-off or promotion. In Japan, however, there is no last-in-first-out. The *nenkō* as the yardstick for determining wages and promotion does not simply mean age/length-of-service (*nen*), but also includes as an essential component merit/ability (*kō*). The *nenkō* system, though, produces a seniority-related wage profile as depicted in Figure 5.1. Usually two main reasons are given: first, the employees with greater length of service can be supposed to be more efficient in performing various jobs, thus deserving higher wages (therefore, length of service is important); second, the older employees ought to be paid more because of their increasing living costs with their families to support (therefore, age is important). The *nen* vaguely stands for age and/or length of service. In the *nenkō* system, nevertheless, the evaluation of *kō* (merit/ability) of individuals is always done in and for itself and reflected in their earnings, however small this part of their earnings might be. Moreover, the accumulated slight differences in *kō* evaluation year by year play a considerable role in determining an individual's future career in the company. Where jobs are not clearly defined in quality and quantity, or where the union adopts a hands-off policy concerning job distribution amongst its membership (the regular employees), the assessment of an employee is solely by his superiors or supervisors. This is often done according to such subjective notions as co-operativeness, trainability, work motivation, potential ability or whatever criteria the superiors choose. This does not mean that favouritism is rampant at the workplace. (An individual or a minority group overtly critical of management policies is ruthlessly discrimi-nated against in wages and in promotion, of course.) The assessment which tends to evaluate the total personality as well as technical skills is important because of its comprehensive nature. In short, the *kō* is concerned with what has been done and what will possibly be done by an employee for the sake of company goals. The *nenkō* system, when put into practice, takes a form somewhere between a more seniority-based and a more meritocratic system.

The enterprise union seems to have failed to counter the employer's initiative to reorganize the system into a more ability-based one. The union's failure to prevent the employer from using the kō-evaluation for selective rewarding and promotion results in a large number of lay-offs among older employees once times have become extremely hard for the firm, though the lay-offs usually take the form of 'voluntary' early retirement. Now we must take a closer look at the internal career-type flexibility which moulds the working life in the innermost trapezoid, which, in turn, forms the very base of the union organization.

Change in workforce deployment entails some adaptation in a series of factors such as the scope of a particular job, its work load, manning levels for specific tasks, overtime working, rotation within a work-place, transfer between different plants, promotion, opportunites for training, and who is to be made redundant first if lay-offs are inevitable. Generally speaking, the degree of workers' independence from their employer depends on how much they can extend their control over these issues. And the success or failure of such auto-nomous control depends a great deal on the strength of the shop-floor solidarity of workers who have a shared view of their job descriptions.

A regular male employee in the innermost trapezoid, however, finds himself in a serious contradiction arising from lifelong career forma-tion within a single firm. Put simply, he is expected to climb the job-ladder, or more exactly, to work his way up a grading system linked loosely with clusters of jobs, by adapting himself to frequent changes in work. In other words, he only secures his lifelong employment in competition with his fellow workers and at the cost of his ties to well-known jobs and to long-familiar work mates. The prospect of lifelong career formation can be influenced by the firm's position in the product market. Describing, rather affirmatively, how skill, that is, a company-specific skill, is developed in a large firm, Koike (1987: 307) says this:

> With this type of skill formation system, workers' skill develop-ment largely coincides with the prosperity of the firm. When the firm grows quickly, workers can be promoted quickly, and the opportunity to attain higher skill levels comes earlier... And when the firm suffers from reverses or decline, workers may be laid off. To a worker with a specific skill, lay-off or redundancy represents great damage; it is not only an interruption in skill development, but it is a sacrifice because he is often compelled to find a job in another company that cannot utilize the skills he has acquired. In order to protect his own skill development, the worker must be interested in the economic situation of the firm. Even without any loyalty to the firm, he has to pay attention to the firm's productivity to prevent it from being bested by rivals.

Even from the employee's standpoint, therefore, there ought not to be any exercise of workers' autonomy which would injure the flexibility in workforce deployment, for the firm's improved productivity depends on it. In fact, shop-floor groups of workers, formal or informal, rarely develop restrictive practices. And the formal collective bargaining system between management and the enterprise union scarcely covers detailed labour process matters which affect workers' immediate jobs. As Shirai (1968: 122) says:

> Generally speaking, while labour unions in Japan express the primary concern over the wages, they pay little attention to the amount of labour supplied in return for the wages... (the) union function is very feeble or rarely seen in such areas as the regulation of production schedules, manning levels, standard output quota, speeds of production and so forth. At least, unions scarcely pick up these issues as the agenda for the formal collective bargaining system.

Under the *nenkō* reward system where the evaluation of an individual employee's merit/ability is at the employer's discretion, the lack of workers' collective control over the daily operations of production reinforces competition among co-workers. It can, therefore, be argued that the flexible-deployment structure is substantiated by highly competitive efforts by each worker, not as an occupant of a certain job but as a holder of permanent employee status, to achieve a more advantageous and stable position in the ever fluid organization. This flexibility–competition nexus is geared to ever higher productivity, intensifying the work effort of an individual.

The small-group activities conducted by quality-control (QC) or zero-defects circles play a similar role. Even when such a circle tackles a purely technical problem arising from a particular production process, it is usual that the circle conducts a systematic survey of its members' performance, using various industrial engineering methods including time and motion studies. Such activities often result in elimination of 'parasitism and superfluous work motions' from the labour process, or simply identification of 'parasitical persons' in the process. (cf. Dohse, *et al.*, 1985: 12). Furthermore, some small-group activity problems arise precisely because of chronically undermanned situations. A QC-circle gave their reasons for selecting the problems it tackled:

> To cover increasing production of bumper shock absorbers for Toyota, our superviser asked us to transfer one operator from our team to the night shift. However, we expected it would be difficult to maintain the whole operation with fewer operators.
> We examined the problem by using the Industrial Engineering method but could not find a satisfactory resolution. So we

decided to rationalize the inspection operation. (Cole, 1979: 150)

The flexibility–competition nexus requires some favourable circumstances in order to keep working efficiently for the company goals. At least, competition should be guided to enhance, not hinder, the sort of productivity improvement as is achieved in 'team work'. Ideologies of 'management familism' or of 'the company as a community of interests' may serve this purpose to a certain extent. But ideological self-identification with the company would soon wither away and be finally lost if employment security and promotion prospects could not be believed by the majority of the regulars.

According to Koshiro (1983: 36), the number of those fortunate workers who acquire a 'desirable employment opportunity' mostly in major companies and public sectors is estimated to be around 10 million. This is only 18 per cent of the gainfully working population (approximately 56 million), and a quarter of total employed labour (approximately 40 million). By 'desirable' Koshiro means the employment opportunity which provides for the employed higher wage-levels, security of employment, various welfare benefits and social prestige. In short, their relative security in employment is because they are organized in the innermost trapezoid of the whole pyramidal labour-force structure. They are supposed to be the last to be discharged when redundancy comes up, only after all measures have been carried out to reduce labour costs among the lower and peripheral sections. Furthermore, provided that a substantial part of the undesirable or 'blind alley' jobs are performed by those in the non-regular sections both within and without the company, the flexibility in deployment often makes it easier for the regulars to go, sooner or later, up the job-ladder to, for example, off-the-assembly-line jobs or supervisory positions after experiencing a number of entry jobs which are sometimes identical with those of non-regulars. In the same way, worker competition is probably relaxed to some extent, since the mass of non-regulars and 'outside hands' will rarely be regulars' rivals in the promotion contest even when both share almost the same sort of tasks.

In addition to the structural segmentation of the labour force, Japan's continued high economic growth has also played a significant part in habituating regular workers to flexibility and competition. The process has two dimensions: one aspect relates to the industrial expansion itself and the other to the unprecedented scale of technological innovation which accompanied the expansion. Throughout the years of rapid growth beginning in the late 1950s and ending with the oil crisis in 1973 (real annual growth rates in GNP were almost always around 10 per cent) the total size of the pyramid-shaped enterprise expanded continuously. This provided permanent employees with palpable opportunities for upward social mobility by way of promotion within a specific company. It is precisely in those days of incessant growth that the lifelong *nenkō* system, in its idealized form with emphasis on automatic wage raises and promotion by age and length of service, appeared firmly established at least among the regulars in major firms. The system then could virtually guarantee capable employees a smooth upward path in the corporate hierarchy, while rewarding even mediocre workers with yearly wage increases until mandatory retirement with a lump-sum allowance.

Lifelong security of employment and rewarding by age/length of service, as a tacit understanding between management and labour, successfully committed an increasing number of regulars to the flexibility–competition nexus. Even in the eyes of workers, competitive effort among them seemed normal and desirable if equal promotion opportunities and 'fair' assessment of each's ability were assured. The enterprise union was there, so its membership expected it to protect them from 'unfair' demotion or dismissal and to see that the minimum annual pay raises according to age or length of service should be granted even to inevitable losers in competition, these being relatively few in the days of growth.

The technological-innovation dimension is more difficult to summarize in a few words. Here it may suffice to say that 'flexibility in using an employee' contributed greatly to the successful implementation and accommodation of the latest technologies which were largely borrowed from the West during the period. An able practitioner-theorist in labour management, Okuda of Nippon Kôkan Co., one of the leading steel producers in Japan, said in this connection:

What is meant by the lack of 'job'-orientedness is that traditionally 'job'-related problems have scarcely made up a serious agenda of negotiation between employers and labour unions, and that the management prerogative in changing 'job' definitions has been rarely challenged by any parties concerned. Therefore, in the days of rapid innovation in production techniques, the employer was quite free to introduce the newest equipment and to reform existing production processes to achieve greater productivity, even if such steps often entailed drastic changes in job content and in the way it was performed. Workers simply tried hard and successfully to adapt themselves to renewed work situations, hardly resisting management's initiatives in this field.

Yet, in all probability, this intensive process of investment in modern capital equipment and of changes in production methods caused workers lots of anxiety, because it ruthlessly ruined workers' skill which might have been acquired through long years of service. The conventional policy of lifetime security of employment and related practices in Japanese firms was intended to ease and to compensate for such probable employee frustrations. Various provisions in the name of management familism were there to prevent workers' psychological disturbances. (Okuda, 1972: 76-7, our trans., but the expression 'job' is his)

As we said before, what made 'lifetime security' work as the 'conventional policy' was almost two decades of incessant growth in firm-size. Furthermore, what was in fact ruthlessly ruined by the technological innovations in the same decades was far more the stability of those shop-floor relations of co-workers which had been formed around traditional skills than simply an individual's skill in general. The degree of mobility increased throughout the period, not only in the workplace but also between old establishments and new ones equipped with the latest technologies. Put another way, the formation of the group cohesion of workers on a particular shop-floor was limited because of the wider career ladder vertically arranged within the enterprise as a whole. In short, the regulars were increasingly obliged to climb the ladder as an individual learning by doing new jobs without any stable autonomous group for her/him to belong to.

The flexibility in deployment coupled with competitive individualism among the regulars had thus established itself as a normative rule under the life-long *nenkō* practice in the later years of high economic growth, long before the employer began to talk about the enormous burdens of this conventional employment practice in face of an entrenched low-growth economy. Now many observers say that the traditional permanent employment custom has finally begun to disintegrate. From our point of view, however, the present transformation of the industrial relations system should be interpreted in terms of further exploitation by the employer of the flexibility – competition nexus. The nexus was once moulded by the lifelong *nenkō* practice but now the former is beginning to remould the latter. The most critical outcome, then, is the relative reduction in the size of the innermost trapezoid of core employees who can expect to be covered by the lifelong *nenkō* system which is now more meritocratic than seniority-based. A closely related outcome of the hierarchical segmentation of the labour force is seen, for instance, in the recent enactment of the Employee Dispatching Business Law. Many major Japanese firms have created miscellaneous subsidiaries in order to hive off potentially redundant senior employees and some of the new subsidiaries are nothing but manpower-leasing agencies.

To stay in the inner-core section one must be ready to accept almost any job change with additional effort to acquire new skill. As an interesting example of changing jobs within a company we quote from a recent study of the effects of technological innovation upon labour relations:

In the Asahi Newspaper Publishing Co., 681 jobs including those of 226 typographers and 125 stereotypers were abolished with the introduction of NELSON [new editing and layout system of newspapers]. But the employment of those affected was secured by means of transfer to other departments such as editing and distribution. The reasons why the transfer between such divergent workplaces (or jobs) was carried out without any substantial friction were, among others: (1) there were no wage-rate differentials between jobs, (2) training opportunity was given in computer-aided editing jobs to all who desired it (though a considerable number could not finish the course), (3) employees were keenly aware of the critical situation in market-share competition with Yomiuri and also knew well of Mainichi's management difficulty [both are the most popular newspaper publishers competing with Asahi]. (Sumiya (ed.) 1985: 34, our translation and notes within []).

What may be called Japanese-style meritocracy is based on the evaluation of trainability or general abilities which can be utilized in long years of service. But the actual content of a competitively won lifelong career will not necessarily suit the individual concerned. It rather depends on the market strategy of the firm. Those ex-senior employees screened off from career formation within the company (represented by [E] in Figure 5.2) are a conspicuous result of the meritocratic principle.

After the oil crises many firms proposed 'voluntary retirement' schemes of various kinds and almost always such schemes successfully achieved their aim. Knowing well enough their weak positions in the external labour market, a remarkable number of middle-aged or older employees 'volunteered' for the early retirement scheme. A major electric equipment manufacturer gave notification of a voluntary retirement plan to the enterprise union in 1978 which included the following statement:

All permanent employees may volunteer, but those in the following categories are particularly encouraged to do so.

(1) Those whose work performance is not good
(2) Those with problems in their work record
(3) Those who have not shown a very high degree of co-operativeness with measures taken by the company
(4) Those who have a source of relative income security after retirement
(5) Those who will be hard put to it to conform to the tough measures the company may have to take in future, for example, those who would not be able to respond to transfer orders which involve changing skills or changing home
(6) Any others who, in ways similar to the above, are not able to make a great contribution to the company. (Dore, 1986: 99–100)

In other cases of similar redundancy measures, who was to quit might not be made so explicit. All the same, those who were supposed to volunteer felt compelled to do so because of pressure not only from their employer but also from their fellow workers. Once this 'downsizing' has been achieved, those still in the core section usually do longer hours of overtime working. These are almost inevitable consequences of shop-floor politics where Japanese-style meritocracy rules.

A brief review and conclusion

In the years immediately after the Second World War, when labour unions were first fully legitimized in Japan, the unionization rate among the employed soon soared to well over 50 per cent. With the employer class in disorder from the devastation of the lost war, both white-collar and manual workers who returned to their old work-places, partly encouraged by the Occupation Authority which was then determined to democratize Japan's economic structure, could organize themselves within the workplace in the same establishment-wide organization. Many of the unions assumed the role of works councils in order to resume peace-time production and thus to secure jobs for their membership.

The most typical two demands of those newly established unions were egalitarian treatment for all the employees and guaranteed minimum wages which should enable every employee to maintain a decent standard of living. The unions' egalitarianism aimed to sweep away pre-war management authoritarianism, and especially tried, fairly successfully, to abolish discriminative treatment between priv-ileged 'regular staff' and ordinary factory-hands. In a sense, the new-born enterprise union demanded that all the employees should be covered by the same permanent *nenkō* reward system as had been enjoyed before only by the staff personnel. The union formulated a characteristic wage-payment system, namely wages based on the cost of living. The idealism in this sort of wage demand was that every employee, irrespective of occupational differences, should deserve wages commensurate with the average cost of living, which could be determined only by age and size of family. In other words, the capacity to pay the wage-bill being strictly limited for the recovering industry, wage differentials of any other sorts should be kept to a minimum. This kind of egalitarianism may be said to be an important premise which has prevented the enterprise-wide union in post-war Japan from becoming merely a company-sponsored union.

In fact, a considerable number of labour disputes seem to have arisen from an unavoidable discrepancy between management and union membership in the understanding of the *nenkō* based security of employment. Employers have always claimed as their prerogatives decision-making on hiring and firing when necessary and selective rewarding by means of merit/ability assessment of individuals. Unions were inclined to assert their primary demand for more egalitarian, if heavily seniority-based, wage-rises and promotion, taking lifetime security of employment for granted at least as far as the long-serving regular employees were concerned. Given lifelong career formation within a firm, the union has rarely undertaken the role of standardizing wage rates, occupation by occupation, across firms in the local labour market. The egalitarianism has been confined within a particular enterprise. Instead of linking wage rates with comparable jobs in the market, the union usually demanded a yearly rise in the level of the overall seniority wage-scale established firm by firm.

It is clear, however, that a strictly seniority-related payment system imposes increasing labour costs on management unless the size of firm itself gets continuously larger through annual recruiting of an increasing number of low-waged younger employees. Besides, when labour shortage pushes up the entry wage rate for school leavers, the burden of the system becomes enormous. It was the management side of the industry, therefore, which tried to introduce various models of wage by job and of job evaluation schemes in order to diversify and to curb egalitarian and automatic wage increases by age/length-of-service regardless of occupation. Particularly from the 1950s to early 1960s, when large firms introduced the latest production technologies from the West, management planned to implement a payment by job as they applied Western industrial engineering methods to the changing production process. Only the continued high growth of the national economy thereafter led both sides of the industry to a compromise in the form of the lifelong *nenkō* system as has been examined in this chapter. To be more precise, it was a tacit understanding ultimately depending on the employer's goodwill rather than a compromise reached after explicit struggles between management and labour. The enterprise union, representing the interests of those who expect to climb the job ladder in an expanding company, largely accepted new methods of production and the consequent frequent changes in job allocation as long as seniority principles were observed for the majority of the membership. From the employer's point of view, also, it was made clear that 'a shift from the seniority to the merit system would involve not a partial or technical change in payment or promotion methods but a drastic reformation of the structure itself, beginning with the basic orientation of native values' (Nakane, 1973: 88). Whether 'native values' or not, excessive rigidity in job evaluation schemes would have contradicted the flexible structure. Consequently, while the technical side of the labour process was rationalized with the aid of scientific methods of job analysis, any close correlation between each job and its wage rate was generally avoided in order to make room for rewarding by age and length of service. The result of personnel assessment was reflected more or less in the bonus-part of individuals' earnings or in promotion a little earlier or later than normal. This is briefly how the sociological base for Japanese-style meritocracy was formed on the shop-floor in the later period of high economic growth.

In an attempt to conceptualize the 'white-collarized worker with intellectual skills', Koike (1987: 304) compares the skill formation of Japanese manual workers with that of their American counterparts:

> mobility on the shop-floor in Japan is far less rigid, and seniority functions feebly, contrary to popular belief. Rather, an egalitarian method of deployment prevails. A kind of rotation system covers most of the positions in the workshop. This frequent mobility can extend even beyond a workshop to similar workshops in the neighborhood. For example, workers in an integrated steel plant in the United States cover nearly a dozen jobs in their career but their Japanese counterparts will experience about three dozen positions.

Koike, on the whole, does not see a possible alienating effect of frequent mobility on the worker's tie to both familiar work and intimate work mates. Neither does he make clear who regulates 'an egalitarian method of deployment'. Although he does say 'deployment within the workshop depends partly on shop-floor custom, rather than on regulation by management or by unions' (ibid., 307), flexible deployment is reinforced by competitive effort among workers and controlled through evaluation of individuals' performance ultimately by management. As Burawoy (1979: 107) says, 'the mobility the internal labour market engenders at the point of production dissolves some of the tensions between worker and management and generates new tensions among workers'. Since the 'tensions among workers' are channelled into 'lifelong' competition for promotion in a large Japanese firm, there hardly develops shop-floor custom which endangers management's goals. As for 'intellectual skills' which Koike thinks Japanese blue-collar workers acquire through frequent mobility, the scope and the depth of each of the 'three dozen jobs' must be examined. Some of them may probably be highly routinized so that other workers can perform them without any real training. Furthermore, it is not unusual that frequent mobility in a workshop arises because of the management policy of operating with minimal manning levels. What can be safely said is only that 'skill' scarcely emerges as a source of workers' autonomous power to regulate how and how much workers should work.

In reference to the industrial dual structure, Dore says that 'the elite ten million (i.e. the innermost trapezoid) includes the most skilled of Japan's manual workers' (Dore, 1973: 305). The observation is correct only in terms of the wage-rate differential. But, as we repeatedly emphasized, the wage differential by firm size does not necessarily reflect actual skill levels among workers in different segments of the pyramid. There have developed no nation-wide social arrangements in which workers' skill could be evaluated for its own sake across the dividing lines of firms which are organized in a powerful hierarchy. The higher wage level of workers in a large firm can be explained only by the persistent existence of the dualism itself. And this explains well why a foundryman most naturally defines himself as a member of the Hitachi Company.

Any craft heritage being almost nonexistent – Japan 'skipped the craft stage of union organization' (Cole, 1979: 103) – the notion of skill as a source of worker's political power on the shop-floor is accordingly very weak on both sides of industry. It is, therefore, quite unnecessary that Japanese managers pursue a deskilling strategy for political reasons. The employer even encourages loyal employees to compete in learning various skills. A part of the high productivity of Japan's manufacturing industries is undoubtedly derived from workers' genuine initiatives in carrying out allotted tasks with ever better performance. Yet, our conclusion is that the skill formation in a large firm has been so far a process of deepening dependency upon a specific employer.

These days hardly a week goes by when a pessimistic feature on the future of the lifelong *nenkō* practice does not appear in popular newspapers or business magazines. Japanese workers, who have seen some of their work-mates forced to leave the workplace in mid-career in one way or another, are certainly aware of diminished security of employment even in a large firm. At the present moment, however, a patient acquiescence prevails among workers. The unemployment rate is still low and commodity prices are stable. Those in the privileged sections of the nation's workforce seem to be further committed to a survival game within their respective companies. After all, the present transformation of the employment practice consists of, on the one hand, a relative reduction in the size of the full-time regular-employee class, and on the other, more meritocratic selection in recruitment, promotion, transfer and timing of retirement for core personnel. It is grossly misleading to interpret the transformation in terms of the end of the lifelong *nenkō* system. We should never forget that the system has been, and still is, in close causal relation to the hierarchical segmentation of Japan's working population.

Appendix

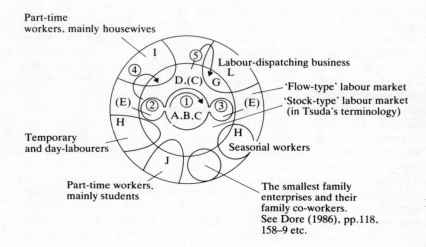

Part-time
workers, mainly housewives

Labour-dispatching business

'Flow-type' labour market

'Stock-type' labour market
(in Tsuda's terminology)

Temporary
and day-labourers

Seasonal workers

Part-time workers,
mainly students

The smallest family
enterprises and their
family co-workers.
See Dore (1986), pp.118,
158–9 etc.

Figure 5.3   Dualistic system of labour market

Key: (1) Male regular employees, i.e. career-oriented, prospective 'core' of the corporate personnel, who are supposed to become 'multi-skilled' or generalist staff also with growing capabilities in supervising and human relations. However, as Tsuda puts down 'changing jobs' in this innermost circle, some may be forced not only to 'change jobs' within the company, but also to change employers, either to work for subsidiaries or subcontractors   (2) under the influence of the company, or to work for venture businesses   (3) created to diversify the business of the company. Whether such arrangements are to be temporary or permanent depends upon both the corporate strategy and merits or abilities of the employees thus transferred. (E) in 2 and 3, therefore, represents ex-employees who have finally been screened and cut off from the main career ladder in the original company. Tsuda's semi-circular arrow here can be seen as symbolizing the flexibility in using individual employees themselves.

The semi-circular arrow (4) stands for the movement of the female labour force. Women who get their first jobs as regular employees of the company retire when they marry or give birth to their first baby. Recently, however, more and more housewives tend to seek jobs as part-time workers either in the previous company or elsewhere when they get freed from child-rearing responsibilities. The other arrow (5) represents a similar movement of workers, female and male, who specialize in a certain field of jobs rather than pursue a 'lifelong' career formation in a specific company.

Source: Tsuda Masumi's 'Is The Dual Structure Being Renewed?' and slightly modified so that Tsuda's original chart can be related to our Figure 5.2.

6 Flexibility and the changing sexual division of labour

SYLVIA WALBY

Introduction

Braverman (1974) developed two major concepts in his analysis of the sexual division of labour which have survived many of the criticisms of his work: 'feminization' and 'reserve army of labour'. Braverman focused on the long-run implications of the expansion of capitalist relations of production into the household, turning women from full-time housewives into a pool of labour for capital to be pulled into the newly deskilled 'feminized' jobs. Subsequently many later writers have used the term 'reserve' to suggest a short-run mechanism in which women's labour is used only in the upturns of the business cycle (e.g. Beechey, 1977, 1978).[1] As Braverman's analysis has been well criticized (e.g. Wood, 1982; Beechey, 1982), I shall not dwell on his shortcomings here. But I would like to draw attention to the new ways in which the central ideas of his analysis have recurred.

Feminization is a concept which has now entered some significant areas of social science discourse (see for instance the work of the Changing Urban and Regional System initiative; Cooke, 1983: 226; Massey, 1984). This refers to the increasing proportion of women in paid work, usually with reference to specific occupations or industries, together with an assumption that this is related to the deskilling of the labour process under consideration. The notion of women as a labour reserve is also present in the developing analysis of the spatial division of labour.

The evidence does not, however, support the thesis that women are used as a short-term reserve army of labour. In 1986 45 per cent of the British workforce was female. While male employment continues to fall from its high point in 1965, female employment, especially that of part-time women workers, continues to rise. There has been no significant recession as far as women's employment opportunities have been concerned in the last two decades. The increase in job opportunities has, however, not been matched by any significant closure in the wages gap between men and women, apart from that resulting from the Equal Pay legislation; women earned 74.3 per cent of men's hourly wages in 1986, as compared to 75.5 per cent in 1977, and 63.1 per cent in 1970 before the Act (EOC, 1987: 38). The increase in women's part-time work has not been at the expense of a decrease in women's full-time employment. The recession is a recession for men, which women experience vicariously through their husbands and fathers and its consequent effect upon household income.

Table 6.1 shows these different trends for men and women in Britain. Women's employment grew faster than men's in the early 1960s, and continued to grow after the wilting of male employment opportunities in the late 1960s. The depths of the early 1980s recession merely momentarily halted the absolute increase in women's employment, but not its relative growth.

Table 6.1   Employment trends, Great Britain, 1959–86

Employees in employment	1959	1966	1971	1976	1981	1983	1986
All persons	20983	22787	21648	22048	21386	20572	21105
All male	13824	14551	13424	13097	12278	11670	11643
All female	7159	8236	8224	8951	9108	8902	9462
% female	34.1	36.1	38.0	40.6	42.6	43.3	44.8
FT female			5467	5366	5290	5125	5321
%FT female			25.3	24.3	24.7	24.9	25.2
PT female			2757	3585	3818	3777	4141
PT female as % of all female			33.5	40.1	41.9	42.4	43.8
PT female as % of all persons			12.7	16.3	17.9	18.4	19.6

Source: Calculated from *Employment Gazette*, Historical Supplement, Department of Employment, Feb. 1987, Table 1.1 for 1959-83; August 1987, Table 1.1 for 1986.

In the face of such data, showing that women's employment has not declined in the recession in the way that the reserve-army theory would predict, theories that women constitute such a short-term reserve put forward by both Marxist feminists (Beechey, 1977, 1978) and neo-classical economists (Mincer, 1962, 1966), cannot hold. Women's employment has been increasing in both relative and absolute terms in times of both economic boom and recession, in times of tight and slack labour markets. Absolute levels of labour demand cannot constitute an adequate explanation for this increased employment of women. Attempts to rescue the reserve-army theory have been made by arguing that the use of women as a reserve is masked by occupational segregation by sex (Breugel, 1979; Milkman, 1976). While men are concentrated in the declining manufacturing sector, women are largely to be found in the more buoyant service sector. It is the expansion of women's employment in the service sector which provides more employment for women than is lost in the manufacturing sector, unlike the case for men. Even if occupational segregation is a major determinant of the pattern of women's (and hence men's) employment, segregation itself stands in need of explanation. Why are employers in the service sector more likely to employ women than men? Why did manufacturing employers historically employ fewer women than men? How is this difference between sectors and across time to be explained? Why were women not used as waged labourers before to the same extent?

Flexibilization?

What light can the recent developments in theories of flexibility shed on this major transformation in the gender composition of the workforce? Are these accounts of the changes in the workforce in terms of a developing differentiation between core and peripheral workers of use for explaining the major changes in the gender composition of the workforce? Hakim (1987b) shows that, if the workforce is divided into two – permanent, full-time on the one hand and 'flexible', either part-time or temporary on the other – then the 'flexible' portion of the workforce rose from 30 per cent in 1981 to 34 per cent in 1986. While one quarter of men were among the 'flexibles', one half of women workers were to be found there. Part-time women workers are the largest single category of non-permanent workers. In 1985 they made up 16.6 per cent of the workforce, while temporary workers (female and male) made up only 5.5 per cent, despite their big increase over 1981 (calculated from *Employment Gazette*, Historical Supplement, Feb. 1987, Table 1.1, and Hakim, 1987b: 93).

So is this flexibility gendered? Is the 'core' masculine and the 'periphery' feminine? Whose flexibility is it? Does part-time work simultaneously meet the needs of women, employers and husbands or merely one of these groups? Is 'flexibilization' 'feminization', given the increase in a 'flexible' part-time female workforce? Can recent changes in women's employment be understood in terms of increases in flexibility?

This chapter will draw out the implications of flexibility theses for gender relations. I will focus on the work of Atkinson (see Chapter 1), both because he and his colleagues have produced one of the most developed models of flexibility, and because the work of the other leading approach represented in the work of Piore and Sabel is effectively discussed by Jane Jenson in Chapter 7. None of these writers on flexibility systematically addresses the issue of changes in gender relations as part of their account of flexibility; but it is my contention that the model they construct is gendered. Furthermore, whether flexibility is the best way of understanding contemporary paid work, and whether it is new are issues to be explored.

Atkinson's model

Atkinson constructs a model of the flexible firm and asks whether there have been significant moves towards it over the last decade. He identifies four main types of flexibility: numerical flexibility, functional flexibility, distancing (especially sub-contracting) and pay flexibility (the first two being the most important). In numerical flexibility employers are able to vary the amount of labour they employ at short notice; in functional flexibility, workers are able to take on a wider range of tasks, which is considered to increase efficiency by, for example, enabling them to perform the work of absent colleagues.

Atkinson constructs a model of the flexible firm in terms of a division between core and peripheral workers, the division being theoretically one of degree, but in practice being effectively treated as dichotomous. Peripheral workers are those who are semi-skilled or unskilled and numerically flexible, as a result of short-term contracts, agency hiring and being employed by subcontractors, and those who are part-time or job sharing. Core workers are likely to be skilled and have secure contracts of employment and be employed by particular firms for a long period, unlike the peripheral ones. Atkinson states that the distinction between these two types of employment has grown since 1980 among the seventy-two firms in which he interviewed. As a consequence he suggests that the labour market has become more segmented over this period.

He suggests that there has been a significant change in management conduct towards workers over the last few years, which has accelerated the move to the flexible firm. He suggests the following as causes:

(1)   the recession, especially in so far as it weakens union power and increases the labour supply (it might, therefore, be a temporary effect);
(2)   technical change;
(3)   legislative change, although this has had only a limited effect;
(4)   changing business objectives, especially changes in the environment demanding faster responsiveness, decentralization and headcount reduction.

The 'permissive factors' encouraging these are summarized as reduced 'union power and slack external labour markets.'

Evidence consistent with the IMS claims about the increase in flexibility is widespread (Cross, 1985; Curson, 1986; Hakim, 1987b; Incomes Data Services, 1982, 1983, 1984), though some writers emphasize national variations in its form (Lash and Bagguley, 1987). Others such as Pollert (1987), are, however, sceptical about its newness in Britain on grounds, for instance, of its similarity to struggles over 'productivity'.

Atkinson's model and gender

How gendered is Atkinson's model of the flexible firm? Does it capture accurately the nature and implications of the different positions of women and men in the labour market? Atkinson makes little reference to gendered processes in his account, but he does consistently note in passing that the part-time workers and 'distanced homeworkers' who make up a significant part of the numerically flexible workforce are usually female. However, this is noted empirically, rather than the significance of the gender of these flexible workers being integrated into his analysis of these changes. Do these processes, which have gendered effects, have gendered social forces as their causes? I shall examine this in stages. First, by asking whether the division between core and periphery is essentially one between male and female workers. Second, by questioning whether the changed environment is critically one in which gender relations have altered, especially in relation to equal opportunity and job protection legislation which differentially affects women and men workers, and in terms of household structure and domestic labour which have resulted in women spending a smaller proportion of their lives as full-time housewives. Third, by discussing the theoretical arguments underlying his model, as to the underlying structural processes. Finally I shall present an alternative view of these rounds of gender restructuring.

Core/periphery

There is a tendency for core workers to be equated with male, and peripheral workers with female workers although there are counter-vailing factors. I shall explore first the reasons which support the notion that these dichotomies are coterminous, and secondly, those which do not.

FOR

It is commonplace to argue that women, on average, hold jobs which are designated as less skilled, low paid, insecure and with fewer promotion prospects than those of men. Taken at the level of the labour market as a whole the typical women's jobs do appear to conform to this model, in that women earn only three-quarters of men's hourly earnings, 73.5 per cent in 1984 (*New Earnings Survey,*

1970–84, Part A, Tables 10 and 11), less if gross weekly earnings are examined, 65.8 per cent in 1984 (*New Earnings Survey,* 1970–84, Part A, Tables 10 and 11). The existence of occupational and industrial segregation by sex means that women are confined to a narrow range of occupations. For instance, while men are evenly spread between services and the production sector, with 56 per cent in services in 1986, 81 per cent of women and 91 per cent of part-time women were in this sector (*Employment Gazette,* Feb. 1987, Historical Supplement, Table 1.1). Women's work is typically designated as less skilled than men's even when the amount of learning time is considerable. Part-time women workers especially appear to fit the model of peripheral workers, particularly in their lack of rights to permanent employment. In Britain, employees must have worked at least sixteen hours a week with the same employer for two years in order to qualify for most of the state-backed employment rights, such as protection from unfair dismissal, maternity rights, and redundancy pay. Those who work between eight and sixteen hours must have been with an employer for five years to qualify. A significant proportion of women fall outside the provisions of the legislation protecting them from dismissal because they work too few hours to qualify for security of employment.

In 1986 42 per cent of women workers were part-time as compared to 7 per cent of men (*Employment Gazette,* Feb. 1987, Historical Supplement, Table 1.1). On average, they earn considerably less than full-time women workers, as well as men. In 1986 the hourly earnings of part-time women were 76 per cent of those of full-time women and 56 per cent of full-time men's (calculated from *New Earnings Survey,* 1986, Part B, Tables 30, 31; Part F, Table 179). Most of this difference must be presumed to be from part-time workers performing different, or differently categorized work, from full-timers, since there is no evidence that the same employer pays the same job at different rates for full- and part-time workers. Typically part-time work is among less skilled areas of employment (Martin and Roberts, 1984; Robinson and Wallace, 1984). As a proportion of the workforce part-time women workers are growing, from 13 per cent in 1971 to 19 per cent in 1986, while the proportion of full-time women in the workforce has been nearly constant over the same period, rising from 25.3 per cent in 1971 to only 25.8 per cent in 1986 (calculated from *Employment Gazette,* Feb. 1987, Historical Supplement, Table 1.1). Part-time workers are less likely than full-time workers to be on the relevant promotion ladder or to achieve the seniority necessary for attaining the status of core worker.

Homeworkers, as women on low rates of pay, working for a few hours a week outside the protection of much of the employment legislation, might be considered the quintessential peripheral workforce. Hakim (1987a) shows that while these women exist, especially among manufacturing homework, they do not constitute all home-based workers. In particular, they need to be carefully distinguished from workers, often male, who merely use their home as a base, and who have high earnings and greater continuity of employer. Hakim (1987b) suggests that the full-time, part-time division is the most important in differentiating the conditions and pay of these workers.

AGAINST

On the other hand there are factors which might mitigate against such an equation of men in the core and women in the periphery. In particular, a case against such a core–periphery dualism can be made if the employment of women is disaggregated, especially if clerical work, which employs so many women, is examined.

In a more disaggregated picture the labour market is revealed as highly segregated and with major differences between forms of women's employment which contradict simple generalizations about women's work. Vastly differing proportions of men and women in the seventeen socio-economic groups (SEGs) demonstrate the complexity of the picture (Bagguley and Walby, 1988). While women are much less well represented in the upper echelons of the SEGs, the pattern is, nonetheless, not simply one of all the men at the top and all the women at the bottom. There are small, but significant, numbers of women in professional jobs such as teaching and nursing, and increasing numbers of women who are gaining qualifications in, for example, accounting and law. And it is the nature and scale of women's employment in clerical work which most significantly challenges the over-simple picture. Of all women in employment 39 per cent are in the junior non-manual category, which typically means clerical work; women make up 71 per cent of this SEG. This work, while at the bottom of any hierarchical classification of non-manual work, cannot be placed beneath the SEGs for manual workers in a simple way. It is better in terms of pay and conditions of service than women's manual work; it is worse in terms of pay than most male skilled and semi-skilled work, but better than the male unskilled. But is it worse in conditions of service than these male workers? In terms of responsibility, control over the labour process in clerical work is varied. There is in fact considerable controversy as to the place of clerical workers in the stratification system (Abercrombie and Urry, 1983; Braverman, 1974; Crompton and Jones, 1984; Goldthorpe, 1980; Klingender, 1935; Stanworth, 1984; Stewart, *et al.*, 1980; West, 1978). Some of this controversy reflects the wide range of situations within clerical work.

This debate has especially focused upon women's skill level, responsibility and control over the labour process of themselves and other workers, and their likelihood of promotion, all of which are generally believed to be low for women clerical workers. Their conditions of service and rates of pay have received less attention in the more theoretical literature, although these have been addressed in some of the empirical studies (e.g. McNally, 1979; Vinnicombe, 1980). It would appear that because of their conditions of service, security of tenure and technical levels of skill a significant proportion of them should be considered to be part of the core, as well as some in the periphery.

Clerical workers often receive 'staff' conditions of service, rather than those accorded to 'production' workers in relation to payment method, length of working week, regulation of working hours (for example, no clocking in, more generous sick leave, pension arrangements), clothing, pleasantness of working conditions, etc. Many, although not all, clerical workers have stable employment of the kind usually associated with primary jobs (although this is partly a consequence of the fact that clerical work is disproportionately located in those industrial sectors which are normally most buoyant).

In the strict Bravermanian sense of control over the labour process, it is now common to consider that such clerical workers are not skilled (Crompton and Jones, 1984). However, many of these workers have levels of technical skill which require better than average schooling, certainly higher than average levels of literacy, and often skills such as typing which require six months training to reach full proficiency, even if these skills are not recognized as socially significant.

This argument is reinforced by Dex (1987), who argues that clerical work constitutes a discrete cluster of jobs within which women experience job movement, and that it is separate from other jobs such as semi-skilled factory work, shop work and personal service work. That is, there is a barrier to mobility for women between clerical work and these other jobs. Dex argues that clerical work is a woman's primary labour market. A significant proportion of clerical work is part of a primary, not secondary labour market, and part of the core not periphery.

So far the analysis has focused upon women, in order to argue that a simple correlation between women and periphery cannot be made. Men, too, do not fit neatly on one side of this divide, although the majority do. One quarter of men do not fall into the permanent full-time category (Hakim, 1987b). Thus, while the majority of the core workers may be male and the periphery female, there are some significant exceptions to this which preclude a simple equation of the two.

Environmental change

Atkinson makes reference to changes in the wider environment as being a factor in the concern for more flexibility within management's strategies. I am going to assess whether these changes are significantly gendered, in particular whether gender is a causal factor in the changing structure of employment. Atkinson's main concern is with changes in the business environment, especially changes in the product market and international competition. He suggests that legislative changes have had little impact and implies that the main changes are ungendered.

If, however, we take a broader definition of the environment, we might observe major changes both in the immediate business context regarding the use of female labour and in the wider environment which have significantly affected the supply of female labour. The changes in the business context include: the dropping of the marriage bar after the Second World War, that is, only four decades ago; the significant lessening of male trade union opposition to women in paid work; equal opportunity legislation which undercuts barriers to women in paid work; employment protection legislation which protects full-time, but few part-time workers (Walby, 1986: 202–42).

Other relevant changes in the business environment include the increased access of women to education. Girls in 1985 obtained 51 per cent of 'O' levels, 46 per cent of 'A' levels (EOC, 1987, Table 2.1), and 42 per cent of university undergraduate degree admissions in 1984–5 as compared to 28 per cent in 1965–6 (EOC, 1985, Table 2.6; 1987: 24). The increased rate of divorce also acts as an encouragement to female career development. This doubled between 1971 and 1983 to 147,000 and is the main cause of the figure of 930,000 single-parent families (EOC, 1985b: 4). Women spend less time on housework, even though the extent and effect of this reduction is very controversial (Cowan, 1983; Gershuny, 1983; Vanek, 1980). The fertility rate continues to fall.

In short the gender environment is very significantly different from what it was even twenty years ago, both within the business context (with the greater rights and protections given to male workers, and to a lesser extent full-time, but not part-time, women workers), and in the wider business environment (in the increased supply of women workers because of changed domestic conditions and gendered educational changes).

While the extent of the impact of the equal opportunity legislation is subject to some controversy (Dex and Shaw, 1986; Hakim, 1981; McIntosh and Weir, 1982; Snell, 1979: Snell, *et al.*, 1981) few would doubt that it reduces the legitimacy of directly discriminatory practices against women. The implication of the employment protection legislation for the gendering of the terrain of industrial relations is less well explored. It would appear to have been important in differentiating the conditions of work of men from those of part-time women. A male-dominated labour movement won legislation which secured protection from arbitrary dismissal of the occupants of jobs which were more often held by men than by women. These were the full-time jobs, and jobs of people who had already been in employment with one employer for some time. Part-time employment typically held by women was much less protected.

On this new terrain there is then greater differentiation of the job security of the average male and a significant minority of female workers, since that of the typical male has been improved to a greater extent than that of the part-time female. There has been a divergence in the conditions of employment of men and part-time women as a consequence of this gendered legislation. A consequence of this one-sided improvement in the job security of male workers is that part-time women workers are more exposed when there is an employer offensive on job security. This is not to suggest, however, that men, even in the 'core', have not been made redundant.

Further differences in the conditions of employment of full-time and part-time workers resulted from state insurance and welfare policy (Hakim, 1987b; Manley and Sawbridge, 1980). Part-timers became more attractive to employers because of state policy relating to the level of the threshold for the payment of national insurance, differential maternity rights and differential eligibility for redundancy pay. This differentiation of the conditions of full- and part-time workers is higher in Britain than many other countries. Britain has the highest proportion of part-timers among the ten EEC countries (see Table 6.2). These differences have historic roots in the particular British experience of the mobilization of women workers in the Second World War (Summerfield, 1984; Walby, 1986).

We should, however, be beware of leaping to the conclusion, as did some of the early theorists on women as a reserve army of labour, that this means that women are less likely to be employed today as a consequence of employers shedding unprotected workers. Rather the reverse is the case. Less-protected workers are more attractive workers to employers, precisely because they have less job security. If employers are indeed seeking greater numerical flexibility, then they are more likely to create categories of employment which are more likely to be filled by part-time women. This is indeed what we see. The flexibility strategy, whether it be old or new, is one which provides employment opportunities to women, albeit under worse conditions of service.

Contradictions between flexibility and labour-market rigidity

One of the motivations of management in seeking to introduce flexible working patterns is said to be the removal of labour market rigidities which impede the efficient utilization of labour. Neo-classical economic theory has long held that a perfectly competitive labour market helps towards an efficiently functioning economy and that any form of labour-market rigidity impedes this goal. One significant aspect of labour-market rigidity is that of occupational segregation by sex (Equal Opportunities Commission, 1985; Hakim, 1979, 1981; Treiman and Hartmann, 1981). Yet, the degree of segregation, at SEG level, has increased between 1971 and 1981. Significantly more men were working in 1981 in SEGs which were at least 90 per cent male than in 1971, and similarly many more women are working in SEGs which are 70 per cent or more female (Bagguley and Walby, 1988). The seventeen-fold division of employment by SEG, using census data, provides a robust measure of segregation. In this way the objective of the flexible firm might be considered to contradict aims for the removal of labour-market rigidities.

This apparent paradox of flexibilization increasing labour-market rigidities may be partly a result of the difference and indeed contradiction between the two major forms of flexibilization. First, functional flexibility, which is designed to remove demarcations, has been largely applied to craftworkers (Cross, 1985; Jenson Chapter 7), who are almost entirely male. It would appear that the removal of demarcation has thus not been pursued across differently sex-typed jobs. Hence functional flexibility has not led to fewer barriers between men's and women's jobs. Second, the strategy needed to implement functional flexibility cuts across that needed to implement numerical flexibility. Functionally flexible workers are not expected to bear the brunt of numerical flexibility. These two sections of the workforce are then further separated in order to sustain these different policies for different groups of workers. However, this is largely speculation based on existing studies which were designed for other purposes and needs further study before a complete resolution of this paradox of flexibilization increasing segregation is possible.

Similarly, the distinction between part-time and full-time work, which is part of the strategy of numerical flexibility is essentially a form of segregation in the workforce; a form of resegregation utilizing the length of the working week as the mechanism justifying it.

Rounds of gender restructuring

Some of the key divisions in the workforce that the flexibility literature is addressing are essentially gendered. The most important and sizeable change in the composition and structure of the labour force over the last couple of decades has been the dramatic increase in the number of part-time women workers. Part-time women workers are the largest single category of non-permanent full-time workers. The above has, however, cautioned against stereotyping core workers as male and female workers as peripheral. While part-time women workers do tend to fit the model of peripheral workers, many full-time women workers, who make up 57 per cent of the female workforce, do not.

Women are entering waged labour in larger proportions, while failing to rise up the occupational hierarchy as a group. Yet women are not simply at the bottom of the pile, nor are they a disposable reserve. There are more of them, at roughly the same position in the vertical hierarchy of paid employment, and they are at least as segregated from men as ever before.

It is because of the erosion of some forms of patriarchal practices in paid work that women have a different place in the new rounds of restructuring than in the old. The attempt to subordinate women in the labour market is not new, but part of a continuing dynamic in the inter-relationship of patriarchal and capitalist structures. It is partly in response to the successes that women have won in terms of entry to the labour market and elsewhere that this new round of restructuring is taking the form that it is. Part-time work for women fits the desire of women for paid work which is compatible with their existing domestic responsibilites, of employers for cheap flexible labour, and of existing male workers to retain the best jobs for themselves.

The employment protection legislation, won under the pressure of the labour movement, gave protection from dismissal to those workers with a period of full-time employment in one firm. Other legislation gave national insurance benefits to employees who worked more than a certain number of hours, and charged employers for this. The new flexibility offensive is an element of the response to that round of labour movement activity. It does not so much contest the advantages given to those workers by legislation, but rather seeks to side-step these issues by both increasingly employing workers on contracts which do not qualify for this state-backed protection, and enforcing lesser job security on these workers who fall outside the protection of the legislation. (It is on the terrain of functional flexibility that the employers are directly taking on entrenched labour movement positions.)

The notions of rounds of struggle, each setting the conditions for the next, as introduced by Edwards (1979) and rounds of accumulation as introduced by Massey (1984) are useful here. We may fruitfully extend these concepts and apply them to the situation which has been developing in Britain in the 1980s. The essence of Edwards' notion is that employers and employees do not engage in simple pendulum-type struggles over the same issues, but rather the terrain of struggle is transformed by each round of struggle, and new issues and forms of struggle.

In the context of full-time female and male workers having won greater legislative protection than part-timers, it is to be expected that, where possible, the next round of jobs created by employers will not be full-time. Further, the forms of resistance that male workers have historically used against the entry of women workers have been undercut by the successful struggles of women against these forms of patriarchal closure. The equal opportunity legislation and changes in trade unions' policies under pressure from their recently enlarged female membership prevent some of the forms of closure that previously occurred, while not guaranteeing women equal access to the better jobs with men.

In Britain then, the growth of peripheral part-time work for women, as an integral and permanent part of the workforce, is a result of a new round of capital restructuring in the context of the new balance of patriarchal, feminist and capitalist forces. This particular balance of forces is not a historical inevitability within capitalism. Indeed Britain is unusual in the Western industrialized world in the extent to which the workforce is composed of part-time women (see Table 6.2).

Table 6.2 Gender unemployment ratios and female employment, EEC 1984

EEC countries	D	F	I	B	L	UK	IRL	DK	GR
F activity rate	40.1	45.6	32.6	35.5	32.7	46.3	32.7	58.4	33.4
% F part-time	28.6	21.1	10.2	20.3	14.8	44.3	13.9	36.7	9.0
% unemployment rate	6.7	9.5	9.8	11.9	2.7	10.9	16.5	8.9	8.1
ratio F/M unemployment rates	1.6	1.6	2.4	2.3	2.0	0.9	1.1	1.3	2.0

Notes: F: Female; M: male. The Netherlands did not participate in the 1984 survey.
Source: EEC Labour Force Survey 1984, Calculated from Tables TO3, T18, T20, T36.

Because this pattern of part-time labour varies between countries, an explanation in terms of the technical requirements of industry (National Economic Development Office, 1986: 22-3; Robinson, 1988; Robinson and Wallace, 1984) is insufficient. Table 6.2 also shows that Britain has the highest rate of part-time women, and one of the highest rates of female participation, in the EEC. It is the only EEC country in which the rate of unemployment among women is lower than that among men. This is because part-time women workers are uniquely open to exploitation in Britain, making their labour especially attractive to those employers seeking cheap labour. The table also shows a general tendency for countries with low levels of part-time work among women to have a higher proportion of unemployment. Further it is countries with the lowest levels of female 'economic' activity (beneath 40 per cent) which show the highest ratios of female to male employment (twice or more).

The balance between patriarchal and capitalist forces is different across nations, and varies between industries. The widespread entry of women into labour-market participation is not new to the post-Second World War period. Historically, men were a minority in the workforce of the first factory employment in the world, cotton textiles in Lancashire. Resistance to women working in these mills, though organized, was too weak to prevent their continuance. At the same time, women were barred from not dissimilar work in engineering by the much more strongly organized male unions. In clerical work, men also lost their battle to exclude women, though they were able to maintain strict segregation, retaining the white-collar jobs. The regional distribution of these forms of employment gave rise to regionally specific female participation rates, which were considerable before the Second World War (Walby, 1986).

Conclusion

The influx of women is not a temporary expedient of employers seeking 'reserves' of labour to use in a crisis, either of an over-tight labour market, or an over-slack one. It is, rather, a long-term restructuring of the gender composition of the workforce. It can occur because of long-term changes in gender relations both within and outside employment. The removal of many overt forms of patriarchal closure in the labour market is as permanent a change as any other (and many less overt forms are under concerted attack from both within and without the labour movement). Changes in gender relations outside employment, in access to education, in marriage and divorce, in political citizenship and in household structure improve women's access to paid work on a long-term basis. Further, many of these changes, such as the educational qualifications attained by young women today, may continue to have a positive impact on women's employment prospects for decades to come.

Old forms of patriarchy are replaced by new. It is only if we hold an over-rigid conception of patriarchy that we would equate these changes with its demise. The wages gap between women and men has not closed. Employment is not less segregated by sex to any significant degree. In women's part-time waged work men do not lose their individual domestic labourers, while employers gain cheap labour. Whose flexibility?

7 The talents of women, the skills of men: flexible specialization and women

JANE JENSON

As Chapter 1 points out, for many people a well-formulated strategy of flexible specialization introduced into the labour process will allow both capital and labour to move beyond many of the problems of the current crisis.[1] For others, however, there is little basis for such optimism, since flexible specialization has an undesirable and costly downside, whose consequences are measured in terms of unemployment, income polarization, and fragmentation of the labour movement. For them, the future will not, and should not, be founded on flexible specialization.

This chapter is also cautious about flexible specialization because of the gender-blind nature of many discussions of it. If one begins with the assumption that workers come in two genders, then one enquires about gender-biased or gendering effects in the social relations prophesized for the future. Gender bias can arise from differential locations of women and men in the new labour processes. Gendering effects are even broader, in that they are the consequences of the articulation of gender and class relations in the social construction of women and men's identities.

To the extent that enthusiasts of flexible specialization are doing more than providing a recipe for management to surmount the current crisis, they must ask whether women and men are located in the labour force in such a way that they will benefit similarly from any new emphases on skilled labour. They must also enquire whether – without substantial political struggle before or at least concurrently with the move to a new wage relation and regime of accumulation – women even have the same potential for positive outcomes from their model of flexible specialization which may exist for some men, at least in certain progressive variants of the theory.[2]

This chapter examines gender bias and gendering effects in particular by exploring the ideas about flexible specialization propounded by Piore and Sabel in *The Second Industrial Divide* (1984). For Piore and Sabel, current changes in the production process reflect a move away from the special purpose machinery of mass production, which relied primarily on semi-skilled and unskilled workers to make standardized goods for mass consumption. New processes have begun to appear which utilize general purpose tools and skilled workers with the know-how to make quick adjustments to changing markets and more differentiated tastes. Out of the observation of such changes in the labour process, Piore and Sabel construct a political programme of 'yeoman democracy'. They suggest that such new political forms could arise out of the greater control over their working conditions and working lives exercised by the skilled workers of the post-Fordist sectors.

In this general argument about capital accumulation, labour processes, and political forms, the concept of skill and notions about influence of skilled workers provide a keystone for the entire edifice. This chapter concentrates on the implications of the observation that skills are historically rather than biologically or technologically constructed and that social construction is part of the process by which unequal social relations are reproduced. Such relations may reflect not only the unequal structures of class power but potentially all other differences, including race, ethnicity, language and sex. It is an argument whose implications strike at the heart of the unproblematic meaning of skill, which so much of the work on flexible specialization assumes. In fact, it problematizes that concept.

Gender biases

Hints that women may not do very well under flexible specialization become especially apparent when reading Piore and Sabel's fond references to Proudhon and suggestions that his utopian visions can be a model for the post-Fordist future (1984: 28ff.). However, the nineteenth-century workers' movement, in France especially, long suffered under the influence of the choice Proudhon gave women – to be housewives or harlots. Embedded at the heart of his understanding of the independent, craft-based working class – which he celebrated – was the belief that women should work only in the home and that any self-respecting working man ought to be able to support his non-waged wife and children. For Proudhon, the family nurtured values which could not survive in the larger world of mutualism, and, in particular, wives' unstinting and supportive affection for their husbands was a consolation and protection against the most vicious consequences of the productivity standard which characterized mutualist society.[3]

These notions of gender and family relations atrophied in the official ideology of the French labour movement when the mass/class unionism of the Second and Third International defeated Proudhonism (Moss, 1976: Chapter 1). Thus, where Proudhon condemned female labour as well as political action by unionists, strikes, and collectivist associations, mass/class unions advocated equal pay for equal work and the organization of women workers who at the time were rapidly entering the paid labour force in the new industrial sectors (Jenson, 1988; Moss, 1976: 52).

Yet, the authors of *The Second Industrial Divide* return to the Proudhonist utopia, using it as a model for their world of flexible specialization where generalized skills are put to work to meet the changing market demands of consumer capitalism. They ignore its gender biases, as they do its lack of emphasis on class solidarity and political action.

It would be wrong, of course, to accuse Piore and Sabel of Proudhon's sins against women, just because they find inspiration for their own utopia of flexible specialization in his enthusiasm for a craft-based world. Nevertheless, in many discussions of flexible specialization, women are either invisible or confined to quite 'different' places.[4] This treatment of women – and the understanding of gender which thus resides at the heart of the analysis – is exemplified in Piore and Sabel's work, both *The Second Industrial Divide* and other pieces written earlier. In none of the earlier books and articles is it common to find a working woman. Moreover, when they do appear, as they do infrequently, they are different, not like the 'real' workers in their work lives and labour market location. In Sabel's *Work and Politics*, where no effort is made to use gender-neutral language, despite the fact that the book was only published in 1982, the problem is clear. The worker is always a 'he', seeking a political strategy for 'his' workplace relations. Any women who do appear are always marginal workers, whose relationship to the labour force is temporary, uneven, and much influenced by other aspects of their life situations.

In Piore's path-breaking work on dual labour markets, women are mentioned only as part of the secondary sector. These important works did make space for discussions of gender bias, by making certain assumptions about women's labour-force participation. For example, in Berger and Piore (1980: 31), women appear as marginal workers in the secondary sector, who along with peasants and migrants differ in their work relations from 'the customary labour force' or 'the traditional working class'. Simplistic assumptions about women's social and economic situation mean Berger and Piore define women as married or otherwise dependent on men. This family relationship gives them access to the economic and social security which their participation in the secondary labour market would otherwise deny them.

> The migrants (foreign and domestic), the rural workers and the women are attractive precisely because they belong to another socio-economic structure and view industrial employment as a

temporary adjunct to their primary roles. They are willing to take
jobs because they see their commitment to these jobs as temporary, and they are able to bear the flux and uncertainty of the
industrial economy because they have traditional economic
activities upon which to fall back. (ibid.: 50)

Similar arguments surface in Piore and Sabel (1984: 167ff.); women
appear in the list of categories of a labour reserve which was called up
in the boom years. However, once these categories come to demand the
status of full participants – wages and benefits comparable to those of
other workers – they cease to have any specificity; they disappear into
the general category of worker. In this way, although the segmentation
literature (in which Piore's work, in particular, is so important) does
mention women, by treating them as any other marginal category the
analysis remains blind to the specific structuring effects of gender
relations which have been uncovered over and over again. SU5
    One can only draw the conclusion that in these works the authors are
assuming that all the real workers are like men; gender, race or
nationality enter into the analysis only to explain divergences from the
norm. There is no room for the notion that women might normally
work or that working women might be the norm in some sectors.
'Women' are presumed to be marginal workers and there is no
consideration of the situation of women in the traditional working
class whose wages are systematically lower or who are confined to the
semi-skilled and unskilled jobs of the primary sector, although their
commitment to full-time employment is as great as men's and their
training may even be as long. Indeed, for Piore it is almost as if
'women' will somehow disappear with modernity in that 'the labour
force for secondary jobs tends to rely heavily, although not
exclusively, upon *preindustrial* groups and classes' (Berger and Piore,
1980: 50 – emphasis added). Actually, it sometimes seems as if, for
Sabel and Piore, a woman working full-time, without interruption, in
a mass-production industry would have to be a man.
    The nub of the criticism is not the language or lack of discussion of
women's work, however. It lies elsewhere, in a concern about the
underlying analytic assumptions. In assuming that all 'real workers' are
the same and/or that women are either non-waged, these analyses close
off the possibility of seeing the gendering effects which exist in the
full-time labour force because they exist in *all* work relations. Thus,
while they may be able to describe – although not necessarily explain –
gender bias, they remain blind to links between the social construction
of gender and of skill. Therefore, they provide a picture which is
inadequate for apprehending the reality of that which they wish both
to describe and control.
    If, for example, employers make use of the female and male labour
force in different ways, if the development of a more 'flexible' labour

force also means rising rates of feminization, if only men are likely to be 'flexible specialists', then a world of post-Fordist flexible specialization is very different – and less benign – than that which Piore and Sabel assume. Furthermore, where the diagnosis of the world is different, the prescriptions for practice are not likely to work. Therefore, the question of where women fit into these analyses is a crucial one.

Recent studies of women in the labour force have found all three of the above statements to be empirically correct. We now know that the level of sex segregation is very high indeed (Bakker, 1988; Hagen and Jenson, 1988). Studies of the industrial sector have often shown that women and men work in different industries. More recent analyses reveal that even in the same workplaces women and men work at different jobs and often in separate locations. In particular, women are increasingly concentrated in jobs classified as unskilled or semi-skilled, which are the classic ones of mass production.[6] Moreover, women and men occupy different lifetime career trajectories with women's being much more truncated than men's. Clearly, female and male workers have not been employed in the same way.

The empirical validity of the second if-statement emerges in studies of the recent efforts by employers to create and manage a more 'flexible' labour force. Flexibility – in which hard-won protection of workers' conditions of employment are lessened – has also brought feminization of the labour force in its trail. It was most often women, especially married women, who took up the offers of part-time and temporary work.[7] With a recognition of both the reliance on women for mass-production industry and the popularity of women for more flexible labour contracts, the economic forces behind the great rise in the female rate of labour-force participation becomes clear (Bakker, 1988).[8]

The detection of gender biases in these aspects of post-war economies makes the third if-statement even more compelling. Much recent work, reported below, demonstrates that women are closed out of skilled work by a variety of social mechanisms. This work also forces us to recall that skill is a socially constructed concept and that its content will therefore be contested not only by capitalists and workers but also by women and men. While Braverman's work made it very clear that definitions of jobs and skilling arise out of struggles among workers and capitalists, further analyses of the labour process have exposed the coexistence of struggles among women and men, which are simultaneously crucial to the development of concepts of skill (Phillips and Taylor, 1980: 82ff.) Such studies cast doubt on the notion that flexible specialization will open new possibilities for many working women.

The social construction of skilled work

One essential aspect of the construction of a skill is the process of differentiation, the erection of distinctions among kinds of work, and therefore the workers who perform them. The result of this process is that differences among workers exist and reproduce within the working class. It was the consequences of skill-based differentiation which since the latter part of the nineteenth century led many militants in the labour movement to advocate forms of organization which downplay craft distinctions. The rising organizations of industrial workers feared the divisive and fragmenting effects of craft bodies founded on principles of exclusion. And, of course, this fear was never groundless. Craft unions which did not extend their sense of community to incorporate the semi-skilled and unskilled industrial workers did not contribute as much to working-class solidarity as did industrial unions or those with a territorial basis of organizing.

The reality of the fear lies in the process of differentiation by craft, which involves both technological and ideological elements. The outcome of skill-based differentiation is the creation and continuing validation of an identity through a labour process which draws boundaries around 'sameness' and 'difference'. Since any particular group of individuals can construct its identity in a plurality of ways, it is very important to the labour movement that it uses the factories and other workplaces of industrial capitalism effectively to bring into being a self-conscious (that is a self-identified) working class. Political struggle culminating in class formation and fostering class conscious-ness is an important ingredient of any successful labour movement's practice (Brodie and Jenson, 1988: Chapter 1).

The difficulties of developing solidaristic class identities among craftsmen have been long understood by the labour movement. It needed strategies designed explicitly to overcome fragmentation based on skill because the nature of skilled work itself had a tendency to encourage identities based on difference. Cockburn's (1983) work on the history of compositors' skills provides a concrete example of this tendency. The compositors worked hard to guarantee that they retained as much control over their workplace as possible. This meant that they had to eliminate the possibility that unskilled women or men would take parts of their work. Compositors struggled hard to maintain the dominance of adult men over women and boys – 'the demon of cheap boy labour' – from the late nineteenth century until the middle of the twentieth. Their recent history has been one in which they have had immense difficulties maintaining their control over definitions of skill and thus over the workplace, in the face of new technology (Cockburn, 1981: 47; 1983: *passim;* Zeitlin, 1985: 195ff).

Each struggle over technological innovation reproduced a compli-cated and nuanced social construction of compositors' identities both as workers and as men. The process involved the compositors' ability, through workplace power, to keep women, boys, and any other unskilled labour, out of the print shops. With regard to women, they managed to do this by refusing to work with women, to apprentice women, to use the type set by women. These actions all discouraged owners from attempting to employ women (whose wages were substantially lower) anywhere where the compositors' union was well-organized (Zeitlin, 1985: 193-5, 214-16). This long struggle culminated in keeping the compositors' craft virtually 100 per cent male, not simply because the men had the workplace power to force employers' compliance but also because women themselves were discouraged enough not to apply.

> Girls were not considered suitable for apprenticeship. Physical and moral factors (girls were not strong enough, lead was harmful to pregnancy, the social environment might be corrupting) were deployed ideologically in such a way that few girls would see themselves as suitable candidates for apprenticeship ...
> The process of appropriation of the physical and mental properties and technical hardware required for composing by a group of men, therefore, was not only a capitalist process of class formation...but also a significant influence in the process of gender construction in which men took the initiative in constituting themselves and women in a relation of complementarity and hierarchy. (Cockburn, 1981: 46)

This example of the compositors' craft clearly illustrates two important points. The first is that identities can only be constructed as part of a process of differentiation. The second is that identities contain elements which order relations between women and men as well as those between labour and capital. Cockburn's historical analysis demonstrates that printers always experienced technology, and particularly the introduction of new technology, not only as affecting the balance of power in class relations but just as importantly as an aspect of gender power. When the compositors faced technology which threatened the dominance of the craftsmen in the shop, they fought it as a challenge to their own power, which included their power to be men. They experienced the innovations as emasculation, and they organized their struggle against them as a fight for virility (Phillips, 1983: 102). For these printers, their identity as skilled craftsmen encompassed not only the boundaries between themselves and the owners and themselves and non-skilled men, but also a gender boundary (Cockburn, 1981: 49). The printing craft involved the social construction of printers as men and as skilled workers. The two elements were inseparable.

Such work amplifies our understanding of the ways that gender relations are reproduced in work relations. One of the major accomplishments of Cockburn and others' work is to demonstate that feminists have paid too exclusive attention to the family as the site of reproduction of women's oppression. [9] They point to the crucial contribution of work and workplace relations in the creation and continuation of relations of unequal gender power, at the heart of which is the very notion of what constitutes skilled work. As a result, the gendering effects of 'public', and especially production, activities have now come under scrutiny. Such analytic correctives have considerable implications for analyses of flexible specialization, where the concept of skill plays such a central role.

Enthusiasts of flexible specialization stress that the positive results for labour in the new conditions will follow only from successful negotiations by workers to capture the potential of new technology and turn it to their advantage (Piore and Sabel, 1984: 277ff. and passim). In any consideration of conflictual social relations, therefore, they highlight only the contest between management and labour. Nevertheless what remains yet to be recognized is that workplace politics simultaneously include the struggles over gender power, which involve, in Cockburn's (1981: 56) words, a 'power play' between women and men, even where the workplace is predominantly single-sex.

The skills of men, the talents of women: gendering technology

Studies of the segmentation of work have demonstrated repeatedly that women and men tend to hold different jobs, to do different kinds of work and, therefore, to have substantially different wage structures. It is important, however, to comprehend how this situation arose. One way is through a process by which both jobs themselves and the appreciation of such jobs are gendered; they exist in social relations of hierarchy reproducing unequal relations of gender power. As Phillips writes:

> The hierarchies of skill are not just an imperative of capitalist production: they express at the same time a system of male dominance in craft identity which is inextricably (if confusingly) linked with masculinity...jobs are created as masculine and feminine, with their skill content continually re-drawn to assert the dominance of men (1983: 102).

The consequence is that the skills so important to notions of flexible specialization are unequally distributed.

Most occupations have a gender and, given existing assumptions about femininity and masculinity, it is those which incorporate the least control over the manipulation of technology which are designated 'female jobs' or which women fill. [10] Therefore, major changes will involve either 'masculinizing' women or finding a way, through political action, to remove the gender designation of jobs. Currently, those gendered jobs are not formally classified as equally skilled. Often what men do is called skilled whereas what women do is considered not skilled, generally because it is thought to involve some natural female talent. [11] The question is why this distinction exists and what practices reproduce it. The most convincing explanation is one which explicates the ideological content of skill definition. [12]

A major factor involved in the differentiation between 'women's work' and 'men's work' is that there is a *real* difference in the relationship of each gender to technology. Managers tend to assign women to jobs which exclusively involve the operation of machinery. In this way, women become the manual operators of the machines while men tend to design, set up and service them. In addition to the highly skilled technicians and engineers who make and/or install machinery, managers value the 'all-rounders', the workers who can turn their hand to anything that needs doing, who can untangle a complicated mechanical or production problem and resolve the difficulty (Cockburn, 1986: 181). That kind of general skill is valued (that is, better paid), while the worker who seems merely to stand aside when a problem develops, and never takes the casing off the machine is not only less valued but more easily replaced. There seems to be an impenetrable, invisible barrier

> between operating the controls that put a machine to work and taking the casing off it in order to intervene in its mechanism... For an operator there is always someone who is assumed to know better than she about the technology of the machine on which she is working. That someone is almost invariably a man. (Cockburn, 1986: 181).

It is these social relations which so often separate women from technology.

There are three basic reasons why women have different relationships to machines than men do. A first reason – which people often overlook in discussing the division of jobs – is the very design of the machinery. Cockburn (1981: 51-2) has documented the ways in which men construct machines which only men can easily manipulate, because the design itself incorporates assumptions about body size and strength of the workers doing the job. Thus the weight of components, the reach required to operate a machine, the general strength needed to perform the job may result from the inventor's presuppositions about who will use the machine. In this way, popular or even individuals' assumptions about the gender division of labour enter directly into the concept of the machine, the work station, and its relationship to other machinery; these then take on a materiality which is embedded in the technology itself. But beyond the design of machines, assumptions about the 'average worker' also enter into working conditions constructed by bargaining between labour and management. When, for example, trade unions negotiate acceptable weight levels, bale sizes, loads, work breaks or sanitary facilities, assumptions about whether women or men will work there shape the discussions and partially determine the agreements the union is willing to accept. The negotiated outcomes may exclude women, if male trade unionists assume they will not – or should not – be in that workplace. Thus, the social content of technological possibilities is very great indeed.

A second reason that men and women hold different jobs – and therefore have different relationships to the machinery – lies in the assumptions of the managers who make assignments. Milkman (1983) explores in detail the ideological construction of work and the division of labour on the part of managers who do the hiring and she has documented how managers make an initial determination of whether a particular job is a 'woman's' or a 'man's'. For example, the notion that 'light industry' was suitable for women whereas 'heavy physical effort' was what men did, led managers in the 1930s and 1940s to fill the jobs of the electrical sector with 'girls and women' (ibid.: 167–8).[13]

There is, of course, little relation between the actual amount of physical effort involved in any workplace and the patterns of employment by gender. Nevertheless, the notion that such differences do exist and are legitimate grounds for differential hiring practices are common; with these assumptions about whether a job is best filled by a woman or a man, the gendering of occupations proceeds. These decisions become part of the relationships of the workplace itself. They help to reproduce a situation which might have initially been an open one but which in time rigidifies along gender lines and itself becomes a major contribution to unequal gender relations at work.

Third, women themselves make a substantial contribution to gender segregation in relation to technology. Women and men's identities tend to contain deep assumptions about what work is proper and possible for each gender. Women's own identity often contains a notion of 'femininity' which, given the prevailing norms in most societies, excludes the notion that technical skill or familiarity with the machinery is feminine (Cockburn, 1986: 186). In the British pottery industry, women who work with men or do not do the traditional work of decorating pottery are thought unrefined and coarse by the other women workers (Sarsby, 1985: 71–3). In addition, many women have learned to escape the monotony of their factory work by defining their lives at work as worthless and trying to use the escape into romance as a way of revaluing themselves and their situations (Beechey, 1983: 29–30). In other words, women participate in the reproduction of their lack of control over the machinery which they tend.

All three reasons lead to the conclusion that operators and 'all-rounders' are made, not born. Men are not born 'handy' any more than women are born without the confidence to turn a screwdriver. The relationship to the machinery is socially created, and as such reproduces existing social relationships, in which ideas about gender play a crucial role. The ethos of the all-rounder – which comes closest to the ideal-typical worker in discussions of flexible specialization – is a masculine one. It involves not only certain abilities to deal with the machinery but also a sense of camaraderie which is highly social and which depends on being accepted by the group.

The politics of skills and talents

The argument thus far is that ideology is crucial for the gendering of jobs, in part through its role in constituting the definition of skill. Studies of working women continue to make visible the failure of women and men, trade unions and employers to acknowledge that much of what women do is skilled work (Beechey, 1983: 29-30; Charles, 1983:5). Very frequently, the work which women perform is classified as non-skilled because it is considered too 'natural' and/or 'merely dexterous' (Cockburn, 1981: 49; Milkman, 1983: 268; Phillips and Taylor, 1980: 6; Remick, 1984: 23). It reflects the supposed talents of women rather than any acquired skill for which recognition in the form of wages or social value is appropriate. This effect is clearly seen when we observe that a secretary's job is probably the ideal-typical form of flexible specialization, albeit in the tertiary sector. Yet, the ability of secretaries to work as flexible specialists is not recompensed but interpreted instead as something unexceptional, especially since it often bears a resemblance, in its multiplication of tasks, to domestic labour.

The most important implication of this gender-based definition of skills is that an on-going system of unequal gender relations is reproduced by the very process of skill acquisition. To the extent that, according to popular conceptions, women have talents while men have skills, a world of flexible specialization will be one in which women are absent. In fact, given this understanding of the definition of skill, the reasons for Piore and Sabel's lack of attention to women workers are more obvious. In the eyes of so much of the world, women are rarely skilled; and therefore, they are not likely to be the flexible specialists who constitute the ideal-typical worker in this brave new world.

This distinction between women as non-skilled and men as skilled is a social construct. As such, it is the product of everyday politics as well as the power relations of organized class struggle. Phillips and Taylor

(1980: 85), claim the distinction 'has been generated through the struggles of male workers to retain their dominanace within the sexual hierarchy'. It is, however, not necessary to assume that male workers *consciously* seek to subordinate women to their desires for sexual power in order to see a social process operating to value men's work over women's.

The conception of identity formation based on differentiation which was sketched above provides a way to understand the reproduction of notions of difference in gender and class identities. That sketch assumed no necessary pattern of gender power. The advantage of conceptualizing gender power relations in a more open-ended way is that it leaves the very production of gender and class identities to political and ideological resolution.

At the very heart of identity formation is, as we have seen, the process of differentiation, the establishment of boundaries of 'sameness' and 'difference'. Thus the process of forming class identities sets boundaries around classes which establish an understanding of those who share a common set of interests and those whose interests are different. Similarly, gender identities form to establish the boundaries between feminine and masculine lives. As we know from generations of politics in capitalist societies, classes neither rise spontaneously to take their place in history, nor do all class actors organize around the same comprehension of class relations. Rather, the variety of possible forms is large and the political consequences of variety are important. By analogy, then, it is easy to see that gender identities may be constituted in a way which allows sexual difference to determine almost all other aspects of life – including the definition of skill. Or, gender identities can minimize the importance of biological difference and men and women can strive to achieve a more equitable and fair world in which the existence of biological differences is simply acknowledged and accepted, but not permitted to culminate in relationships of unequal social power. Whether the former or the latter occurs is an outcome of real historical struggles, ones in which progressive actors such as trade unions and feminists must choose a political strategy which will have, as one of its consequences, an effect on the formation of gender identities. [14]

Workers and their organizations through their political struggles are implicated in the constitution of identities. Obviously other actors are involved, just as identities are not only constituted out of workplace relations. With this caveat about the multiple sources of identity, it is, however, also important to recognize that workplace actors and actions do have a role to play. One central way in which this happens is that they help to determine the grounds for differentiation and the actual form that it takes. Thus, their strategic behaviour will be important in influencing whether there is a move towards equality despite the recognition of differences or one in which hierarchical inequities accompany the recognition of difference. In this way political struggle is crucial for achieving an egalitarian and progressive result.

It is the very importance of the outcome of this historical process which makes the absence of considerations of gender in discussions of flexible specialization so problematic, given that most authors see their work as an intervention in practice as much as theory. Gender-blind analyses will only allow the reproduction of existing social relations, in which gender identities have thus far been not only different but also profoundly unequal. They will not help to overcome gender biases nor alter the gendering effects of work relations.

A number of strategies is available which affect the conditions under which identities are constructed. Examination of the example of work groups, which are so crucial to situations of flexible specialization is helpful to make this point. The observed importance of social acceptance in work groups as well as the entrenched idea that women's relationship to machinery differs from that of men is crucial when evaluating the differential gender effects of flexible specialization. If, as has been argued, workplace relations contribute to identities constructed around both class and gender, the work groups are a major locale where that occurs.

One form of restructuring under post-Fordist regimes of accumulation has involved a move away from the more rigid forms of labour discipline appropriate to assembly lines. In response to technological change in which a knowledge of the machinery is required, new management practices emphasize small groups which work together, job rotation and workers' participation in regulating production. These are all very different from the habits of the traditional assembly line. But studies are already demonstrating that these new procedures are not without gender bias in their application. In an examination of work reorganization around participation schemes in the automobile industry, Wood (1986: 426) found that women and men were differentially affected:

> For example, on the final inspection section, it fostered genuine group working; for many of the male production workers, who were working individually, the scheme had basically facilitated regular small group (quality circle) meetings; whilst for the women who were working on short assembly lines at various points in the production process, it largely meant job rotation, that is increased mobility between very limited tasks, albeit on a basis worked out by the women themselves. This example illustrates how the different relationships which various groups of workers have to technology ... remain even in the modern, more integrated factories, and more importantly mediate the effects of worker participation schemes.

In part what is involved is the constitution of work groups which can respond in a flexible way to the new automated work by adjusting quickly to changing needs of production, deploying effort where attention is needed at any moment and thus increasing both productivity and the intensity of labour. What is unclear is whether such groups will mix together workers who are 'different' in ways which are relevant to the actors involved. Such groups are encouraged to develop ties among themselves and even to compete with other groups over meeting production norms, and improving efficiency. In such tightly knit work collectives, the topic of group composition comes to the fore. Thus questions of difference – whether to include and co-operate with workers who are ethnically, racially, or sexually 'different' – can appear in the workplace. Where the practices of Fordism de-emphasized differentiation among workers to some extent, uniting them by the moving line, stress on co-operation, on consultation, and on planning can make it seem compelling to find 'pals' with whom one feels comfortable. In this way, as a by-product of the new management form of work organization, internal lines of cleavage in the working class around visible differences may be accentuated. Work groups, by their very form, foster 'we/they' feelings and relationships; boundaries are drawn which differentiate.

Technical jobs are often made up of teams of men used to each other and accustomed to working together. As Cockburn (1986: 182) found in her field work, for managers and male workers, if a woman should 'present herself for the work she would not, it was explained many times, fit into what was an existing all-male team'. Therefore, to the extent that work groups constitute themselves around ideas of who 'fits in', mixed groups are unlikely to form, both because notions of masculinity and femininity exclude the possibility of female competence ('she couldn't pull her weight') and because managers and workers recognize implicitly that the very process of group bonding includes reinforcement of gender identities ('she wouldn't like the language and the jokes of the lads'). Thus sexual difference, often carried by a discourse of sexual innuendo, becomes a powerful limit to the development of mixed work groups. Therefore, the work teams that enthusiasts of flexible specialization predict with such relish are likely, under current workplace politics, to be single-sex groups, for which gender difference becomes a boundary.

Conclusion

This chapter has examined flexible specialization through the lens of gender. Beginning with the assumption that workers are both female and male, it asks about gender bias and gendering effects which might result from a shift to flexible specialization. The conclusion which we can draw is that, without political challenges, gender bias is clearly likely to result not only from the effects of segmentation of the labour force but also from the social construction of skill. In other words, 'new' social relations will continue to reproduce the situation in which women's skills are not recognized as any more than natural talents as well as the numerous social processes which divert women from mastery over new technology. These are the gendering effects of work relations – including the relation to technology and innovation – which most discussions of flexible specialization ignore. Exploration of the modes of gendering clearly demonstrates that there is a great risk that if flexible specialization is accepted in a gender-blind way it will reinforce and even strengthen unequal gender relations.

Restructuring the labour process so as to privilege skilled work and workers will further marginalize women unless political actors challenge long-standing processes which isolate women from machinery and which define women's skills as talents. Carefully constructed strategies in pursuit of equal pay for work of equal value – which by their very nature politically question popular notions of skill and value – may be part of such a process. Unions and other actors must also reject notions of 'difference' within the working class which can be the basis for legitimation of a two-tier labour force in which the 'real workers' all seem to be skilled men, and women and others who have been historically without power fill the marginal categories. Acceptance of such a politics of fragmentation can only be a step backward.

8 *The transformation of training and the transformation of work in Britain*

DAVID LEE

Training is an important, if somewhat neglected, aspect of work organization and its development. Organization theorists have shown how national differences in training systems can influence the configuration of work roles in an individual firm or business (Maurice *et al.*, 1980).[1] But training also influences work organization in a profounder sense, going beyond the study of the workplace alone. This is because it is one of a number of major costs which employers face in relation to labour quality and effort. These costs in turn fundamentally influence the division of labour between economic units as well as within them. At one extreme managements can attempt to minimize overheads by developing methods of organization and control which are internal to the workplace. Alternatively, they can attempt to limit costs externally through 'market forces': for example, by purchasing already trained labour or by 'outsourcing', that is, subcontracting another organization to provide a good or service (Ascher, 1987: 8). How these strategies are combined will depend on a whole range of very variable factors in the wider economy and society.

In particular, there is a political dimension to this choice of strategies, very clearly illustrated in the case of training costs. By creating training subsidies and reform packages the state can influence employers' calculations of the return on in-house facilities. But in the absence of state initiatives, employers will have a strong incentive to avoid training altogether, hoping either to recruit skilled labour from the external labour market or, if labour shortages become acute, to mechanize and deskill jobs currently requiring trained workers and to tailor any training to their immediate production needs.

Most important of all, studying training forces us back to what was the central concern of Braverman's *Labor and Monopoly Capital* (1974): the close association between work organization and class relationships. This theme has tended to become somewhat displaced during the critical debate stimulated by his work. Instead much effort has, quite properly in the light of concern about the lack of good data bases (Wood, 1982: 10), been devoted to demonstrating the minutiae of industrial labour processes and the non-linear character of technical change. But arguably the reaction against Braverman has gone too far. Work organization, especially in the wider sense used here, has major implications for class. The same applies to any actions of the state which impinge upon work.

In this chapter I hope to demonstrate the importance of these points by discussing the reorganization of youth training which has occurred in Britain during the 1980s. The British situation offers a 'critical case', first, because of the distinctive character of state training policy. Throughout most of the twentieth century, governments have expected 'industry' largely to absorb the expense of training and refused to intervene in any decisive way to affect the quantity or quality of vocational preparation. British experience thus provides a long-term example of how firms and organizations are affected by having to face the full expense of a major labour overhead.

A second reason is that the British case 'is especially apposite for discussing changes of work organization in the recession' (Wood, 1987: 15). Economic decline and unemployment in the early and mid-1980s weakened union resistance to rationalization in the plant and made feasible greater flexibility in labour usage, tighter work discipline, self-inspection and the speed-up of operations. It also intensified trends in the distribution of jobs and forms of employment which were already affecting the working population generally, as we shall see below. Lastly, it produced a crisis in the voluntary system of industrial training.

In what follows I shall describe this crisis in greater detail. I shall then consider its consequences in relation to three topics which represent crucial aspects, not only of work organization but also of the class situation of workers, especially young workers, in contemporary Britain: employment conditions; skills; and labour control. In the conclusion I shall return to the general debate about the transformation of work.

Voluntarism, market forces and youth training

As I have already stated, British governments have insisted throughout most of the twentieth century that training is the responsibility of industry and that employers should bear in full the costs of providing it (Sheldrake and Vickerstaff, 1987). Political intervention has thus largely been confined to exhorting employers in their own interests voluntarily to expand the supply of trained labour. The principal departure from this 'voluntarism' occurred in the brief period after the 1964 Training Act which subjected employers to a system of training levies and grants. It soon became clear that employers themselves were not especially anxious to see greater central direction (Perry, 1976:

273–300). The levy–grant system was effectively abandoned after 1973 and training opportunities in Britain have otherwise remained in the hands of market forces over a long period.

'Voluntarism' as a way of managing the national labour force has been the subject of persistent criticism. According to a powerful strand of research and theory in the economics of training, exclusive reliance on employer initiatives means that where training has been most needed it is least likely to be provided. The more costly and transferable the skill, the greater the risk of any one employer not recouping investment in the training of workers; and the greater the incentives to undertake no training at all (Chapman and Tooze, 1987: Chapter 2; Lindley, 1983). Employers requiring skilled labour in these circumstances have at least two options: either to 'poach' already-trained workers from other employers, or to dilute the skill teaching to those elements specific to their own firm's requirements, perhaps inducing workers so trained to remain with the organization through the development of internal labour markets. For this reason Marsden (1986: Chapter 8) has argued that competitive market in transferable skills will be inherently unstable unless there is intervention from the state or some other non-market institution to sustain it.

Admittedly, several other industrial societies also rely upon a system of employer-led as opposed to state-led training. But in each example the full impact of market forces is offset by special factors absent from the British case. In Germany, for instance, there are strong legal and union controls over the content of employers' programmes. Even so, the dysfunctions of a market-based system are not wholly absent (Casey, 1986). In the United States general skills are developed within internal promotion chains in a manner that would have been inconceivable in the industrial relations context of post-war Britain (Ryan, 1984). But the majority of British employers have applied strict profitability criteria to any training they do, depleting and closing facilities and programmes in times of recession.

A further consequence of voluntarism in Britain has been that training became an especially sensitive industrial relations issue. Ryan, for example, has shown in detail how, during the inter-war period, employers in the engineering industry created bogus apprenticeships in order to use young people as cheap labour. In the post-war period, when trade unions were stronger and more militant, they reacted against such practices, effectively raising the pay of all young workers relative to those of adults (Ryan, 1987). Political pressure was also exerted to provide statutory control over youth wages in industries where the influence of collective bargaining was weak.

The recession of the 1980s induced a crisis in the policy of voluntarism due to the fact that in Britain, as elsewhere, young workers have been among the hardest hit. For example, about a quarter of 18–19 year olds were out of work in 1983 compared with about 14 per cent of adults (Ashton and Maguire, 1986: 47). The prospects for young people who are unwilling or unable to remain in education beyond the statutory leaving age (16) – still around half of the age group – and even some who do, were especially bleak (Roberts *et al.*, 1986: 244). They had already been worsening during the 1970s as a result of the long-term decline of both traditional apprenticeship and other forms of training. Between 1970 and 1985 the total number of apprentices in manufacturing industry fell from 218,000 to 73,000. 'Other trainees' declined in number from 200,000 to just under 40,000 (Chapman and Tooze, 1987: 92, Table 3.3). But over half of this contraction took place between 1980 and 1985 as firms closed or cut back on their training facilities and commitments.

In responding to this situation the British government set itself two major aims. The first assumed that youth unemployment had risen because both union and statutory wage controls had made the labour of young people too expensive relative to that of adults. To cure unemployment it was necessary to reverse the trend and dampen wage aspirations. The second addressed itself to a structural problem of the economy as a whole, namely, shortages of skilled labour. These shortages, it was argued could be met by an improvement of the supply of so-called 'transferable' skills among the young.

Intervention in youth training was proposed as the most effective way of achieving both objectives at once.[2] In fact, the device of using training and work experience programmes as a disguised form of unemployment relief was first used in Britain during the depressions of the inter-war years (Sheldrake and Vickerstaff, 1987). The practice was reintroduced in the mid-1970s well before the access of the Conservative Party to power in 1979 (cf. Chapman and Tooze, 1987: Chapter 5). The common feature of all these state training programmes was that they effectively gave a labour subsidy to any employers who were prepared to offer temporary traineeships within their organizations to jobless school leavers.

In the 1980s, however, as youth unemployment grew, government training programmes of this type underwent an unprecedented expansion. This chapter concentrates on what is by far the largest and most important example, the Youth Training Scheme (YTS). Initially introduced in 1983 as a one-year programme, from 1986 YTS has offered to unemployed 16-year-old school leavers two years of on-the-job training and work experience on the premises of a 'work provider', combined with three months each year of off-the-job training in a vocational college or special centre. (Seventeen-year-olds are offered a one-year programme.) Employers are encouraged to provide extra training places because trainees are not paid a wage but paid an allowance by the government. Initially, therefore, employers received trainees at no cost to themselves. With the introduction of the two-year version of the programme a variable employer contribution to the allowance was introduced. Even so, this payment still falls well below the cost of paying the trainee a wage for the full two years.

YTS thus contains the prescribed combination of a job creation package and reform of industrial training. The official blueprint for the scheme is in fact based on a version of human capital theory, albeit largely unstated. It assumes that most employers will instruct the trainees in the transferable skills which industry is said to need most. The possession of these skills will in turn ensure the employability of the trainees, either at their work placement or elsewhere. This will in due course revolutionize training for skills in industry, eliminating traditional apprenticeships altogether and stimulating the internal reorganization and modernization of industrial production.

But despite government claims to have created a new start for British industrial training practices, YTS is not so much a departure from the policy of voluntarism as a radical reformulation of it. It still depends on employers being willing to offer training places for unemployed youngsters. Furthermore, the Manpower Services Commission (MSC)[3] which administers YTS for the government, actively campaigned from the outset to get private firms and companies, acting as 'managing agents', to organize the actual training progammes to which the placements are attached. According to a report by a former member of the staff of the Confederation of British Industry, who was involved in the planning of YTS, political expediency, the need to deal quickly with rapidly rising youth unemployment, was partly responsible for this privatization of training (Keep, 1986). But it was also in tune with the free-market ideology of the government. In 1986 over three-quarters of training places were privatized in this way. As YTS has expanded into a two-year scheme the subsidy element, though still important, has been steadily reduced, leaving more and more of the basic provision to commercial initiatives.

> The main principle has been to reduce direct state intervention and public spending in this area and return responsibility for training activities to the level of the individual firm. Market forces would then determine the scale, scope and style of training provision. (Keep, 1986: 6)

Voluntarism is less in evidence as far as the trainees are concerned. So far school-leavers have, in theory, joined YTS on a voluntary basis if only because government plans to withdraw unemployment benefit from those who refuse a place were effectively opposed when YTS was set up. Nevertheless, the element of 'workfare' in YTS schemes has grown over time. Workfare refers to the principle that the receipients of state unemployment relief should be required to work for their benefits. YTS 'refusers' had already been put under considerable pressure by benefit offices, as well as by the lack of any real alternative to YTS, except unemployment. Since 1988, young people who 'unreasonably' refuse a training place have been disqualified altogether. Arguably, this drift to workfare, against a post-war background of welfare policies in Britain, is the most truly innovatory aspect of current training policy.

So how is the scheme working out in practice? In particular, what effect does the availability of a growing labour force of jobless trainees have upon employers' training costs and work processes?

Labour costs, training opportunities and changing patterns of employment

One way of approaching these questions is to look at the direct impact of YTS on young peoples' training and employment prospects. The evidence can be divided according to whether it relates simply to the number of training places and jobs created or to their quality as training and experience.

Without doubt, the quantitative expansion of YTS has been rapid and extensive: by 1986, 400,000 16-year-olds (46 per cent of school-leavers) became trainees and so additionally did 29,000 17-year-olds (Department of Education and Science, 1987). Furthermore, according to the MSC's regular surveys, about 60 per cent of trainees each year have either been kept on by their original sponsors or have soon found jobs elsewhere. Firms had derived considerable economic benefits from YTS. An independent survey of employers in six key industries found that, though some training places were provided by employers for social and philanthropic reasons, taking on trainees helped businesses to survive the recession and/or to expand, so increasing the availability of employment generally (Deakin and Pratten, 1987). These conclusions corroborate previous findings reported by the Commission itself (Gray and King, 1986; Sako and Dore, 1986).

Yet critics of YTS qualify this relatively optimistic picture in four main ways. First, wide regional variations exist. The Commission's own statistics show, for example, that in areas with above average unemployment, YTS graduates have a much poorer chance of finding work than in more prosperous localities, where as many as 70 per cent or more later get jobs (Lewis, 1986). Compared with a favourable labour market YTS training is a minor factor in getting a job. Second, a proportion of YTS job success is bought by substituting trainees for other kinds of workers. Third, some YTS placements are 'deadweight' in the sense that they would have existed anyway but as *jobs* for young people. Surveys have repeatedly indicated that about a third of the YTS traineeships in large firms can be ascribed to this substitution or deadweight effect. In smaller concerns, where a high proportion of the trainees is believed to be, the proportion is still higher (Deakin and

Pratten, 1987: 25–6, 53–62; National Labour Movement, 1987: Part II). A final objection is that much of the information about the job success of trainees, including the independent study by Deakin and Pratten cited above, depends upon reports by managers, employers or managing agents. It can be argued that these informants are not likely to be either completely knowledgeable or completely impartial about the destinies of the less successful trainees. Unfortunately, possible undermeasurement of 'failure' is also a problem with the Commission's postal surveys of former trainees (the main alternative data source) because of the effects of non-response, which is highest amongst the least able.

It nevertheless would be surprising if YTS did not increase the number of training and job openings for youth. Lowering the price of a commodity should enhance demand for it and there is no obvious reason why youth labour should be an exception. As well as quantity, however, there is the question of the quality of the work experience which young workers have as a result of a change in their 'price' (Marsden and Ryan, 1986).

One indicator of quality is the type of industries and employment conditions over which trainee and youth labour is distributed. Consequently, it is necessary briefly to consider trends in the types of jobs available generally in Britain and the way recession has accentuated them. Britain shares with many other industrialized societies a long-term drift of employment from manufacturing into services. Whereas in the mid-1960s some 37 per cent of the workforce was in manufacturing, by the mid-1980s the proportion was about 25 per cent. Recession greatly intensified this trend: one estimate suggests that between 1981 and 1984, nearly 750,000 jobs were lost from manufacturing while almost 500,000 service jobs were created (Department of Employment, 1987, Table 1). Growth and decline did not necessarily affect the same individuals or localities, which is why unemployment, which rose to over 3 million, was unevenly distributed.

As manufacturing employment declined so too has employers' reliance upon a conventional workforce of full-time employees. The new firms and industries make greater use of a so-called 'flexible labour force' made up of the self-employed, labour-only subcontractors, part-timers and casual workers (Hakim, 1987b). Here too, the trend existed well before the onset of the recession because of technical change and the shifting work preferences and job orientations of the population itself. But an equally important cause is the expansion of the service sector. Industries such as catering, distribution, repair work, professional and business services are very labour intensive and firms control labour costs by using various flexible employment arrangements. Additionally, manufacturing industry itself increasingly contracts out costly business services once performed by in-house employees (Ascher, 1987: 8; Rajan, 1987: 200). This has encouraged the rise of small independent white-collar organizations, such as financial or computing consultancies, which may offer well paid employment but exist in highly competitive and/or high-risk environments.

Flexible employment is a general term for several tendencies which respond in differing ways to cyclical economic influences and its precise meaning and extent are a matter of some dispute. Especially contentious is how far flexibility is synonymous with exploitative and uncongenial work situations. For present purposes the main point is that almost by definition flexible employment means an alteration to the life chances of individuals and groups of workers, due to the reduced availability of conventional promotion chains and traditional career moves from firm to firm.

Precise statistics on the relative size of the flexible workforce do not exist. The recession of the 1980s, however, was associated with a spurt in the growth of certain forms of flexible working presumably because of the additional pressure (or opportunity) it created to cut labour costs. One estimate claims that because of the simultaneous contraction of conventional employment, the flexible labour-force in Britain may now account for about a third of employees of all kinds (Hakim, 1987b: 551).

YTS has been absorbed into these deeper seated trends. The MSC's own statistics show that the main expansion of training places has in fact been in the administrative and services sector whereas, apart from construction, production industries tend to be under-represented. I shall argue here that this is because the distinctive manner of the scheme's development complements and parallels the widespread use of flexible labour, especially in service industries.

First, some trainees have simply become part of the flexible labour force directly by virtue of their obvious value as cheap labour. Exploitation of youngsters was rife under the predecessors to YTS and in its own early days (Raffe, 1984a, 1984b). Subsequently, the Manpower Services Commission has commited itself to eradicating bogus training and low quality work experience, though, in practice, many YTS schemes have yet to meet the quality criteria laid down by the Commission for approval (Leadbetter, 1987). Some reasons why quality controls will be hard to enforce are discussed in the next section.

But even if exploitation of trainees themselves is discounted, the conditions under which they train have conferred considerable organizational flexibility on firms. All YTS trainees are recruited on a temporary and legally non-contractual basis. Employers' formal commitment to them is therefore extremely low. Research on how firms use YTS has shown that it has valuable functions in the recruitment, selection and development of staff, acting, to quote one of our own respondents, as 'one long interview'. The government and the Commission acknowledge and welcome the substantial contribution which YTS trainees make to firms' output, the extent of this contribution being, by now, well-documented. It was found to be especially high in labour-intensive service industries, noted for low-pay levels, specifically retailing, hotels and catering and in repairs and personal services (Deakin and Pratten, 1987: 493, Table 3; National Labour Movement, 1987: 61-2). It seems likely, therefore .that the general cheapening of youth labour together with the specific provisions of YTS have encouraged employers in industries of this sort, and maybe elsewhere, to substitute young people for other low-paid groups (such as married women) and to use government trainees as an indirect extension of the flexible labour force. This possibility can be investigated further by enquiring into the calibre of the actual training itself and the kind of skills typically acquired by trainees.

Market forces and the structure of skills and training

We saw above that one of the aims of government training policy has been to reduce skill shortages in the British economy, especially of workers trained in broad transferable competences. But the available evidence suggests that creating temporary traineeships during a recession has had quite the opposite effect. The network of placements is in effect a surrogate labour market which is subject to commercial pressures in the same way as real labour market (Lee *et al.*, 1987). Direct or indirect cheapening of training costs by the state is predominantly taken up by labour-intensive firms and organizations whose skill requirements are narrow and whose training costs are low. But the subsidy has not been sufficient to defray more than marginally the high cost of training in transferable skills. As a result, the majority of skills learned by the trainees are not really transferable at all but relatively specific to the organizations in question.

The scale of YTS means that the sharp distinction between transferable and specific skill breaks down in practice and the numerous individual schemes and placements form a complex hierarchy of very unequal opportunities. The 'top' end of this hierarchy is largely constituted by firms in the manufacturing sector who merged their existing apprenticeship programmes into YTS. They did so for two reasons: to get the benefit of goverment funding for the initial years of training they would have done anyway; and to use training capacity which had become surplus to requirements in a time of contraction (Chapman and Tooze, 1987: Chapter 7; Rickman *et al.*, 1986). But Deakin and Pratten (1987) found that half of the skill shortages in traditional apprenticeship-based industries, such as engineering, required a level of prior education not possessed by the typical YTS trainee. Turbin (1988) has suggested that YTS traineeships created by the use of spare training capacity actually led to skills for which there is no longer any demand in either local or national labour markets.

This is corroborated by a study of engineering companies in the Coventry area, a number of which continued to make a sharp distinction between their (much reduced but genuine) apprentice intake and their YTS trainees (Dutton, 1987: esp Chapter 8). The latter were generally reckoned to be of 'poorer quality' than the apprentices, though Dutton's report points out that a proportion of them might have expected to have got apprenticeships in the past. They nevertheless ended up as semi-skilled process workers doing firm-specific tasks.

The ability of YTS to offset the decline in traditional training is constrained by the changed industrial relations climate of the 1980s. In the recession, craft-union controls over apprenticeship were decimated along with the occupations they attempted to regulate. Trade union opposition to government-sponsored training schemes like YTS has been, in the opinion of most commentators, confused and weak (Eversley, 1986; Ryan, 1986). Nevertheless where unions can make their presence felt they actually reinforce the effect of market forces. Shop stewards encourage employers to supplement the allowance given to trainees by the government and to offer permanent contracts from the start of training. Trade unionism thus raises employers' training costs. And because unions are strongest in large firms and high-skill areas their actions have the effect of restricting the supply of training places in transferable skills. On the other hand their influence is weakest in small firms and private service industries, leaving employers there free to turn government interventions in the youth labour market to their own advantage.

The service industries and clerical occupations which dominate YTS are disproportionately to be found at the lower end of the YTS hierarchy. In general they too generate very few transferable skills which are not based on a good level of prior education (Deakin and Pratten, 1987). Below that point, traineeships and surrogate jobs tend to be low-skilled and/or specific to particular firms or outputs (Rajan, 1987: 222-6). That many YTS youngsters in these circumstances are contributing to output instead of being trained is suggested by Deakin and Pratten's finding that the productive contribution of trainees to output is greatest in firms with low training overheads. Comparable findings have emerged from a study of YTS which I and colleagues are conducting in a thriving south-east town with an above-average amount of service employment. In many of the cases examined, YTS has been a straightforward wage subsidy to organizations whose actual job-training requirements are widely recognised as minimal. The more responsible managers of schemes in these cases are embarrassed by the extension of the training period to two years, which the type of work does not, in their view, justify. At worst, YTS has encouraged the proliferation of bogus training in areas of employment where little or none existed previously. Despite the declared aims of YTS, trainees who leave their schemes, who are not taken on at the end of the year, or who eventually leave their employers, have relatively little transferable labour-market capacity except their experience of 'real' work and any tacit but largely uncredited skill they may have acquired.

The off-the-job component of YTS training might, of course, confer a degree of marketability on trainees, especially where linked to pursuit of a recognized qualification. But we have found that very specific or even bogus workplace training undermines the effectiveness of off-the-job training. The narrowness of the workplace instruction which many trainees receive creates severe problems of integration with the off-the-job curriculum. Trainees are often in a state of considerable anxiety as to whether they will be kept on and intolerant of any off-the-job training which seems to have been fabricated or not of immediate relevance to their own work placement and hope of employment there. In some cases they conspire with their employers to be absent from classes. Problems of integration are severest in the 'new' areas of training pioneered under YTS. Quite often a recognized credential did not exist prior to YTS and a variety of minor vocational certificates have been created or colonized for the purposes of getting approval from the MSC.

There is thus considerable discrepancy between the 'human capital' assumptions of British government training policy and the actual practice of many YTS schemes and placements. This explains one finding of Deakin and Pratten's otherwise laudatory review of YTS: that many trainees are being trained for skills 'which are not in short supply' (1987: 495).

The discrepancy between theory and practice has arisen because the representatives of industrial firms on the Youth Task Group, which designed the structure of YTS, insisted on 'black boxing' the content of on-the-job training as a price of agreeing that employers should provide work placements (Keep, 1986: 26). Black boxing means that what trainees do on work placements is not directly vetted but placed largely at the discretion of the trainee's employer. It is constrained only by agreed 'end-product' criteria which the MSC has found difficult to enforce. Admittedly, over time the quality of workplace training has become a sensitive matter and, as mentioned above, the Commission has endeavoured to ensure that two-year YTS is subject to stricter controls. But since 1986, when YTS was extended to two years, employers have had to make a small payment towards the training and maintenance costs of each trainee taken on. They are consequently even less likely to tolerate supervision and monitoring of their use of trainees (Lee *et al.*, 1987a). Supervision in practice is increasingly privatized by being devolved onto the agents who are managing individual schemes.

The unintended effects of current youth training policy in Britain are not, however, restricted to the mere content of tasks. They also extend to the way in which the gender division of industrial labour is perpetuated, both within firms and between types of employment. The youth labour market has always displayed a marked gender segmentation (Ashton *et al.*, 1986) and the creation of more equal opportunities in training and employment has been a declared intention of YTS, notably as reformulated in its two-year version. Organizers of YTS schemes are in theory required to satisfy MSC field staff on their provision for equal opportunities before schemes can be approved. But statistics published by the MSC show that marked occupation gendering of the take-up of YTS placements persists (Marsh, 1986). Empirical research has shown that commitment to equal opportunities is not necessarily shared or understood by the Commission's field staff and still less by those running individual YTS schemes – and hardly at all inside the black box of on-the-job training (Cockburn, 1987). The record on racial and ethnic discrimination is no better (National Labour Movement, 1987: 22-7, Part IV). The preconceptions which trainees and their parents bring to the situation are thus rarely challenged.

This is very important because traditional gender stereotypes help create the wider segregation between the traditional and flexible sectors of the adult labour force, and sustain the kind of advantages, such as dispensability and low wages, which employers can derive from it.

Training policy and the control of the workforce

Some critics claim that the underlying but undeclared aim of British government training policy in the 1980s has been to increase political and economic control over labour. Ranson (1985: 240) argues that recession conditions have created an acute political problem: to manage expectations and aspirations in the face of 'the surplus capacity of persons and communities'. From interviews and discussions with officials in the MSC and the Department of Education and Science he concludes that government and state agencies had quite deliberately set out to alter the curriculum of school education as well as industrial training. Known as the 'new vocationalism', these curricular initiatives tried to redefine, channel and limit the 'aspirations that are carried into the labour market' (Ranson, 1985: 237). The needs of industry and the economy are stressed and the hierarchical nature of economic life emphasized. In the words of one of Ranson's respondents: 'People must be educated once more to know their place' (ibid.: 241).

From this perspective, YTS is part of the new vocationalism. As Green (1986) points out, the training paradigm underlying the scheme has drawn upon a number of key themes of 'progressive' educational theory and adapted them to the changed context. Thus the ideal of 'relevant learning' has been reinterpreted and narrowed to 'task/work oriented instruction'; the progressive stress on active involvement of the learner has been assimilated into performance-related methods of instructing and assessing trainees in limited workplace competences. That control *is* an aim of policy seems to be supported by the current Chancellor of the Exchequer's description of the kind of workforce the economy needs: not only equipped with the 'right skills' but also 'adaptable, reliable, motivated and...prepared to work at wages that employers can afford to pay' (Finn, 1987: 54).

Yet the effect of what can be achieved through curricular change and reorganized training packages can be exaggerated, as can the unity of purpose within the state itself. The actual development of YTS has revealed differences of approach between the various agencies which had a stake in setting it up and between the heads of these agencies and government ministers (Jackson, 1986; Seale, 1984). Moreover, disputes remain between government and employers over YTS funding and organizational structure. And as long as employers, because of black boxing, retain decisive control over the content of the workplace training, curricular activities by the state will remain largely cosmetic.

Admittedly, in the short term, programmes like YTS extend employers' repertoire of internal control because of the hold they give them over recruitment, selection and progress. But arguably what makes these sanctions effective is simply the impact of the recession itself on youth expectations. Our fieldwork indicates that it is the limited range of alternatives to surrogate employment and the lack of real jobs which reinforce an employer's control. Trainees are encouraged to think of the placement as an opportunity whereby they can 'work themselves into a job' if they show willing. This is why from the employer's point of view the placement is a chance (as one employer put it) 'to mould them to our way of thinking'. But it is not just the young who are vulnerable: other categories of employee face the threat of displacement with what has now become the cheaper labour of young trainees and workers.

It may be misleading to assume that young people themselves necessarily attach much significance to the content of their work experience which is, after all, transitory, to be tolerated, hopefully as a route to a real job. Survey research suggests that youngsters and their families are coming to accept YTS as an inevitable feature of the transition from school-days. The effect is to encourage 'hard realism' and 'instrumental attitudes' (Raffe and Smith, 1986). But the meaning of the recession for young people varies with the opportunities available in the locality (Ashton and Maguire, 1986). This in turn affects the exact meaning of the trainees' dependence on the employer. The more permanent control of aspirations and behaviour through youth training may in fact be occurring in the more buoyant areas of the country. Our case study, being based on a relatively prosperous locality, suggests that because YTS typically *did* lead to a job at the end its effect was to create among the youngsters a sense of what we have called 'moral rescue' ('what YTS did for me') and to emphasize the separateness of YTS refusers and the unemployed 'who do nothing to help themselves'. In less prosperous localities many trainees, as we have seen above, simply drop back into unemployment, and its associated demoralization and anomie, at the end of their programme (Roberts *et al.*, 1986). In both cases, it is the economic context of YTS, not its curriculum or its repertoire of direct sanctions, which lowers expectations.

What appears to be most important, then, is the way YTS seems to have facilitated a shift in the balance of control from employers' internal systems to flexible control over youth labour in general by the impersonal forces of the labour market.

Conclusions

My immediate aim in this chapter has been to draw attention to training as a crucial aspect of work organization. By considering what has happened in Britain during the 1980s, I have tried to show that training and training systems are important, not simply as another aspect of the labour process which has to be accounted for, but also as an important *cause* of variation, both within and between labour processes. This is because training is a major cost of production. Its causal influence is especially important at the point where employers choose between in-house management and outsourcing of resources and activities.

In making these points, I have had the further aim of encouraging a broader conceptualization of work organization – and of its transformation – than is generally found in the literature. The division of labour, in which tasks are devised and allocated to persons, is determined not just in the workplace but at many levels. Braverman's celebrated deskilling thesis, and especially its oversimple attempt to 'read off' changes in class relationships from changes in task content and control at the point of production, was criticized for precisely this reason (Garnsey, 1981; Lee, 1982). Contributors to the post-Braverman literature have not wholly ignored the point. But empirical studies still tend to focus only on flexible labour use and other transformations of work generated within (mostly manufacturing) organizations by new technology and managerial control systems. As a result, the central category of analysis, work organization itself, remains unnecessarily restricted.

I have, lastly, sought to emphasize the close relationships between the study of work and the study of class. Even though his own account may have been flawed, Braverman's basic concern with this issue remains highly relevant to contemporary events. We have seen, for example, that in Britain major changes have been taking place in the distribution of workers between different labour processes and forms of employment which are bound to have implications for the balance of power between labour and capital, many of them unexamined as yet. Arguably, these effects have intensified during the recession. State training policies have had considerable importance in this context, enabling firms with flexible employment systems and low-training costs to benefit from the growth of a labour force of young jobless trainees on government training programmes. They aim to reduce real wages as well as wage expectations. They enable firms to survive the recession and at the same time affect the bargaining power of organized labour. There are also likely to be consequences at the level of class stratification, involving changes to the market situations of different individuals, occupational groups and class fractions. From the viewpoint of workers, in fact, especially young people seeking jobs for the first time, 'transformations of work' which affect the distribution of life chances in the market are arguably the most important. Broadening the way that we think about work organization and the division of labour hardly diminishes the importance of class. It moves it back to its proper place at the centre of analysis.

9 'New production concepts' in final assembly – the Swedish experience

CHRISTIAN BERGGREN

The future of assembly work. Between Taylorism, flexible specialization and new production concepts

Work in automobile production has for a long time attracted interest from students of industrial work. This is for good reasons. One is the importance of this industry for the economic life of the Western countries, another is its role in developing and spreading new technology and forms of rationalization. In this chapter the focus is on the assembly processes in the production of cars, trucks and buses. Based on a long-term research programme, it is an attempt to analyse the changes in the Swedish automotive industry during the 1970s and 1980s.[1] The core question is the possibility of ending Taylorist forms of production design, above all the assembly lines, 'the classic symbol of the subjection of man to the machine in our industrial age' (Guest and Walker, 1952).

In the first phase of my research on the automotive industry a critical assessment of Braverman was an important point of departure. Two of my main objections to Braverman were his tendency to treat control as an absolute interest of capital regardless of any costs and his theoretical rigidity which identifies scientific management with capitalist rationality (Berggren, 1980). At the end of the 1980s the problem of the theoretical debate is quite the opposite one: are the vitality and prospects of Taylorism being dismissed a bit too easily and sweepingly?

New technology is, as was suggested in Chapter 1 – as it was in the 1960s – seen as a progressive force making requalification and an end to the division of work possible. The main theme in this discussion is not so much if, but how, and to what extent, these possibilities will be realized. For the Germans Kern and Schumann (1984) the new possibilities definitely are linked to the process of automation, though not directly, but within the context of a new production concept. The old strategy of capitalist rationalization was the maximum elimination of human work, and minute control of the residual tasks which could not be automated. The new concept of production, according to Kern and Schumann, is based on an understanding of the qualitative importance of human work, and the productivity gains to be had through employing more qualified workers and utilizing integrated tasks.

Piore and Sabel (1984) associate the new possibilities with a new technological paradigm, a modern craft model. At the basis of their theory is the dichotomy of mass production – craft production. After the first 'industrial divide' mass production characterized by giant firms, specialized equipment and standardized work became the dominant paradigm. This development started in the US, but during the economic boom after the Second World War it spread to all industrial countries. Today, with increasing demands for flexibility and a technology which is liberating itself from economies of scale, there is the historic possibility of a new divide, in which the craft principles of flexibility and skills could come back to the forefront. Since some concepts such as flexibility and skill development are central to the work of Piore and Sabel and also this chapter, I will first consider their position in detail.

The new divide

In Piore and Sabel's study, skills and flexibility are correlated negatively with mass production. However, 'mass production' is here extremely narrowly defined, in fact more or less identified with the *American* way of mass production, with large and vertically integrated corporations and a mass of strictly regulated job classifications. The other main concept, 'the craft paradigm/model', is on the other hand elusive. 'Shorter' production runs, 'less rigid' technology, 'more skills'/less strictly defined job roles are mentioned, but the authors refrain from any real analysis of, for example, the qualities of craft labour.

This is no small problem because using this diffuse dichotomy, Piore and Sabel proceed to classify various production patterns over the world. And like all Americans who are eager to get the ears of management, they try to enlist Japan on their side. The Japanese production system is thus presented as a leading representative of the skill-based 'craft paradigm' which is superseding the mass production model.

This really is a misrepresentation of the Japanese economy (see also Chapters 5 and 10) made possible only by their rigidly ethnocentric definition of mass production. As we saw in Chapter 1, far from breaking the principles of standardization, large-scale economy and Taylorism, the Japanese are the modern masters of them. This is born out by studies of their competitive edge – which is consistently confined to areas where mass production has been possible, and not primarily in customized design and production involving a lot of 'software' (see e.g. Franko, 1983). The Japanese successes have come precisely because of their capacity to introduce mass-production principles to new areas, such as the machine-tool industry (a case misinterpreted by Piore and Sabel), and to proceed very rapidly from product concepts to mass production on a scale of millions, as in the case of video tape recorders. The question of a 'divide' in the historical development of industrial work, making flexibility, skills and integrated work central themes, really is an important one. But Piore and Sabel's gross dichotomization of the world and of industry confuses the issue.

'New production concepts' without automation?

The work of Kern and Schumann (1984) is much more to the point. Their notion of a new production concept, based on a new pattern of rationalization, will be an important heuristic tool in this chapter. It is, however, by no means an unproblematic concept. Two problems stand out. The first problem concerns their overall assessment of the development. In their book *Ende der Arbeitsteilung* they devote a major section to the technical and organizational changes in the automotive industry. Here, their favourite instances of new production concepts are the robotized body shops with their novel skilled jobs, such as *Strassen-fuhrer* and *Anlagenfuhrer* (monitor of complex equipment). Such positions can be found also in the Swedish body shops. But, it is also quite easy to find counter evidence, instances where robotization of body processing has generated more restricted and fragmented work. Thus, the consequences of automation in one instance may not be generalizable to others.

The second problem is the supposed correlation between automation and new production concepts. What then of a process such as assembly? In the work of Kern and Schumann assembly operations are dealt with summarily. Admittedly, automation is starting to make inroads even here, but they provide only a very few examples of qualitative changes in assembly work. The same is true for another German study concerning new concepts in the automobile industry (Jürgens *et al.*, 1986). In this chapter the 'new production concept' presupposes some kind of changes in technology (or industrial engineering), but need not, however, entail automation. A central aim is to examine the meaning of 'new production concepts' in a process which remains manual and to analyse its prerequisites and prospects.

This chapter consists of four main parts. The first presents some basic information concerning the production of cars, trucks and buses in Sweden. The second part discusses automatization and changing rationalization interests. The third contains an overview of continuity and change in assembly design 'since Kalmar' (the first Volvo plant to experiment with job redesign), and an analysis of the state of the art in 1987 regarding assembly design and work organization in Sweden. The fourth part is devoted to a case study of an assembly plant, which for several years was a flagship of new assembly work–organization within Volvo.

Assembly operations in the Swedish automobile industry

The automotive industry in Sweden consists of two manufacturers, Saab-Scania and Volvo, each with product programmes comprising passenger cars as well as trucks (chassis) and buses. Part suppliers and sub contractors are not considered here. Some basic data of these two companies are presen ed in Table 9.1.

Table 9.1   The Volvo and Saab-Scania companies, 1987

Production (in 1000)	Total volume	in Sweden
Cars:		
Saab	127	86
Volvo[a]	300	200
Trucks & buses:		
Scania (> 16 tons)	31	16
Volvo (>7 tons)	51	17
Employees (in 1000)		
Saab	16	13
Volvo Cars	34	28
Scania[b]	23	16
Volvo Trucks[b]	23	10

(a) Only 200– and 700–series.
(b) Including buses and diesel engines.

In an international perspective the car operations of both companies are of a small-scale nature. For trucks the opposite is the case, Volvo being the second and Scania the fourth biggest producer of heavy trucks in the world.

Assembly operations have two main forms, final assembly and component assembly. The main focus in this paper is on final assembly. An overview of assembly operations in the Swedish automotive industry, according to companies, products and production facilities, is given in Table 9.2.

Final assembly plants (shops) normally consist of pre-assembly and final assembly (traditionally on the line), as well as such functions as quality inspection, materials handling and maintenance. The relations between pre-assembly and final assembly vary. For passenger cars

Table 9.2 Assembly operations in the automotive industry in Sweden

Product	Production facility	Production volume (in 1000)	Employment (BC)
Volvo			
Pass. cars	TC, Gothenburg	164	4200
	TUN, Gothenburg	13	300
	Kalmar	31	1000
Gas. engines	E-plant, Skövde	300	800
Diesel engines	Skövde	60	400
Marine engines	Vara	14	100
Truck:			
cabin	VUV, Umeå	33	300
chassis	LB, G-burg	6	300
chassis	X-hall, G-burg	9	600
Bus chassis	Borås	3	200
Saab–Scania			
Pass. cars	Trollhättan	65	2200
	Arlöv	29	1000
Gas. engines	Södertälje	135	500
Diesel engines	Södertälje	30	300
Trucks:			
cabins	Oskarshamn	14	300
chassis	Södertälje	14	800
Bus chassis	Katrineholm	2-3	200

most of the work is done on the assembly line (normally 70–80 per cent), whereas the assembly of bus chassis to a large extent (60 per cent or more) consists of pre-assembly. The focus here is on final assembly.

A remaining manual process

In a study of the 1960s, Kern and Schumann's *Industriearbeit und Arbeiterbewusstsein* (1977), technological development and mechanization play a central role. This is, however, not the case in their analysis of assembly work. Here instead they emphasize the various obstacles to mechanization. In their follow-up study *Das Ende der Arbeitsteilung* (1984), they emphasize how the German automotive industry is trying to overcome these obstacles. However, they do not distinguish between different types of manufacturers.

Generally, it is true that the technological front has moved forward. Automation has started to have a substantial effect on *component assembly* (even such complex and varying products as gasoline engines). Nevertheless, in *final assembly* the obstacles to mechanization are still great. Here the number of product variants is much greater, the tolerance chains are longer and therefore the dimension spread, and many items are to be handled in a very limited space and with awkward assembly routines. Another difference is the more extensive and complex materials flow in final assembly. The situation is quite different from the stamping and body shops, where the range of output is much smaller, materials flow is simpler and volume is higher, one press plant typically serving several assembly units.

On the one hand, the technology of assembly robots has developed significantly during the 1980s. At the same time the obstacles to automation of final assembly have, however, become even more pronounced. There has been in Sweden a substantial increase in the number of model versions, in the frequency of product changes and in product complexity and quality control requirements. The automated installations, e.g. assembly robots, which today can be found in assembly operations in Sweden, are mostly of a test character ('after all, we must start to try the technology somewhere, even if there is no profit', to quote the chief of the industrial engineering staff at Saab in Trollhättan).

It is difficult to make a general comparison between West Germany, where some of the most automated production facilities are located, and Sweden in this regard. The conditions vary greatly between a high volume manufacturer, such as Volkswagen, and the Swedish companies. In 1987 Volvo's volume of assembled cars in Sweden was about 200,000 and Saab's 100,000 which taken together is not more than the output of one single, large European plant.

Investments are being made in advanced forms of information and transportation technology. But even by the beginning of the 1990s, according to current estimates, the level of assembly automation will represent only a tiny part, for existing products a few per cent at the most, of the total number of assembly operations. For buses and trucks, with significantly lower volumes – thousands and tens of thousands respectively instead of hundreds of thousands – the prospect of automated final assembly seems even more remote.

To conclude, in both the short- and medium-term final asembly will remain labour intensive and particularly so in firms like the Swedish ones. What then are the prospects of a qualitative change in manual assembly? The basic issue here is the future of the assembly line and the forms of control associated with it.

Contradictory rationalization interests

Ever since the principle of the mechanically-paced assembly line was introduced on a large scale by the Ford Motor Company in the 1910s it has been the ideal of efficiency for the world's automotive industry.

Traditionally companies have seen the following advantages in this model:

- High work intensity;
- Short training period;
- Simple supply system for materials with few delivery points;
- Central control over the flows and pace, a guarantee for stable output.

Rationalization measures within final assembly based on this model have been aimed at two targets. First the development of special tools and selective automation. One current Swedish example is the automation of the so-called marriage point, where the body is fitted together with the power train. Second the development and refinement of production and job design in order to secure maximum availability and work intensity.

At the beginning of the 1970s the assembly line as an extreme of Taylorism was met with a great deal of worker discontent all over the Western world. But in countries like the US, 'the blue collar blues' were soon replaced by job insecurity in the middle of the 1970s, without it having had any great effect on job design. In this respect Sweden was different (Wild, 1975a). Massive personnel problems at the beginning of the 1970s led companies to try new types of production design and organizational forms. This process has continued since then, even during economic recessions.

One reason for this is the changing product markets which are deemed to require more flexibility. The product strategies in the 1980s of Saab and Volvo have deliberately been based on going upmarket and high value-added production. Another reason is the persistently high levels of labour turnover in the traditional assembly plants. Compared to other auto-making Western countries Sweden has enjoyed a uniquely low level of unemployment during the 1970s and 1980s (see Table 9.3).

In the 1960s the recruitment problem was solved by the import of *Gastarbeiter*. Since the middle of the 1970s this has not been possible any more. Taken together, these developments in product and labour markets have highlighted a growing number of efficiency problems in traditional assembly line design. We will discuss briefly the most important aspects:

DECREASING WORK INTENSITY

There have always been difficulties in achieving 100 per cent labour utilization on the assembly line, since the work cannot always be

Table 9.3   Relative unemployment in Sweden, 1970–86

Year	Proportion of the pop. in the labour force	Unemployment as per cent of labour force
1970	65.7	1.5
1971	65.5	2.5
1972	65.4	2.7
1973	65.7	2.5
1974	67.0	2.0
1975	68.5	1.6
1976	79.0	1.6
1977	79.4	1.8
1978	79.9	2.3
1979	80.9	2.1
1980	81.5	2.0
1981	81.5	2.5
1982	81.7	3.2
1983	81.8	3.5
1984	81.9	3.1
1985	82.6	2.8
1986	83.0	2.7

Note: 1970–5: population 16–74 years of age; 1976–86: population 16–64 years of age.

divided up so no labour inefficiencies exist. Thus, there is normally idle time at some stations, so-called *balance delay*. This did not cause any great problems with a standardized type of production. But when the number of variants expanded quickly during the 1970s, it became increasingly difficult for industrial engineers to achieve a perfectly balanced line. This was particularly apparent in the production of trucks and buses. Another problem is that the mechanical line cannot take into account variations in the working-pace of the assembly workers. When the workers are short of time they have to allow half-finished products to go through, leading to so-called *system losses* (Wild, 1975b).

HIGH SENSITIVITY TO DISRUPTIONS SUCH AS LACK OF COMPONENTS OR PROBLEMS OF FITTING

This feature also has become more difficult to master with increasing model variation (and thus a more complex materials flow) and high labour turnover.

THE RIGID PRODUCTION LAYOUT OF THE LINE

The line design is effective for production of long series, but expensive and time-consuming to change over for the production of a new product. Here again it comes into conflict with the new demands of the market, requiring the ability to quickly adapt the production process.

WORKERS' DISSATISFACTION WITH THE CONSTRAINED
AND MONOTONOUS WORK

This not only involves the costs of recruitment, training and excessive 'manning'. The continuous influx of new people on the assembly line also increases the need for control, inspection and adjustment, in other words it increases system losses and levels of inventories.

To summarize, the companies' interests in changes in layout and organization involve achieving: maximum work intensity, i.e. a minimum of balance delay in spite of variants; a capacity to build 'RFB', Right From the Beginning, i.e assemble without any need for adjustment; flexibility; reduced susceptibility to disruptions; more attractive jobs, which can reduce turnover, thereby improving quality and increasing commitment.

Also important in Sweden is the Metalworkers' Union which, during the 1980s in increasingly articulated ways, has criticised short-cycled, constrained line-work and demanded alternatives. It has taken an active part in the planning of new plants in order to promote these demands. This policy should of course be viewed against the background of the favourable labour market.

The 'new rationalization interests' are only one side of the coin. There are also other concerns, particularly management's interest in control, security and training costs. Here arguments for the line have remained strong (the line concept here is not limited to its traditional physical form, the conveyor belt, but includes modern forms, such as computer-controlled carrier lines): the line is safe and tested, it involves the minimum of risks; the line ensures discipline and pace – the line is the best foreman; the line design and short cycle times are necessary to keep quality up and costs down – long cycle times increase the risk of errors and lead to unreasonable training costs.

Other arguments in favour of the line concept are of a more technical nature, e.g.:

– the line guarantees an unbroken sequence (the same order of variants at the beginning as well as at the end of the flow). With a free flow the sequence is broken and there may be problems regarding the supply of materials;

– 'future automation will require a high frequency flow.' To be sure, the realization of automation is far away, as I said before. But its very prospect has in the 1980s become an argument in production design, being used to support the retention of a basic line structure (only modified to allow assembly on stationary objects, so as to permit precise positioning).

Line revival from Japan

In this context it is impossible not to mention the impact of Japan. The extraordinary efficiency levels of Japanese automotive firms have set new performance standards and provoked a broad Western interest in their methods. Anglo-American automotive industry researchers have called the Japanese system of car manufacturing the 'third major transformation' in the history of the automotive industry (the two previous being the ones directed by Ford and Sloan respectively). They have even asserted that the Japanese production system has 'turned the principles of Scientific Management upside down'.

This alleged 'turning upside down' never has, however, included the production design. On the contrary, production managers visiting Japan have found a hard-core Taylorism in the automotive plants, such as long, mechanical lines with short-cycled and highly constrained tasks. Fundamental Taylorist principles are propagated by leading Japanese industrial writers (e.g. Shingo, 1981). Consequently, 'if the Japanese are exploiting the line design so profitably, why should we change', has been a widespread reaction by managers, thus reducing their interest in basic reforms, and reinforcing arguments for the line. Furthermore, some features of Japanese-style rationalization, above all the principle of non-inventory production systems (elimination of all stocks and buffers in order to increase capital turnover and overall discipline), contradict a central aspect of work improvement, namely increased technical autonomy. This point can be illustrated by contrasting the planning of two truck plants, the LB and Oskarshamn plants (discussed further below, p.184–6), which took place simultaneously at the beginning of the 1980s.

In the planning of the LB plant, the importance of buffers was asserted, both because of the availability of parts problem and the need to make jobs more attractive. At precisely the same time, the new cabin plant in Oskarshamn was being planned. But there, inspired by Japanese examples, a completely bufferless design was outlined. Products were to 'run through the factory', which meant a drastic decrease in autonomy in the body shop, and a lot of protests among workers. Eventually some buffers were introduced in the body shop in order to guarantee reasonable availability of supplies and working conditions.

The Kalmar plant and beyond – the difficult search for alternatives in car assembly 1974–87

In my discussion of the search for new assembly methods I will separate passenger cars from commercial vehicles. The pressure for change in the early 1970s was roughly the same for both product lines. However, the business cycles for passenger cars and commercial vehicles as well as their market conditions, are different, with the spread of model variations and demands for customized design being much larger in truck and bus manufacturing.

The Kalmar plant, started in 1974, represents the first and most well-known example of a new type of assembly design in car production. Its most noticeable innovation was the individually controlled carriers, which replaced the traditional, mechanically paced moving belt. It was thereby possible to test a new type of layout, which combined a basic series structure with parallel substructures. The total assembly was divided into twenty different sections. These were connected in traditional series, the cycle time remaining short, normally 3–4 minutes. Within some of the subsections, it was possible to dock the carriers into parallel stations, thus increasing the work cycle to 20–30 minutes. With the help of buffers between adjacent sections, workers within a section would have some opportunity to vary their work speed independently of the main flow. In addition, the carrier technology made ergonomic changes possible, through so-called tilting of the car bodies. One of the purposes of the plant architecture and the division of the line was to foster in each section team responsibility and spirit.

For many observers the new carrier technology and the novel kind of building disguised the fact that the basic structure remained essentially unchanged (see the official evaluation by Agurén et al., 1985). The carriers in Kalmar were operated in the same centralized way as any conventional line. No organizational changes to support the development of teams were introduced. For example, no additional tasks were transferred to the teams, and the workers did not get any rights to exercise discretion. At specified predetermined times the carriers started moving, monitored by a central computer, regardless of whether or not the assembly workers were finished (thus in practice constituting an indexing line, an intermittently running line). This even applied to the so-called dock assembly, where it created a considerable amount of stress. Furthermore, the buffers between the subsections failed to function as expected, and in practice, the same pace was maintained throughout the factory.

During the same year as the Kalmar development, a new engine plant, the E-plant, based on the same principles, was also started by Volvo in Skövde. Scania tested a new assembly concept as well, going a step further than Skövde's E-plant. In a new gasoline engine plant in Södertälje final assembly work was organized in a number of parallel lines, so-called loops, with relatively long cycle times (a maximum 30 minutes as compared to a few minutes in Skövde). This design has often been described as one of 'autonomous groups'. However, no change occurred in the organizational structure and control. What it involved was job enlargement and some freedom from centralized line pacing. Within the groups operators were obliged to keep the same work speed (each loop being in practice a short line either with moving operators, or divided into stations).

Some further experiments were carried out by Volvo in Skövde and Gothenburg. In 1976–7 Skövde tested the concept of individual assembly of complete engines and Volvo Torslanda tested the idea of allowing teams of workers to build entire passenger cars (that is a genuine form of dock assembly). They attempted to satisfy both the industrial engineer's interest in increasing work intensity by eliminating balance delays, and the more general interest the company had in developing attractive jobs in final assembly, so as to make labour recruitment easier.

Skövde's experiment turned out to be economically viable compared to the line assembly, but it did not lead to any significant change in regular production. Torslanda's dock assembly was the subject of great suspicion in the factory (e.g. the union remained completely outside of it) and the groundwork for its implementation was inadequately prepared. It was a flop, with much lower productivity than the line, and was quickly abolished. For a long time 'the failure of dock assembly' was used as an argument within the plant against any radical changes. Shortly afterwards a new, more efficient balancing system was introduced on the lines, and the industrial engineers lost much of their interest in experimenting with alternatives.

At about the same point in time the first evaluations of the E-plant and Kalmar were issued. Both were judged as constituting improvements in working conditions, but as having clear limitations. For example, the Kalmar report stated that 75 per cent of the assembly workers felt that they had little or no chance to influence their work. Economically the E-plant was a success, as was Scania's engine assembly plant (which later however developed problems of another character, see p. 184). On the other hand, Kalmar's economic performance two years after it started was far from convincing. Direct and indirect labour per unit, as well as the quality level, was the same as in Gothenburg, i.e. there was no noticeable improvement. This was considered unsatisfactory because of the significantly more expensive equipment (e.g. the carriers) in Kalmar.

The economic records of the new plants were then far from being unambiguously successful; at the same time a dramatic change occured in the demand conditions of the industry. The first half of the 1970s had been years of growth and expansion for the automotive firms. In 1977 an economic crisis came, with reduced production programmes, financial losses in passenger car production, and rising unemployment in the economy at large. The pressure for change from labour market strength decreased substantially.

The design of new production lines during the late 1970s and early 1980s at Saab and Volvo Passenger Cars was approached cautiously. When Saab started a long-awaited renovation of its final assembly plant in Trollhättan in 1982 (a renovation which is still in progress), management chose the most conventional of the several alternatives considered during its planning stage, a so-called mini-line system. This is merely a segmentation of the traditional line, each section being separated by buffers. Mechanical pacing is retained within the sections. Since there are no parallel systems the cycle time is short, 2–3 minutes. The gains for the company are decreased susceptibility to disruptions (because of the buffers) and reduced final adjustment and repair work (due to the inspection and adjustment being performed at buffers at the end of each section). The use of job rotation is expanded as pre-assembly is placed within the same supervisory area as line assembly. On the other hand, due to a new balancing system accompanying the reform, work intensity also increases.

The same segmentation of the line into mini-lines was introduced at Saab's factory in Arlöv from 1985 onwards. In contrast to Trollhättan the mini-lines in Arlöv are indexing lines with intermittent rather than continuous running (cycle time 6 minutes), which enables work on stationary objects. The pacing remains, however, centralized.

These very restricted reforms in final assembly at Trollhättan provide a stark contrast to the dynamic development in the body shop at the same factory. During the 1970s this shop was a forerunner with its parallel 'lineout' system for manual welding and grinding (Rubenowitz, 1980). During the 1980s this plant was similarly leading the way by combining the new technology with qualified teamwork in the automatized body processing, which was introduced in 1984 and 1985, when the new 9000 series was launched and the number of robotics jumped up from 10 to 110).

The same cautious line-buffer system as in Trollhättan's assembly plant was also introduced in the TUN plant, which Volvo constructed for the introduction of the 700 series in 1982. The management's policy was that no experiments with organization or design which could threaten the introduction of the new model would be allowed. The 'failure' of the dock-assembly experiment in TC was used as a strong argument for keeping the line structure. In contrast to Trollhättan, however, at the TUN plant there was a conscious effort to develop a group-based organization with the delegation of administrative and quality inspection responsibilities to workers.

During the early 1980s intensive rationalization measures were carried out at Kalmar. In comparison with TC, productivity was increased substantially. At the same time most of what was intended to be a departure from the strict line principle disappeared. The buffers between the subsections disappeared, except for those considered necessary for supply reasons. Dock assembly was eliminated too, the definitive step being taken in 1984 when the 700-series was introduced. Thereafter assembly design at Kalmar is basically the same as a traditional line. The main difference for workers is the possibility of job enlargement (from 3 to a maximum 25 minutes) through their being able to follow the carrier on its way through the subsection.

At Södertälje's gasoline engine plant, too, the concepts of the 1970s were to a large extent eliminated, though they were not replaced by a conventional line, but rather by new technology. The layout from 1972, with its parallel loops, led to increased worker satisfaction, lower turnover and fewer complaints. But at the same time the group pressure in the loops was tough (all the assemblers working at a high speed in order to be ready early and have long breaks). The combination of this fast pace with a low labour turnover led to serious health problems for the totally female workforce. Allied to an increase in production volume in 1983 the shop was redesigned and robotics introduced for much of the internal assembly of the engines. The remaining manual assembly was allotted to individual stations with operators working in a completely individual way, and the group structure thus dissolved.

Assembly of commercial vehicles – prospects of genuine requalification?

Volvo's truck assembly operations had roughly the same problems during the early 1970s as the passenger car side. When, as part of an increased production programme in 1974, Volvo opened a new, minor production facility in Arendal, the opportunity to test new concepts was taken. The assembly system here was structured as a 'two-stage dock', where a single, large work team assembled the complete chassis at a rate of two vehicles per day. The cycle time was four hours. When the production programme was lower, the cycle could be up to eight hours long. This work team enjoyed a high degree of autonomy concerning work speed, work methods, job allocation and weekly planning. In spite of its long cycle time, compared to traditional assembly work, Arendal quickly achieved the same level of productivity as the main factory (the X-hall). Quality was considerably better.

During the mid-1970s, Volvo was planning a new bus chassis factory in Borås. Arendal served as an inspiration. The old bus plant (in Gothenburg) had utilized an indexing line. In Borås this has been replaced by four parallel docks each containing three assembly steps between which the assembly workers move the chassis on air-cushioned platforms. Each dock has one work team of 10–12 persons. The station time varies between 2 and 4 hours. Although this does not constitute a complete departure from traditional concepts (each dock being in reality a three-station line), Borås is an important step toward a more integrated form of assembly work. In its first year of operation (1978), it had however great difficulties in achieving its production goals.

At the same time the Arendal plant had problems in maintaining its output. The reasons for this were primarily external, but management blamed it on the layout and the long cycle time. This, together with the problems at Borås, contributed to something of a Taylorist backlash within the truck production organization in Gothenburg which lead to a rejection of dock assembly as a realistic option for assembly operations. This was the situation when the planning of a new assembly plant for heavy trucks was started (The LB-plant). Management was not willing to take any risks, and wanted a production system which could be run as a centrally paced line if 'necessary'. At the same time dissatisfaction and worker unrest at the traditional line in the X-hall was evident. Many industrial engineers within the organization were strongly in favour of a change in assembly design and organization. The union also actively campaigned against the idea of a line. The result, when the factory opened in 1981, was a compromise.

The production layout turned out to be more conventional than Borås with final assembly in two parallel carrier flows, each with four assembly groups and buffers between the groups. The important step here was that control over the carriers in the flows was allocated to the assembly groups. In other words there was no centralized pacing as at Kalmar. At the same time both the company and the union supported the development of a group-based work organization with substantial delegation of responsibility to workers.

The 'LB organization' has subsequently become the subject of controversy, many managers thinking that things in the plant went too far. When the old X-hall was renovated in 1984–5, much of the traditional organization was retained, particularly the job structure and supervisory responsibilities. The assembly design of LB, however, with its unpaced and buffered flows, soon became the norm for the truck division in Gothenburg and was also introduced at the X-hall. In 1987, after some years of conflicts and hesitation, organizational development at LB got a new start.

The truck cabin factory in Umeå, VUV, too, is an example of uneven development. During the 1970s the body shop of this plant introduced essentially the same production design and organization as at Saab's body shop in Trollhättan (the 'lineout' concept). During the 1980s both increases in volume and new products paved the way for a partial automatization of body processing. The effects on skills and working conditions have been ambiguous. On the one hand, some of the experienced or better educated workers have got more qualified robot handling jobs. On the other hand, there has been a return to the principles of centrally paced lines in the body shop, implying a substantial reduction of autonomy in the remaining manual work.

The situation is the same in the assembly shop, which has eight short lines for the final assembly of cabins. The large number of lines was chosen partly because of the model mix and partly because of the desire to avoid cycle times that are too short. (The 1987 average cycle time was approximately 30 minutes.) At the beginning of the 1980s none of the lines was mechanically paced. But during recent years production management – despite opposition from the union – has introduced centralized pacing of six of the lines in the form of computer-controlled intermittently running shuttles. At the same time, however, VUV has introduced dock assembly, beginning with special variants (the Globetrotter cabins) which were difficult to handle on the conventional line. Here skilled workers are assembling finished cabins at one station. This dock assembly is in a process of rapid expansion; in 1988 it will take care of at least a third of final assembly.

Within the production of diesel engines (Skövde) there has been no renewal of basic assembly design and organization. There is one exception, however, the Vara factory, a plant for the machining and assembly of marine engines. Organizationally a part of Volvo Components in Skövde, it was planned as a conventional factory. The assembly was designed as an unpaced line, the only new departure being the placement of the motors on manually controlled air cushioned carriers to provide greater flexibility. Plant management and the union jointly, however, started a broad, local development process which began in the mechanized machining section but spread to the assembly operations. By applying the principle of 'following the engine through the flow' (moving operator), the content of the work became substantial with a 2–3 hour cycle time. A qualitative change, however, occurred in the organizational and management structure. An all-encompassing team organization was developed, with production groups being made responsible for maintenance, quality inspection and reporting. Several specialist staff, including the traditional supervisory level, were eliminated. Thus the factory has a compressed management apparatus, with only three hierarchical levels, a plant manager, two general supervisors ('department heads', one for assembly and one for machining), and the production groups. The plant and its management were, however, looked upon with suspicion by the parent organization, and the ideas introduced did not spread elsewhere.

The Scania Division, a heavy truck specialist, has succeeded very well in matching the design of new products and production systems to the demands of the market. Automation in the machining sections has been taken quite far, but management has been reluctant to take any risk with the organization of work. This is especially true for the final assembly operations in the main factory in Södertälje. In the countryside plants, however, we do find some interesting innovations in the Scania division.

One example is the cabin plant in Oskarshamn. In 1980–1, when a new cabin programme was introduced it was extensively renewed. The old mechanical assembly line was replaced by a carrier-based flow, containing fourteen steps in series. Most of these steps have several parallel stations (the maximum being four). For assembly workers these changes involved work on stationary objects and a lengthening of cycle times to a maximum of 36 minutes. However there has been no real relaxation of traditional flow discipline. Pacing is as centralized as before. The carriers pick up the cabins at pre-programmed times. Computer terminals in the shop could be used to get a few extra minutes, but to do this operation a special code is necessary. This is given only to foremen. Each interruption is logged and checked by the process control centre. The local union took the issue of the assembly workers' right to control the carriers as far as central negotiations, but then lost the issue. The system creates a tension between the actual centralized pacing and the technological possibility of autonomy. For the assembly workers it is desirable to obtain the code and thereby the control of the carriers. So management, to prevent it from falling into the wrong hands, changes it often, sometimes several times a day.

Oskarshamn also introduced a new material handling system in order to cope with the growing number of variants. This means that all so-called medium-size articles are chosen centrally and placed in individually specified boxes, instead of being delivered in batches within the shop. Then, the boxes are loaded on to the relevant carriers at specific stations in the flow. This system can both handle breaks in the sequence of cabins and cope with parallel systems without sending the same parts to several different locations in the shop.

Another instance of innovation is the chassis shop at Scania Buses in Katrineholm. Scania Buses is an operation which since the end of the 1960s has enjoyed a great deal of autonomy. In contrast to more large-scale automotive production, it has retained certain traditions of craftmanship, especially in the body and painting shops (where the volume is only one tenth of that in the chassis shop). Up to the beginning of the 1980s the chassis shop had a conventional line layout, of the same type as, for example, Volvo's old shop in Lundby. Admittedly the cycle times were relatively long because of the low production volume, but the work was fragmented and had a very low status. Labour turnover was high and the chassis workers applied as quickly as possible for the skilled jobs in the body shop.

In 1982 the chassis shop was opened. Final assembly here takes place in three parallel, unpaced flows. Each flow has basically five stations and the assemblers move the chassis between them on air-cushioned platforms. The interesting point about Katrineholm is that the assembly workers are not assigned to fixed stations (as is still done in Borås). Instead they follow the chassis through the flow. In this way two assembly workers build the complete chassis, at a rate of 3–4 chassis per week (making total cycle time 10–12 hours). This resulted in the upgrading of chassis assembly to the status of skilled labour, a requalification which makes Katrineholm an exceptional plant in the Swedish automotive industry.

A new phase?

Up to the mid-1980s reforms in car assembly were, as we have seen, of a relatively cautious nature, implying no great departure from the line model. In recent years the possibility of a breakthrough in the car industry has, however, grown considerably. The background is economic. During the years 1983–4 the sales of the Swedish passenger car producers moved sharply upwards and their profits and production figures started to rise steeply. Expansion of production capacity became necessary. In 1985 Volvo commenced planning for a new assembly plant in Uddevalla and in 1986 Saab started preparations for a new plant in Malmö. According to the plans as of 1988, both are to be in full operation by 1991.

At the same time the economic boom in the metropolitan and auto-producing regions led to a considerable increase in labour turnover and recruiting costs at the old-style assembly plants in Trollhättan and Gothenburg. Though not unimportant, the comparatively low pay of Swedish auto-workers is less significant than the working conditions on the assembly line. A 1986 study at Volvo's main assembly plant showed that: 80 per cent of the final assembly workers considered their work to be degrading; 36 per cent felt disgust about the idea of going to work, either daily or several times a week; and 48 per cent never felt any satisfaction with their work. Since the mid-1980s young people in Sweden have definitely begun to reject Taylorized types of work. In addition, the Metalworkers' Union in a quite new way has started to press for qualitative changes in the conditions of assembly work. In conjunction with new product requirements, pressure for change has thus again increased. Both Volvo and Saab managements now realize that at least in Sweden they cannot build new factories based on traditional assembly lines. (In their plants in Belgium, Holland and Brazil there are, due to high unemployment, no real problems of recruitment and turnover, so the pressure for reform is not strong.) However while Saab tends to limit its ambitions in Malmö to reforms within a basic line concept, Volvo's approach in Uddevalla has gradually become more radical. At first the plant was planned as a variant of the Kalmar layout, with basically one 120 station-long assembly line. When the draft of this was presented in 1985, it was strongly opposed both by the Metalworkers' Union and top management, both of whose ambitions went beyond a straight copy of the Kalmar solution. A group of innovative industrial engineers suggested the possibility of a radical alternative, the 'Kalmar solution' was dropped, and the planning department got a new senior manager.

In 1987, after two years of intensive planning, experiments and debates, the outline of quite a new type of automotive plant emerged. Although the total production of one shift will only be 40,000 cars a year, the factory will be subdivided into six parallel, autonomous plants, each producing one sixth of the output. Each small plant will consist of a number of teams, each team building a complete car (apart from the testing and anti-corrosion treatment). Such an assembly concept requires many associated innovations: a new material handling system; a new computer-aided system for technical information and documentation; a new model of learning and training; and a flexible technology which is cheap to add to.

It further presupposes a centralization and partial automatization of those parts of the process where economies of scale are highly significant, such as material handling and some of the pre-assemblies. The Uddevalla planning is a production concept for final assembly based on skill development, a composite technological strategy and a new look at supposed economies of scale: small-scale, manual skilled work in the final assembly, centralized, large-scale and possibly automated operations in the material handling and minor pre-assemblies. A definite assessment of the economic performance of this concept has to wait until the plant has been run in full-scale production for some years. But already it has had important repercussions within the Volvo company.

Another important step within Volvo is the investment programme for TC, Volvo's main assembly factory, which was decided in 1985. In 1987, a first major step was taken with the introduction of a new shop for assembly of power trains. The mechanical lines were replaced by a complicated carrier system, involving both line and dock sections. A major part of the assembly is being done in a dock section of fourteen parallel stations (one system for each main model series), thus enlarging cycle times to a maximum 37 minutes. This enlargement was considered a risky step by production management, but was immediately successful – an important experience for the further development of the plant. The system was, however, too sensitive to disruptions and too much of a compromise with the line concept. So in 1988 it will be rebuilt in 'the Uddevalla direction', that is, with more parallel autonomous units and integrated assembly.

In the last fifteen years there has been a rich variety of production layouts, systems for material handling, control and pacing principles and organizational forms in final assembly within the Swedish automotive industry. The above review has focused on some central, recurring issues:

- *The production layout* (assembly concept), the two extremes being, on the one hand, a strict series layout (the traditional mechanical moving belt) and, on the other hand, complete parallelization, (dock assembly). Kalmar was an early attempt not to abandon the line but to combine it with certain elements of dock assembly. This attempt was not successful. Basically the same concept has, though, been realized in Oskarshamn where the materials handling system has been developed to match this idea.

- Oskarshamn has (as Kalmar always did), retained the centralized *pacing and control*, allowing computer control to replace the conveyor belt. Excluding bus production, only Volvo Trucks in Gothenburg (and for a part of its production, Volvo Umeå) has abandoned the principle of centralized pacing in their final assembly operations.

- A third, central issue is the *vertical division of work* in final assembly operations. The range here is from traditional authoritarian management forms to far-reaching decentralization and multi-skilled team-working, with the teams having responsibility for planning, training and production scheduling.

During the 1980s there has been a great deal of discussion about changes in the vertical work organization, aimed at giving workers more responsibility. In most cases the actual results have been limited. This has to do with a central contradiction in manual assembly between the managerial interests of worker commitment and initiative on the one hand, against those of subordination, and securing a high work intensity and a stable pace of work on the other. Departing from established production and organizational principles endangers for many managers their capacity to achieve subordination, which explains their reluctance to engage in comprehensive reforms.

Like other 'Japanese' organizational devices, quality control circles and action groups have been tried in the Swedish automotive industry, as everywhere else. Basically, they are 'add on' arrangements designed to tap employees for ideas which can be used in the rationalization of production and the modification of products. The intentions are not to change the hierarchy of authority (but rather to strengthen it, especially the first line supervisors) or encroach on traditional management prerogatives. These devices will not be considered here.

State of the art of assembly design in 1987

I will now present the 1987/8 'state of the art' of Swedish assembly operations in terms of the central issues discussed in the preceding section. These issues, production design (layout and control) and work organization can be related to the familiar dimensions of horizontal and vertical division (or integration) of labour. That way we can get a simple analytical tool as used in Figure 9.1 for classifying the various plants.

Here the horizontal axis stands for the assembly design and the division of labour in production work. The value assigned increases relative to the extent to which the work is integrated and autonomous.

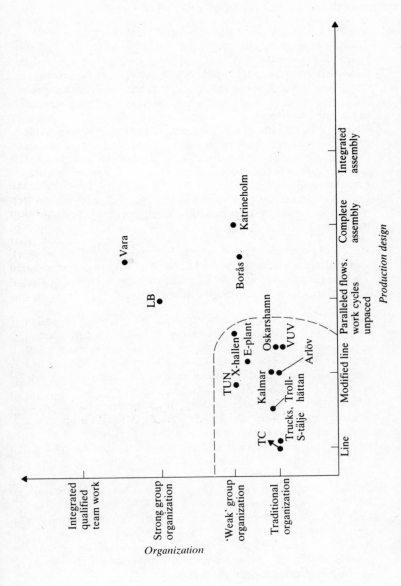

Figure 9.1 Assembly design and work organization. State of the art in 1987 Swedish automotive industry.

In other words this axis indicates the work content, the technical autonomy and the assembly-skill levels. The following levels have been distinguished:

(1) Traditional line, highly repetitive and restricted work with a normal cycle time in passenger car production of a few minutes, at the most.

(2) Modified line with somewhat longer cycle times (10–30 minutes), and perhaps some chance of varying the working pace and/or moving between line assembly and the less restricted pre-assembly work.

(3) Parallel flows without central pacing, with relatively long cycle times (30 minutes to a few hours).

(4) Complete assembly, whereby an individual, a pair or a group of workers carry out the entire final assembly with long cycle times of hours or days.

(5) Integrated assembly as in level 4 (complete assembly) but with quality inspection/testing and adjustment being totally done by the groups.

The vertical axis represents the organizational structure and the workers' chances of exercising influence. Levels 2 to 4 presuppose group-based work. The values assigned increase in relation to the degree of organizational integration and workers' degree of influence:

(1) Conventional hierarchical and individually structured organization. A typical chain is plant manager, line manager, general supervisors, foremen, assistant supervisors, and assembly workers. Hardly any issues are influenced by the workers. (On a line under a traditional organization workers cannot even decide for themselves when they can go to the lavatory.)

(2) Weak-group organization within the structure of traditional management. Production groups determine such things as the internal allocation of tasks, but have no powers which encroach upon managerial prerogatives. If there are group leaders they tend to be a part of the ordinary hierarchy (often in practice appointed by the foremen).

(3) Strong-group organization. This is a group-based organization where the work teams have taken over a large number of the tasks traditionally done by foremen and/or industrial engineers (one example, the LB plant, is analysed below).

(4) Integrated, qualified teamwork. The traditional supervisory level is eliminated, and there is close co-operation between the teams and various technical functions.

These scales are, naturally, not of a quantitative type, and are not interval scales (in terms of association one could speak of logarithmic steps). A more complete analysis would require additional dimensions. For example, a third axis representing performance requirements and economic control would be necessary to provide a more complete view of work loads and production strains. There are however, distinct advantages with using only two dimensions, simplicity and clarity. In Figure 9.1. they have been used for plotting the positions of assembly plants in the Swedish automotive industry.

Flexible Taylorism is the dominant trend

A number of observations can be made from Figure 9.1:

(1) Ten years ago the lower left corner was even more crowded. The field is moving, and the front is being shifted towards 'north-east', that is the upper right corner. In the Swedish automotive industry today no one is building assembly lines of the old type.

(2) However, it is far too early to say 'farewell to the line'. An absolute majority is still left on the inside of the line which marks the boundary between 'modified solutions' and 'qualitative changes' ('new assembly concepts').

(3) Flexible Taylorism in production design combined with group work within rather restricted forms is the dominant trend. Using Figure 9.1 'flexible Taylorism' could be defined as a combination with at least value two on one of the axes. That is: *either* traditional line layout ($x = 1$) combined with a modified, group-based organization and a more flexible personnel usage, that is $y = 2$, *or* a modified production design, for example a carrier line ($x = 2$), connected with a traditional or modified organization (that is $y = 1$ or 2).
The latter form is the most frequent one in the Swedish automotive industry. As could be seen in the figure, the changes in the Swedish automotive industry have not been simply restricted to making the line more flexible.

(4) In the production of commercial vehicles there are today a number of plants 'on the other side of the boundary', indicating a real departure from the line. There are no experiments, but regular production units. But at several factories there are parts of the assembly operations which are carried out in accordance with new principles, for example, the dock assembly operations at Volvo Umeverken (VUV in the figure).

The new assembly plants for passenger cars which are being planned for the 1990s have not been plotted in Figure 9.1 since their forms, especially in organizational terms, are far from settled. But the Uddevella factory will 'cross the boundary' and definitely incorporate new assembly concepts, and will constitute a breakthrough in this part of the industry. In the rest of this contribution I will try to assess what it means to go beyond flexible Taylorism, mainly by focusing on the case of Volvo's LB-plant outside Gothenburg.

Going beyond flexible Taylorism: the case of the LB-plant

The LB-plant assembles heavy trucks, with a capacity of approximately 6,000 vehicles per year. In 1986 the plant had twenty salaried employees and about 300 workers, of which about 120 worked in the final (chassis) assembly operations, 80 worked in pre-assembly including cabins and motors, and the rest were employed in materials handling, quality inspection and the adjustment and 'customizing' shop.

The new ideas in this plant are:

(1) A production design with two non-mechanical flows which have been structured for group work, with assembly at stationary vehicles, worker-controlled carriers and buffers between the groups. A cycle time of between 30 and 45 minutes, depending on the programme.

(2) A group-based organization comprising all workers. The groups are responsible for the allocation of all tasks and training, daily planning, detailed balancing and choosing group leaders. The leaders take care of time reports, quality inspection and contacts with superiors, industrial engineers, etc. Job rotation within groups is the norm. This rotation includes, for workers with enough experience, the position of group leader.

(3) A wage system with individual grades (the group leader position being the highest) and group bonuses for different areas of responsibility.

(4) An organization with only three levels, plant manager, supervisor and production groups (the groups being listed in the organizational chart of the company).

(5) New forums for union participation with joint labour-management committees for information and consultation at both department and plant level.

The plant was started up in 1982. Field work for an evaluation of it was conducted in 1985–86, at a time when the plant had sufficient experience of production to permit a robust analysis. A general problem in social science focusing on change is of premature evaluations. Five aspects of the LB-case will be treated below: economic performance; worker evaluation; participation and shop floor 'power relations'; role of industrial engineers; and role of unions.[2]

Systematic comparison of LB for the years 1983–5 with the traditional X-hall, also producing heavy trucks, showed that it had successfully fulfilled four of the six goals which were laid down by the company at the planning stage: higher productivity; less tying up of capital (mainly by being able to build customer-ready vehicles directly in the chassis flow); more mixed production; and reduced down-time.

The last point is particularly interesting. Departing from the system of central control and pacing of the assembly was regarded by management to be a risky step. The analysis of the years 1983–85 showed that production losses at LB were consistently lower than in the X-hall, in spite of a significantly higher degree of capacity utilization. On the other two goals set for the plant, quality and labour turnover, the performance of LB was roughly the same as the old plant. But here the analysis revealed significantly that LB was a success in those parts of the factory and organization which had really adopted new forms of work design. The absence of substantial improvements was found in those areas of the 'LB-compromise' where the old line ideal (under the motto of 'minimal risk-taking') was accorded most significance. Thus the fairly high labour turnover of the plant largely resulted from the fact that the workers in these areas considered the job to be too much like conventional assembly. They therefore tried to move on to more skilled and less constrained jobs, or left the company.

In this context it is worth comparing LB with another assembly plant based on a novel concept, Katrineholm's new chassis plant. It was started at the same time as LB, but with greater changes in the assembly work: assembly workers, having previously worked on a line, in the new parallel, short flow units, now build complete chassis. In 1982 the company was not sure whether this new work form would prove to be economically viable or whether it could survive labour turnover and increases in volume. A study in 1987 showed that the shop has passed the test, in spite of heavy pressure for production. The new job design had resulted in significant improvements in both productivity and quality, as well as increasing personnel stability. The flow of employees away from the chassis plant had ceased. The chassis assembly workers now belonged to the factory's category of skilled workers.

Workers' comparisons of the work at LB with their previous assembly jobs produce a very distinct picture, as is shown in Figure 9.2. Compared with the traditional plants, the assessment of LB is very positive. This is even the case when the comparison is with 'TLA' which is a shop for final adjustment and customization of the chassis. Though the work there is more skilled than at LB, the organization is

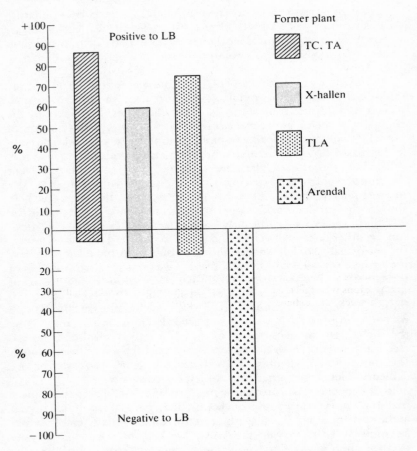

Figure 9.2   Evaluation of work at LB in comparison to jobs of the same kind at other Volvo plants. Workers at LB were asked to compare their current jobs with their previous ones. Percentages of positive and negative responses, respectively. (Proportions which did not indicate any difference are not shown).

Note: the columns do not represent the same number of people. The overwhelming majority of LB-workers with other Volvo experiences came from TC and the X-hall. The Arendal group is small, but has a very distinct profile.

very traditional with an individual piece-rate system. Among other things, jobs at LB are considered to be more varied, to involve more responsibility and challenge, and to foster more helpful attitudes. The majority of the ex-Arendal workers are however *negative* about LB.

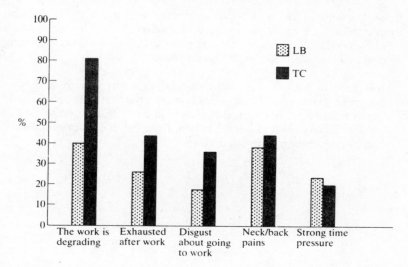

Figure 9.3 Working conditions in assembly work at LB compared to TC (proportions who feel the work is degrading; proportions who, daily or several times a week, are exhausted after work; proportions who feel disgust about going to work; proportions who have neck/back pains; proportions feeling they are under strong time pressure at least half the day)

A cross tabulation of the responses of final assembly workers at LB and TC illustrates both the advances made and the remaining problems at LB (see Figure 9.3).

– At TC 80 per cent find the job to be degrading. This proportion is reduced to 40 per cent at LB. A clear improvement, but still a high percentage, especially if the goal is to achieve labour stability in final assembly.

– The proportion of workers exhausted after work is significantly lower at LB, in spite of the fact that the performance demands there (measured in Methods Time Management) are objectively higher because of the new balancing principles. This appears to reflect the increased autonomy and less repetitiveness.

– The proportion of workers with a feeling of disgust about going to work is significantly lower at LB.

– Physical work loads, measured by a question about 'frequent neck/back pains' are, however, at roughly the same high level in both plants.

– Similarly, both plants have about the same proportion of people who feel they work under 'strong time pressure'. LB's high level reflects the fact that the complexity of the product mix has increased significantly since the plant was planned, which creates problems because of the 'line compromise' that was chosen. The buffers between the assembly groups in the chassis flows are too small both to cope with this mix flexibility and to create autonomy for the groups. The result is an uneven work rhythm, causing considerable stress.

The overall assessment of the LB plant is reflected in the following interview from a worker in the chassis flow:

> It is good here if you have something to compare it with. If they are going to change TC, then this system is the best. It is definitely better than a line. Better health, better quality...but nevertheless I do not feel any pride about what I do, the work is so monotonous and boring that anyone can do it.

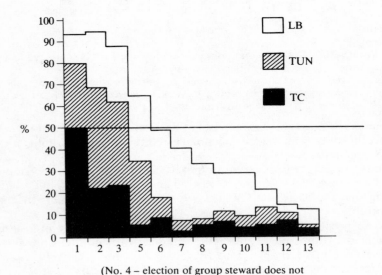

(No. 4 – election of group steward does not exist at TC and was therefore excluded)

Figure 9.4   Direct worker influence at three Volvo assembly plants measured for proportions of workers answering that they decide the issue

Notes:
1. Job rotation.
2. Allocation of work, who is going to do what.
3. Planning of the daily jobs.
4. Who is going to be the group steward.
5. Choosing replacements.
6. Requisition of repairs.
7. Time off.
8. Choosing new employees.
9. Manpower needs.
10. Planning 2–3 week perspective.
11. Changes in production design.
12. Production pace.
13. Making up for lost production.

This is a reflection on the working conditions. We also asked about participation and worker influence. Figure 9.4, compares the direct influence of the workers at TC, TUN and LB, on 12 specific items. It shows the proportion who answered that workers do have influence on a particular matter (the term 'workers' means individuals, groups or the group leader, which at LB is elected by the group).

We can see that LB consistently has the highest proportion on all items, that TUN has a middle position, and that the proportion at TC is very low. (Compare this with the first three levels on the y-axis in Figure 9.1.) There was no one issue over which the workers at LB (or the other factories) wanted less influence than they actually had. On the contrary, the pervading opinion was in favour of increased influence, particularly over long-term issues.

The dual role of industrial engineers

The industrial engineers in manual assembly have a dual role. One is to control and maximize work intensity. From the workers' perspective, this is the labour intensification or 'sweating out'. The industrial engineer also has the role of preparing new products for production, thus constituting a link between design and manufacturing. The activities of industrial engineers are often the subject of harsh worker criticism. In traditional assembly plants, this is mainly concerned with the intensification function and involves standards, times, performance, and payment, and can often be hard and bitter. For example, in the X-hall, a 1981 company investigation showed a markedly negative attitude towards the industrial engineers:

> The opinion about the industrial engineers is clear-cut along the entire line. They walk around here with their damned papers and do not understand a thing, you cannot talk to them, they must be brainwashed. Already on his first day a new employee can hear from his workmates that the methods people exist for the purpose of making life sour for the assembly workers.

What happens now when the conditions are changed, when production becomes less standardized, when workers become more skilled and when responsibility is delegated to the shop floor? There are various possibilities. At LB worker criticism of industrial engineers remains strong. But – and this is very interesting – most of the criticism no longer involves the 'sweating out' function. It concerns instead the industrial engineers' function as a link between shop floor and the design department. The workers are of the opinion that the industrial engineers have too little interest in collaborating with the shop floor, and that the information they receive on new variants and product changes is too little and too late. Many of them claim that the groups could do much more of the engineering work, if they only had a little more time and training. Such types of discontent and demands for change are much stronger at LB than at TC and TUN. To some extent this relates to the character of production – LB has a significantly broader range of variants and product changes than the other two factories. This means that the products are necessarily less 'designed' when they come into the shop. However, it also relates to LB's different type of organization and quality of personnel.

> That people at LB experience the industrial engineering staff as being sluggish also has to do with the level of the guys. Here people do not ask questions; the only things that count are times and wages. It is different at LB. There the guys have more skills and they make demands regarding equipment, layout, etc. (former foreman at LB, now at a traditional plant).

We can compare LB with the bus plant in Borås which is also an instance of new assembly principles. Here there is also strong worker criticism of the industrial engineers' role in the preparing and planning of new products as workers recognize that collaboration in the product planning process is of vital importance to this non-standardized form of production. But in Borås there is also a strong criticism about their 'sweating out' function. Borås, in its production layout, has taken a more distinct step away from the line than LB. But as a method of control management instead utilizes a very strict piecework system in the docks. This leads to many acrimonious conflicts with those who set the rates for piecework, that is, the industrial engineers.

To conclude, the changes in products, production design and organization with their associated new skill demands bring to the forefront the role of production engineers. A new role for them, however, will not be created without conscious efforts. Two conditions seem necessary. First a changed form of economic control, concentrated on overall effectiveness, rather than the narrow counting of man-hours in direct production. Second, new structures, forms and routines, which allow for an ongoing collaboration between skilled asssembly workers and industrial engineers.

The changed position of the union

To conclude the LB case report, we will discuss the role of the unions in the new organizational settings. In the discussion of participation we have thus far concentrated exclusively on the direct influence of workers, suggesting a strong correlation between actual and desired levels of influence. What then about the interest of the workers in union influence? An analysis of data not shown here from the three-plant survey using the same items as in the previous measures of workers' direct influence gave a very clear result: there is no immediate connection, positive or negative, between the direct influence of workers and their interest in union influence. The proportions of workers regarding union influence as important were nearly identical in each of the three plants, and so were their rankings of the 12 different items. Group organization or not, mechanical line or unpaced flow, in some essential aspects work in final assembly p ants is of the same nature, and issues concerning work intensity and work pace continue, from the workers' perspective, to be central union concerns.

A correlation analysis of the LB-data on the individual level reveals no correlation between actual direct influence and desired union influence, or between desired direct influence and desired union influence. Union consciousness and interest form a dimension which is separate from, and determined by, factors other than those which relate to an individual's or his own group's direct influence. When, however, we study the overall effect of the LB-model the result is different. The higher skill level of the workers has also helped to 'upgrade' union activities. The local union at LB is much more concerned than is the case in conventional plants with questions of long-term relevance to the work organization, such as education, production planning, and, last but not least, the structure and manning of shop management. Thus, the LB-model with strong worker groups, its union–management organizational agreement ('the organizational handbook of the plant') and its new forms of union participation in decision-making has given the union a significantly strengthened role. Also union commitment to new concepts is a very important element in their realization. This was certainly the case in the preparation of the LB-organization, and was also the case in the strategic shift of the planning of Uddevella, moving from consolidation of the old to the creation of new concepts.

Conclusions. Prospects and prerequisites for new concepts

Are there possibilities for new production concepts, in Kern and Schumann's terms, even in manual assembly operations? Briefly stated, the conclusion will be: yes, definitely, for certain product ranges. But in regard to the industry as a whole it is quite difficult to make a prognosis. However, the following observations can be made:

(1) Within the Swedish automotive industry, production design is changing along a broad front. The classical assembly line is being abandoned. But – thus far – it is mainly a question of a transition from rigid lines to flexible Taylorism.

(2) However, alternatives which really point toward new production concepts have also been established. Thus far this has occurred within the manufacture of commercial vehicles. Today, however, there is also the possibility of breakthroughs in passenger car production.

(3) During the 1980s the assembly plants with new types of production design and organization have demonstrated their economic viability in a number of cases.

(4) Workers are strongly in favour of these new principles. However, from their perspective, the changes have in most cases been far too limited. Upgrading of what was previously unskilled assembly work to skilled labour is of decisive importance. This presupposes a different model for assembly work: a builder of vehicles instead of an assembler of parts.

(5) Union commitment and influence is of vital importance for a development from flexible Taylorism to new production concepts. This holds true both in the planning of new kinds of plants and their successful operation and development. Also, strong group organization, qualified workers and extended forms of labour–management cooperation may upgrade and strengthen the role of unions.

(6) Increased model variations and proportions of multi-skilled groups pose a challenge for industrial engineers. If they continue to work in the old way, conflicts at the shop floor will, if anything, increase. At the same time the new type of organization, if combined with new forms of economic control, provides opportunities for management–worker collaboration in the preparation of new products. Also, such collaboration is essential for a continuous development of the technical insights and skills of the assembly workers, and is thus a prerequisite for a lasting upgrading of this work.

Looking at developments elsewhere, it is obvious that flexible Taylorism is not unique to Sweden. The Japanese assembly system could be viewed as another case of innovation, but one in which the basic coordinates are quite different. The Japanese keep an orthodox line structure, but compensate for its rigidity in two principal ways.

One is the elaborate, multi-tier subcontractor hierarchy (the *shitauke*-system) which both reduces risks and increases flexibility for the *oya* companies, that is the main automotive firms.

The other is the personnel policy with its flexible usage of labour. Key elements include: broadly defined job roles (which transferred to the American context means extremely few job classifications); extensive job rotation; training programmes and career-planning for blue collar workers; and comprehensive group organization involving strong group pressures (Tetsuo, 1987; Cole, 1979; see also Chapters 5 and 10).

Another important aspect in the Japanese production organization is the celebrated commitment of workers despite a basically very authoritarian organization. This must be understood against the background of three social conditions which make workers in large firms extremely dependent on their employers (see Chapter 5). First, the lack of any global welfare systems, the only ones available are the arrangements set up by the companies; second, a highly segmented labour market, making jobs in large companies very attractive (Clark, 1979). Third, the lack of an independent union movement within the private sector, the 'in-house unions' of the big firms being effectively subordinated to company interests (Yamamoto, 1980).

In sum, the Japanese system involves flexible usage of personnel within a basically rigid production design. In contrast to Sweden there are no signs of a fundamental departure from Taylorism in Japanese firms. But, since the first oil crisis the Japanese automotive firms have – in contrast to their Swedish counterparts – faced no recruitment problems.

The idea of new production concepts in Germany, as we noted in the introduction, has been closely linked to automation, and has taken the development in the body shops as the main example of new types of integrated work. In contrast to this, we have emphasized that final assembly of cars still is very far from being automated. The principal factor distinguishing the automated body shops from (manual) final assembly is, however, not the technology in itself, but the different cost structures. New production concepts in assembly operations require a qualitative break with Taylorist principles, and specifically with the assembly line, albeit within a type of production where work intensity is still a central managerial concern. That makes the departure from Taylorism difficult. The role of the labour market and of the position and policies of unions, therefore are of crucial importance. Without a concerted union effort backed by a strong labour market position it is hard to envisage any real development of new production concepts in such labour intensive operations as final assembly.

10   The transfer of Japanese management concepts in the international automobile industry

ULRICH JÜRGENS

As we saw in Chapter 1, learning from Japan has been an important aspect of the development of management theory and practice in the 1980s. The interest in Japanese management concepts seems more than a passing fad and extends beyond a straight transplanting of certain techniques. A large number of concepts has already been taken over, and especially prominent in this process have been the automobile manufacturers. This chapter is concerned with the process of transfer of Japanese productivity concepts. The central question is which elements of the Japanese employment system and Japanese production methods are of the most relevance outside Japan, and how some of these concepts will be transformed in their new surroundings. The observations are based on interviews with management experts and union representatives at US British and German automobile companies.[1] The most important protagonists of a transfer of Japanese management concepts are still the two major US automobile groups, General Motors and Ford. Accordingly, they will be found more frequently at the centre of our account.

Since the real transfer process depends on a large number of individual measures, pilot projects, plans and strategic concepts, we can only attempt to evaluate presently discernible trends. Nor is it possible within the scope of this chapter to investigate systematically the national and company-specific peculiarities in the transfer of Japanese management concepts in every country and company in the international automobile industry. Ideally, developments in Italy and France, where there has so far been hardly any discussion about such a transfer, would have to be investigated to discover whether this is more a matter of unevenness or only non-simultaneity in international development.

We should make clear at this point that the new management concepts of the 1980s are not just ideas imported from Japan. The adoption of Japanese ideas in the early 1980s must be seen in the context of other reform concepts, as otherwise one would run the risk of ascribing many of the changes in the plants currently going on in North America and Europe solely to the 'learning from Japan' movement. This other context has, for example, contributed to the readiness to transfer group concepts. Two such approaches to a solution to productivity problems developed relatively independently of each other in the 1970s: (1) organizational development strategies developed by US companies; and (2) new production concepts, the prototypes of which were developed by Swedish companies (see Chapter 9).

Since the early 1980s the transfer of Japanese concepts has been taking place largely parallel to a spreading of the methods and concepts of the other two approaches. All three approaches converge on the question of the decentralization of production responsibility. In this connection the 'Japanese model' performed the important function of being the confirmation and reinforcement mechanism for reform ideas being developed elsewhere.

Points of departure for the practical transference of Japanese methods

The Japanese competitive advantage is by no means solely a question of production organization and productivity. According to the UAW (unpublished) Telesis study roughly 20 per cent of the Japanese cost advantage is accounted for by lower wage costs, 24 per cent by the value of the Yen, 18 per cent by tariffs and only 38 per cent by higher efficiencies in manufacturing and assembly (McElroy, 1985). The tremendous difference in productivity compared with their own automobile production was, however, the first real 'discovery' of Western management. In one of the 'Japan Reports', for instance, a US company estimates the manning difference between one of its assembly plants in North America and a Japanese plant with comparable product to be around 100 per cent: 28 hours of blue-collar work were needed in the US plant to produce one car as compared with about 14 in the Japanese plant! Especially striking was the difference in indirect labour: 9 hours were needed in the US plant, little more than 3 in the Japanese (Jürgens, *et al.*, 1988).

Western management experts went to Japan in the early 1980s to get a closer look at the individual peculiarities of the Japanese system which could explain the productivity advantage. This pragmatic and inductive process of discovery resulted in a listing of the individual factors which contributed to the Japanese success in production without, however, an analysis of their internal context and the preconditions specific to their system and culture.

At first it did not appear easy to shape practical policies using this list. After all, the central principles of the Japanese production system are diametrically opposed to the traditional principles of Western management that have so far applied. For example:

- the principle that it is only possible to produce efficiently in large batches or production runs; the Japanese prove the opposite;
- the principle that production quality can only be improved if higher production costs are tolerated; in the Japanese production system the opposite applies;
- the principle that an increase in plant utilization times presupposes the maintenance of large intermediate stores of materials and primary products; in Japan it has been seen that it is precisely the minimization of intermediate stores and the just–in–time supply of qualitatively perfect parts that help to increase the 'process yield'.

The puzzlement was even greater since Japan obviously did not take the traditional North American and European path. She did not step up the level of various indirect functions such as quality inspection and industrial engineering to control the work performance of direct labour. The central message from Japan was, namely, that higher efficiency and greater intensity of direct production work could be achieved without a greater amount of these control functions. 'There are very few policemen in the system', concluded a manager in the controller's staff of a European company in our interviews.

The paradox lies in the fact that Japanese management apparently has greater control over the work and production process without having to differentiate this control organizationally and socially. In this way fewer personnel are required, especially in the indirect areas of production, quality control and maintenance, but also in the salaried-employee functions such as industrial engineering and financial control. If a transfer of ideas is to be more than simple experimentation with individual concepts, it is necessary to apply a more systemic approach to the explanation for the Japanese productivity success.

A large number of factors affecting productivity have been debated within discussion of the Japanese model. It is possible to isolate five such important elements, and hence possible 'transfer rails': (1) the level of qualifications and methods of vocational training; (2) the forms in which problem-solving knowledge is mobilized; (3) the specific forms in which technology is used and production controlled; (4) the importance of groups and group relations; and (5) the ways in which behaviour is steered and conformity assured.

Qualification level and plant qualification

The level of qualification necessary for even the simplest production tasks in Japan, given the current pattern of recruitment, corresponds almost with that of English A-levels (in Germany, *Abitur,* in the USA, high-school graduation). Even at this level there is a rigorous selection process (with entry exams, for example). It is apparent that strategies for the use and qualification of labour have totally different preconditions than those in the traditional manufacturing countries where work in the auto industry has a relatively low position in the social hierarchy. The high initial level also sets quite different preconditions for further qualification and specialization. There is a wide range of courses available for this purpose on which the control and bonus mechanisms place great importance. On-the-job training is the principal method by which qualifications are acquired. The long-term career development of most workers is based on a more or less systematic pattern of job rotation and on internal mobility. In this way qualification reserves are created for every kind of activity, which greatly facilitate flexibility and the ability to co-operate.

More important than the entry qualifications and formal structures of further training courses seems to be the 'system of collective apprenticeship' (Nohara, 1987). This relates to the way in which the work tasks with a new content such as programming and maintenance of new technology are progressively delegated by engineers to maintenance workers, and then by these to production operators as the new production system gradually settles down. In this way, the knowledge and skill associated with new technologies diffuses down through the job structure. 'The dynamic of their collective apprentice-ship is helping to make innovation in Japanese firms a genuinely endogenous process' (Nohara, 1987: 22).

Mobilization of problem-solving knowledge

Japanese management makes greater use than the traditional manage-ment of Western countries of the knowledge and experience of people at the lower hierarchy levels, and of the knowledge and experience of production workers themselves. "Bottom-up" decision-making characterizes many management decisions' (Marsland and Beer, 1983: 52). Lower management levels and adjoining staff areas are also included in the decision-making process in a more comprehensive fashion in order to introduce criticism and corrections (the *ringi* system). Thus what has been adopted outside of Japan is the attempt to use the knowledge and experience of the 'shop-floor' so that produc-tion groups are set up with various names – the best known one is quality circle – in order to solve production problems. Originally oriented to quality goals, the groups have become increasingly involved in topics such as work-flow optimization and questions of work safety.

This system for the mobilization of production knowledge and experience among the rank and file not only provides inputs for management decisions, but is also a way of evaluating those decisions: for example, why didn't they arrive at appropriate ideas for improvement themselves? This results in communication structures for plant problems between employees and management outside the system of industrial relations.

Technology and production management

The Japanese production system is based on three principles: flexibility in utilization of facilities; minimization of quality problems as they arise in production; and minimization of production-flow buffers, whether material, manpower or time-buffers. The realization of these principles is not apparently dependent on a specific technology; in fact most of the experts conclude that the Japanese 'competitive edge' is not based on technology. One of the most important factors is, in fact, the intense manpower utilization resulting from the interaction of the above-mentioned three production principles. According to Abernathy *et al.*, (1983: 84ff.) the process yield and the quality control system stemming from this kind of production management explain about half of the Japanese advantage in productivity; workforce management regarding absenteeism, structuring of jobs and work-pace explain about 34 per cent and technology (process automation and product design) 17 per cent.

That Japanese automobile groups work on the just-in-time principle in their relations with suppliers, without large material buffers, has been widely noted in the literature. But the emphasis is on the productivity gains due to rationalization of the supply process. The just-in-time system is, however, only part of a more comprehensive zero-buffer system of production management that also includes staffing questions and aims at rationalizing the entire work process. Schonberger (1982: 32) characterizes this principle as follows:

> The Japanese no longer accept the buffer principle. Instead of adding buffer stocks at the point of irregularity, Japanese production managers deliberately expose the workforce to the consequences. The response is that workers and foremen rally to root out the causes of irregularity. To ignore it is to face the consequences of work stoppages.
>
> The Japanese principle of exposing the workers to the consequences of production irregularities is not applied passively. In the Toyota Kanban system, for example, each time that workers succeed in correcting the causes of recent irregularity (machine jamming, cantankerous holding devices, etc.), the managers

remove still more buffer stock. The workers are never allowed to settle into a comfortable pattern; or rather, the pattern becomes one of continually perfecting the production process. Toyota's small group improvement activities (SGIAs) never run out of new challenges. Whether the cycle of improvement can be sustained indefinitely, remains to be seen.

This principle of a constant increase in the pressure for rationalization underlies not only reductions in material buffers but also reductions in personnel and working-time buffers. After a visit to five Japanese automobile plants a vice-president of an American multinational automobile company noted in a memorandum in 1978 that the Japanese avoided 'surplus manpower' or even operated systematically with understaffing:

> There are no standby men to cover for personal necessities, no emergency staff for absenteeism, illness or personal days off. Everyone has a full job to do and works the whole time. The assembly lines are typically manned to an extent of only 97 per cent. The remaining 3 per cent has to be made up for by 'extra effort'. (Company document, unpublished)

Exposing the under-utilization of capacity is frequently used to recognize time and personnel buffers. At Toyota, for example, there is an 'arrangement that makes it immediately possible for others to recognize when a worker has surplus time. This shows him and others that the workers have too much time, that objectively, therefore, there is no reason not to increase his work' (Shizmizu, 1979: 335). The same function is performed by the warning lights mounted over many of the assembly lines to show when workers are having problems. Schonberger (1982) points to the contribution this form of exposure has on work intensifi tion. According to his studies, a situation of no warning lights also signals management that there are personnel or working-time buffers on the line and that, consequently, staffing can be reduced. This management practice, like other forms of the zero–buffer principle, can only avoid costly production disturbances when the employees are highly flexible in job assignment and performance. Workers must be prepared to jump in when there are bottlenecks elsewhere or take over the activities of co-workers who have been pulled off the line.

Production teams and group relations

The scope of the group, the basic unit of work organization in Japanese plants, is broad. It represents a 'family' and social contacts; it is an educational authority (for late-comers, for instance) and training agency (including its role as a quality circle); it is responsible not only for guaranteeing efficiency and improvements at the work site but also for product quality. According to Koike (1983 the typical pattern of labour deployment in Japanese industry (such as on-the-job-training, job rotation, broad job classification) emerged from the work groups which were also the basis for the decentralized regulation of the work process. It should be mentioned, however, that the group in the Japanese context is not an element of industrial democracy with, for instance, the group members electing their leader or through making redundant the foreman's functions. The Japanese groups have not weakened the supervisory functions of lower management and do not form a counterveiling power to the management hierarchy. The 'supervisory density' is, in fact, far greater in Japanese plants than in Western ones (Jürgens and Strömel, 1987).

Individual conformity and 'compliance'

A whole array of factors must be mentioned here. To be noted first is the system of the lifelong job security for many employees. This employment relationship is frequently viewed as the most important precondition for the high degree of loyalty to the company on the part of Japanese employees, their acceptance of technical change and, even more, their willingness to participate through rationalization measures even if it eliminates their own job. At the same time, the close bond between individual and company perspective increases the dependency of the former on the company. A change in employers would be seriously damaging for members of the permanent staff. Individual dependence on the company is strengthened by many other mechanisms.

The central position of the group does not mean that individual achievement and personal evaluation do not play a role. The opposite is true. One cannot imagine finding in a Western concern a system for personnel evaluation so ingenious and complicated in its application as that which we see in Japanese firms (Demes, 1989). The fundamentals are self-evaluation, personal goal-setting and rating by superiors. The results of the evaluation play a major role in the determination of individual pay, promotion and work placement, and its importance relative to seniority is increasing.

The expenditure of Japanese companies on staff evaluation is high. The precise criteria and pattern of weighting employed at this level to measure individual work performance and behaviour are also impressive. One is easily reminded of the comparable expenditure by Western companies for performance standards and workplace controls.

The 'human engineering' basis for the Japanese staff evaluation system is, in a sense, a 'functional' equivalent to the role 'industrial engineering' plays in the regulation of individual performance in Western companies. This also accounts for the increased importance of personnel policy and the size of personnel departments in Japan in comparison to Western companies.

The closure of the system is cemented by the principle of the company union: the lack of autonomous, collective factors for the articulation of employees' interests is viewed in this case as an explanation for the 'compliance' of Japanese employees. The bond the Japanese employee shares with her/his company is thus secured in many ways. The conformity in the consciousness and attitude of the employees is not solely the result of the historical, social and cultural peculiarities of Japan. It is, rather, the result of carefully designed control systems.

The thrust in the transfer of concepts from Japan

Qualification and plant training

The recruitment of automobile workers at the level of A-level graduates is hardly conceivable in the immediate future in the countries of North America and Europe, not even under exceptional labour-market conditions like those at the new Nissan plants in Tennessee where in 1983 130,000 applications were received for 1,760 jobs. Forms of production organization aimed at the utilization of a high initial level of qualifications among the production workers are most visible in the Federal Republic of Germany, where simple production activities are also being done by, for example, skilled turners, fitters and electricians. There, the preconditions for integration of production and maintenance work, or for the formation of mixed teams of skilled and non-skilled workers, have been met or are being put into practice. The mix of skill within the teams and the presence of skilled workers even on the production line also facilitate the exchange of knowledge in technical problem-related matters. There is, however, nothing coming close to the system of collective apprenticeship described above. But there are indeed tendencies to decentralize the technical staff functions and to bring those of engineering closer to the shop-floor (related to concepts of area management).

Mobilization of production knowledg

The idea of quality circles has been adopted all over the world as a management concept. Wide-scale introduction happened first in the

USA. The fact that the establishment of quality circles was not necessarily a costly measure, especially in times of recession when the line could even be stopped for discussion in the circle, helped plant management to accept the idea. In the USA the spread of quality circles in General Motors and Ford was part of the former's specific organizational–design (OD) and quality of work life (QWL) programmes and the latter's employee involvement (EI) programme. With union headquarters supporting the programmes and most of the branches at least tolerating quality-circle activities, around 20 to 25 per cent of the two companies' employees were at least occasionally involved in quality circles in the first half of the 1980s.

In Great Britain this method of using production knowledge to solve management problems has been rejected by the unions as unpaid extra work and criticized as an attempt to brainwash workers. The companies, on the other hand, do not seem eager to offer a trade-off in terms of extra pay in order to pursue quality-circle activities. This does not mean that there are no informal activities in some plants which come close to those of quality circles. In the Federal Republic, too, quality circles have so far become relevant in only a few companies. The stumbling block has been the demand of the works council for a general agreement with the union on the terms of the circles' activities. The union is especially worried that the circles, by electing their own spokesmen, may become a parallel organization to the shop-steward system (*Vertrauensleute*). In a recent agreement between the company and the union at Volkswagen the first breakthrough was reached which gives the work council full control over quality-control matters. The other companies do not seem prepared to follow this example. Though, at Ford and BMW quality circles have been working since the late 1970s, with the works councils tolerating or even actively supporting these activities.

The incorporation of quality circles and the programmes of participative management into the US industrial relations scene (in the form of GM's QWL and Ford's EI programmes) do not appear to represent a decisive turning point (see Wood, 1986). But although many plant programmes have failed, withered away or exist only symbolically, this movement has by no means lost its drive. In many US plants, problem-solving groups have been incorporated into the institutions of industrial relations and may, to some extent, shape workers' expectations. In Europe the spread of quality circles has been slowed down in some companies, by union demands, while others have already had some experience of such activities and have in the meantime adapted the Japanese concepts to their own specific needs.

Nevertheless, in every traditional manufacturing country and company, institutions like quality circles have so far remained foreign with, for example, still unresolved questions of incorporating them into the industrial relations, payments and disciplinary systems, and problems of inclusion in and acceptance by lower- and middle-level management. Without parallel and accompanying measures and developments in industrial relations, increased training and participation they will remain such foreign bodies with their future significance uncertain, and current effect doubtful.

Technology and production management

As we have seen, the difference between the productivity of Japanese and non-Japanese manufacturers is not explained primarily by technical factors. In many cases it is also obvious that the simple transfer of a particular technical or organizational feature from Japanese plants (like push buttons used to switch off the assembly lines at every work place to avoid faulty production in the event of overload) is no guarantee that it will be used in a like manner to Japanese practice. Nevertheless, the three central principles of the Japanese production system (flexibility, zero errors, zero buffers) have gained acceptance in principle by Western manufacturers.

The goal of a more flexible utilization of machines and facilities has had a considerable influence on the investment strategy of Western car manufacturers since the early 1980s. The increasing use in production of robots instead of single-purpose welding presses is a visible expression of this. In the pressing plants of most Western companies the practice of producing smaller batches with more frequent tool changes has also been adopted.

The longer the planning perspective of Western companies, the more profound and comprehensive the impact of Japanese production principles. An example is 'Buick City' near Detroit, USA. This is not a town but a sweeping concept for a production location. The location was to be planned as a 'city' right from the beginning, since it is in a city that the sought-after closer relationship between outside firms and final manufacturers can best be realized, just as in its model, Toyota City. The orientation to Japanese production systems goes so far in this case that even the cramped spatial conditions of Japanese plants are to be copied. According to the plans for 'Buick City' the space per employee is to be roughly half that of other comparable GM prodution plants (Rohwand, 1984) and thus approximate the Japanese standards. There will, in consequence, no longer be room for repairing defective vehicles by taking them out of the assembly-line flow as is normally done in Western plants (thereby causing disorder in the planned model mix which, in turn, makes the pre-plant work allocation obsolete and thus causes considerable inefficiencies in manpower utilization as well as reducing productivity). The philosophy behind it is explained by a Ford manager in whose plant this idea has already been put into practice:

> Historically, we would have repair bays coming out our ears...now, we've eliminated the repair bays, the philosophy being, if there is no repair bay, you'd better not generate a repair. You're going to make sure your productive maintenance schedules are adhered to...(McElroy, 1985: 44)

In view of the long-term nature of this strategy and the considerable, related investments and capital risk, an extensive organization-wide transfer of all the production methods is not imminent. The experiences gained from the pilot projects must be awaited. Only after these concepts have proved themselves and adjustments been made in the course of the projects to meet the special national and organizational features will their spread in this area continue. The present degree of diffusion is not, therefore, a reliable indicator of the future relevance of Japanese concepts.

Limited capital must, in particular, be considered in relation to the realization of the zero-buffer principle. Due to the costs entailed by a completely new stock-keeping and material-flow system, which presupposes changes in all aspects of the production process, according to the American Production and Inventory Control Society, a more extensive change to just-in-time is mainly a question of capital, and here it is not very likely that just-in-time can be quickly realized in the automobile industry.

The technology/capital-induced brake on diffusion allows time to conceive, try out and negotiate work structures which are more likely to be accepted by the employees than any attempt to copy wholesale present Japanese practices. For any element of Japanese management concepts would probably run counter to union policy and to concepts of job design influenced by moves for the humanization of work. Since, for instance, buffers built into the work flow play an important role in enhancing the work groups' control over time.

Production teams and group relations

So far the actual spread of production teams does not correspond to their central importance within the Japanese scenario. Even so, at General Motors in the USA there are now more than twenty 'team plants' with some 30,000 employees. (Small intergroup component-making plants are included in this figure.) In Europe, the engine plant in Aspern near Vienna opened in 1982 serves as the pioneer team plant for GM in Europe and has become a pilgrimage location for visitors from other European car companies.

In Great Britain, British Leyland (BL) has so far only introduced the team concept in a very limited way in some of its plants (Willman and Winch, 1985; Wood, 1988c). In Germany, only one company, Audi, has as yet entered into team-based production on a larger scale. At Audi the experimental stage, which all companies have entered in certain areas of production, has passed and their management seems to be fully committed to the team concept. The other German producers remain wary. In Sweden, after much scepticism as to the success of the Volvo–Kalmar experiment, the team principle has been retained even if some of the advanced concepts, such as process layout, have been abandoned. The new factories of Saab and Volvo are again planned to be team-based (see Chapter 9).

If future trends are looked at, the importance of the team concept comes out more strongly. Work is to be done in teams at all production facilities presently being built and at plants being planned. General Motors' Saturn project is the most prominent example. Here, it is expected that the team principle will merge with new production concepts, as in Sweden, which will be based on, for example, assembly islands and decentralized product shops, marking a break with traditional assembly-line work organization.

Although the conceptions of the different strategic approaches overlap in the formation of production teams, and developments in various countries seem to be converging on creating production teams, the differences which still exist should not be ignored. Teams can, as we have seen, be viewed and used in many respects as a productivity resource. Nevertheless, they typically have a different function for management in various countries. In Japan the group is an integral part of the system of production management without which the zero-buffer and zero-defect principles could not function.

This close linkage of the group principle and production organization does not exist in the USA so far. There, the introduction of group principles seems to be primarily linked to changes in the field of industrial relations. The expectation placed on the production team is that it will help abolish present union rules on work assignment (seniority rules) and the division of labour (demarcation rules). To reach this goal, as has been seen, it is not enough to gain union concessions regarding greater work-assignment flexibility and less rigid work descriptions for individual categories of employee at the bargaining table. Only by transferring the full responsibility for production tasks, which are flexibly divided up among the members of the team, is it possible to reduce down-times and waiting times which stem from skill demarcation and hierarchical gradation.

In the Federal Republic, on the other hand, different driving forces can be observed for the spread of the group principle. For example, groups were introduced in the highly mechanized areas especially of the newly modernized body-shops to address teething and technical problems or contemplate preventive maintenance and assure maximum machine-up time. In these highly mechanized areas the required qualifications are extremely wide-ranging, from system monitoring and preventive maintenance on the one hand, to supplying materials and inserting parts on the other. But, at the same time, the remaining 'crew' in charge of this machinery has become so small that its members have to work more or less in isolation within the mechanized area. To assure maximum system availability, everyone working in the area should then be able to recognize malfunctions and help to prevent or eliminate them. The spread of the group principle in the German context is not primarily intended to overcome traditional work practices and job demarcations guarded by the unions. Rather it is the consequence of the 'systems approach' to rationalization by management (Altmann *et al.*, 1986) involving the introduction of new technology. Its main function will be to reduce the gap between skilled and unskilled workers.

This point of qualification is taken up positively in union policy as well. Group work with rotating work tasks and correspondingly higher qualifications of every group member is viewed as a protection against wage down-grading and the loss of jobs if 'residual jobs' within the area are subjected to further rationalization measures. These are jobs such as stacking parts into magazines and feeding machines which it is technically foreseeable will soon be rationalized, and the union wants to make sure that this will not automatically mean 'residual workers' tied to these jobs.

So far, among the big final producers only Audi seems to have committed itself fully to the group principle. But it can be expected that other companies will follow. At Opel, both labour and management are carefully watching the development of the production teams in the new engine plant in Aspern. At Ford, a new job category of group leader has been created and this may in the future serve as the nucleus for a formation of teams which would then also cover the final assembly area. Thus, in the German context companies and unions are pushing towards introducing the group principle as the basic unit of work organization.

The system of attitude control

Taken together the factors described above are often characterized in the discussion of Japan, on the one hand, as an expression of the 'wholistic concern for people' (Cool and Lengnick-Hall, 1985: 10), or, on the other hand, as a 'subtle compliance system' (ibid.: 14). This is also where criticism frequently starts. Worker participation and group autonomy in Japanese organizations do not signal a democratic organization. They are seemingly based on factors which are regarded as not transferable or not worth being transferred:

Pressures on the individual to conform to group norms and

goals, 'exam hell' for students and the attendant suicides, systematic discrimination against women, and the 'closed world' of the corporate employee who lives in a company house, vacations in a company resort, and usually associates only with other company employees. (Marsland and Beer, 1983: 66; see also Zussman, 1983)

Such means of regulating attitudes would hardly appear to be transferable. But since, as we have seen, peculiarities of the Japanese production system are sometimes simply copied in order to find out whether they will have the same effect in other conditions, it is by no means certain that some forms of 'repressive control' will not also be transferred as functional equivalents to the means of insuring worker loyalty and union co-operation if they cannot be achieved. In many ways, the labour-market conditions, the fear of losing one's job, have been such a functional equivalent thus far, that is in the first half of the 1980s.

Summary

The worldwide adoption of Japanese concepts in the early 1980s was not a fad. The spreading of structurally effective but investment-intensive measures for a transfer of Japanese production principles appears instead to be a growing trend for the early 1990s. What is probably involved, however, is the adaptation of concepts to the conditions of the guest country and company, particularly through pilot projects at selected plants and production locations. In Europe, Japanese concepts are in any case being adopted to a greater extent via the discussion engendered and the concepts developed in the USA – due partially to the interdependence of the European subsidiaries.

The question of the selection pattern of Western manufacturers was dealt with in terms of five central factors widely assumed to explain the Japanese success in productivity. A highly uneven selection pattern is to be seen, a pattern that also varies between the traditional manufacturing countries of North America and Europe as well as between the companies.

Of the five possible 'transfer rails', that of qualification based on on-the-job-training and rotation between jobs seems to be followed by General Motors especially in its team-based plants with pay-for-knowledge wage schemes. The vocational training system in the German context, though, seems to offer a functional alternative to the Japanese system as regards the supply of qualified labour.

The mobilization of problem-solving knowledge among the rank and file is a concept that was widely adopted as early as the beginning of the 1980s. Although it is fairly widespread, outside of Japan it still appears to be foreign to the industrial-relations setting. This applies to every country investigated, although institutional incorporation seems to have developed furthest in the US context.

In the field of technology and production organization the main principles of the Japanese production system (flexibility, zero errors, zero buffers) have been accepted by companies in the West and have triggered gradual processes of change there. Much of that is still in the conception and planning phase. There are still no evaluative reports on the experience gained with such concepts in Western companies.

The introduction of production teams and the decentralization of responsibilities and decisions regarding the allocation of, for example, work, represent a broad international trend in which the adoption of Japanese concepts fits. The mechanisms for assuring conformity and regulating attitudes seem to be too embodied in Japanese social structures and their conditional factors for their transfer to be systematically developed. The implications for individual and social relations are also frequently commented on critically by management. Indeed, the group principle would be put under too much stress if the groups were also to be formally entrusted with measures such as controlling absenteeism.

The scientific discussion about the Japanese model keeps centring on the question of whether Japanese productivity success is primarily due to compliance, that is the submissiveness of workers and the mechanisms for its creation, or whether it is based on consent – authentic approval and the willingness to perform resulting therefrom. The practical transfer process so far was directed more at consensus-oriented concepts under the influence of OD approaches. But this must not hide the fact that since the early 1980s, and due to the continuing, tremendous pressure of labour-market conditions and individual fear of job losses, a great amount of compliance has been generated.

11 Automation, new technology and work content

WILLIAM CAVESTRO

This chapter outlines the main results of work which I have carried out concerning the relationship between new technologies, the evolution of skills, and work content (Bernoux *et al.*, 1987; Cavestro, 1984a, 1984c, 1986a, 1988 a, b, c).[1] It deals, in particular, with the application of microelectronics to both continuous and discontinuous industrial processes, focusing on the qualitative changes which French firms are undergoing during the current period of automation.

It is based on the observations made during detailed field studies which included interviews with operators, technicians, programmers and managers. Starting from these studies, I shall try to demonstrate that, far from reducing work content, automation and computerization bring a new diversity of tasks as a result of a general transformation of working activities, skills and areas of competence. The deskilling thesis, developed by writers such as Braverman (1974), Freyssenet (1979), and Friedmann (1963), raises a number of questions. Can one accept the idea that the human factor can be integrated into machines? What happens to the experience and tacit skills which underlie everyday practice? I shall first of all examine the nature of work in continuous industrial processes (refining, cement and float-glass manufacture), in order to uncover the exact nature of human intervention and the way in which it operates within automated systems. Random problems and the control of breakdowns will play an important part in the analysis. The evolution of skills in discontinuous industrial processes will then be considered. A comparison of automated and non-automated mechanical engineering processes will be the starting-point for an exploration of the changes affecting work content. The principal aim of the chapter is to underline the importance of tacit skills and the intellectual aspects of work with reference to the introduction of new technologies.

Skill in continuous processes: random problems and breakdowns

The first section is devoted to the analysis of work content in continuous industrial processes (e.g. chemicals, cement-making) with reference to breakdowns and other unpredictable problems. In these automated sectors, skill clearly appears to be a question of dealing with breakdowns and information-handling systems. The difficulty of the work lies in the ability to obtain information concerning the state of the process, to make comparisons and to use the results to deal with incidents. The vision of the operator as a relatively passive agent would appear to be incompatible with what I have observed during my field investigations of work content.

Refining: skill and incident control

The introduction of automatic regulation and the centralization of data processing and control operations in the control room during the 1960s constituted the first stage of automation in refining. This stage was quite distinct from manual control, in which the operator sought information on a given parameter (such as temperature or pressure), compared it to the instruction and acted manually upon the parameter by opening or closing a valve. With automation, an automatic control mechanism which kept the variation of the parameter within fixed limits tended to separate the operator from the process of chemical reaction, and thus from direct regulation activities. Automatic regulation was marked at this stage by the centralization of information in the control room where the state of the chemical reactions was presented analogically by means of synoptic display panels (needle gauges). The second stage of automation was the introduction of microprocessors at the end of the 1970s. Synoptic display panels were replaced by video displays. Numerical information took the place of analogical displays.

In most control rooms in the 1980s the control and supervision of the plant is indirect. Contact with automated installations is maintained using video displays with external installation supervisors and workers operating on the spot. The control-room operators' key role has three dimensions – detection (of any abnormalities in the operation and state of the plant), stabilization (of the chemical reaction), and optimization. The first two functions are particularly important and are not limited simply to start-up situations.

In everyday practice, control-room operators distinguish between two types of operating conditions: 'quiet periods' and 'disturbed periods'. During the quiet periods the operator is continuously occupied with variations in the parameters of the control system (for example, pressure, temperature, gas and liquid flow rates) on the display screens. The actual values of the parameters are shown along with their set-points. A set-point is the limiting value of a parameter beyond which one passes into a disturbed period. In all the installations visited, the set-points were fixed by the operators themselves. In a disturbed period the incident is identified by an abnormal difference between the set-point and the true value which is shown for each parameter, or by warning lights. Problems crop up constantly and are far from exceptional. Table 11.1 summarizes the principal tasks of the operators in continuous industrial processes (in a number of cases including chemicals, cement-making, float-glass) and in discontinuous processes (mechanical engineering). The last two columns show the problems which are typical of each process and the diagnostic elements used by operators to identify problems.

In the case of refineries, for example, control-room operators often observe inaccuracies in the sensors which register the parameters' real values. A complex installation can have as many as 1,000 sensors. Whenever any one is faulty, the value of the parameter is altered and the control loop is no longer effective. If the loops are automatically controlled, a number of other adjustments are, in consequence, no longer accurate, in particular the opening and closing of valves. Automatic control can be too fast or too slow, in which case the operator has to revert to manual control.

The result of such incidents is to induce the operator to actively seek information. In order, for instance, to control a distillation column, the operator has to compare three types of information:

- a permanent knowledge of the lay-out of the installation, the process being used, normal operating temperatures, pressures and flow rates, and the reaction time of the system;
- occasional information concerning the state of the system at any given moment;
- immediate information concerning the progress of the chemical reaction and parameter values.

In the event of a problem, the operator makes a preliminary diagnosis on the basis of the information shown on the displays (see Table 11.1).

In addition, the operators often seek supplementary data from two sources. First, they may call up partial views of the regulatory system on the screen – in one installation which I visited, the operator had access to 960 partial views grouped in 16 numerical tables of flow rates, temperatures and pressures – which allow them to increase the precision of their preliminary diagnosis. Second, they may engage in intensive information exchanges between the workers supervising the plant and the foreman, either by telephone or radio. The preliminary and final diagnoses are collective tasks in which the installation supervisors and the control-room operators exchange information on the state of the installation and on the appropriate decisions to be taken.

Centralization of information in the control room and automatic control do not eliminate this interactive exchange between operators and installation supervisors, for the preliminary diagnosis which the

Table 11.1 Examples of human activity and control in work

1. Continuous industrial processes				
Type	Control system: automatic (A) or manual (M)	Operator activity	Problems/ breakdowns	Elements of preliminary diagnosis
Chemical industry refinery	A M	– supervising screens – collecting data – controlling valves, boilers, pumps, set-points	– sensor or transmission breakdown – deviation of parameters – leak in pump – valve jamming	– abnormal variation in parameters – rise in temperature of a column
Cement	A	– supervising alarms – foreseeing incidents – controlling parameters (flow of ammonia, etc.)	– granulation – percentage of lime – temperature of furnace	– poor granulometry
Bio-chemical industry	A M	– supervising temperature – controlling deviations and set-points	– pressure delivery too low – irregular temperature – contaminated culture – pH	– pH is too high – impurities in culture environment – cultures late
Float-glass	A	– supervising the appearance of the sheets of glass and of the smears that remain on them – controlling temperature and speed	– widening the sheet of glass – sheet sticking to the sides of the float – temperature too high, slow-down in speed	– thickness variation – presence of bubbles in the glass
Nuclear power station	A	– parameter control (boric acid, advance of uranium bars, temperatures, neutron flow, etc.) – specific action on each parameter – checking of results – consulting instruction manual	– variation in thermal power	– irregular temperature
Coal-fired power station	A	– control of delivery pressure, temperature of superheated steam – control of turbine speed variations, of coal and gas output, and of pipes and tubes	– deviation of parameters	– difference between parameter and set-point

2. Discontinuous industrial processes				
Type	Control system: automatic (A) or manual (M)	Operator activity	Problems/ breakdowns	Elements of preliminary diagnosis
Mechanical engineering: numerical control machine tools, FMS	A M	– feeding – unloading – repairing minor breakdowns and restarting – correcting parameters	– warped parts – broken tools – mechanical and electronic breakdowns	– abnormal parameter values – sparks, particular noises – poor surface quality
Sheet metal work NC folding machines NC punching machines	A M	– programming (NC folding machines) – feed-in – supervision of evacuation of parts – dimension control – unjamming sheet metal and restarting – programme correction	– jamming of sheet metal – faulty parts (warped, crushed, etc.) – faulty tools – crushing of parts between punch and die	– torn parts – marked parts, burrs – change in punching cycle
Welding robots	A	– supervision of installation on screen – welding quality control – change in welding parameters, or in direction of robot – action from control box – change in welding rods	– warped metal sheets – jammed parts – wrongly positioned parts – geometrical variation in parts – wear and tear of clamps	– poor quality welding – burrs – some welding incomplete
Transfer lines	A	– feed-in – changing and grinding of tools – transfer line control and supervision of the movement of parts – part and dimension control – diagnosis and repair of breakdowns	– broken tools – machine or circuit failure – overshot dimensions (diameter, surface, quality, etc.) – faulty circuit boards in control unit	– abnormal noises – small defects on parts – abnormal parameter values shown on panel

operator establishes within the work group is developed in a situation of partial uncertainty. Because of this, the ability to gather accurate and reliable information about the state of the system (taking account of inaccurate sensors, changes in the parameters, or faulty pumps) is an essential element of an operator's know-how.

The construction of a preliminary diagnosis thus plays an important role in the handling of disturbances and in the stabilization of chemical processes. The initial diagnosis leads to a more definitive one which allows the operator to monitor the automatic control or to interrupt it and switch over to manual operation.[2] In order to correct the breakdown, the operator develops a problem-solving strategy.[3]

As we have seen, the operator's intervention is part of a continuous sequence of information-gathering and selection, and of actions affecting the evolution of the chemical process up to the moment at which the incident is under control. The operator's reasoning is based on categories or types of incident. To take a particular example, the operator recognizes a loss of pressure in a column as belonging to a specific class of incident: pressure-drop in the gas or steam circuit, abnormal triggering of a column, boiler overheating. The different categories are established from experience. This method of categorizing incidents allows the operator to anticipate events from the moment that the first signs of a problem appear.

As one operator explained to us, as soon as a return pump between columns shows signs of failure,

> I am aware of the failure as a result of the increase in temperature in the first column. However, there is still no disturbance in the second column, but I know what is going to happen. I have to anticipate the problem and order the back-up pump to be put into operation. I then check the state of the parameters and their evolution with reference to the set points ... I have to be able to foresee this type of incident, otherwise the plant will be down for two days.

In reality the complexity of the job is due to the fact that every problem is different. In addition, each problem creates a link between the upstream and downstream control loops. The operator constantly has to analyse the situation in terms of the origin and evolution of the incident, and the products and of links with other circuits within the plant (water and chemical reactions, for example). During my investigations, the operators insisted on the fact that they worked from hypotheses in order to identify the causes of incidents and to deduce possible scenarios of where these might occur. The gathering and comparison of data allowed them to reduce the number of likely scenarios and to take action such as reducing the temperature, putting back-up circuits into operation or opening a by-pass or safety valve.

Experienced operators can identify scenarios and hypotheses much faster because they have a much larger repertoire of control procedures and solutions. This lets them integrate the data–gathering phase directly with that of diagnosis. The difficulty of fully describing these activities highlights the complexity of the work of control-room operators in automated refineries. The anticipation of incidents, the resolution of random problems, and breakdowns, are a central part of the operators' skills. The ability to respond successfully to such events requires the construction of complex mental images which allow their identification.

The control of breakdowns in continuous industrial processes

The conditions which prevail in continuous industrial processes, such as cement and glass manufacture or nuclear power, result in the operator constantly intervening in the process. Breakdowns are numerous, even within the automatic control systems themselves. As one recent French study has shown (Du Roy *et al.*, 1985) the start-up of automated plants is often long and fraught with difficulties. According to Berry (1985), automated plants are theoretically supposed to run at 90 per cent capacity in terms of their operating time. In reality, however, this figure is nearer to 50 per cent. More specifically, de Montmollin (1984) has shown that the theoretical operating conditions of automated equipment bear little relation to actual running conditions. In one continuous soap-making firm, he highlights the fact that the main automated machinery is equipped with a 'perfectly' designed computer. But the worker who is supposed to supervise this machinery has to physically intervene every 2 to 3 minutes to deal with problems in several parts of the equipment. It turns out that the machine stops more often than was planned, and that it is out of the question for management to have maintenance technicians permanently on tap. Thus, in this ultra–modern, technically sophisticated plant, workers are to be found crawling under a moving conveyor-belt in order to carry out adjustments as part of their normal workload. In France, such an example is not an extreme case. Machinery design is done by specialized services (engineering consultants and production engineers) which do not fully take account of the constraints encountered in the work situation. These services base their decisions on the reliability of the technique and on the incorporation of human factors into the automatic control systems. But as Berry (1985) has pointed out, the operators' work, reckoned to be straightforward and adaptable, is seldom analysed before the equipment is designed. Yet breakdowns are a normal part of the operators' everyday tasks.

In automated cement works the operators play a decisive role in following the process from the crushing of the lime to the cooling of the mixture after being burned in the ovens. The process is regulated from the control room by means of a synoptic display panel and a main control console. Television monitors or video displays show the state of the flame in the ovens and the appearance of the granules when cooked. But in some plants, the system is not sufficiently well designed to prevent upsets in the granulation process. The quality of the granulation depends on the limestone content which varies from one delivery to the next. Poor granulation creates disturbances both in the cooking and in the cooling processes. The operators' role is to anticipate such random changes by making a preliminary diagnosis of the granulation and by changing the cooking temperature and cooling rate (see Table 11.1). In order to do this, they over-ride the automatic control system and supervise the variations in the parameters 'manually'.

Similarly, in the biochemical industries numerous random problems occur as a result of the uncertainty and variability of biological processes. These processes are controlled by sensors, television monitors, video displays and computerized systems. But, because the sensors are not sufficiently sensitive, the control of such plants remains largely beyond the engineers and designers. In fermentation processes, the sensors can detect only some of the random incidents: temperature irregularities and contaminated cultures, for example (see Table 11.1). For this reason only the operators are capable of anticipating and handling such incidents. Their task is all the more complex because the fermentation processes are not synchronized from one vat to the next. Here too the elaboration of a preliminary diagnosis based on a survey of the parameters (pH and impurity levels), and of a firm diagnosis based on the comparison of different data sources is a central part of the process of anticipating and coping with these disturbances. The same active approach on the part of the operators is found in other automated continuous industrial processes (e.g. float-glass manufacture and coal-fired power stations). Table 11.1 shows the different types of incidents and the diagnostic elements used by operators.

According to research carried out by de Keyser (1987), Leplat and Cuny (1984), de Terssac and Coriat (1984) on human work in continuous automated systems, it has become increasingly necessary to take breakdowns and hitches into account when planning this type of work activity. Automation creates a new context in which the optimal use of technologies necessarily involves rapid human intervention. According to my own observations, automation does not restrict the operators' scope of action. On the contrary, the need for human intervention becomes virtually permanent. This involves a cognitive and iterative approach, moving repeatedly back and forward between data intake and action until the situation is brought back to normal. Also, with the introduction of automation, the operators work increasingly from a symbolic representation of the process, in coded language form. A symbolic system of data representation is set up between the operators and the automated installation. The operators must learn how to code and de-code the data which is part of their stock of knowledge. They are confronted by several types of information – visual, aural, symbolic – which accentuates the intellectual dimension of their work.

Automation and work content in discontinuous processes: the case of mechanical engineering

In this section I shall emphasize the principal changes in work content resulting from microelectronics applications in discontinuous industrial processes. In this type of process, the material is transformed in stages, with intermediate stocking between the machines (as, for example, in textiles, mechanical engineering, shoe-manufacturing and electronics). I shall concentrate on mechanical engineering (sheet-metal and machining). A great variety of forms of automation have developed in this sector – transfer lines and numerically controlled (NC) machine tools (NC lathes, machining centres, NC folding and punching machines, and welding robots). My survey of firms having introduced these technologies since the 1970s covered both large firms of over 500 employees and smaller firms of 200 to 500 employees. In all, thirty-two firms were covered by the survey. Two trends in work organization and skills will be stressed in relation to automation: the increased formalization of work activities and programming, and the treatment of breakdowns and utilization of tacit skills.

The increased formalization of work activities and programming

Here I will discuss the main aspects of the evolution of work organization and work content. In order to highlight the tendencies which have been observed, details will also be provided concerning work organization and work content on conventional non-automated machine tools. It will be seen that automation has involved the transformation of tasks and skills around programming.

CONVENTIONAL MACHINES: WORK ORGANIZATION AND WORK CONTENT

Even without the introduction of automated systems there is already a great diversity of forms of work organization. The relations between the production engineering department and the shop-floor, in particular, vary according to the size of the firm. In large French firms, production engineering takes place in a specific department which is responsible for the preparation of the parts to be manufactured, for production programming and for the routing of the different batches.

Production programming defines the mode of fabrication and the necessary machine, and decides which tools should be used. Within the production programme the different batches are routed between machines according to time constraints and the size and technical characteristics of each batch. In big firms the work of the production engineering department has long since been formalized, although there are substantial differences between sheet-metal work and machining. In sheet-metal work, job routing and production programming developed during the 1970s. The setting up of production engineering departments in machining had already become commonplace before the 1960s in large firms.

In small firms employing fewer than fifty workers, the production engineering function is less well-defined. In non-automated processes, it is not necessarily integrated in a particular department. In small- and medium-sized sheet-metal manufacturers, for example, work preparation is often minimal. The markers copy the outline of the part directly onto a metal sheet which is then used as a model by the operators who punch the sheet-metal blanks. The formalization of these processes is less important than in machining, since the operations involved are generally less complex.

Nevertheless, no matter what type of work organization has been adopted, with conventional technology the shop-floor organization (machine setters, markers and machine operators) does not necessarily conform to the details in the production engineers' recommendations. The shop-floor has some degree of potential autonomy in relation to the production engineer concerning its way of organizing the work. Lastly, conventional machine operators' skill depends on their intellectual competence, capacity to adapt, training and work experience. Manual dexterity remains the fundamental dimension of skill. This involves being able to change the speed or stop the machine, and to adjust the rhythm of gestures according to personal dexterity and competence. As Naville (1963) has pointed out, the work rhythm was imposed above all by the operators themselves and by the type of work organization. Similarly, the control over machining sequences was carried out by workers who could adapt their gestures and follow up directly on the movement of tools and parts.

DECOMPOSITION-RECOMPOSITION OF TASKS

Automation has completely transformed the relations between production engineering and the shop-floor. The production engineering function has become the key to the new work organization. Substantial changes are brought about by the introduction of NC machine-tools. Machining procedures, such as production programming, tooling, machining speed, are now formalized, and are also coded into the programme. At the same time, new relations between the various functions are established within the firm. In all cases the production engineering function becomes a specific department, even in small firms. The formalization of work is accentuated and the links between the shop-floor and the production engineers tightened, since the use of computers and programming compels them to use the same formal language. This constitutes a major break with conventional technologies.

The introduction of automated machinery has brought about a transformation of tasks, some of which disappear altogether. Some examples will help to illustrate this point. In sheet-metal work, marking is no longer necessary after the introduction of NC punching machines because of their high degree of precision and incorporated automatic tool-change. Similarly, shearing and finishing operations, again in sheet-metal work, are no longer necessary because NC machine tools are polyvalent. In the course of my survey of machining firms, I also noted the disappearance of machine-setting as a skill. On NC machine tools machining speeds and tool changes are controlled by the programme instructions, and they can be modified from one batch to another without manual intervention.

On the other hand, automation also gives rise to new types of worker competence. The most important new proficiency is in using and understanding computer languages. With NC machine-tools and robots the machine operator must constantly interpret data in the form of coded language. As in continuous industrial processes, the operator works from symbolic systems of representation of machining sequences. The coding and de-coding of information and instructions contained in the programme are complex intellectual activities which involve a substantial amount of memorizing, comparing and processing of data. Simply to read a programme involves all of these mental activities. Moreover, the successful handling of automated machining calls for a greater ability on the part of the operator: to anticipate problems unlike conventional machining, it is not possible to immediately rectify errors (such as badly placed parts and inaccurate dimensions). Manual dexterity is no longer essential. Skill becomes much more a matter of competence in programming tasks.

Programming tasks are of crucial importance in the transformation of work. They can be subdivided into two types: (1) programming in the strictest sense of the term; and (2) corrections and programme improvement (see Table 11.1). This distinction is helpful in determining levels of proficiency. Programming in the strict sense is still the most complex activity. In machining, it is either manual or automatic. In manual programming the programmers give all the instructions to be entered on the basis of a geometrical definition of the part. The programmers proceed through two phases: the breakdown of the part into elementary geometric elements (arc and straight line, for example) and the transcription of these elements into technical language. The programmers thus define the type of tool and its travel speed, the rotation speed of the cutting bar, the depth of the cut and the necessary tool changes. In automatic programming the programmers only specify the dimensions, and this partly eliminates the need to define the parts geometrically. In punching operations in sheet-metal work programming is done on a tool-by-tool basis. The programmers work in two dimensions using a standard sheet-metal blank. In most programming systems the programmers indicate the type and thickness of the metal and elaborate each programme on a tool-by-tool basis, indicating precisely the sequence of movements of the tool, its form and the punching speed. Programming calls for a knowledge of engineering drawing, trigonometry and metal resistance.

Who is in charge of the programming? We will distinguish between two situations, mechanical engineering and sheet-metal work. Of the twenty-three mechanical engineering firms in survey, it would appear that in 20 per cent of cases the programming is carried out by programmers who have had two years post-school training in mechanical engineering (the French technical diplomas BTS or DUT), or by former machine-setters who have secondary school technical training in mechanical engineering. Programming has, however, tended to move towards the shop-floor, particularly in small high-precision mechanical engineering and machining firms.

In this case the operators are skilled workers with a sound secondary school training in mechanical engineering. I have also observed that for simple machining operations workers who have had some training in programming are able to write the programme themselves when using NC machine tools with integrated computers (Computer Numerically Control tools – CNC).

In the sheet-metal industry I have observed two contradictory trends. In punching, the programming is carried out by skilled programmers who have had two years further education in mechanical engineering. On the other hand, in metal folding it is almost always carried out by skilled workers with experience on conventional folding presses (Cavestro, 1988a, b). These differences within the same firm are explained mainly by the role which the machine operators played within the conventional work organization. As one executive we interviewed pointed out:

> Folding is essentially an intellectual skill, since the workers have to manage their tools and have responsibility for the finished part. On the other hand, punching is more often repetitive work, unless the worker also has to mark the metal.

The observations which I have just outlined underline an overall tendency for machine operators in France to play only a secondary role in programming, as compared with the programmers, which is broadly consistent with Kelley's findings in the USA (see Chapter 12).

However, my survey nonetheless reveals the decisive part played by the operators in programme correction. This involves modifying the machining parameters – the length and form of the tool, travel and cutting speed, and the depth of the cut. This activity calls for a thorough knowledge of computer language, as well as the interface between this language and the identification of machining sequences. In practical terms, the worker who tests the programme must check, for each sequence, how the parameters behave as a whole and in combination with each other, the aim being to optimize machining conditions.

In 70 per cent of the machining firms which I have surveyed, these corrections are made by the machine operators, either by themselves or in collaboration with the workshop technicians or programmers. In sheet-metal work the situation is more diverse. The workers in charge of metal folding carry out their own programme corrections, whereas in punching operations the machine operators correct the programme in only 50 per cent of cases. There are many reasons for this. The size of the firm and the type of technology used are determining factors. It is undeniable, for example, that CNC can facilitate the transfer of programming and programme correction towards the shop-floor. On the other hand, when the technologies used are complex (e.g. FMS) there is less likelihood that the operators will have access to programming. Overall I have observed that the existing form of work organization and the traditions of the skilled workers play a decisive part in the allocation of programming tasks. Examples from metal folding and punching illustrate this. The traditions and competences of skilled metal folders have enabled this group to take over programming activities without much difficulty. On the other hand, in punching, where the skill level is lower, the operators have found it more difficult to do so.

Tacit skills and the handling of breakdowns

As in continuous industrial processes, automation brings to light a great variety of tasks related to the handling of breakdowns. Table 11.1 indicates the main types of incidents with which operators have to cope according to the type of automated technology being used. In many cases the machine operator must register, or even identify and resolve problems, in collaboration with the workshop technician, the programmer or the technician in charge of machine maintenance. There is nothing new in the notion of random problems. However, with the introduction of automated machinery the identificaiton of such problems becomes much more complex. This involves developing new abilities in diagnosing the causes of breakdowns, particularly in the electronic parts of machines (for example, command controls, control boxes and sensors). In my survey I observed that machine operators often carry out light maintenance work in small firms. They are in charge of changing the circuit boards, lubrication and fluid control, as well as grinding and repairing smaller tools. Worker competence is shifting towards two activities: maintenance and product quality control. Clearly the spread of quality circles in French industry in the mid–1980s confirms this trend towards the collective involvement of workers in the improvement and maintenance of machinery, and in product quality. Thus it appears that the so–called 'expression groups' (set up by the Auroux industrial legislation in 1984 under the socialist government), as well as quality and 'total quality' circles are being used to bring out hidden but effective know-how which the workers have accumulated through their work experience but which they are reluctant to reveal (Troussier, 1987).

Given the difficulties involved in mastering the new technologies, company management has encouraged these forms of worker involvement in technical and organizational change. Over the last two or three years, however, worker participation in quality circles has begun to wane because of workers' determination to keep a hold of their acquired know-how and competence. In this respect automation has given rise to a tendency to formalize some of the workers' implicit knowledge: for example, rules of metal strain, modes and speeds of machining operations. However, the idea of a straightforward transfer of workers' knowledge into the computer software is illusory. The term transfer implies a one way movement which our observations do not corroborate.

A few examples may illustrate this. In conventional sheet-metal work production engineers define the tools to be used (dies) depending on the theoretical tensile strength of the metal. Using a parameter chart and mathematical calculations they set the following parameters (folding strength and matrix width) according to the thickness of the metal sheets. However, on the shop-floor the workers in charge of folding operations do not necessarily follow in detail the instructions given by the production engineer, since they have a practical, intuitive knowledge of metal strain which they know to vary, for example, according to the quality and the outward appearance of the metal. In metal folding, automation does not mean the disappearance of skills. On the contrary, the workers in charge of folding remain in control of programming and programme correction. Their field of competence is simply enlarged to include the formalization of folding rules. Parameters are given in terms of numerical data. Automation does not eliminate the need for a good working knowledge of folding techniques, nor does it do away with the rules of metal folding or metal strain. As in Jones and Wood's observations (1984), I have observed the continuing use of the operators' tacit skills and the know-how of their trade in my study of machining firms. A skilled operator summed this up as follows:

Once the programme has been set up I do the correcting myself. The programmer cannot possibly integrate all the data. For example, with a given quality or type of metal I will have to modify the depth or the number of cuts. The cutting tools tend to become blunt and I therefore have to correct the length of the tool. Very often I also correct the tool path when I discover a quicker way of carrying out the same operation.

When using carbide tipped tools on NC machine tools machine operators also elaborate new and indispensable knowledge. As one worker pointed out:

I am the only one to have precise knowledge of the real cutting conditions, according to the metal to be used, the rotation speed of the cutter bar and the probable wear and tear of the tips. These three parameters must be optimized simultaneously. The quicker the tools rotate the quicker they become blunt. I therefore have to obtain an optimal combination of the parameters depending on the metal I am machining. This type of adjustment is impossible the first time round. You have to see the machine in action. The programmer cannot integrate all these data when he's writing his programme. That's why I correct the programmes. This helps to avoid breakdowns, broken tools, inaccurate cuts, etc.

These examples show that experience and practical knowledge play a determining part in the handling of automated technologies. The tacit knowledge stored up in the work place makes it possible to clear up many incidents and to correct errors in the programmes and in the running of automated machinery This is now recognized to a greater or lesser extent by company managements and is taken into account in a variety of ways from one firm to another, or within the same firm among the various professional groups (production engineers, programmers, workshop technicians, folders, punchers and NC machine operators).

Conclusions

In the automation of industrial processes we can see several characteristic trends emerging in work content and job skills. The first trend is that of a growing complexity and variety of technologies. Workers have to cope with information systems which are increasingly difficult to master. Faced with this, the demarcation of older forms of work organization tends to be fragmented so as to improve the operation of automatic installations. In mechanical engineering shop–floor operators and production engineers are brought closer together. In France, a break with classic Taylorist forms of organization can be observed. The most obvious symptom of this break is the emergence of new working groups which involve both programmers and operators in work preparation and in programming.

The second trend is the lasting, unresolved contradiction between the increased formalization of work and the existence of breakdowns, unforeseen incidents and errors. Automation introduces formal work preparation procedures using algorithms. Programming is a typical example of the use of algorithms. But the formal procedures alone do not ensure the successful operation of automatic control systems. Various unpredictable problems do crop up, the handling of which becomes part of the workers' exercise of skills. Work content is shifted more towards the anticipation and handling of the various incidents which constantly occur.

The work is increasingly characterized by data gathering, and the construction of hypotheses and strategies leading to the resolution of malfunctions. At the same time, the level of abstraction of the tasks tends to increase due to the fact that with automation the operator works with information in symbolic form. Codes and computer languages constitute the basis of her/his intervention. The worker–machine dialogue takes place in a coded language. Within such a framework, incidents and malfunctions thus play an important part in the learning process and in the successful handling of technologies. In order to deal with such incidents, the operator often resorts to heuristic procedures of trial and error, hypothesis-forming and problem-solving.

Deskilling theories tend to overlook the emergence of new skills. In addition, the notion of a simple transfer of workers' know-how to programmes does not appear to be validated. Automation in part formalizes operators' practical knowledge. But it also creates other forms of knowledge, notably in programming, tooling, the operation of machines, breakdowns, maintenance and quality. Work content largely depends on work organization which can facilitate or inhibit such a widening of know-how. But it also appears that operators' practical knowledge is not simply digested by programmes. Programmes are themselves reappropriated by the operators. In other words, automation produces a symbiosis between the formal, programming, computer languages and the informal tacit skills rooted in experience.

12 Alternative forms of work organization under programmable automation

MARYELLEN R. KELLEY

Introduction

Programmable automation (PA) – the use of computers to direct and control the operation of machines – is a new technology aimed at batch manufacturing processes that have proved difficult to automate in the past. There is a widespread view in the United States and elsewhere that the microprocessor applications of PA, particularly computerized numerically controlled (CNC) machine tools and flexible manufacturing systems (FMS), will play a key role in restoring US competitiveness in world markets.

Yet considerable disagreement exists about what that technology portends for the social organization of work. To 'post-Taylorist' theorists such as Hirschhorn (1984) and Piore and Sabel (1984), PA provides the greater flexibility needed by small-batch, niche-seeking small firms to respond to the growing instability and unpredictability of product markets. To exploit PA's capabilities as a 'flexible' form of automation, these scholars argue, a radical devolution of existing bureaucratic structures and a concomitant rise in collaborative, skill-enhancing forms of work organization seem necessary. This contrasts with the deskilling thesis (hereafter referred to as labour-process theory), promulgated by Braverman (1974) and supported by Noble (1979) and Shaiken et al. (1986). Labour-process theorists see PA technology as a management tool for enhancing its control over production and reducing its dependence on the skills of workers directly engaged in production activities.

Implicit in both these theories is a model of PA adoption in which management is compelled for technical and economic reasons alone to use the technology in a particular way. Were PA mainly a tool of management for wresting greater control over the machining process from blue-collar workers, as Shaiken et al. (1986) argue, we would expect to find the assignment of programming duties to machining occupations to be very rare. On the other hand, were PA technology to be applied mainly to small-batch production in generally small establishments (i.e. work places), as Piore and Sabel (1984) suggest, we would expect to observe a dominant pattern of decentralized control over programming in which such tasks are exclusively the responsibility of those who are directly involved in the set-up and operation of PA machines.

Until quite recently, research on this question consisted of establishment case studies showing how computer-controlled machines permit management to exert greater control, or how decentralized operator-programming permits management to exploit the technology's advantages as a flexible form of automation. The lack of consistent methodological approaches made comparisons across studies difficult. A recent re-examination of the available data from my own and others' case-study research (Kelley, 1986) concluded that neither theory fits the empirical evidence very well. Indeed, that cross-study comparison suggested there were three discernible management approaches to the deployment of blue-collar workers with PA technology, reflecting different trade-offs between centralization of control and flexibility. These alternatives were characterized broadly as representative of a *scientific management*, a *technocentric-participative*, or a *worker-centred participative* approach. In this chapter, that typology is refined to focus on the organization of programming tasks with PA technology. New findings are presented from a comprehensive national survey of US manufacturing plants on the prevalence of alternative forms of work organization. These new data enable me to consider how much specific organizational characteristics and technical attributes of the machining process at plant level influence management's predilection to organize programming work according to each of these three modes.

The data were collected from a stratified random sample (stratified by size of plant) of US manufacturing establishments in 1986-7 as part of a larger study undertaken by myself and Professor Harvey Brooks of Harvard University on the patterns of diffusion of programmable automation technologies throughout American manufacturing industry (Kelley and Brooks, 1988).[1] Our sample was designed to include a representative cross-section of US manufacturing plants from the smallest (fewer than twenty employees) to the largest (more than 250 employees) in twenty-one different industries at the three-digit standard industrial classification level. Production managers in 1,015 plants completed our mail survey, for an effective response rate of 50 per cent.

Forty-three per cent of the 1,015 plants responding to our survey were found to have adopted PA technologies in some form. Among PA-using plants, 86 per cent reported using the new microprocessor form of the technology with more than half of these tools having been adopted in the past five years. ('Micro–PA' machines include stand-alone CNC machine tools and their more complex variant, the FMS, in which groups of CNC machines are co-ordinated and controlled by a central computer.) With such tools, it becomes technically feasible to write programmes at the machine, thus removing the logistical impediments to operator programming that Kelley (1986) and Jones (1982) found to be associated with the pre-microprocessor form of PA: the numerical controlled machine tool. The analysis of the social organization of programming tasks presented in this paper is confined to that subsample of PA-using plants which have adopted micro–PA.

Alternative forms of organization for programming tasks

On 'conventional', that is continuously human–controlled machine tools in batch manufacturing, a machine operator's responsibilities may include planning the sequence of actions to be taken, laying out the work piece, setting up the machine, selecting the appropriate cutting tools, positioning the tool in relation to the work piece, and controlling the cutting action of the tool and its (or the work piece's) movement. Of course, not all operators of conventional machines have such planning and set-up responsibilities. Moreover, in an analysis of the skill differences among conventional machining occupations, I found that control over set-up and planning is usually limited to one type of machining operation, for example, grinding or milling operations (Kelley, 1984).

With programmable machines, instead of the operator continually controlling the metal–cutting actions of the machine by adjusting hand levers, a set of instructions or a programme, written and recorded on tape (or some other electronic medium), directs the machine to execute automatically a sequence of cutting operations. Control over programming permits machine operators to exercise discretion in varying the pace of work through control over the speed and feed rate settings of the machine. Were programming solely an engineering or management function, or the exclusive province of a new white-collar speciality, then control over these aspects of the work process would become more centralized, shifting the locus of control from the blue-collar to the white-collar occupational domain. I call that approach 'strict Taylorist'. It is consistent with what labour process theory would predict to be the dominant managerial approach to the organization of work under micro–PA technology.

In contrast to the strict Taylorist approach, programming functions could be delegated exclusively to blue-collar jobs. This approach I term 'worker-centred control'. It implies a decentralization of control over programming. If programming responsibilities were widely distributed among workers in blue-collar occupations, it would also imply a flattening of the occupational hierarchy. Post-industrial theory suggests that worker-centred control should be the dominant pattern for the small batch operations typical of the machining process.

The third approach, what I call 'shared control', occurs when responsibility for programming is not limited to only the white-collar or only the blue-collar domain of work. Rather, control over programming is shared among a combination of white-collar and blue-collar occupational groups. Under shared control, programming tasks are at least occasionally performed by workers in blue-collar occupations even though there is a professional programming specialist, a manager or an engineer, who also has responsibility for writing programmes. This form of the distribution of control over programming most closely matches the technocentric-participative approach, in which management relies on workers in blue-collar occupations for programming whilst retaining a formal chain of command and responsibility for the programming function within the managerial and professional ranks. This more contingent approach to the distribution of control is a strategy by which management hedges its bets—attempting to gain some flexibility through decentralization of programming while maintaining traditional authority relations between white-collar and blue-collar work roles. We would expect to find shared control in establishments where there is neither a strong pull towards centralization (as would tend to be true of large organizations) nor particular technical conditions favouring complete decentralization (as would be the case for small-batch, small-scale production operations).

Prevailing patterns

As Table 12.1 indicates, neither strict Taylorist nor worker-centred control dominates the application of micro-PA technology in US manufacturing. The modal pattern of organizing programming tasks in the machining process is shared control. Nearly 45 per cent of the plants in the twenty-one industries studied can be characterized in this way. Moreover, more workers in machining occupations (42.6 per cent) are employed in plants where control over programming is shared than in plants where control is exclusively confined either to the blue-collar domain (worker-centered) or to white-collar occupations (strict Taylorist).

PA is clearly not used mainly to enhance managerial control at the expense of workers in machining occupations. As a share of all work places, strict Taylorist control is the least common form of work organization. In only one-fourth of plants using micro-PA are blue-collar workers found to have no responsibility for programming. Nor does the adoption of micro-PA, by itself, imply a dramatic shift towards a new worker-centered form of organization in which control over the technology is highly decentralized. Plants characterized by worker-centred control comprise just 31 per cent of micro-PA-using plants.

In terms of employment, worker-centred control is the least common form of organization encountered by the machining work force. Only 18.6 per cent of all machining workers and only 13.1 per cent of all those who operate PA machines are employed in work places characterized by worker-centred control over programming. A larger share of total production employment takes place in plants with strict Taylorist control over programming than for any other type. But when we consider the share of employment in machining occupations, or more narrowly only in PA-using occupations, we find that shared control edges out strict Taylorism as the most common form of organization.

Table 12.1 Distribution of establishments and employment by type of work organization, in plants using micro-PA technology[a]

	Plants (%)	Total employment (%)	Machining employment: any technology (%)	PA machining employment (%)
Strict Taylorist[b]	24.0	47.1	38.8	42.5
Shared control[c]	44.8	41.1	42.6	44.4
Worker-centred[d]	31.2	11.8	18.6	13.1
Total	100.0	100.0	100.0	100.0

(a) Micro-PA refers to microprocessor applications of programmable machine technology, i.e., CNC or FMS installations, excluding those cases where only NC technology was reported in use. Data on all variables shown in this table were available for 477 Micro-PA using plants (representing 95 per cent of the respondents reporting some Micro-PA use).

(b) In a plant with a strict Taylorist form of work organization, program-writing is a task performed exclusively in white-collar occupations, i.e. a manager, engineer, or professional programmer (22%), or not at all (2%).

(c) In a plant with Shared Control, programming is not exclusively performed in white-collar occupations but is a task that is at least occasionally performed by workers in blue-collar occupations as well.

(d) In a plant characterized by Worker-Centred Control, programming is exclusively a task of blue-collar occupations.

Note: These estimates from a survey of machine tool-using plants, stratified by size and randomly selected, in 21 industries in 1986–7 are weighted to reflect true population proportions (Kelley and Brooks, 1988).

In sum, when both shared control and worker-centred control are considered, we find that for 76 per cent of the US plants in which the new microprocessor form of PA technology has been adopted, workers who set up and operate programmable machines have at least some responsibility for writing parts programmes. Moreover, more than half of total production employment in the industries studied occurs in such work places. Thus, contrary to Noble (1977) and Shaiken, *et al.* (1986), our data indicate that the prevailing pattern of work organization associated with the adoption of micro-PA technology in US industries is operator programming.

If few PA-machine operators were actually permitted to write parts programmes and only did so on occasion, we might conclude that operator-programming involves only a modest supplement to the skill repertoire of machining occupations and exacerbates the differences between high- and low-skill production jobs (skill polarization). But if the creation of new programmes is an established job responsibility for most workers, then we would conclude that operator programming implies a substantial change in the skill requirements of machining occupations. How widely such regularized programming responsibilities are distributed among the machining workforce at a plant depends on whether control over programming is jointly held with white-collar occupations, or is exclusively a responsibility of blue-collar jobs. In plants exhibiting the latter form of organization, i.e. worker-centred control, 62 per cent of all PA machine operators were, on average, found to regularly write programmes for these machines as well. By contrast, under shared control, an average of 40 per cent of the PA-using machining workforce at the plant performed programming tasks as a normal, everyday practice. Hence, when management depends solely on its blue-collar workforce to perform programming tasks, the skill demands for most machining occupations at the plant are enlarged, which is indicative of a flattening of the occupational hierarchy, not skill polarization.

Factors influencing the organization of work

Similar to what Jones (1988) observes with flexible manufacturing systems in the UK, our survey results indicate that it is neither the technology as such nor the demand for greater flexibility alone that shape the division of labour in the machining process within the United States. Rather, the distribution of programming responsibilities among various work roles is mediated by the specific technical and organizational conditions of production in which micro-PA is introduced. At any given plant, the resulting arrangement of work roles with some programming responsibilities reflects a constrained choice by management that is in part determined by organizational size and unionization as well as by the technical requirements of volume and product variety.

For each alternative, Table 12.2 displays the characteristics of plants exhibiting that form of work organization. When no one in a blue-collar occupation does any programming (strict Taylorist), the plants are likely to be large and unionized. Where programming is a shared responsibility of blue-collar and white-collar occupations (shared control), plants are moderately large in size and mostly non-union. Plants in which programming is solely a task of blue-collar occupations (worker-centred control) seem to be the smallest in size and least likely to be unionized.

Table 12.2 Selected characteristics of plants, using micro-PA technology by form of work organization[a]

	Strict Taylorist	Shared control	Worker centred control
No. of employees (mean)	260	121	50
Unionized plants (%)	42.3	10.7	4.9
Small-batch producers[b] (%)	53.2	49.4	70.2
High technical flexibility requirements (%)[c]	31.3	27.3	43.1

(a) Micro-PA refers to microprocessor applications of programmable machine technology, i.e. CNC or FMS installations, excluding those cases where only NC technology was reported in use. Data on all variables shown in this table were available for 477 micro-PA-using plants (representing 95 per cent of the respondents reporting some micro-PA use).

(b) A small-batch producer is defined as a plant with 50 per cent or more of its total machining output in batch sizes of fewer than 50 units per lot.

(c) A plant with high technical flexibility requirements for its machining operations is defined as having a median batch size of fewer than 10 units and producing more than 50 different parts.

Note: These estimates from a survey of machine tool-using plants, stratified by size and randomly selected, in 21 industries in 1986–7 are weighted to reflect true population proportions (Kelley and Brooks, 1988).

Seventy per cent of the plants exhibiting worker-centred control were found to specialize in small batch production (with median batch size of fewer than 50 units per lot). While this is indeed a considerably higher incidence of small batch production than we found for the other types of plants, note that small batch size is typical of the machining process in general. More than half of the plants with a strict Taylorist form of work organization also specialize in small batch production, as do half of those characterized by the shared control approach. Truly mass production is the exception, not the rule, in machine tool-using industries.

To evaluate the likelihood of each of these alternative outcomes under different technical and organizational conditions, I estimated separate multivariate logistic regression models and used the results to simulate the independent influence of plant size, unionization, and typical batch size on the choice of one type of work organization (for example, strict Taylorist) against both other alternatives (for example, shared control and worker-centred control).

Bureaucratic control and plant size

Table 12.2 presents evidence that plants which have adopted micro-PA differ greatly in size. In large plants, we would expect to find a more detailed division of labour and a tendency of management to rely on bureaucratic means of control – that is, on formalized rules detailing job responsibilities and methods of work. Moreover, since direct managerial control of production is problematic in large-scale operations, we would expect to find a greater reliance on technical systems of control and a tendency to centralize decisions concerning how micro-PA technology is used. This, in turn, implies that in large plants machine operators are not likely to be assigned any responsibility for programming. Our findings support Edwards' (1979) perception that large bureaucratic organizations have a tendency to rely on a high degree of differentiation among work roles. Large plants are much more likely to exhibit a strict Taylorist form of organization. Holding other variables (that is, the rate of unionization and the share of plants specializing in small-batch production) at their sample means, I estimate the chances that programming will be exclusively a white-collar job responsibility at better than 1.5:1 for plants with 1,000 or more employees.

Just as large-scale operations tend to have a highly differentiated form of work organization, small-scale facilities are much less likely to completely isolate programming from operating work roles. For small plants of fewer than fifty employees, the chances are less than 1:3 that the programming of PA machines will be assigned to jobs other than machine operation.

Industrial relations considerations

A simplistic interpretation of labour process theory would lead one to predict that in unionized work places, blue-collar workers would have the best chance of at least attaining shared control over programming. Were unions effective at resisting management efforts to diminish the power that workers derive from their skills, we would expect the presence of a union to increase the chances that PA machine operators would have some programming responsibilities. But the impact of unionization on the distribution of control over programming cannot be understood merely as a reflection of organized worker resistance to management control. The industrial relations system, management's power to circumvent union pressure, and the so-called 'job control' approach that US industrial unions have taken in collective bargaining over technological change need to be considered in explaining how we might expect unionization to matter (Kelley, 1989).

Kochan et al. (1986) argue that over the past twenty years – a longer period than the life of micro-PA technology – US managers have taken an increasingly aggressive posture towards unions with the objective of restricting their growth and limiting their power. Braverman's analysis might have been more complete and plausible for US manufacturing had he noticed and explained that in unionized work places, a strict Taylorist approach to the organization of programming work can be as much an industrial relations tactic, aimed at weakening the bargaining power of a unionized workforce and freeing management from the restrictive practices of the collective bargaining agreement, as a means of lessening the skill and work role status of individual workers. Assigning programming to a white-collar occupation increases managerial discretion by removing job control issues from the collective bargaining arena – for example, who gets to perform programming tasks and how those asks should be executed.

Within a US manufacturing plant, the extent of unionization is always incomplete. Plant management and most (if not all) of those employed in white-collar technical and clerical occupations are usually not covered by the terms of a collective bargaining agreement. In a unionized work place, we would expect there to be a sharper demarcation between white-collar and blue-collar work roles in order to keep the distinction between unionized and non-unionized occupational groups clear. The union has as much interest as management in maintaining that boundary, since it delimits the union's legal representation responsibilities. With respect to programming, that separation could be achieved by either worker-centred control or a strict Taylorist approach. The latter would reserve programming responsibilities to the white-collar occupational domain and the former would imply a complete delegation of programming responsibilities to blue-collar workers. The worker-centred alternative might enhance (but certainly not diminish) the control that unionized workers as a group exercise in production – an outcome that would not be desirable or consistent with the long-run objective of management to diminish the power and influence of in the work place unions. Thus, at least in the United States, managers of unionized plants can be expected to try to impose a strict Taylorist form of work organization. Whether or not they can be expected to succeed depends on the union's approach to bargaining.

The job control system of bargaining characteristic of US industrial unions seeks to preserve control over skill through contract compliance. One consequence of a clear specification of the rights and obligations of employers and unions in a legally binding contract is that, for historical reasons, there is little room for unions to effectively challenge management's attempt to impose a strict Taylorist separation of programming from work roles involving machine set-up and operation. Only when contract language can be interpreted to mean providing protection against the removal of a bargaining unit's work do unions have a legal basis for challenging management's right to exclude programming from blue-collar work roles. A one-time acceptance of the separation of programming from protected unionized job classifications may undermine any later claim by the union that such tasks customarily belong within the traditional domain of blue-collar work. The usual collective bargaining mechanism may, therefore, be too weak, relying as it does on customary practices, to counter management's power to reorganize work roles when a new technology is introduced.

Our analysis indicates that a strict Taylorist form of the distribution of control over programming is quite typical of large, unionized plants. For example, in a unionized plant with 1,000 employees, the odds of a strict Taylorist approach are more than 4.1:1. Even in moderately large, unionized plants of 250 employees, the chances are better than 2:1 that programming will be designated as the exclusive responsibility of white-collar occupations. In non-union plants of the same size, by contrast, the chances of a strict Taylorist form of control are practically reversed, only 1:1.6.

When we consider management's desire to avoid the restrictions and pressure to bargain over new wages and work rules that would apply were programming to come under the terms of a collective bargaining agreement, together with the tendency towards specialization associated with large bureaucratic organizations generally, it is not surprising that we find the chances of worker-centred control to be the smallest in large, unionized plants. In unionized plants with 1,000 or more workers, the odds that control over programming will be exclusively worker-centred are very small: more than 29:1 against. Moreover, when there is a union, the chances of blue-collar workers having even limited, shared control over programming are significantly lower than for workers in non-union plants. Holding other variables constant at their sample means, when there is a union the chances of shared control are less than 1:2.3. By contrast, without a union, the chances are that blue-collar workers will share responsibility for programming with white-collar workers are nearly 50:50 for our hypothetically average plant.

Technical requirements for flexibility: low volume and high product variety

Until the development of programmable machines, automation of the fixed-cycle type had hardly penetrated the machining process where products are usually made in small batches, that is, fewer than fifty units at a time. Because of the capability to re-instruct the machine rather than having to completely replace it, PA is a more flexible alternative to fixed-cycle automation, capable of producing a wide array of different parts in small volume. Likewise, continuously human-controlled conventional machines (such as a general purpose lathe) are a more flexible alternative to fixed-cycle machines. Compared to operator-controlled machines, however, the major technical advantage of PA seems to be cheaper and faster set-ups and re-tooling, that is, a gain in efficiency when many different small-batch runs are to be carried out with the same equipment.

The 'flexible specialization' thesis of Piore and Sabel (1984) suggests that management can only fully exploit the technology's flexibility and greater efficiencies for small-batch production provided that the workers who perform other machining functions also write the programmes. Our survey results provide limited support for this thesis. Holding plant size and the rate of unionization constant at their sample means, we find that the chances of worker–centred control nearly double when machining output at a plant is disproportionately small batch, going from 1:4 to 1:1.8. The only scenario where the chances of worker–centred control can be considered even moderately strong is the case of the very small–scale operation (i.e., with only ten employees) specializing in small batch production. The chances are at best 50:50, but only among non–union plants of this type.

Although the scale of production operations is not important in distinguishing shared control from the other two alternative forms of work organization, the volume of production runs is quite important in an unexpected way. Specialization in small batch production actually reduces the chances of shared control to less than 1:1.6. When machining output is disproportionately large batch (that is, more than half of the output is in batch sizes larger than fifty units), the chances that management will adopt a shared control approach are better than 50:50, perhaps indicating that when control over programming is shared, PA is used to achieve greater standardization and consistency of production flows.

A more restrictive definition of Piore/Sabel-type (1984) flexible production would be the combination of specialization in very small batch production (a median batch size of less than ten units) and a large array of product types (more than fifty different parts or products). Plants with such a high degree of technical flexibility in both batch size and product variety have about the same chances (1:1.6) of having programming characterized by worker–centred control or by shared control. In other words, even in the most technically flexible production operations, there is only a small chance that the distribution of control over programming will be organized in a manner consistent with the flexible specialization thesis of Piore and Sabel (1984). Once again we see evidence that organizational structure and technological capability are independent dimensions.

For further evidence of this, consider that neither specializing in small-batch production nor producing a large number of parts in small volume has any influence on the likelihood of a plant exhibiting a strict Taylorist form of organizing programming work. In other words, we find no evidence that production in large volume or relative inflexible technical requirements for the machining process is related to a strict Taylorist division of labour. A Taylorist approach to the distribution of control over programming is determined mainly by organizational, rather than technical, factors.

Conclusions

Across a broad spectrum of US industries, the modal approach to the organization of work under the latest microprocessor application of programmable automation is the compromise solution of shared control, in which responsibility for programming PA machines straddles the white-collar and blue-collar domains of work. Neither the strict Taylorist form predicted by labour-process theory nor a completely worker-centred approach as anticipated by post-industrial theory dominates industrial practices.

For US manufacturing, our analysis clearly demonstrates that the flexible specialization thesis of Piore and Sabel (1984) holds true (at least through the spring of 1987, when our survey was completed) for only a certain class of work place. Indeed, compared to organizational size and unionization, the influence of technical flexibility or of small batch production on the resulting division of labour is small. For the very small non-union plant specializing in small batch production, there is an even chance of worker-centred control over programming. There is no evidence supporting the obverse of the flexible-specialization thesis – that large batch, more standardized production is associated with a strict Taylorist form of work organization. Instead, our results show that Taylorism is largely a product of bureaucracy – associated with large-size plants – and constitutes a reaction by management against the elaborate 'web of rules' codified in collective bargaining agreements (Dunlop, 1958). Faced with a union, US management is more likely to adopt a Taylorist approach to work organization and less likely to choose a worker-centred control approach, even if the technical conditions favouring the latter are present. Labour process theory provides no explanation for the sharp differences we find between union and non-union work places.

The controversy over whether programmable automation implies a loss of blue-collar worker control over production (as happens with a strict Taylorist approach to the organization of programming tasks) or leads to enhanced control over production (as seems to occur with worker-centred control) has been mistakenly cast as a debate over an underlying technological imperative allegedly driving management's approach to the organization of work. The analysis of US industry practices presented here suggests that there is no technological imperative shaping the division of labour but rather a combination of organizational, institutional and technical factors which act as a set of restraining influences inhibiting (or promoting) the degree of centralization or decentralization of control over programming responsibilities.

13 Computer rationalization and the transformation of work: lessons from the insurance industry

EILEEN APPELBAUM and
PETER ALBIN

Introduction

The diffusion of computerized control, communication, and information technologies is transforming the production of services as well
as goods. Market forces play a role in mediating this transformation;
but relative changes in the prices of capital and labour are not sufficient
guides to action in the face of rapidly changing technology, and
outcomes are not uniquely and efficiently dictated by an impersonal
market mechanism. Instead, as was true of earlier waves of technological change and market extension, this latest transformation occurs
within the bounds and restrictions of an industrial culture oriented to
past techniques. The flexibility of computer-based production processes and their associated systems' architectures, however, means that
managerial choice in developing production systems and designing
jobs is increased. The development and diffusion of computer
technology and solid-state circuitry advanced the technology for
processing information and controlling machinery far beyond what
could be accomplished by earlier electromechanical devices. In addition, computerized-control technology alters the balance of work tasks
and decision-making between people and machines, increasing the
scope managers have to redesign jobs so that the skill content of work is
increased or decreased. As a result, organizations face a wide range of
choices in implementing automated production systems based on
computerized-control technology; that is, in implementing computer
rationalized production. More so than with past innovations, the
pattern of productivity and skill characteristics is shaped by managerial
discretion in choosing among alternatives.

Organizational change, however, occurs slowly. In the USA, rules
of thumb based on older, Taylorist principles of fragmenting tasks,
routinizing jobs and maintaining tight managerial control of produc-

tion and decision-making survive as managerial strategies. Such rules may have yielded satisfactory productivity gains in the context of assembly-line technologies, but applying them to the computer rationalization of production can prove short-sighted. Computer and information technologies, after all, are also well suited to the integration of tasks and the decentralization of control and decision-making. Alternative approaches to job design and work organization which make better use of these attributes, while not widely employed in the USA, can already be identified. In many applications it is reasonable to assume, as Piore and Sabel (1984) do, that such alternative patterns of technical development will be associated with high requirements for skilled workers and sustained productivity growth as well as with the ability to produce better quality, more diversified, or higher value-added goods and services. It is less clear that managers, following past practice in implementing technological change, will choose these alternatives.

The institutional framework of the USA provides managers with few incentives to incur either the higher initial costs or the risks associated with investment in the training of workers and with innovations in management and work organization designed to utilize new worker skills. Unlike Japan, where job tenure and consensual decision-making are norms in primary industry, or Germany, where strong trade unions and the legal protections afforded workers by codetermination provide managers with economic incentives to make productive use of a skilled labour force, US managers face few external constraints. Conventional wisdom regarding work organization and job design persists, even in the face of disappointing productivity gains.

These may, by now, be familiar themes in the debate over technology and worker skills. They have, however, been framed largely in terms of the auto, steel, chemical and machine tool industries where production workers are overwhelmingly male. This chapter extends the discussion to the service-sector workforce where a majority of workers are women. In examining the computer rationalization of production in the insurance industry, we draw on a case study of computerization and the redesign of work in the US insurance industry (Appelbaum, 1984 and 1988), and on methodology developed for job content analysis (Albin, 1985). We shall focus on what we view as the key domain of technological change in knowledge-based service industries (see US Congress, Office of Technology Assessment, 1987: 35-7, for the distinction between knowledge-based and traditional service industries).

Job design in the insurance industry

In contrast to other 'office' industries such as government or law, where office automation technologies have mainly affected support activities like word processing and document control, in the insurance industry computer and information technologies are automating the core production activities. Although the extent of automation varies by product line, the use of computers to carry out underwriting and rating procedures, to issue policies and attachments, and to process claims is increasing in all segments of the industry. In this respect, it has been suggested more meaningful parallels can be drawn between automation in insurance and automation in manufacturing than between insurance and other service industries (Baran, 1987).

Another useful parallel can be drawn between insurance and manufacturing. The production process in the insurance industry was rationalized decades before the introduction of computer and information technologies. Taylorist principles of work organization were well-entrenched in this industry (De Kadt, 1979). At every level, jobs were fragmented and functionally specialized with simpler functions performed by less skilled workers. Paper was routed around the insurance office floor as surely as if it were on an assembly line.

Mail handling provided the most obvious examples of routine and monotonous jobs, but all forms of clerical work had been fragmented and rationalized to a large extent. After the underwriting and rating functions were completed, it was not unusual for an insurance policy to pass through the hands of five clerical workers before being issued (Appelbaum, 1984). For the claims department to issue a cheque also required five clerical workers – one to type it, a second to verify it, a third to audit it to insure the charges were appropriate, a fourth to take apart the carbons, and a fifth to put the cheque through the signing machine (Baran, 1987). Including supervisory personnel, it took six or seven different people to carry out the routine clerical aspects of underwriting or claims activities.

As was noted in Chapter 1, the service sector has been neglected in the literature on flexible specialization. Piore (1984) briefly mentions it in an unpublished paper. He, however, seems more uncertain where to place the insurance industry, including it at one point among mass-production industries (ibid.: 6) and speculating later that 'the bimodal job structure associated with computers in the insurance industry ... probably reflects the re-emergence of craft structures' (ibid.: 8).

As this chapter attempts to make clear, firms in the insurance industry face a broader range of choices than is suggested by any dichotomy such as craft and flexible resources versus mass production and narrowly specialized resources. Nearly identical computer hardware is utilized by the firms described in this study; yet very different skill and occupational structures emerge. While product market characteristics play an important role, job structures associated with computer rationalization do not, as Piore (1984) suggests, depend primarily on the product markets in which they are introduced.

Instead, we find that some firms using computer rationalization eliminate semi-skilled clerical work and push conceptual skills and decision-making responsibility down the ocupational hierarchy while producing standardized products and retaining the mass-production mode. Other firms have used the computer to facilitate the writing of specialized policies, which in some ways resembles craft production, but they have simultaneously combined this with computer monitoring of work time and decision-making. A consequent loss of autonomy for skilled workers is not what would be expected in the craft mode of production.

Our analysis of the insurance industry suggests that computer and information technologies allow a variety of solutions to questions of job design, work organization, and structure, with actual outcomes lying along a continuum whose extremes are characterized below as 'algorithmic' or 'robust' organization. Decisions about design and structure require the evaluation of economic trade-offs, often difficult to specify in advance; observed outcomes represent the differing conclusions drawn by firms about the terms of these trade-offs. In evaluating the form which the implementation of computer rationalization should take, the immediate cost factors – especially the costs of attracting more educated workers, retraining the existing workforce, restructuring the work-floor, developing innovative managerial techniques, involving workers in decision-making and increasing internal communication – must be weighed against the potential productivity gains associated with learning by doing, responsiveness to changing conditions, and effective management of unexpected failures. The volitional element in such decisions is conditioned by the objectives and sophistication of managers and their prior experience of training production workers (in this case, female clerical workers), as well as the strength of workers or their unions and important cues communicated by policy makers.

Automation and information technologies

Mainframe computers, widely introduced in the insurance industry in the 1960s, automated discrete tasks but left the production process largely unchanged. Computers were used at first to process routine or repetitive transactions such as claims disbursements or premium transactions. In addition, the computer was used from the beginning to generate the numerous reports required by the accounting department. Automated data processing activities were centralized in a separate department in which work was organized according to the same hierarchical principles that prevailed in other insurance activities.

The introduction of large, often noisy, machines, the even more intensive fragmenting of work and the further narrowing of job content raised the spectre of the office as a factory. It appeared to threaten the elimination of skilled clerical tasks and to further routinize clerical work. Some observers anticipated the polarization of skills between highly trained professional workers and less skilled clerical workers, with the associated problem that clerical workers are overwhelmingly female while professional workers are predominantly male (see Glenn and Feldberg, 1979).

During the 1970s, as insurance firms began to use the capabilities of the computer to automate key insurance production activities – underwriting, claims adjusting, and the insurance of policies and attachments – and as word processing and other office automation technologies began to diffuse through the industry, the outcome for worker skills, especially those of clerical workers, became less clear. Automation eliminated the least skilled clerical jobs, such as mail handler, and upgraded entry-level skill requirements; but it also eliminated the most skilled clerical job, that of the rater who determined the price of the policy. The most profound effects on the work process in insurance have, however, occurred following the introduction in the mid-1970s of on-line processing capabilities and their subsequent diffusion – a process that is not yet complete. In implementing these technologies and redesigning jobs, managers have a range of options in distributing tasks between workers and machines and among workers in different occupations. A key question is whether routine data entry is to exist as a distinct job to be performed by a data entry clerk, or whether routine data should be entered as they are generated.

Algorithmic organization of production

Some of the largest insurance firms, such as Prudential, have utilized telecommunications technology to remove the processing of insurance applications for personal lines of insurance (health, life, auto and homeowners) from field offices and have centralized these operations in large clerical processing centres in suburban or rural areas far from the firm's other operations. Typically, in these operations, the agent collects customer information manually on a standardized application form and mails it to a processing centre. There, a data entry clerk enters the information into the computer which then performs both the underwriting function (assessing risk and deciding whether to issue a policy to the customer) and the rating function (determining the premium to be paid for the policy) on the basis of decision rules or algorithms programmed into the machine. If the application is accepted, the computer prints the policy and any necessary attachments and assembles them for mailing to the customer. Applications which fall outside pre-established parameters – between 10 and 50 per cent of those of the firms selling personal lines (Baran, 1987) – are flagged by the computer and sent electronically to an exceptions underwriter, a skilled professional working out of a field office or the firm's central office who assesses the risk and determines whether a policy should be issued.

Clerical entry of client data is common even where agents have access to computer technology. At one large life insurance firm, 3,000 of the 9,000 agents selling the company's products have been provided with personal computers (PCs). The PCs are used to aid marketing by quickly pricing new, individualized life insurance products. They are, however, not being used to enter data into the firm's data base or to process applications. Agents still record client information on forms that are sent to the company's processing centre where data entry clerks enter it into the computer.

As computer rationalization proceeds along these lines, skilled clerical jobs such as those of rater or underwriter's assistant, as well as less skilled professional jobs handling more routine types of underwriting, are eliminated. Their functions become automated. What remains are routinized data entry jobs. For these, some firms prefer to hire married women whose child care responsibilities preclude full-time work and whose husbands' jobs provide health and other benefit coverage. Whether there are or are not productivity gains, the companies can benefit from pecuniary savings in compensation and other employee costs. Technology is used to organize work so that it can be done by lower-paid part-time workers who receive few or even no fringe benefits, who require very few skills beyond the typing accuracy they must demonstrate to be hired, and who have no access to training for other positions and no opportunities for promotion to them.

We have termed this reorganization of the production process in the insurance industry algorithmic because its goal is to push the routinization of the work performed by people as far as possible and to reduce decision-making as much as possible to a set of self-contained rules (algorithms) implementable by a computer. It connotes a proliferation of routinized data entry jobs with a reduced number of more highly skilled professional jobs. Though frequently viewed by managers as desirable, algorithmic organization is actually far from fully implemented within the insurance industry. It has proved easier to automate the underwriting of personal than of commercial lines. While some firms have developed computer-assisted underwriting for commercial auto, small stores and small apartment buildings, no one expects to automate the underwriting of elevators or ships which carry varied freight under widely differing conditions. As a result, automation of underwriting has proceeded much further in the life and health segment of the industry, where personal lines form a larger share of business than they do in the property and casualty segments. But algorithmic organization is widely viewed as state-of-the-art use of technology – to be emulated by smaller firms, and to be extended via expert systems to exceptions-underwriting and commercial lines-underwriting as well as to claims-adjusting.

Alternatives to algorithmic organization

Yet contrast this use of computer technology with the approach taken by a smaller firm that markets only standardized personal lines, including both group and individual policies. It sells its policies through direct mail advertising rather than relying on agents. By 1980, the firm had already automated mail handling and filing, thus eliminating nearly all of the least skilled clerical jobs. Policies were entered on-line and the system could handle inquiries for current information. The work process was, however, extremely fragmented. Rating and underwriting were still largely manual operations. In 1980 the company lost a contract representing one-third of its health insurance business. Only then did a dramatic restructuring of the work process begin, resulting in the integration of some clerical tasks, the elimination of all assistant supervisor and manager positions with some staff positions as well. At first, no use was made of computer technology. But by 1983, information technologies had been used to create highly integrated, multi-activity jobs in the operations areas – underwriting and claims adjusting – where the new technologies have had their greatest impact.

Underwriting and rating were entirely computerized and the corresponding jobs eliminated. Instead of these positions, a new, highly skilled clerical position had been designed – customer service representative. Initially these representatives used to handle complaints. Now they are responsible for selling insurance, accessing the computer programmes that assess risk and rate policies, explaining the rating procedures to customers, answering their questions and responding to complaints. They are knowledgeable about insurance products and are authorized to make decisions up to a certain dollar limit. Advances in telephone technology, which have increased the volume of incoming calls, have also played a key role in this job redesign. The technology enables the company to do a lot of measuring – how many rings until a phone is answered, how many minutes to answer a question, how many calls are answered; and employees have company-established standards to meet.

The claims representative is the other main skilled clerical position at this company. With the assistance of software that processes automatically the most routine claims and provides parameters that guide decision-making in other cases, claims representatives are able to settle most claims themselves. The policy and any related files are called up on a terminal, the claim processed, the policy updated, and a settlement cheque issued – all from the claims representative's terminal. All less skilled clerical jobs – typing, coding, key-punching and verifying the claim – as well as most of the professional adjuster positions have been eliminated. The company has set standards for the number of files to be handled and the number of claims to be closed each day. New entrants in skilled clerical positions are about evenly divided between high school and college graduates. Despite the skills and responsibilities involved in these jobs, the starting salary in 1984 was typical for clerical work ($11,000). The company provides customer service representatives and claims representatives with five weeks classroom training in insurance fundamentals, telephone and computer skills. This is followed by 3 to 6 months of on-the-job training, after which the employee is expected to be proficient in her area. Clerical employees are then encouraged to take additional insurance courses on their own time, paid for by the company.

In principle, possibilities for promotion to supervisor or manager still exist for clerical workers who can demonstrate knowledge of insurance. In practice, the thinning of lower level management ranks and the direct hiring of college-educated professionals into upper management ranks have greatly reduced upward mobility. Clerical workers who make it into management ranks do so by returning to college. Clerical jobs in claims or customer service are now highly skilled, but they have become dead end by design.

While data entry positions have been entirely eliminated from the underwriting and claims adjusting functions, traditional clerical jobs do exist elsewhere in the company. Data still has to be entered when, for example, premium payments come in. Legal requirements mean that insurance companies must continue to maintain some paper files, especially in relation to claims, despite the fact that they have a complete set of electronic files. A centralized word processing pool supports the work in the claims and customer services departments. A handful of jobs remains in the mail-house facility which co-ordinates the company's direct mail advertising in addition to receiving premium payments, written enquiries, and complaints. The number of such traditional clerical jobs at this firm is, however, small. A high school degree is required for entry into these jobs, but not the writing and speaking skills needed for entry into skilled clerical jobs. There are no established avenues of mobility from traditional to skilled clerical work.

Part-time and temporary workers are not widely used by this company. There are about 100 part-time workers, usually senior citizens or students who have been given the same training as full-time employees. They are used to manage peaks in the volume of claims or customer service.

In its two main operations areas – underwriting and claims – the company has used computerization to support skilled clerical workers in carrying out multi-activity jobs in which tasks are integrated and where they have responsibility for decisions that, until this decade, were made by professional employees. The company measures the success of its work reorganization and the pay-off to providing female clerical workers with training in excess of industry norms in terms of the resulting productivity gains. In the three years following its first lay-off in 1980, it reduced employment at its main location by more than one-half, from about 5,000 employees to about 2,300. By 1984, this drastically reduced number of employees was handling a volume of business greater than that being done by the company at its previous peak.

In contrast to the firm discussed previously which uses computer technology to fragment and routinize clerical jobs, computer rationalization at this compnay has enhanced the skills of clerical workers, increased decision-making in clerical jobs, and increased the complexity of clerical job tasks. It has, in general, supported a more robust organization of the insurance production process, where robustness connotes an organizational capacity to adapt to changing conditions. Unskilled clerical jobs have largely been eliminated and routine data entry reduced. The computer has been used to move skills and decision-making down the organization, and skills in the remaining jobs have been increased. As noted earlier, training provided to female clerical workers is more extensive than that generally available in clerical positions, though wages are about average and seemingly low in comparison with the skill and responsibilities of the jobs performed. The company provides a full range of fringe benefits as well as the training and tuition expenses. Cost savings have been realized as a result of productivity increases, and not through reductions in compensation.

While production is more robustly organized at this firm than at most companies dealing in personal lines, the extent of its robust organization is limited by the fact that its product lines are standardized. Skill levels are higher and decisions are made at lower levels than at most other companies. Nevertheless, a standardized product line limits the richness of these decisions.

Non-standardized products and work organization

Unusually high interest rates at the end of the 1970s and beginning of the 1980s and the resulting opportunity to make exceptional profits in the insurance industry unrelated to underwriting success increased competition for the premium income from commercial accounts. In particular, premiums on small or unexceptional commercial risks – condominiums, stores, commercial auto and worker's compensation – were driven down, substantially reducing the profitability of these lines. These increasingly competitive market conditions in property and casualty insurance lines led the property-casualty division of one of the largest US firms to turn to computer rationalization to reduce processing costs and improve the efficiency of the division's distribution network.

Property-casualty risks are characterized by this company as (1) commodity transactions which include both personal lines and small or routine commercial risks, and (2) special risks which are usually large and never routine. In marketing its products, the company relies on independent agents for commodity transactions and on brokers for special risks. The agents and brokers are employed by independent agencies and work on a commission basis. Traditionally, the firm has done the underwriting of applications, provided marketing support and taken care of the clerical processing of applications. The firm does not expect to be able to automate special risks, which in any event account for only a small part of its employment. Instead, the company felt itself driven by rising costs and declining premiums to automate commodity transactions.

Computer rationalization of personal lines products, along the algorithmic lines described above, had already occurred at this firm. Personal lines are processed at five large centres located in suburban or rural areas. Initial increases in productivity were substantial, though still below what vendors had suggested was possible and what the company had hoped to achieve. By 1984, productivity gains from this reorganization were exhausted and, blaming the clerical workers for the slowness of further gains, the company was considering plans for electronic surveillance of clerical workers in an attempt to raise productivity by increasing key strokes per minute.

The computer rationalization of commercial commodity lines at this company began some years later, in 1983, with workers' compensation. Computer rationalization of commercial lines is proceeding in a very different manner than in personal lines. In its workers' compensation line, the firm has eliminated the underwriting function and, using an interactive, distributed data system, has shifted the underwriting, rating and quoting systems to the agents who operate from independent agencies associated with its seventy-four commercial risk marketing offices. Using intelligent terminals connected to the firms' mainframe and with direct access to its data bases, agents provide clients with policy alternatives and use the computer to underwrite and rate the various policy options. When the sale is made, the agent can issue a policy immediately using printers at the point of sale.

Not all agents are being provided with terminals and software. Of the 10,000 agents marketing commodity lines for the carrier, 20 per cent actually write 80 per cent of business volume. The company intends to include half of these agents, chosen on the basis of sales volume and what the firm terms the professionalism of the agency office, in its automated product delivery system. As these procedures are implemented, all clerical processing associated with these product lines is being eliminated. In addition to clerical jobs such as policy typist, rater and underwriter's assistant, many underwriting jobs are being eliminated. The agent's job has become more professional, in part because the agent now has responsibility for, albeit computer-assisted, underwriting. On-line access to the company's data base facilitates the design of more individually tailored policies as well as a more professional approach to marketing. The firm expects eventually to do 100 per cent of its usual volume in commercial commodity risks with 10 per cent of its sales force.

The content of the remaining underwriter jobs is undergoing a profound alteration, shifting with computer rationalization from underwriting risks to managing nominally independent agents in the field. Skilled underwriters oversee the agents's 'book of business' – assessing the agent's success at underwriting, developing customer profiles, focusing marketing efforts, assuring the professionalism of the agency and encouraging the agent to do the volume of business necessary to justify the firm's investment. Supervision by underwriters on the firm's payroll is the price exacted from the agents in exchange for hardware, software and on-line access to the company's data base.

The company is now extending the agent's ability to market, underwrite, rate and issue policies at the point of sale to other commercial commodity product lines. It expects to realize increased market share in commercial commodity insurance because of improved marketing capability and the ability to tailor policies more precisely to client needs, and to achieve substantial cost savings through the elimination of clerical and most underwriting support jobs for this type of risk.

When automation comes late

A final example may help to illustrate the range of strategies available for automating the insurance production process. A large, established property/casualty company, which has used mainframe computers for billing and accounting purposes since the 1960s, was late in beginning the process of automating other insurance functions. As a result, it faced the task, in 1982, of simultaneously automating rating, under-writing and claims adjusting, excluding special risks, for both personal and commercial lines. This presented the firm with both a challenge and an opportunity. The company has drawn its own lessons from the experiences of competitors who automated earlier. It views its goals as a computer-assisted rather than a computerized production process, by which it means that it does not intend to establish clerical processing centres to deal with personal lines of insurance. Among the advantages of automating late is that its software for policy management includes claims functions as well as underwriting in an integrated system which shares the same client data base.

The firm has organized an operations unit at each of its forty-two branch offices to provide all clerical support required by the underwriting and claims adjustment units. The operations unit services personal and commercial lines, and special risks. There are no plans to isolate personal lines and establish a small number of processing centres to deal with these more routine policies.

Skilled clerical jobs are increasing in the operations units as the firm decentralizes decision-making and transfers responsibility from the home office to the branches. Rating for commercial lines is only 50 per cent automated, so raters are still required. They are taught the rating of routine risks, even though these functions are entirely computerized, in order to be able to respond to customer questions and requests for information which are also handled by the operations unit. Underwriter's assistants are skilled clerical workers who take care of the routine aspects of both personal and commercial underwriting. Jobs in the operations units span a wide range of skill levels and provide opportunities for mobility within clerical work; but the job of underwriter's assistant has been transformed into a 'career clerical' position. For the first time, at this company, it will not be possible to move from clerical to professional positions.

For entry into the job of underwriter, the company now requires a college degree. Further study of insurance is encouraged through a tuition support programme. Decisions on commercial underwriting risks which were previously made at the home office have been decentralized and are performed by underwriters at the forty-two branches. The position of insurance agent is also being upgraded. About 10 per cent of the company's 4,000 agents are being equipped with computers. Computer-assisted agents selling personal lines are now responsible for underwriting and rating functions. Underwriters of personal lines are now used as field representatives and marketing managers. They supervise the agents and help with underwriting problems. The company has increased its hiring of women into underwriting positions. Women are 85 per cent of new hires in the revamped personal lines underwriting positions and 50 per cent in commercial lines. The company reports that it expects this to offset and negative effects on opportunities or affirmative action goals from the decision to develop career clerical positions and cut off traditional avenues of mobility.

Decentralization of decision-making and on-line processing capabilities has led to large reductions in home (as opposed to field) office employment at management, underwriting and clerical levels. The home office now provides support for the branches through a new insitutional support department responsible for systems analysis, applications programming and computer auditing, and still provides underwriting support for very large risks. Despite hiring for this new department, employment at the home office and company headquarters has been reduced 15 and 25 per cent respectively since 1979. It should be noted, however, that the insurance industry in general has experienced more difficulty than anticipated in developing fully automated underwriting and claims processing in commercial lines. It has not been possible to push the automation of these lines as far as personal lines. For example, one of the firms that favoured highly algorithmic organization in its personal lines is pursuing the use of expert systems to fully automate commodity risks, but with mixed results to date. Difficulties have been encountered in eliminating manual rating of these risks and in developing software. In addition, the expert systems that have been developed institutionalize accepted-rather than best-practice in underwriting these risks, since management studies of professional productivity are rare and best-practice techniques have not been identified. Understandably, underwriters resist using the expert systems that have been developed and claim to be superior to the programmes. In view of the difficulties, the flexibility of computer-assisted branch operations is seen by this firm as a definite advantage over fully computerized operations.

The transformation of work: the range of outcomes

The reorganization of production and the redesign of jobs as computer rationalization proceeds in companies using essentially the same computer hardware and information equipment can, as we have suggested, fruitfully be described as lying along a continuum, from more algorithmic to more robust. We will draw on the case studies described above to refine these concepts.

The algorithmic approach

Production organized along algorithmic lines replaces worker skills and knowledge in decision-making with pre-programmed decision rules. The goal of this approach is to limit worker skills and reduce the role of human knowledge and judgement in the production process by designing self-regulating systems that require little input from the human operators who work with them. Routine data entry characterizes clerical work at firms that follow this path. Technology is utilized to separate the entry of data from the processing of applications. Removing the latter work to remote locations is an extension of the Taylorist organization of work that was already prevalent in the insurance industry when computer rationalization was introduced a decade ago. Productivity gains, and they can be substantial in comparison with the manual processing of applications, are realized in the period immediately following computer rationalization and then exhausted, at least until a new generation of improved hardware is installed. Firms dissatisfied with these productivity gains, or pressured by increased competition and the deregulation of financial services, find themselves with few options for increasing productivity or reducing unit labour costs. Increased surveillance and computer monitoring of clerical workers is viewed by some managements as a way of increasing productivity. In the workers' counter-view the increased stress leads to increased sickness, absenteeism and turnover. In effect in these applications, productivity advances from powerful information and computation technologies are limited by the dexterity of a woman's fingers.

The routinization of clerical work typical of algorithmic organization relies on the fragmentation of work and requires no knowledge of insurance products or claims adjusting procedures. The skills that remain – routine keyboarding and word processing skills – are related to the computer and not to the firm's business lines. This organization of production facilitates the use of part-time or temporary workers as a strategy for augmenting limited productivity gains with reductions in labour costs. The firm may realize substantial savings on wages or fringe benefits in the switch from a full-time clerical staff at field offices to a workforce which includes a large proportion of part-time workers at processing centres. High turnover among these workers holds down wage growth and training can be accomplished in days. In addition, routinization of clerical work facilitates the increased use of temporary workers in home and field offices.

More robust alternatives

In contrast, more robust alternatives proceed by increasing the amount of information about products, procedures and clients available to workers at every level within the organization. The decision-making capacities of all workers, including clerical workers, are enhanced. Decision-making is decentralized and moved down the organizational hierarchy which is often streamlined or simplified in the process. The most robust forms of computer rationalization proceed by using microprocessors to monitor the production process (for example, to route requests for information or the processing of applications according to pre-established priorities), and to process and transmit data on the operation and performance characteristics of the production process to workers at all levels. The associated work organization is designed to promote and value learning, flexibility and adaptive behaviour on the part of employees. In this, it differs fundamentally from computer-based automation that proceed by standardizing and reducing information inputs and applying algorithmic decision rules to fully anticipated situations.

The case studies should make it clear that more robust organizations of production, despite the value placed on worker skills and flexible use of technology, need not imply socio-technical work settings in the 'Tavistock tradition'. An increase in job complexity and responsibility was often accompanied by a loss of autonomy, increased stress and more stringent regulation of working time. Clerical workers who are required to handle clients in a given number of minutes and nominally independent sales agents who are now monitored by company employees are obvious examples.

Robustness has implications for the work setting but it cannot be characterized simply in terms of it. Robustness refers, instead, to the degree of organizational adaptiveness and, as such, is a systems property describing how the firm, or a significant subset of its production activities, is organized. The defining characteristics of robust forms of organization have to do with relationships among the employees at different levels within the firm. Workers at higher levels are familiar with the work done at lower levels as well as with the people doing it. Confidence in workers at lower levels allows managers to delegate problems with current products or services to lower levels for solution while freeing those at the upper levels to develop new products and markets. Workers at each level have some knowledge of the whole production system, though the extent of this knowledge increases at higher levels. The depth of access of workers into the company's information systems and heir capacity to alter entries are among the formal indicators of the extent of algorithmic or robust organization. In the most robustly organized firms, communication among peers and between workers at one level and those just above or below them is extensive. There are many cross links between the levels in such an organization. While the organization is still hierarchical, there are fewer levels of hierarchy, and communication is not intended or formally structured to be primarily top down. Two-way communication is both encouraged and facilitated.

Decisions about organization and structure involve the evaluation of many trade-offs. In particular, there are costs associated with implementing robust forms of organization. Investments in human capital are necessarily high in such firms. In service sector industries, the cost of investments in physical capital is often low in comparison with these. The higher training costs for workers at lower levels are problematic for some firms. There may be costs associated with rearranging the work-floor, developing new management techniques and involving workers in decision-making. In addition, robust organizations pay an overhead for all the internal communication they require.

These costs can only be justified if the firm is in a position to take advantage of the increased adaptiveness that robust organization provides. In a stable environment, where products are standardized and technology is expected to change slowly, firms will still want to be as fully adapted as possible to the conditions in which thay are currently functioning. As the earlier examples indicate, even here, the reductions in unit labour requirements may be dramatic, off-setting the higher costs of training and communication. Where firms face a changing environment, however, the costs associated with robust organization are less important to profitability than the productivity gains associated with the ability to move rapidly up the learning curve or to adapt easily and flexibly to new conditions. Robust firms achieve efficiency in the long run, rather than in shorter time periods, because the primary advantage of robust firms is their ability to reorganize as conditions change.

Thus, the choice of organizational structure reflects managements' evaluation of the trade-off between higher costs in the present and the potential for higher productivity, higher quality or greater flexibility in the future. Not surprisingly, examples of more robust organization in the insurance industry tend to be found in the property and casualty segments where products are less standardized, the flow of the premium income is less certain and profits exhibit greater cyclical variation. Even here, however, the difficulty of evaluating uncertain future gains may result in undue weight being attached to the higher short-run costs, and the uncertainty itself may lead managers to rely on rules of thumb that favour fragmenting tasks and centralizing decision-making as the accepted means of increasing productivity.

Furthermore, the decentralization of decision-making characteristic of more robust organizations requires managers to relinquish control over parts of the production process to workers on the floor. In the insurance industry, more robust organizational structures have transferred some control to clerical or sales personnel. Resistance to providing training to clerical workers has been one factor favouring more algorithmic organization in this industry. Distrust by carriers of the independent agents who frequently market their products, and an unwillingness to provide them with access to the client data base necessary for point-of-sale underwriting and issuance of policies is another. The possibilities for more robust organization increase where carriers have a prior history of training female clerical workers, and where the sales staff is employed by the carrier or can be made to accept close supervision. Evidence from a large-scale study (Baran, 1987) suggests that reliance on centralized clerical processing centres for data entry and underwriting predominates while use of agents for this purpose is rare.

Implications for worker skills

The routinization of work in more algorithmic firms and the premium placed on adaptive behaviour in more robust firms suggests the important influence that organizational design choices exert on worker skills. In evaluating the effects of computer rationalization on worker skills, there are two key dimensions along which algorithmic and robust firms diverge. In addition to the fragmentation versus integration of tasks discussed previously, it is necessary to consider the extent of contextual knowledge required in jobs. Furthermore, the transferability of some important skills required by the robust computer rationalization poses job-design problems.

Contextual knowledge requirements

The contextual knowledge requirements of a job refer to the extent to which acceptable performance requires the knowledge of the firm's products, production processes, customers, clients, procedures or regulatory environment. The role of contextual knowledge in job design is an important dividing line between more algorithmic and more robust forms of work organization. Many jobs in firms organized along algorithmic lines are low in contextual knowledge requirements. Job skills in these firms are related solely to the sophistication of the software employed in the firm. The valued skills, from word processing to graphics design or programming, are not firm specific but relate instead to the technology.

The extent of contextual knowledge required for a particular function is generally not technologically determined. In robust organizations, multi-activity service jobs are filled by workers with substantial training and knowledge of the firm's products, processes and procedures, and with the authority to make decisions and resolve problems. Increased communication within robustly organized firms implies a need for highly skilled administrative support staff knowledgeable about the firm's operations. While jobs other than professional or managerial positions in algorithmic firms are designed to be low in contextual knowledge requirements, less complex jobs in robust firms may require substantial amounts of such knowledge in order to be performed with a minimum of supervision and to integrate properly with other related tasks.

Transferability of skills

In addition to the contextual knowledge requirements discussed above, sales, clerical and administrative support jobs in robustly organized firms require mastery of a range of worker skills not previously associated with such work. These include:

(1) social and communication skills in order to meet and integrate the needs of customers, clients, marketing staff, and product designers;

(2) managerial skills related to planning, organizing time effectively, thinking more comprehensively about the enterprise, and acting in a strategic manner; and

(3) general skills related to computer technology – how to hook up microcomputers to larger networks via modems and telephone lines, how to access a data base to store and retrieve data, how to turn data into useful information (perform searches, identify potential customers), and how to use standard software packages.

These skills are required in a large number of emerging jobs that are more properly classified as 'para-professional' than as clerical or sales occupations, and are increasingly transferable across a variety of specific job titles and industries. Because thay are transferable, firms are reluctant to utilize internal labour-market mechanisms to provide them, particularly as many of the jobs in which the skills could be utilized are held by women and fall outside the traditional boundaries of the internal labour market in many firms.

Employers have been reluctant to provide training, or to reward increased skill levels with higher pay and status – the phenomenon referred to in the US as the up-skilling and down-waging of clerical work. The skills required in occupations that are dominated by women have long been 'invisible' and under-paid (see Chapter 7). What is new in the current situation is that more robust uses of technology require high level skills beyond those taught in secondary school and that cannot easily be learned on-the-job. New educational mechanisms, perhaps along the lines of experimental community college programmes, may be used. Not least among the reasons for such training programmes is that the widespread availability of high level skills in the female workforce reduces the costs to firms of more robust uses of technology and increases the incentives favouring the development of multi-activity, integrated and responsible jobs.

The degradation of work?

Algorithmic uses of computer technology in underwriting personal lines appear to be extensions of Taylorist approaches to job design and work organization which were already firmly in place in this industry more than two decades ago. Many firms are currently engaged in the attempt to routinize the underwriting of ordinary commercial risks, and some are even attempting to develop expert programmes to automate exceptional risks. As the algorithmic uses of technology eliminate routine underwriting and economize on clerical skills, the remaining professional skills in claims adjusting and exceptions underwriting appear to some firms as the next place to get labour costs 'under control'. Pessimism about the future of worker skills in the insurance industry derives from the momentum behind the move to centralized clerical centres and the conviction on the part of many firms that this use of technology represents the state-of-the-art.

Innovative uses of computer and information technologies that break with the Taylorist forms of work organization, as we have seen, have been quite successful. Reductions in unit labour requirements in these firms have sometimes been exceptional, with positive effects on both profitability and sales growth. Optimists point to the capability of on-line processing to eliminate entirely the centralized data entry performed in large processing centres, leaving the industry with a streamlined workforce of highly skilled employees. While this is correct, it has so far not prevented centralization, which firms may favour for a variety of non-technical reasons including a shortage of specialized skills in the female labour force, an unwillingness to provide substantial training for clerical workers, the perception that centralized processing allows productivity gains to be augmented by savings in compensation from utilizing a part-time labour force, and the firm's desire to retain control over the client data base. Whilst no simple answer to the question of the effect of new technology on the skills of workers employed by insurance companies emerges from this analysis, it should not then be concluded that at some stage the determinants of the choices cannot be specified.

14 The limits to industrialization: computer software development in a large commercial bank

SARAH KUHN

Computers have been at the centre of much of the recent debate about the transformation of work. Will computers remove the skill content from most jobs, as some predict? Will they, as others claim, enhance the skill requirements for the average job? What will happen to the jobs of people who programme the computers? Finally, what can we learn from studying computerization about the broader question of how work will be transformed? Through a close examination of the changing content of computer programming work, this chapter points to a new way of thinking about the development and alteration of work in general.

Predictions about the transformation of computer programming

Few social scientists have examined the changes taking place in computer programming as the occupation, and the technology, matures. Greenbaum (1979) and Kraft (1977) studied the work of programmers and both predicted the progressive routinization and simplification of programming work. Their studies drew heavily on the work of Braverman (1974), and echoed Braverman's predictions about the nature and direction of change in the labour process.

Braverman identified three ways in which capitalist competition, which leads employers to assert greater control over the labour process, transforms work:

(1) the conception of work and its execution are separated;
(2) work becomes fragmented and a detail division of labour is created;
(3) skill requirements become polarized, with a significant reduction in skill requirements for the mass of jobs.

Although Braverman's principal concern was with manufacturing and routine clerical work, he briefly discussed the effects of this process on computer programming. Greenbaum's and Kraft's studies, which were based on open-ended interviews with programmers from a variety of work settings and on participant-observation, provided detailed extensions of Braverman's model to programming tasks and work places.

Programmes and programming

'A computer program,' says Brooks (1975: 164), software engineer and author of a widely cited book on programming, 'is a message from a man to a machine. The rigidly marshalled syntax and the scrupulous definitions all exist to make intention clear to the dumb engine.' A programme is a written text using letters, numbers and symbols. This text expresses a set of instructions to be read and executed by a computer. The instructions must be complete and unambiguous, and must follow exacting rules of, for example, syntax and punctuation. Although any of the terms which are used to describe written expression in natural language are also used for computer languages ('text', 'language', 'syntax', 'word', 'writing') and although many programming languages make heavy use of English words among the mathematical expressions, a computer programme has more in common with the holes punched in the paper cards which controlled the Jacquard loom than it does with *Moby Dick* or the poetry of Shelley.

This study focuses on the programming labour process and its context; it is therefore concerned with programming as an activity, not with the occupation called 'computer programming', nor with programmers themselves as individuals. Programming is a generic term used in this study to signify the central activities required to generate a computer programme or to construct a computerized system. These central activities are of two main sorts: analysis, which consists of the variety of tasks necessary to understanding the overall system, the purpose it should accomplish, and the general design of the computer programme which will accomplish this purpose; and coding, the actual writing of the programme in a computer language.

Testing the 'industrialization' hypothesis

To test whether programming is indeed becoming routinized, a case study of business applications programmers in a commercial bank was conducted. Because programming work in financial institutions is generally said to be the most routine, and because a large company offers a greater opportunity for the division of labour, a large bank seemed the most likely place to find the routinization or 'industrialization' of programming.

The bank described in this study is a US commercial bank with world-wide employment of roughly 24,000. Like other financial institutions of the mid-1980s, the bank was undergoing radical change in its competitive environment. The stepwise deregulation of financial institutions during the 1980s had rocked the generally staid world of banking, and the bank was beginning to respond with internal reorganization, the development of new products, and an increasing emphasis on elaborating a corporate strategy. All of these changes affected the systems area, yet at the time of this study the bank was neither particularly advanced compared to its competitors nor unusually backward in its use of computerized systems. The data for the study were gathered primarily during open-ended, in-depth interviews, averaging two hours in length and conducted during 1985 and 1986 with twenty-five bank employees.

The evidence from the bank did not confirm Braverman's (1974) predictions about the reorganization of programming work. First, conceptual work, or 'analysis', was not substantially separate from execution, or 'coding'. Although some employees performed analysis but wrote no code, there were no programmers who were solely coders. Everyone at the bank believed that the systems development process was made more effective when coding and analysis were done by the same person. Second, the opportunities for fragmentation of work were severely restricted, and even when a programmer worked on a part of a system, such work was integrated with the work of others. An internal labour market provided promotion opportunities, and even entry-level employees had jobs which required them to perform a variety of tasks. Finally, while the minimum skill requirements for technical proficiency seemed to have dropped for applications programmers',[1] narrowly defined technical skill is only one of the skills required for effective programming. Programmers must also be able to analyse a work process and to communicate with their clients, the system users, to design and maintain successful systems. In recent years, there has been a shift in skill requirements for applications programmers, with a growing emphasis on analysis and communication and the decreasing importance of strictly technical skills, especially coding.

Separation of conception and execution

The idea that the managerial control of work entails the separation of conception and execution is as central to Braverman's (1974) theory as it was to Frederick Taylor's model. Braverman, Greenbaum (1979) and Kraft (1977) all identify analysis as the conceptual element of programming, and coding as execution. Analysis, in their view, encompasses the planning work required for the production of a programme, and coding consists merely in transforming what is already planned into computer-readable form. In drawing these parallels, Braverman, Greenbaum and Kraft also affirm the conventional view that there is a hierarchical relationship between analysis work and coding work: the analysis is done by upper-level workers and the coding by less skilled detail workers.

In fact, this research uncovered no systematic and wholesale separation of coding and analysis. Some who did analysis work did not code, and some who wrote code were involved in projects for which they did not have primary responsibility for overall analysis, but there were no cases found of regular bank employees who did coding but no analysis.

Why is there no separation?

There appeared to be no single reason why execution and conception were not segregated. Instead, there were many factors contributing to this outcome.

MOST LARGE SYSTEMS ARE ALREADY DEVELOPED

The proportion of systems analysts and programmers occupied in the construction of large systems has fallen as smaller-scale projects and maintenance work come to dominate the time of systems people. In the 1980s, it appears that fewer development projects for large transaction-based systems are taking place since many of these systems have already been built. Smaller projects, like maintenance work, offer fewer opportunities for the division of labour, and therefore also for the separation of conception and execution.

LABOUR MARKET CONSTRAINTS

Managers in the systems area seemed concerned about recruiting and retaining capable and motivated systems people. Past experiences with uncomfortably high rates of turnover and difficulty finding technical specialists for positions above entry level have prompted the bank to show increased concern about salaries, working conditions, and intrinsic interest and challenge in systems work. One of the consequences of this is that no one in the systems area is expected to work full time writing code. Coding, especially writing COBOL code (a programming language developed in the 1950s) for banking applications, is considered by most to be unattractive as a full-time task. In general, systems people said, the smart liberal arts graduates from 'starvation majors' whom they recruit for entry-level positions do not want to spend the rest of their careers writing code.

HIGH LEVEL OF AMBIGUITY IN WORK

Several systems people spoke of the great ambiguity which sometimes characterized their assignments. It is certainly true that programmers, because of the nature of their work, never do quite the same thing twice. Unlike workers on an assembly line or in a routine clerical work situation, the work of programmers is not standardized. Given this fact, it seems likely that the separation of conception and execution would be impossible, or at least seriously counter-productive.

CONTEXTUAL KNOWLEDGE NEEDED FOR GOOD SYSTEMS WORK

Because the vast majority of all systems failures at the bank was caused by poor communication between users and systems people and other political factors, more stress was being placed on careful analysis and improved understanding of business problems. Many systems people emphasized in interviews the importance of knowing the business context when working on system development. One manager saw the increasing emphasis on context and on understanding contextual factors as serving to *increase* the skill required of programmers in the systems area, saying 'Deskilling is doing a job with no context'.

Such knowledge is useful even at the detailed and technical level of writing the code, so it is important for coders to understand the uses to which their system will be put. This suggests that coders will do a better job if they are also privy to the analysis work involved in system development.

A related advantage of having programmers who are both analysts and coders is that the same people can follow the project through from beginning to end. While this does not always happen, it does seem to be the norm. More than one manager argued the advantages of having analysts who also do the coding, reducing potential communication problems.

PROBLEMS DEFINING THE TERMS 'CONCEPTION' AND 'EXECUTION'

Braverman and his followers discuss conception and execution as if the meaning of these terms were clear and unambiguous. The evidence from the bank reveals, however, that this distinction can be quite difficult to make in practice. Programmers found it difficult to say where analysis ended and coding began, and when pressed one programmer seemed to suggest that analysis was endemic even to the writing of code itself. Any reflection that took place during coding she considered to be analysis, and reflection seemed to be a common component of the coding process. This suggests a degree of overlap – even an inseparability – of conception and execution for which Braverman's theory does not allow.

Fragmentation and a detail division of labour

Although work in the systems area was organized hierarchically and most projects involved multiple participants and a division of labour, there was no generalized evidence of the sort of fragmentation and detail division of labour which makes individual tasks routine. Several findings support this conclusion.

NO OCCUPATIONAL GHETTO FOR CODERS OR MAINTAINERS

At the bank, writing code was not considered a dead-end job, and entry-level people could expect promotion, often into jobs involving little or no coding. On some projects senior members of the project team also wrote code, so that coding was not just an entry-level task. Furthermore, systems programmers, who were highly esteemed for their technical ability, wrote code as part of their jobs.

Maintenance, considered by many to be the most routine work done by systems people, in fact contained many challenging elements, including the necessity to solve technical puzzles crucial to the continued functioning of the bank. Although maintenance was still stigmatized at the bank, a growing number of people – including experienced systems people – were said to consider maintenance important and attractive work.

ASSIGNED TO A PARTICULAR BUSINESS UNIT, WHICH LIMITS THE DIVISION OF LABOUR

Although it has been an article of faith since the time of Adam Smith that the extent of the market limits the division of labour, the fact that the bank operates in a mass market does not mean that there are extensive opportunities within the systems area for a detail division of labour. Indeed, because each system built by the bank's programmers and analysts is 'custom-made', there are distinct limitations on the bank's ability to fragment, routinize and divide labour. While a group or an individual may be assigned a module of a programme to develop, a routine and factory-like division of labour in which work is done by rote is not created.

MOVEMENT FROM DETAIL WORK TO 'WHOLE' WORK AND BACK, DEPENDING ON THE JOB

On the whole, even entry-level systems people seemed to have jobs with significant variety in them. While a person could be assigned to a large development project and work on the same system for a matter of a year or even considerably more, systems people more commonly worked on a variety of projects of different sizes, often tackling more than one project at a time. On one project their role might be larger or require more of an overview than on another (perhaps because the projects were in different phases), so that a systems person would experience a shift in the scope of work when going from one project to another. This gave considerable variety to the daily schedule of a programmer or analyst.

FRAGMENTATION IS NOT EQUIVALENT TO SIMPLIFICATION

Implicitly or explicitly, Braverman (1974), Greenbaum (1979) and Kraft (1977) treat fragmentation and simplification as intimately linked. While it may be the case that, by any meaningful measure, the fragmentation of work also leads to its simplification, the reverse is not true. The history of the computerization of work offers many examples of situations in which work was simplified but not fragmented. At the bank, the use of higher-level languages by programmers allows them to write simpler code more easily, but it does not fragment their work. In some cases, in fact, use of such languages may lead to more unified work when it allows the size of project teams to be reduced. Fragmentation and simplification, then, are separate concepts, and should be treated independently when analysing the changing organization of work.

Degradation of skill for the mass of jobs

In the larger community of software specialists, work in the systems area of banks and insurance companies is regarded as routine and relatively unskilled. A software engineer from a leading computer company referred to these work places as 'sweatshops' and suggested that a significant decline had taken place in the skill requirements for these jobs – if indeed high levels of skill were ever required.

This study suggests, although it cannot prove conclusively, that programmers at the bank are less *technically* skilled than their counterparts five, ten, or twenty years ago. It certainly seems to be true that applications programmers, who are the majority of programmers in the bank's systems area, know far less about the hardware with which they work than was true when their precursors worked in an area adjacent to the machines. It also appears that applications programmers can be effective with a lower level of technical programming knowledge than was true in the past. While there may have been little change in the computer language used by programmers, a variety of aids – such as code editors, compilers, and Job Control Language – have been developed to expedite the other tasks associated with producing applications software. These aids do indeed remove the requirement for certain kinds of technical knowledge among programmers.

Far more important, however, is that the 'sweatshop model' overlooks some of the most significant aspects of software work at the bank. To measure the skill required to be a successful programmer at the bank simply by examining the amount of technical skill required is to use too limited a yardstick. Certainly technical skill – proficiency in coding, ability to understand the hardware and so forth – continues to be a key element of systems work. What the interviews at the bank document, however, is the large and growing component of systems work which is not strictly technical (or related to 'bits and bytes', to use the language of some interviewees). Systems work has always been conducted within the context of a business objective, and everyone in the systems area stressed the importance of the ability to understand the business of the bank, as well as to communicate both with other systems people and with the user-community about how a system should be designed and built.

These abilities are skills which are crucial to an effective systems development process. They are not, however, generally considered technical skills by systems people. Instead, they are a different sort of skill, requiring a different set of abilities and a different outlook on the process of programme production. As such, they are measured on a different scale than that which measures technical proficiency. Both technical and non-technical abilities are required for good software work.

An increased emphasis on analysis and communication as a proportion of all programming work has evolved over the course of years at the bank. Many factors have contributed to this shift in emphasis. Each of these factors is discussed briefly below.

REASONS FOR SYSTEMS FAILURE ARE LARGELY NOT TECHNICAL

As one manager emphasized, the vast majority of systems failures are the result of problems in human communication, not the result of technical faults. For this reason it has made sense for managers in the systems area to put increased stress on analysis and communication, the areas of greatest weakness in the process of systems construction. Many systems people said that time spent getting the specifications right saved time at every subsequent stage of the systems development process, and that such time was therefore well spent.

TO RETAIN MANY EMPLOYEES, EMPLOYERS MUST PROVIDE INTERESTING NON-TECHNICAL WORK

The sort of people the bank hires for entry-level programming work have non-technical backgrounds. While they may be interested in the technology, they are unlikely to be satisfied for a long period working at a job which is purely technical in its preoccupations. Increasing the exposure of systems people to the context of their work serves the purpose of expanding their horizons to include analysis and communication.

FEWER NEW DEVELOPMENT PROJECTS, MORE MAINTENANCE

Because there are a growing number of systems which need to be maintained, maintenance has become a larger part of the total workload in the systems area. Since maintenance is said to involve a higher proportion of analysis and a lower proportion of coding than does new systems development, the increased importance of maintenance increases the share of work time spent on analysis rather than on coding.

MORE OUTSIDE PURCHASING OF PROGRAMMES

The bank is increasingly turning to the outside purchase of 'packaged' software, and is building proportionately fewer systems in-house. All the software used on personal computers (PCs) has been purchased outside the bank, and many mini-computer and mainframe systems are also purchased packages. These packages may be adapted for use by the bank, but much of the coding that would otherwise be necessary to build an entire system is eliminated. Outside purchase does not, however, eliminate the analysis work involved in system design and implementation. Analysis work is required as a prerequisite to choosing a software package, and user training and support are not eliminated simply because an outside vendor has supplied the software. Packages purchased for PCs represent the limiting case of this trend, since their installation requires analysis – that is, an assessment of the job to be done and the tools available to do it – but no coding.

PROGRAMMING TOOLS ARE BECOMING EASIER TO USE

The bank makes some use of new software tools which expedite the process of coding. Although still heavily invested in COBOL (still the most widely used programming language in business settings), systems people have also used at various times some of the database packages and fourth-generation languages available on the market. These tools can have the effect of significantly reducing the time spent on technical issues, particularly coding. As such, they con ribute to the shift in emphasis away from technical concerns and toward analysis and communication.

In addition to these tools, the use of aids which expedite the aspects of the work which are not simply involved with the production of the code itself – for example, the areas in which programmes intersect with data sets and operating systems – have reduced the minimum technical knowledge required of applications programmers.

FALLING HARDWARE COSTS MAKE OPTIMIZATION LESS IMPORTANT IN SOME SITUATIONS

In the past, one of the activities programmers engaged in was the process of trying to write a programme so that it used machine time and space as efficiently as possible. This process of optimization could be enjoyable for those who liked to solve technical problems, but it was also time-consuming and therefore expensive for the employer. Today, hardware costs have fallen so significantly that machine efficiency, while still significant, is less important than it was.

MORE EMPHASIS ON COMPUTERIZING PROFESSIONALS' AND OTHER POORLY UNDERSTOOD SUBJECTS' WORK

When work processes that are rationalized, fragmented, and well-understood are automated, the analysis process can be relatively straightforward. Many of the early bank systems were computerized versions of work that had been done manually by clerical workers. The analysts generally saw themselves as simply the translators of a paper process into computer terms.

At the bank today, most of the large, rationalized, transaction-based systems have been computerized. More recently, systems people have been turning their attention to more conceptually difficult problems: the construction of systems which have not previously existed in paper form, and the automation of some aspects of professional work. This new kind of work takes more time for two reasons. First, it is conceptually more complex, and requires more analysis, and second, systems people generally approach professional users differently than they do the clerical workers who work in the rationalized environments. With professionals, systems people feel they have to 'sell' their product, while managers generally present clerical workers with a 'take it or leave' situation.

Conclusions

Braverman predicted that under modern capitalist conditions the mass of jobs will become degraded: fragmentation and a detail division of labour, the separation of conception from execution, and the destruction of craft skill with a polarization in skill requirements will prevail. Both Braverman (1974) himself and his followers, Greenbaum (1979) and Kraft (1977), have applied this prediction to the work of computer programmers and have concluded that programming, too, will follow the assumed course of other occupations. The evidence from this study, however, suggests that Braverman's predictions for programming do not hold, at least in one large commercial bank. Where Braverman, Greenbaum and Kraft predict fragmentation, this study finds a division of labour which undergoes considerable modification from project to project but which never relegates programmers to the position of detail workers. Where they predict the separation of conception and execution, instead it appears that coding and analysis are generally not separated, and that no one spends all their time simply writing code. Where they predict reduction in skill demands for most jobs, a shift in skill requirements – emphasizing analysis and communication and de-emphasizing coding and other technical matters – is found.

There are several possible reasons why the findings of this study are at odds with those of Greenbaum (1979) and Kraft (1977). The most likely is that their investigations focused on changes in strictly technical skill requirements, overlooking the shift which placed greater emphasis on analysis and communication. Since their evidence was based on interviews with individual programmers in a variety of firms, the broader corporate context – and thus the significance of relationships with users and others – may have been underplayed. It is also possible that there has been a real about-face in managerial practice since the 1970s, as managers discovered the limitations of an 'industrialized' approach to programming, and as many programmers' tools became easier to use, but the evidence from this study does not corroborate such a hypothesis. Despite the fact that ten of the interviewees had been at the bank since the early 1970s, they had no recollection of serious managerial attempts to apply Taylorist techniques to programme production, or of an era when programmers had been more restricted than they were in the mid-1980s.

These findings do not by themselves disprove Braverman's theory about the transformation of work. In the recent history of industrialization there are many instances of the transformation of work following the pattern laid out by Braverman, with the automobile assembly line serving as the classic example. This study does, however, call into question the applicability of Braverman's theory to programming work in financial services and in other settings, and even perhaps to all work in non-production settings.

A defender of Braverman's model might review the evidence presented here and conclude that it poses no significant challenge to his notion of the degradation of work because programmers can be said to be in the same relationship to workers in the white-collar work place as the industrial engineers in Frederick Taylor's shops were to the machinists whose work they reorganized. That is, programmers are the rountinizers, not the routinized, in the work place. To some extent, this is correct. It is the job of the programmers at the bank to examine and rationalize the work of others, and one can reasonably expect that the brunt of routinization will fall elsewhere. However, there are three serious qualifications which must temper this position.

First, Braverman himself (1974: 328-30) invites us to conclude that there is a process of degradation affecting computer programmers. In so doing, he permeates the boundary Taylor was trying to establish between the 'office' – that is, the industrial engineers – and the shop-floor. Braverman may simply have been wrong about the possibility of applying his model to computer programmers. If programmers are exempt from this process, though, one must establish why, and what the implications of this exemption are for the overall occupational structure.

Second, while programmers at the bank did work to automate many of the bank's clerical functions, these functions were in many cases extensively rationalized long before the programmers arrived. This makes it less obvious what the effects of computerization will be. It seems likely that computerization eliminates many jobs and perhaps constrains others, but in an already rationalized environment the impact of computerization may be quite different in character from that in a less highly codified situation.

Finally, the bank's programmers are spending increasing amounts of time on providing computerized tools for professional workers at the bank. The aim of these tools is to increase the productivity of professional workers, with the possible result that professional jobs will be eliminated. It is an open question, however, whether the application of these tools makes professional work more routine.

Why has standardized, routine work developed in some work places and occupations, but not in programming at the bank? Assembly-line-like programming work has not developed at the bank, nor does it show any sign that it will in the future. The presence of the assembly line in some manufacturing and clerical work but not in programming may be explained by distinguishing between two different phases of the production process: *development* and *reproduction*.

The development phase comprises the design work and strategic and tactical decision-making that are the prerequisites for manufacturing or clerical production. In the development phase the product is designed, the policies set and the infrastructure constructed which allow the actual production of a product or service. Reproduction is the phase which follows the development process, during which the actual products and processes conceived during the development phase are brought into being. In the production of automobiles, for example, the work of the engineers who design the car and the production process is part of the development phase, while the shop-floor workers who manufacture and assemble the autos are reproducing the product design again and again as they perform their jobs.

Programmers, in this analogy, are like design engineers, not like automobile production workers. They are not involved in the reproduction of a product; instead, they are designing programmes which remain, in effect, as one-of-a-kind objects. This is true regardless of whether the software is intended for a company's one-time internal use or for reproduction for sale as a commodity in the market-place. The matter of whether the programme will be reproduced or not may have only minor effects on the nature of programming work in a given setting. The size of the market for a particular programme – be it a market of only one customer or a market of thousands – has no systematic effect on the nature of programming work, since it is development work and not reproduction.[2]

There is always a significant element of 'custom' work in each programming project. Although there are similarities among programmes, no two are ever identical. Instead, programmes exhibit a 'family resemblance' in that they may contain common elements, use a common language and share similar purposes. Because of these common elements, tools can be developed which expedite the programming process. While these tools may simplify the technical aspects of programming work, they do not routinize programming itself. Even at a lower level of technical complexity, successful programming still requires analytical insight and the capacity to respond to a variety of potentially ambiguous situations. The judgement of the programmer is still an essential element of the systems development process. Tools that reduce the technical complexity of the work have not led, at the bank, to the routinization of programming but rather to a change in the job content of programmers.

The distinction between development and reproduction helps to clarify the relationship between these findings and the work of Piore and Sabel (1984). While Piore and Sable make a broad argument about production methods, technology, and social and political institutions, much of the attention paid to their work focuses on the notion of flexible specialization, a craft-oriented organization of production which they contrast with mass production and assembly-line techniques. They argue that mass production and flexible specialization are the two alternative development paths for production work, and that as a society we face a choice between them. Yet Piore and Sabel focus in their examples on 'reproduction', not on 'development' work. In programming – and therefore presumably also in development work in general – these two alternative paths are not viable. Because programming work is fundamentally a design activity, programmers are sheltered from the threat of true mass-production techniques.

'The Henry Ford of software hasn't come forth yet,' quotes Greenbaum from an article in *Computerworld* (Greenbaum 1979: 105). Nor will such a person ever come. Software development is not suited to the methods of the automobile assembly line. The conditions which Kraft (1977: 52) describes as prerequisites for the routinization of work – 'an unvarying good or service and...an unvarying way of turning it out' – are not met. Fordism will never make it to the programming shop.

15 *Work organization and product change in the service sector: the case of the UK National Health Service*

ROD COOMBS AND KEN GREEN

Introduction

The service sector in all advanced economies is currently the site of many technological and organizational changes. Study of the changes in output and employment in the various industries which make up the service sector suggests that some of them (particularly financial and leisure services) will be major growth points as advanced capitalist societies move into a so-called post-manufacturing, information stage.[1] Issues of work organization within the service sector have received less attention. The majority of the studies that have been done tend to concentrate on office work (Collinson and Knights, 1986; Crompton and Reid, 1982; Storey, 1986).

This chapter is not a general survey of work transformation in the service industries since there is insufficient unity within those industries to allow many general statements. Indeed, it is our contention that it is not possible to make meaningful predictions about the shape of the organization of work without first establishing the likely shape of the service-producing enterprises and, just as important, the nature of the output of those enterprises, the service products. Changes in work organization are connected to broader changes in social and economic institutions as well as to changes in technologies. We will here explore the relationship between technological and organizational change by using examples from current innovations in one service sector only – health care. But first, we set our discussion in the broader context of service provision, summarizing what we have written elsewhere (Blackburn *et al.*, 1985).

The services do not exist as a sector; they are a heterogeneous collection of industries. The main thing they have in common is that their products, the resultant service, are not in the main physical goods but are in some way intangible, impermanent or immaterial. A lot of ink has been spilt in attempting some embracing definition of what constitutes the service sector, much of it wasted by trying to bring unity to what is better left as diversity. Gershuny and Miles (1983) have pointed out that the definitions are of limited value since the term services has at least four meanings:

1   *Service industries:* including tertiary industries (transport, communications, utilities), personal services (hairdressers, dentists, catering), goods services (maintenance of cars, consumer goods and buildings), producer services (finance, banking, legal and research work), cultural industries (publishing, broadcasting, advertising) and public services (education, health and public administration);

2   *Service products:* which are also produced by manufacturing industries who offer them for sale (for example, computer manufacturers who offer maintenance services) or who consume them internally;

3   *Service workers:* people who actually produce the service products are distributed across all industries both service and manufacturing; and

4   *Service functions:* necessary human requirements which can be satisfied in a number of historically specific and changing ways.

The interesting question from the point of view of analysing work organization is how the changing structure of service industries and employment is linked to changes in the mode of satisfaction of various human service functions. Gershuny and Miles (1983) have used these distinctions to demonstrate a characteristic shift in services over recent decades. Some service functions have been satisfied with new manufactured products rather than by an expansion of a service industry of waged workers. Using these manufactured durables, consumers fulfil the ultimate service function with their own labour, in so-called 'self-servicing' modes; the motor car as a means of meeting the transport service function and the television and video as a means of meeting the entertainment service function are obvious examples. Huws (1985) notes others, in the use of consumer durables for food preparation and in the washing of clothes. These examples illustrate that there are profound 'social innovations' in consumption which accompany the transformation of a service product to a manufactured product, a process we can call 'commodification'.

If one sees information technology as the main component of the next wave of technological change and extrapolates the self-servicing thesis into the immediate future, interesting possibilities emerge. For example, some services could be transformed as people buy information technology equipment to substitute for some services which were previously externally provided but have now been cut back, because they are highly labour intensive or relatively too expensive. Some service functions could then be fulfilled by means of bought software running on mass-produced information technology devices operated by individual consumers. As new technologies profoundly change the means of producing physical goods and services, so new consumption patterns are established with a radically different mix of service provision. At the same time some aspects of a wide variety of services previously provided by the state could, in a radically new technological form, be brought into the household creating large consumer markets for private firms. In education, for example, educational and training packages using interactive video discs and telecommunication links for 'distance' learning are already beginning to be used. In health care, the example of medical self-testing kits will be discussed later in this chapter.

The commodification/self-service argument is, however, less straightforward with regard to services such as education and health than it is for transport, entertainment and domestic tasks. First, education and health require much more highly skilled, professional labour. Second, health and education are frequently closely tied to the state which may financially support them or even organize them as part of the state's historically acquired function of shaping the institutions which reproduce and organize civil society. The combined support and control functions of services within the welfare state arose out of the inability of market mechanisms to satisfy health, education and welfare demands. Since commodification is a process which is more in the market than in the state administrative realm, there are difficulties in penetrating the state welfare areas. Nevertheless, technological developments do present the possibility of changes in the delivery of these professional services as well as in the nature of the service product itself. We will explore what this means by discussing two aspects of the delivery of health care which are currently undergoing organizational and technological change – administration and management, and diagnostic laboratory testing. The first focuses on changes in management information systems and the resulting distribution of managerial power and authority between administrative and clinical personnel; the second on how existing ways of organizing diagnostic testing are changing with the availability of quicker and cheaper tests which are less reliant on the services of skilled laboratory technicians.

Health care administration: organizational and technological changes

The British National Health Service (NHS) is a particular institutional form of health care service provision which is specific to the conditions of the evolution of health care politics in Britain. Since the mid-1970s, however, successive governments have pressed for the NHS to emulate or adopt procedures and structures which are present in other, less socialized health systems, so its development extends beyond the British case. In what follows we focus on the interplay of organizational and technological changes in the internal management procedures of the NHS, and its possible implications in the light of the preceding discussion.

Organizational changes

We cannot here do justice to all the organizational changes in the NHS which have been especially numerous since the mid-1970s. We shall concentrate on the changes in management structure and in budgetary procedures recommended by the Griffiths Report (1983). The events following this report have perhaps been the clearest expression of the growing tendency on the part of successive governments, through the Department of Health and Social Security (DHSS), to require the NHS to function in a more commercial manner.[2]

From the early 1980s the NHS has been involved in a drawn out transformation from its previous state as a medical service organization with limited administrative needs met by specialist administrators. The new target form and ethos for the NHS is a so-called tight and cost-effective service in which activities are planned and operated with detailed knowledge of the opportunity cost to other activities, and within a budget. Nothing will ever be allowed to 'grow like Topsy' any more; at least this is the dream of some in the DHSS. The attitude is that even though the NHS is not a profit-making business, it can be run using the rules of 'good husbandry' which businesses are supposed to employ, and that this is the appropriate way to frame discussions between doctors, managers, politicians and patients about what the content of the service should be.

The impetus to this managerialist tide has three components. First, and most obvious, is the pressure on the overall NHS budget. This is due to the increased demand for health care induced by an aging population and the use of more expensive medical technologies, as well as high inflation of health costs and Britain's poor economic situation restricting room for manoeuvre in public spending. The second reason concerns the changed ideological and political situation in Britain since 1979. Conservative governments have been more zealous than the 1974–9 Labour government in trying to squeeze economies from the NHS and wish to see a more market-based relationship between suppliers and consumers of health care. The third reason concerns the increasing size and complexity of the NHS and the increasing professionalization of health administration.

The aspect of the Griffiths Report (1983) which has attracted most attention outside the NHS has been the creation of general manager posts at all levels down to that of individual hospitals, replacing the system of administrators and consensus management. In the NHS, doctors' decisions are the main influence on resource consumption, but doctors are not managerially responsible for those resources, so the creation of general managers is clearly important.

Another of the recommendations of the Griffiths Report, however, was the implementation of NHS management budgets. In essence, these budgets are negotiated agreements between 'budget holders' (such as a senior consultant running a specialist hospital department) and district treasurers or unit general managers. A given level of clinical activity is related to a resource level for a budgeting period, usually of one year. The budget holders are then charged with moderating their behaviour in accordance with their budget, subject to provisos concerning unforeseen changes in activity, and uncontrollable (external) effects on costs. Penalties and incentives for over- or under-spending are a possible component of the scheme. The philosophy which underlies the scheme is that the clinicians who control the level and character of activity in the NHS are the immediate influence on resource consumption and that they should therefore be the 'natural managers' of the service. The proposers of the scheme hope that if information on activity and resource consumption is regularly fed back to a budget holder he or she will identify and exploit opportunities for increasing efficiency which might otherwise be overlooked. These management budgets were being actively developed in the second half of the 1980s in some parts of the NHS.

Such an approach to the management of the NHS calls for a very substantial increase in the sophistication of the information systems of most hospitals and District Health Authorities. Depending on how ambitious a local district management is in following this approach, changes may be necessary to the data sets collected on finance, manpower utilization and clinical activity (for example, patients treated in each diagnostic category, drugs used and theatre times). This will normally involve substantial increases in the use of computer hardware and associated software. The detailed design of the system, involving decisions about the level of budget holder (for example, medical speciality, consultant or group of consultants), the content of the information fed back, the method of presentation and the rules for the use of money involves considerable discussion between different sections of the administrative machinery and the clinicians themselves. An issue of fundamental importance here is the differing perceptions which occur both between administrators and clinicians, and within those two groups, concerning the merit and purpose of budgets. Amongst clinicians, there are opinions ranging from enthusiasm and energetic participation to scepticism and outright opposition. Some believe that resource management has its rightful place in the clinical competence of the doctor whilst others are suspicious that budgets are a covert device for reducing overall resources. There is evidence from studies of the health systems of other countries (Coombs, 1987) that a group of doctor-managers could emerge as a distinct elite within the medical profession. It is not yet clear whether this will happen within the NHS.

NHS administrators have usually been in favour of the principle of devolved budgets but there are differences as to how they should be introduced, what the degree of devolution should be and what forms the financial information should take. This makes for an intricate framework of values and attitudes shaping the changes in information systems in which fundamental issues concerning the quality of the service, the effectiveness of delivery, the balance of types of activity and the appropriate devices for measurement of these concepts are continually being raised and contested.

We now turn to the role of information technology in the context of the organizational changes under way, looking both at aspects which result quite closely from the issues we have discussed and others which have different origins.

The role of information technology

Information technology (IT) is diffusing into a variety of managerial activities in the NHS.[3] These fall into three broad categories. First, IT is being used to store data on normal everyday operational activity of hospitals. Examples of this are patient administration systems in which remote terminals are used to record admissions and discharges on a computer network, at the time at which the event occurs. It is a relatively straightforward extension of this system to include data on primary diagnosis, the patient's doctor and planned medical procedures. Second, IT is being used in manpower planning and control systems in which staff allocation between wards and larger units is monitored and planned on microcomputer systems. Third, IT is being used as computer-based budgetary packages in financial control systems in which cost data are allocated to defined cost centres (ranging from clinical departments, through individual doctors, to individual patients). The management budget systems already mentioned are current examples of this trend.

There is considerable scope for the interlinking of these three uses of IT both in straightforward technical terms and in permitting novel analyses and calculations by linking together data in new ways. In technical terms, the existence of increasing numbers of computers and terminals and the facilities to connect them together is creating an environment in which combinations of the three types of system (activity, manpower and financial) have become more and more feasible. The movement from central batch-processing systems to decentralized on-line systems is a powerful impetus here since it increases both the range of data that the systems can acquire and the range of potential consumers. Among software specialists, the motivation exists to mesh the three types of data in order to generate novel indicators of organizational performance and to provide a richer information base for the planning and control of the NHS. The possibility of doing this is of course facilitated by the fact that the data can be easily defined and captured in compatible forms and moved around within the connecting computer systems.

Examples of new performance indicators are the experiments in diagnostic costing which borrow some of the methodology of the accounting systems of private health care organizations. These experiments are based on the American Diagnostic-Related Groups (DRG) system in which average treatment costs for closely defined diagnostic categories are calculated from national data on the costs of treatment in hospitals across the USA. In the USA these are then used as the basis for reimbursement by insurers, thus imposing a market discipline on hospitals. In the UK and other European countries the investigations and experiments are centred on creating DRG–type data for internal management control, thus inserting 'internal market' discipline into the control system. The ten–year regional and district plans which are now in use in the NHS base their allocations on a crude form of this principle, though working at a much higher level of aggregation than the DRG system.

The two trajectories of organizational and of technological change that we have identified do not, however, follow clear and predetermined paths. The organizational developments surrounding the measurement and control initiatives are fraught with disagreement and conflict. The culture of the NHS is dominated by the medical profession and the dualism in the locus of managerial control between administrators and doctors. The very notion of control is an anathema to a substantial proportion of medical professionals because of the deep-seated ideology of clinical freedom. The actual content of initiatives to expand the scope of control information in the NHS is continually subject to bargaining, disagreement and local particularism. Furthermore the vast size and federal character of the NHS, as well as the distance of the national management from the units, means that the general exhortation to increase management control is essentially a political campaign within the organization. As of 1988, there were no clear nationally agreed rules for cost allocation and managerial responsibility to be followed in the creation of the control systems. Thus the central directive can be interpreted in widely differing ways by different parts of the organization.

Similarly, with regard to information technology equipment, there is no clear path laid down by any central agency. There are some centralized NHS initiatives in 'demonstration sites' which could provide the basis for a more consistent set of procedures but there is no requirement on individual district managements to use these systems. A plethora of systems ranging from the small to the very large has in fact sprung up everywhere in the NHS. Some of these are packages purchased or commissioned from consultants and systems houses – and they are frequently imcompatible with each other. Others may be entirely home-grown and therefore even more likely to be context-specific. Thus the particular performance indicators and planning initiatives which arise in any local site are the outcome of some national and shared pressures, some local peculiarities, and some mixture of standard and customized pieces of information technology.

These changes are enhancing elements of competitiveness within the system in two ways. First, there is the issue of the overall effectiveness of health provision as shown by the information systems' indicators. In the public service context, competitiveness is translated into cost effectiveness and pressure is being exerted to prove this more 'scientifically'. Second, the information generated by the systems, in the context of overall resource shortage, is creating a much more intricate bargaining environment in which all sub-units within the NHS – wards, doctors, medical specialties, hospitals, district authorities, regional authorities and community services – have to compete for resources by demonstrating effectiveness. This in turn highlights the difficult problem of the incommensurability of different activities such as, for example, between preventive and acute medicine.

Information technology is thus not a static bundle of technical attributes; individual systems' features can be seen to be the result of interactions between the enabling features of a technology, and the culture, control systems and competitive circumstances within and surrounding the organization. However, local particularism is not absolute. 'Solutions' generated in one location can diffuse to other locations and partly predetermine or even pre-empt rival local developments. The organizational desire for management budgets is stimulating the use of IT in so-called 'feeder' systems (such as those generating pathology or radiology costs and assigning them to the consultant originating the requests). Also the availability of the IT is making possible initiatives such as those based on DRGs, which would not otherwise be feasible.

Laboratory testing: technological and organizational changes

New technologies for the *actual* output (service product) of the health care service sector – namely the diagnosis, treatment and care of the sick and incapacitated – are legion. The non-communist world market for medical equipment in 1985 was approximately $30 billion and is a manufacturing growth industry (ACARD, 1986). In treatment and care in the 1980s new technologies have included implantable devices and synthetic organs based on new materials, computer-aided electronic patient monitoring devices and new techniques of surgery and anaesthesia. In diagnosis there has been substantial investment worldwide in hospital-based computer-aided devices for imaging which provide better internal 'pictures' of patients, through new techniques of scanning tomography – Magnetic Resonance (MRI), Ultrasound, Positron Emission (PET). Also for diagnosis there is a growing market for devices based on microelectronics for the measurement of body electrical signals (electronic blood pressure measurement devices, electronic thermometers and miniaturized portable, 'ambulatory' equipment for the measurement of cardiac signals).[4] Finally there is a widening range of new techniques and electronic devices for the detection of substances in body fluids (blood, urine and infectious discharges) – the sort of tests of patients' samples done in biochemical and microbiological laboratories. (The world market for diagnostics in 1985 was $5 billion and rising fast.) This is the subject of the present section of the chapter.

As with our discussion of NHS administration, we will review incipient technological developments in the context of organizational changes in diagnostic testing. This includes changes in the formal health care services, organized in state-financed or state-regulated Health Services, as well as those in the informal sector of self-care, self-diagnosis and self-medication. Discussion is principally confined to Britain with its centralized hospital laboratories which carry out the majority of analyses of hospital and general practice testing with only a small over-the-counter (OTC) market which has so far been mainly for pregnancy test kits. Other advanced countries with different health care financing systems have different organizational structures for testing and a more dispersed usage of new tests, with primary care clinics performing many tests in their own small laboratories and a larger OTC market.

Forty years ago most hospitals had limited testing facilities – siderooms off wards and clinics performing a few, almost exclusively urine, tests. This changed during the 1950s; testing began to be centralized in large hospital laboratories or, particularly in the USA, subcontracted to privately owned pathology laboratories, staffed by a growing number of laboratory technicians. The growth of laboratory testing and the explosion in the number of tests performed on patients' blood and urine were associated with the mechanization and automation of testing and the ready availability of pre-packaged reagents. The first automated machine, Technicon's AutoAnalyzer, introduced in 1957, reduced the test for the analysis of blood sugar, important for the control of diabetes, to a fraction of the time and cost of previous manual methods. By 1970 a number of other manufacturers had introduced machines which could perform simultaneously a number of biochemical tests on blood or urine samples in automated analysers, each additional test costing little more than the cost of the reagents. Doctors began routinely to order all the tests that their laboratory instruments could do – obtaining elaborate data on the profile of each patient's sample. In addition, from the late 1970s instrument manufacturers started to sell semi-automatic devices for the more rapid culturing and identification of micro-organisms, to introduce more mechanization into the microbiology laboratory.

There has been much criticism of this application of Parkinson's Law to testing. Doctors have been criticized for over-ordering, and then being unable to analyse properly the resulting reams of machine print-out data whose relevance to the particular patient's illness might be obscure. Over-ordering is one result of the methods of financing health care consultations in which the actual cost of the tests is borne by neither patient nor doctor directly. It has also been stimulated, especially in the USA, by fears that omitting to perform some readily available test might open a doctor to legal action for malpractice (Fineberg, 1979).

However, from the mid-1970s completely new techniques which do not rely on large automatic machines to perform accurate analyses have been introduced. These tests involve new biochemical methods, sometimes in combination with new microelectronic-based devices.[5] One of their central 'selling points' is that, apart from being quick and individually cheap, they are simple to perform (though interpretation and diagnosis may still be difficult). They can, therefore, be done by non-laboratory workers – by doctors themselves (not necessarily trained in the complexities of laboratory equipment operation), by nurses and, in some cases, even by patients themselves with or without the supervision of health care personnel. They are thus useful for what is called 'bedside' or 'near-patient' or, less colourfully, 'decentralized' testing (Marks and Alberti, 1985, 1986). The near-patient test most familiar to readers will be the do-it-yourself pregnancy test though there are many others notably for the detection of glucose in blood (useful in monitoring insulin therapy) and the detection of blood in faeces (an early indicator of possible bowel cancer). Advances in biotechnology, based on monoclonal antibodies, have extended the range of possible new tests for the detection of micro-organisms and 'tumour markers'. This opens the possibility for quick, simple and cheap home tests for various bacterial and viral infections, particularly sexually transmitted diseases (STDs) and for otherwise as yet undetected (asymptomatic) cancers. Screening for the earlier detection of many conditions, particularly cancers, therefore becomes economically conceivable (Steering Committee on Future Health Scenarios, 1987).[5]

Many of these technological developments are being promoted by US firms both in the diagnostics industry (where firms are keen to exploit the potential of monoclonal antibody technology) and in the laboratory instrumentation industry. There are strong links between the developers of the test kits and of electronic devices and many companies are actively promoting the sales of their new testing devices directly to doctors rather than to laboratories. There is also direct promotion to individual consumers. Since 1986, US TV stations have been encouraging viewers to screen themselves for faecal blood, using a quick screening kit made by SmithKline Diagnostics; the kit is picked up free of charge from your local chain pharmacist – donated as a loss leader for its other products – and processed by a local hospital laboratory. It is recommended that you perform this self-screening annually from the age of 40, purchasing a kit and calling on your health insurance to finance any further internal examinations.

Some may see these near-patient tests as a classic example of technologies of deskilling – if performed by laboratory workers at all they are intended to be simple enough to be done by less-trained staff. But this would be a rather one-dimensional view. The tests can also be carried out by doctors themselves or by nurses either in general practitioners' (GPs) or consultants' clinics, or by the patients themselves at home. This can have a number of advantages: the results are obtainable more quickly than from centralized laboratories so patients do not have to revisit the doctor just to get the test results; testing can be done at times and places otherwise inconvenient for the laboratories (for example, at night). Near-patient testing may also be cheaper than centralized testing: though the cost per test might be higher, reduced transport costs from sample points to central laboratories may counterbalance this. In addition, in the USA quick tests allow GPs to present a more efficient image, thus attracting patients – testing in this case is a competitive weapon in the health care business. If more testing were to be done by patients themselves then there could be an extension of self-care. So far, however, the use of such tests for self-care in Britain has been limited. The market for pregnancy and fertility tests is the largest but even that runs at only about £4 million per year though forecasts expect it to grow rapidly in the early 1990s, even if not so rapidly as in the USA.

The advent of near-patient testing raises, we should stress, only the possibility of a different organization of diagnostic testing, both within the formal health care service and in the extent of OTC do-it-yourself testing. A number of other organizational factors have to be considered concerning two general policy disputes – between professional control and managerial control of health care organization (as discussed earlier) and between preventive and curative medicine.

There is frequent criticism of the increased centralization of laboratories. Some see centralized automated testing as too inflexible, resulting in the slowness of transport of samples from clinics/GPs surgeries to laboratories; indeed the very cheapness of automated testing encourages its over-use. Some doctors are, however, keen on decentralization so that they can do the testing in their surgeries and clinics.[6] In particular over the last fifteen years there have been changes in the status of GPs within the NHS due to their improved training and the increased emphasis on primary health care. GPs are, therefore, both keener on, and more capable of, carrying through innovations, but this is thwarted in the UK (unlike in the USA) by the lack of any significant fee-for-service system; so ACARD (1986) thinks that technological innovation at the primary health care level is held back in Britain to the detriment of British firms in the medical equipment and diagnostic market. GPs are now keener to be involved in management of chronic conditions (such as hypertension or diabetes) and there is patient pressure for more autonomy, all of which encourages more self-testing though with clinician support (such as in the management of some types of diabetes).

However, the managerial/cost-controlling forces might not be so clearly in favour of decentralization in the NHS. Certainly, changes in hospital financing as described earlier might favour decentralization of testing because it promises reduced costs per department; but doctors might not see this in such narrow financial terms, preferring to emphasize the positive aspects for patients of quicker testing, such as speedy diagnosis in outpatient clinics. The economics are not then so clearly in favour of decentralization. As the large laboratories will still be needed for more complicated tests, the cost of each test might rise considerably if expensive equipment were to be used less intensively.

The increased national emphasis on preventive medicine might promote demand for cheap screening and self-monitoring. But there is in addition the opportunity for manufacturers of diagnostic equipment to develop new markets for tests for certain medical conditions thought embarrassing. This might be particularly true for STDs: in the USA an infection self-sampling kit for gonorrhoea can be purchased in drugstores and posted for analysis at a private pathology laboratory. Quick tests are also marketed for home use detection of some cancers. One might expect some change if quicker tests for STDs and particularly for the AIDS virus could be marketed. There is already a large market for pregnancy tests used to get quick confirmation prior to arranging ante-natal care or, perhaps, an abortion.

There is a substantial non-medical/political element to the growth of screening tests of this sort. For example, in the summer of 1986 in the USA, a stimulus was given to extra-medical system testing in Nancy Reagan's anti-drugs campaign (Sims, 1986). The US drug test market was worth $80m in 1986 – 70 per cent of the world market. The US military does 3 million tests a year and 30 per cent of US companies do mandatory tests. The latest urine test takes three minutes to detect morphine, cocaine and amphetamines by colour change in a sheet of specially impregnated paper. So far the market in Britain for drug tests of this kind is small, though growing (Blackhurst and Inman, 1987).

It is too early to see how the new testing technologies and the on-going changes in the organizational structure of testing will interact. How will they change the balance between testing in centralized hospital laboratories and in (decentralized) consultants' and GPs' clinics? What will the balance be between the growth of informal OTC home testing and testing from within the formal health care service? It is not possible simply to 'read off' the future organization forms – including the division of testing labour between existing laboratory workers and the new near-patient or do-it-yourself testers – from the technological possibilities. Organizational change can be induced by changes in funding levels for the different types of health (primary versus hospital), in the level and type of demand for health care services, as well as the strategies of equipment suppliers, and in external political demands. At the same time possibly unconnected changes may be occurring in available technologies. These technologies will offer new possibilities – because they are cheaper, easier and/or more promising – in addressing the new questions thrown up by on-going organizational change.

Conclusion

We have discussed a number of features of the organizational and technological trends in the NHS which bear upon the future evolution of patterns of control in administration and laboratory testing. The variable character of the technological systems being adopted or likely to be adopted is interesting and important. In some commercial organizations, such as some private hospitals, conditions are such that uniformity of control systems can be sought and achieved; but this is not the case in the NHS. The factors which appear to be specific to the NHS, and thus interesting in terms of their ability to shape managerial control strategies, are these:

- the fact that the state is the source of many of the initiatives, and is therefore both more distant and more internally differentiated than a conventional management;
- the great uncertainty surrounding the formulation of agreed objectives in the planning, delivery and quality of medical care, and the inability of non-medical personnel legitimately to specify how medical work should be done;
- the unique blend of bureaucratic and professional control systems which overlays the formal management structure of the NHS and the peculiarly public nature in which some of the resulting conflicts are conducted; and
- the prospect that redesigned institutions, in which either markets, or decentralized budget systems, or some combination of the two, might modify behaviour of clinicians in

ways which conventional managerial strategies have been unable to achieve.

The new forms of organizational structure of the NHS and, by extension, the organization of work in its different sub-units, are thus heavily dependent on struggles within the NHS and between the NHS and the state, the outcome of which cannot be ascertained in advance. Nevertheless we can speculate, drawing on some of the ideas discussed earlier regarding the way service industries are restructured around new technological forms.

The presence of an increased number of computer terminals as part of the office furniture of hospital departments might be thought to have radical consequences for work organization. However this is unlikely to be the case, at least until the late 1990s. Most terminals will only substitute computer operations for paper-based operations in relatively modest portions of individuals' work roles. The scope for Fordist specialization will be low. More important, there is little evidence of a managerial motive, or even real management capability, to implement such specialization. The work of non-professional groups is conditioned by, and organized to reflect, the rhythm of work of clinical professionals. As we have emphasized, these professionals have great autonomy in the organization of work and exercise by far the most important influence on day-to-day operations of all hospital workers. One possible counter-tendency to this inertia in work reorganization is the possibility thatthe managerialist tide could eventually penetrate the ethos of the clinical professionals, resulting in their seeking work reorganization directly. The form of such work reorganization will, however, still depend on local circumstances.

For reasons we have described it is quite likely that some changes in hospital laboratory organization will occur and it is into those changes that the new testing technologies will be fitted. Such changes will alter personnel requirements, the skills demanded and the patterns of work of laboratory employees. Increased decentralization is opposed by some laboratory workers on the grounds that training of ancillary/ nursing staff in the performance of the tests will be inadequate if not centrally directed and the results of the tests will be of low quality (Browning *et al.*, 1984). Laboratory managers are more likely to be in favour of controlled decentralization, emphasizing potential econo-mies of scale and cost control resulting from centralized testing so long as suitable curbs can be placed on doctor's ordering of 'unnecessary' testing. Other changes would follow if GPs were permitted to charge the NHS for carrying out tests in their own clinics. Obviously, this wouldreduce the number of tests ordered by GPs from hospital laboratories and encourage the larger primary health care clinics to set up their own laboratories. If preventative screening campaigns become more popular or diagnostic firms were able to convince the medical profession that there were no health dangers from mis-diagnosis in an extended range of OTC tests, then the market for such tests would increase considerably.

Technological changes of the kind service industries are currently experiencing are, then, not just significant because of associated changes in work organization. Especially in large service industries, particularly those with close connections to the state, the content of the service and the manner of its delivery – the constitution of the service's product – can be substantially altered. New technologies will make possible new products which may substitute for the existing service products, forcing the substituted service industry to restructure, or permitting other industries, both manufacturing and service, to expand.

Not all elements of health care can be refashioned into marketed manufactured commodities – as opposed to marketed service commodities (such as private hospital surgery). As we have tried to show, the technological conditions are however being established for a refashioning of the testing component of diagnosis. It is conceivable therefore that the current organizational arrangements for testing could also change with the emergence of markets for testing kits in a direct relationship between manufacturer and 'patient' rather than as at present with the doctor acting as a mediator. The possible use of new testing techniques in this way is admittedly limited in Britain by the low privately financed input into health care. There is no direct financial stimulus to the diffusion of the tests. However the situation is different in the USA and in some European countries where expansion of extra-laboratory testing is encouraged by the prevalence of fee-for-service medicine. Indeed the high cost of ancillary medical services encourages doctors in a competitive health care system to adopt cheaper tests and even to externalize testing costs by encouraging patients to self-service. Coupled with the greater public interest in illness prevention and higher costs of consultation this encourages the growth of the US OTC self-testing market. Nevertheless the growth of OTC testing for some medical conditions cannot be ruled out in Britain.

Even within the formal health services, technological changes can be associated with changes in what constitutes the output of the service. As we have described, the powerful pressures on the NHS to use resources more economically and to justify its activities have created an impetus toward measurement, calculation, analysis and cost control. At the same time, the rapidly maturing hardware and software of information technology is creating ever-expanding possibilities for the capture, transmission and manipulation of the data involved. The construction of a richer, more extensive database, facilitated by IT, permits strategic options in the delivery of health care to be explored more extensively. This means that the types of conditions to be treated and the mix of them (for example: how many hip operations? how many open heart operations?) can undergo changes. The same is true of who treats them (in the sense of the balance between medical, nursing and ancillary labour required) and of where they are treated (in GP clinics? in day surgery? through preventative methods?). To put it another way, the combination of changes in management systems and in the use of more efficient information processing systems can result in improvements in health care productivity and efficiency (the declared aim of the NHS reorganizers) and also a re-cast of what the NHS actually offers as health care. The combined effects of financial pressures and improved awareness of the actual costs of procedures has resulted in the NHS contracting out some medical services (such as surgery) to the private sector, whilst simultaneously selling other services (such as scanning) to the private sector.

Any changes that are possible in a service product, to return to Gershuny and Miles's terms, will be part of an ongoing reorganization of the service industry concerned, both internally and in its transactions with its customers or clients. These changes, may, however, be under way for reasons unconnected with technological changes, caused instead by shifts in resources or straightforward political intervention. These trajectories of organizational change interact with, and change the opportunities for, the utilization of new technologies. Changes in the work tasks of the various groups of workers in these organizations will depend on how these interactions work out. It should be clear that it is not possible to forecast in detail changes in the work organization of the NHS, or of groups within it, which are deemed to flow from the use of new technologies, whether for information processing or for clinical diagnosis. Information technologies and new diagnostic tests only affect work organization by way of their interaction with organizational innovations which are taking place for reasons not directly connected with the technological innovations. Detailed studies of changes in work organization for particular groups – nurses, secretaries, doctors, laboratory technicians – must not over-concentrate on changes in the details of day-to-day work that the use of new technology requires. They must also be concerned with broader transformations in the overall work-organizations. But it must also be remembered that new technologies and new organizational imperatives alter not only the way in which the service product is delivered, they alter what the service product is.

16 *What is socialist about socialist production? Autonomy and control in a Hungarian steel mill*

MICHAEL BURAWOY and
JÁNOS LUKÁCS

Are there features which distinguish production in state socialist societies from production in capitalist societies?[1] Can one talk of a capitalist as opposed to a state socialist production process? At similar levels of the development of the forces of production is the work organization in industrial societies essentially similar, irrespective of differences in their political and economic systems? After undertaking case studies which compare advanced capitalism and state socialism, specifically the United States and Hungary, we have come to the provisional conclusion that the two types of economy do incline toward different forms of work organization. Specifically, Braverman's (1974) thesis that the tendencies toward the separation of conception and execution shape the character of capitalist production finds indirect support from the reverse tendencies we observed in state socialist enterprises.

Criticisms of Braverman have often been misplaced. His focus on domination at the expense of resistance, his mistaking ideology for reality, his recognition of only one strategy of control where a number are operative, his essentialist view of development without adequate analysis of social mechanisms, are all important shortcomings when explaining variations among and within capitalist economies. But Braverman set himself the task of identifying features common to all forms of the capitalist labour process, so his claim that its tendency is toward the separation of conception and execution can be properly evaluated only through a comparison of the labour process in capitalist and non-capitalist societies. This chapter explores the more undeveloped side of this comparison, namely the socialist labour process.

Braverman (1974) was primarily concerned with domination and exploitation, the vertical dimension of production, not with the horizontal conditions that make production possible. That is, Braverman took as unproblematic the supply of inputs to and the demand for products of enterprises. Neither supply nor demand can be taken for granted and we follow Kornai's (1980) distinction between two types of advanced industrial economies, one in which supply exceeds demand, the modern capitalist economy of over-production, and one in which demand exceeds supply, the state socialist economy of shortage. Contrary to Piore and Sabel (1984) who argue that demand-side constraints generate tendencies toward the reunification of conception and execution, we argue that this is the result of supply side constraints.[2] Our task will be to identify, on the one hand, pressures toward and compatibility between expropriation of control from the shop-floor and over-production under advanced capitalism and, on the other hand, pressures toward and compatibility between workshop autonomy and shortages under state socialism.

Theoretical framework

We define a mode of production as composed of two sets of relations: relations of production through which goods and services are appropriated and redistributed, and relations in production which define the labour process, the production of those goods and services. Under capitalism appropriation is private with a view to accumulating profit in a context of market competition. The pressure here is to gain a competitive edge either by process innovation (including reducing wages, developing mass production, reducing inventories and introducing new technology) or by product innovation. This has two consequences. First is the tendency toward over-production, for supply to exceed demand. Captialism is, therefore, characterized by demand constraints and, following Piore and Sabel (1984), one can plot the development of capitalism and its national variations in terms of changes in those constraints as well as the way enterprises and states respond to them.

But there is a second consequence of the search for profit in a competitive market which Piore and Sabel (1984) overlook. That is, it leads to the insecurity of both capital and labour. Profit is realized in the market but generated in production. The reproduction of the relations of production depends first and foremost on the relations in production and so the capitalist can afford the latter little unfettered autonomy, and all the less so the more intense the competition. Although management might subscribe to all sorts of ideologies defending greater participation by employees and in certain cases put these into practice (see Chapter 9) this is concerned with achieving control over and co-operation from employees. The contemporary context of global competition has created pressures toward centralization within large enterprises, for example, through the elimination of middle managers, whilst simultaneously managements are pursuing 'involvement' strategies at 'local levels'.

Since labour depends on capital over which it has little control its fate is doubly insecure. It has to cope with an arbitrary subordination to capital, itself subject to the caprice of the market place. Anxiety at this level concerning material livelihood is inimical to forms of self-organization that do not bring immediate economic gains or may further endanger jobs.

In state socialism, central appropriation incorporates enterprises into a hierarchical bargaining structure.[3] The accumulation of resources, whether of materials or investment, depends on the enterprise's bargaining power with the centre which may depend upon its size, its profitability, the political influence of its director, plan fulfilment or other criteria. None of these are 'hard' criteria but are themselves subject to bargaining. The results are twofold. First, enterprises develop a seemingly inexhaustible appetite for investment resources, leading to shortages. The source of that appetite cannot be reduced to a universal urge for expansion (Kornai, 1980) but more important in our view is the allocation of new resources which makes it impossible to effectively utilize existing ones. Supply constraints, that is, stem from the discrepancy between the logic of allocation and the logic of production.

Central appropriation and redistribution give rise to a second set of consequences. The success of an enterprise is less dependent on the production process than bargaining power with the centre. Insecurity lies in the competitive relations among enterprises for resources which are centrally allocated. The result is a split within management between strategic management, looking upwards to reproduce and expand the relations of production, and operational management concerned with relations in production while middle management negotiates relations between the two. The independence of operational management creates the possibility of autonomous adaptation to supply constraints. As we shall see this autonomy can become quite coercive when materials and machinery are so inadequate as to make adaptation more and more impossible. At the same time employees do not work in fear of losing their jobs – a security which conditions the possibility of their self-organization.

In other words, centralized appropriation – the separation of conception and execution at the level of relations of production – goes hand in hand with decentralized production – the unity of conception and execution at the level of relations in production. This is made possible by guarantees of employment and of enterprise survival while it is made necessary by the need to adapt to shortages. In capitalist appropriation, on the other hand, the mutual interdependence of the relations in production and relations of production leaves no space for autonomous self-regulation of the former without corresponding regulation of the latter. Any attempts at self-organization of work are made more difficult by the insecurities facing both capital and labour as well as by the centralizing pressures from demand-side constraints.

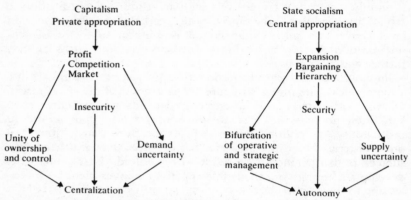

Figure 16.1 Ideal type models of capitalist and state socialist enterprises

In this chapter we illustrate this theoretical framework by an analysis of Red Star Steel Works, one of Hungary's three integrated steel mills. We will examine, in particular, one section of the plant where the steel is actually produced. Here the use of the most modern equipment, imported from advanced capitalist countries, allows us to control for the effects of technology in studying how the political economy shapes work organization. Following the model outlined above, we focus on problems in the supply of both investment resources and material supplies, and how shortages are exacerbated by demand constraints. We then turn to the way a shortage economy structures management. At the enterprise level strategic management negotiates external relations, in particular bargaining with the state over, for example, new investments, subsidies, prices and production profiles. In the plant middle management acts as a co-ordinating umbrella for operational management, the majority of whom are formally skilled workers. Middle management finds its influence restricted, on the one side, by strategic managers who hand down decisions arrived at through accommodations with the state and, on the other side, by operational managers who have to enjoy considerable autonomy if they are to adapt to the exigencies of shortages. We describe the forms of this self-organization on the shop-floor and managerial attempts to undermine it. In particular, we studied two cases of attempted centralization – the use of computers to regulate the system of production and the imposition of a centrally directed system of quality control – and a further case of the scrap yard where shortages were too intense to permit meaningful self-organization. Finally, we draw some conclusions about the potentialities and tendencies of the socialist labour process.

Shortage constraints at Red Star Steel Works

The problem of shortages becomes more or less intense according to pressures from the demand side and from the character of the technology. We examine each factor in turn.

Demand pressures

Red Star Steel Works produces steel for domestic and foreign industry, including quality carbon and alloy steel. Of Red Star's total steel production in 1985 63 per cent was used domestically, 14 per cent was exported to socialist countries and 23 per cent to the West. The specific site of our study within Red Star was the Combined Steel Works, completed in 1980 at the very height of the international steel crisis. Its purpose was to introduce 'state of the art' technology into the production of quality and alloy steel, primarily to supply the growing need of domestic manufacturing industry for specialized quality steels. Proudly boasting that it can produce any type of steel, Red Star management faces intense pressure from the state to accept orders for almost any type of alloy steel required by Hungarian industry. The relatively small scale of manufacturing ventures and a general unwillingness to use higher quality steel in Hungary has given rise to lots of small-batch production with a wide range of quality specifications.

Diverse and small-batch production is also the result of state economic policy. The construction of the Combined Steel Works was part of a larger government plan for the steel industry, namely that in addition to supplying domestic demand it should export finished products to the dollar markets while importing its raw materials from the ruble markets, complementing the opposite strategy of the machine and vehicle building industries which import capital goods from the West and export to the Soviet bloc. The success of this venture has been substantially thwarted by the unanticipated international crisis in steel production, marked by world steel surpluses, competition from both advanced and industrializing countries with their new steel complexes, and falling prices for finished steel. The strategic management of Red Star has sought to enter into the world market by accepting orders which Western steel makers reject as uneconomic, namely small-batch production of high quality steels at huge losses. Only by establishing its reputation in such steels can Red Star begin to attract orders that might be profitable but to achieve the necessary reliability is virtually impossible given the constraints on small-batch production posed by shortages in and/or poor quality of raw materials and investment goods. A further consequence is that the state has to make up the losses of the steel enterprise with subsidies, leaving no resources for the investments necessary to alleviate some of the problems responsible for the losses.

Uneven development of technology

Irrespective of demand-side pressures Combined Steel Works has to operate in a very unfavourable technological environment. On the one side, the backwardness of the technologies that produce the basic ingredients for steel production – the blast furnaces and scrap deliveries – and, on the other side, the antiquated rolling mills that are often poorly equipped to deal with processing high quality steel undermines the effectiveness of the new steel making complex. While this problem of uneven technology due to under-investment can be found in captalist countries it is accentuated in the shortage economies of state socialism. Here the distribution of investment resources is based on bargaining with state organs, that is, on political as well as economic criteria. Rather than concentrate all new investment at a single steel enterprise it becomes politically imperative to distribute resources among all three enterprises, thereby leading to the development of uneven technology.

To understand some of the problems of installing capitalist technology in a socialist economy we have to look more carefully at the character of that technology. The new steel producing complex gradually replaced the eight, old Siemen's Martin open hearth furnaces with an eighty-ton basic oxygen converter from West Germany, known in the shop as the LD. Like the Martin furnaces before it the LD reduces pig iron to steel by combining it with scrap (roughly in a ratio of four to one) under high temperatures. But whereas the Siemen's Martin furnaces used gas to maintain the necessary high temperatures this is accomplished some eight times as quickly by an infusion of high pressure oxygen. Here operators face a number of typical supply problems. For example, the amount of oxygen 'blown' has to be carefully controlled to produce high quality steel. The computer assumes that the oxygen is 97 per cent pure whereas in fact its purity fluctuates between 87 per cent and 94 per cent so that operators have to blow more oxygen in than prescribed. Exactly how much depends on the quality of the oxygen, which is often unknown. In addition to the LD the combined steel works contains an eighty-ton electric arc furnace from Japan, the UHP, which operates in conjunction with a Swedish vacuum degasser, the ASEA, to provide the highest quality steel.

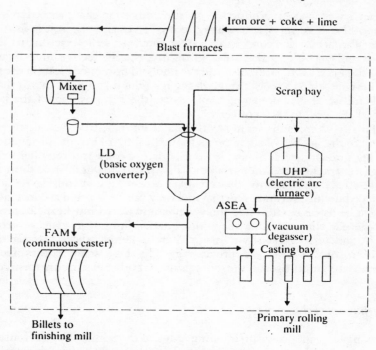

Figure 16.2 The Combined Steel Works at Red Star

Within the same complex are casting facilities. There is a five-strand continuous caster, the FAM, from Japan which accepts steel mainly from the converter. Money did not permit the two continuous casters, originally planned, to process the bulk of the steel produced. Even with the best continuous casters, casting sensitive alloy steel is a difficult operation usually confined to one or two qualities and not the wide range that would have to be cast at Red Star. So there remains a casting bay where ingots are cast and from there taken to the more primitive primary rolling mill via an ill-equipped soaking pit where they are reheated. Stoppages at either of these points affect the casting of ingots at the casting bay as well as the final quality of steel produced in the fine rolling mill. To ensure continuity in production at the rolling mill, that is avoid frequent change of the rollers, they try to maintain the same shape of steel for long periods of time which results in frequent changes in the quality of steel, exacerbating problems in the steel making process.

Pig iron (hot metal) coming from the blast furnaces is *teemed* (poured) into a mixer which can hold up to 1,300 tons, enough for almost twenty *heats* ('vessel' or 'ladle' of steel). As well as acting as a buffer, the mixer is designed to homogenize the content of the hot metal so that steel production in the converter can proceed more smoothly. It is important when the quality of the pig iron from the blast furnace varies considerably over time, as is the case due to the poor and variable quality of the iron ore, the ineffective sinter plant which processes the iron ore, and the now old fashioned blast furnaces. In practice, due to the shortage of pig iron the mixer is often less than half full so that it does not homogenize the composition of the hot metal charged into the converter.

Finally, there is the scrap. As the major ingredient of the electric arc furnace the quality of scrap poses the critical barrier to the production of high quality steel. Scrap is also used in the converter together with pig iron and here too the variable quality means that it is more difficult to control the production proccss. In an advanced steel mill the scrap is divided up into several grades so that they can be selected according to the steel to be made. Here the scrap is not sorted but heaped onto a single pile. It is often of very poor quality and unprocessed – loose, light and often mixed with slag. There is neither the space nor the equipment for effective processing. The best scrap comes from within the enterprise but most of it is used at other electric arc furnaces.

Tightly-coupled technology

We have seen how surrounding advanced technology with more backward technology intensifies the problems created by shortages. But the character of that advanced technology is itself a source of tension. The different parts of the Combined Steel Works are tightly interconnected and interdependent at the same time that they have their own cycles of production so that the entire operation is very sensitive to mechanical breakdowns and to the availability and quality of raw materials. Take the relationship between the converter (LD) and the continuous caster (FAM). The cycle of production at the FAM dominates the production process at the LD but only within limits defined by the LD's own cycle. Once the FAM begins to cast it must be continuously fed with heats from the converter about every forty-five minutes (the exact time depending on the size of the billets being cast and the number of strands working). To be efficient the FAM must be fed at least five consecutive heats. This requires advanced planning. There must be enough hot metal and scrap for all five heats and the temperature of delivery (around 1,600 degrees) is important otherwise the FAM will not work properly. It can happen that by the time the heat reaches the FAM it is too cold, or it reaches the FAM too late, or something happens at the FAM so that it malfunctions – the strands get clogged up with aluminium coating, steel can leak from the strands due to the presence of bits of slag or it may have too low a viscosity due to low temperature before entering the strands – then the heat has to be sent to the casting bay where it can be cast at lower temperatures. But that is a complicated re-routing process and whether there will be space at the casting bay depends on the availability of ingot molds. Such an elaborate co-ordination in time and space of tightly-coupled technology is very susceptible to the type of supply problems that a socialist firm faces. What are the implications for the organization and direction of work?

The squeeze on middle management

Based on the demarcation of three levels of management – strategic, middle (directing the plant and working on day shift) and operational or shop floor (distinguished by shift work) – our thesis is that the shortage economy tends *de facto* to polarize managerial direction at the lowest and the highest levels, leaving middle management dependent on both. This is a consequence of a shortage economy which requires strategic management to negotiate with the environment, particularly the state, at the same time that responsibility for dealing with shortages must lie in flexible organization on the shop floor. We shall show in later sections how attempts by middle management to appropriate control over the shop floor undermine effective adaptation to the exigencies of a tightly coupled technology in a context of supply uncertainty. This is not to say middle management is superfluous. It does carry out important recognizable functions to which we now turn.

Routine functions

First, middle management performs certain routine functions. The highest levels create a buffer between the actual shop-floor practices and the attempts by the front offices to dictate alternatives. Here the authority of the plant manager is critical – both with those above and those below. He has his agents on the shop-floor, work site managers and foremen working permanently on day shift. They mediate dictates from above, as when some urgent order requires immediate production, an experiment is run or preparations have to be made for the visit of a delegation. They are supposed to plan ahead, for example, the supplies needed at the work stations. They redistribute personnel on a temporary basis when there are shortages as well as controlling promotions and demotions. Foremen and work site managers are responsible for co-ordinating relations among the parts of the plant. In their daily managerial meetings they are held accountable for failures at their work sites. At the same time, we shall argue, steel making in the context of shortages of materials and uneven, tightly coupled technology requires that immediate production decisions be made on the spot by skilled workers who are elevated to what we have called operational managers, specifically the steelmakers at the LD, UHP and ASEA, the casting bay master and the process controller at the FAM.

Development functions

Second, middle managers attempt to improve the efficiency and safety of the plant and during the three years of our research we observed considerable increases in the output of the converter. When we began in 1985, the average number of heats was as low as 6 or 7 per shift; when we left two and a half years later it was as high as 9 or 10 with a maximum of 14. This was made possible by the greater availability of pig iron from the blast furnace and higher quality scrap steel. The crucial factor was the final closure of the remaining four Siemen's Martin furnaces in October 1986, so that all the pig iron could be directed to the converter as well as an improvement in the supply of scrap. But who decided to close down the Martin furnaces? Confronted with the necessity of new investment there, strategic management decided to close them down altogether, exploiting the move as a sign of Red Star's commitment to modernization. Once they were closed many of the advantages to the Combined Steel Works fell into place.

Another achievement of middle management is the increased rollability, that is improvements in the quality of the steel coming from the Combined Steel Works, permitting more efficient production in the rolling mills. It attributes this to improved organization and a new incentive system. Further investigation shows that the improvement in the rollability can be attributed to the improved quality of the casting powder used in the casting of ingots, although here, middle management was involved in obtaining the new material. Finally, in the second quarter of 1987 middle management proudly announced a considerable increase in the number of heats per converter lining, from a record of 861 to 1,294. The major reason appears to have been the use of magnesium oxide which reduces the corrosive effects of the slag. This is a textbook solution to the problem, raising the question why it took so long to be adopted. It seems that the problem became particularly acute when, in a short period of time, the price of the heatproof bricks that make up the lining more than doubled from 6 million forints to 14 million, to be paid in foreign exchange. Strategic management transmitted gradually increasing sensitivity to budget constraints by offering middle managers considerable bonuses for extending the life of the lining. Such innovation bonuses are a major way for middle managers to increase their income but not all innovations receive significant rewards. Here middle managers have to take their cue from strategic management who set the system of rewards. Again the initiative for development lies with top managers. There is a reluctance to take up small-scale changes on the shop-floor which would advance production but offer few material rewards.

Regulatory functions

The third and perhaps the most important function for middle managers is to establish the incentive system for shop-floor operations. While all production workers in the Combined Steel Works releive bonuses according to the performance of their respective sectors, output is beyond the control of all but the key operators, such as the pivotal figure of the steelmaker who directs production at the converter. Given a programme of production of certain types of steel, the steelmaker faces three problems: the first is to obtain hot metal and scrap, that is, backward co-operation; the second to ensure effective production of steel at the converter; and the third to deliver steel which is of appropriate quality and temperature which can be teemed at the FAM or casting bay.

The official incentive system corresponds to these three problems. Thus the steelmaker tries, first, to minimize the percentage of hot metal per ton of steel. This in turn minimizes the cost of inputs, since at Red Star hot metal is more expensive than scrap. Second, he tries to minimize the number of kilograms of charge (hot metal and scrap) per ton of steel produced. This is a measure of the efficiency of the converter. Finally, he tries to maximize the ratio of steel teemed to steel cast. This involves producing steel that is of the right temperature, right quality and right quantity so that it can be used at maximum efficiency at the FAM or casting bay. At the FAM any amount of steel can be cast, so that the steelmaker does not worry about the number of tons; but the temperature is critical. At the casting bay, on the other hand, only fourteen ingots each of 5.8 tons can be cast, that is 81.2 tons. Anything over this will have to be scrapped, bringing down the steelmaker's rate of teeming. Here the operative temperatures are lower because the casting is quicker, giving more flexibility to the caster. As far as the steelmaker is concerned, the quantity of steel cast is critical and therefore the steelmaker develops an interest not just in the provision of hot metal and scrap but also in what happens at the FAM and Casting Bay.

For those whose efforts affect production the official incentive system functions quite well. Sometimes, however, there are break-downs, most frequently at the FAM, that are beyond the control of the operators but which can adversely affect their pay. On one occasion the personnel officer explained how the FAM had not been working well and workers' wages were being threatened. Extra premiums were introduced to create an effective bottom to their pay – absent in the official pay incentive system. If the official system had operated by itself then the FAM would not work as efficiently as it does, there would be continual turnover of workers and their spontaneous co-operation would be lost. A bargain has to be struck on the shop-floor between workers and managers outside and, indeed, in opposition to the official incentive system.

If this incentive system is the carrot there is also the stick, a punishment system that hung heavily in the minds of operators, arousing fear and fury. In a system so sensitive to shortages, there were ample cases of hold-ups, breakdowns and failures, whether these took the form of production stoppages, production losses or production of scrap. Here the punishment system took its toll. If operators failed to deliver the expected number of heats then, irrespective of the problems they had faced, they were subject to reprimand and verbal harassment. A more serious failure, such as the production of scrap, elicited threats of fines, some of which were actually carried out, for those declared negligent. Any failure to meet expectations, any malfunctioning has its culprit who must be punished. The punishment system is ritualized in the morning meeting the plant managers hold with night shift operators, known to all, after the TV talent show, 'Who knows how to (defend himself)?' Each operator has to give a persuasive account of any production failures. Later on there is a meeting of the day shift managers where fines and reprimands are sometimes distributed. Those who run the meeting are not particularly interested in excuses or explanations, but rather are concerned to allocate the blame to some irresponsible action.

Managers responsible for implementing this punishment system say it is necessary because the steel works is such a dangerous place. This is less than an adequate response since danger is often the stimulus to self-organization and autonomy. Another explanation lies in the seemingly crucial role the Combined Steel Works plays in the overall profitability of Red Star but in a system of such tight interdependence the role of the blast furnaces and the rolling mills are no less crucial. More likely is the view that strategic management is no less interested in the complaints and excuses of plant management than the latter is in those of its operational managers. The punitive system is passed down from above. Further, the unwillingness of plant managers to examine the causes of failures lies in their lack of control over the crucial factors of production (supplies and machinery) and their dependence on shop-floor operators to deal with breakdowns, disruptions and crises as they spontaneously develop on the shop-floor. The punitive system represents a frustration with their own powerlessness. What then is the response to this system of positive and negative sanctions on the shop-floor?

Self-organization on the shop-floor

Given the constraints under which Red Star has to operate, it is perhaps remarkable that its productive system is as effective as it is. As we will argue, its success can be largely attributed to the adaptive responses of operators on the shop-floor. What are the elements of their autonomy?

Lateral co-operation

On the basis of criteria established from above, shop-floor management's attention is directed laterally toward co-operation with other units in the Combined Steel Works. Take the steelmaker at the LD, like most of the other operators always a male. Since he is dependent on the co-operation of others he must command the confidence of his fellow operational managers at the other work sites. We observed the strivings of a recently promoted and inexperienced steelmaker to establish himself among his peers, his furnacemen and middle managers. Whenever he made a mistake, for example, they would say how young he was, how much he had to learn and how in the old days the steelmakers were really experienced. The steelmaker who does not command respect may find himself waiting for the teeming ladles, for the 'pots' into which the slag is poured, for hot metal from the mixer, for scrap from the scrap bay, for space and ingots to be prepared in the casting bay. Co-operation is particularly crucial when steel is being made for the FAM since its operation requires an uninterrupted flow of heats from the converter. The steelmaker's adrenalin begins to run and tempers can flare. If operators at the other work sites are not keen to co-operate he has to somehow persuade them that it is in their interest to do so.

But the steelmaker seeks more than simply co-operation from others. In order to protect himself against unforeseen adversity, such as breakdowns at other units, poor service from the overhead cranes which often need repair, inferior quality or inadequate supply of materials, arbitrary interference by higher managers, he asks them to undertake two types of manipulations: routine manipulations that make his production record look good and exceptional manipulations to cover up mistakes. First, the amount of scrap and hot metal registered as charged into the converter can be made less than that actually charged, so that at the FAM the amount of steel produced gives a better charging rate – ratio of scrap and hot metal to steel produced. At the casting bay the extra steel gives the leeway necessary to guarantee minimum production of 81.2 tons and if the casting bay master co-operates there will not be too much officially recorded excess. Such manipulations require the co-operation of crane drivers, supervisors at the casting bay, scrap yard, mixer and FAM.[4]

The second set of manipulations take place when there is a failure at the converter. For example if the chemical composition of the heat is outside the limits stipulated for the steel being made, it is possible to change the steel being produced to a different type. This requires the co-operation of the dispatcher – another operational manager – who plans production of steel from blast furnace to rolling mill during the shift. The steelmaker may ask the FAM to accept a heat that is slightly cooler than prescribed. Or he may ask the casting bay master to discount the scrap that was produced from a heat, or ask the FAM to submit a sample from a good piece of steel rather than from the bad one actually produced. In his turn the steelmaker can extend favours to those upon whom he depends. He can record lost time due to shortage of scrap, for example, which otherwise would be blamed on the scrap master as time lost due to shortage of hot metal, for which no one is blamed if there is less than 600 tons in the mixer because officially this is the minimum. In practice there usually is less than 600 tons so that such a doctoring of the record is easy. In short, a system of reciprocal favours develops around the objective of producing steel on the one side and the protection of operational management from the punitive sanctions of middle management on the other.

Any attempt by management to eliminate such manipulations would lead to narrow self-protection on the part of each work site, involving continual and heated arguments as to who was responsible for a given failure, for example, in teeming. As it is the manipulations are the basis of joint co-operation. The steelmaker accepts the risk involved; for example, that his teeming ratio (amount teemed to amount of steel produced) may be adversely affected by what happens at the casting bay or the FAM but in return he expects his counterparts to undertake compensating manipulations that will make his production record look good and cover up his mistakes. Instead of interfering directly the plant manager allocates fines to those held responsible for lapses. Operators and steelmakers do not forget their punishments in a hurry – not only because the fines are considerable but also because of the public humiliation. In this way middle management defines what is acceptable and what is not. Out of this emerges the norms that govern relations and practices on the shop-floor in conditions of uncertain production.

Shop-floor culture

This shop-floor culture is further elaborated through a network of social ties. While drinking groups forge solidarity between operators and their team of workers, football competitions and outings, all of which are organized on a plant-wide but shift-specific basis, establish ties between the different work points. Although workers and operators may move around from work place to work place they rarely change shifts. This facilitates the development of social ties and a common set of norms. It is interesting to note, therefore, that the majority of complaints are made against those who are outside the control of this system of co-operation, that is, against the laboratory and maintenance workers. Both groups are outside the moral order of steel production and their co-operation is more difficult to extract.

Shifts compete with each other to teem the greatest number of heats and to avoid breakdowns. This leads to antagonisms as each shift tries to push problems onto the next shift. One shift may postpone repairing the tap hole which has become too large or spraying the inner wall of the converter that has worn thin. Rules about the relative composition between hot metal and scrap may be flouted to get out a last heat, thereby emptying the mixer of hot metal and leaving the next shift stranded. At the casting bay there might be no ingot moulds or the place may be left in a mess, at the scrap yard the new crane drivers must begin afresh with empty boxes, or there may not be any pre-heated ladles or slag dishes. Any of these can lead to considerable time loss at the beginning of a shift. Moreover, the quarterly production con-ferences are held separately for the different shifts. All of which cements solidarity within a shift across work points while building up distance between workers at the same work points but on different shifts. While middle management complains about 'shift chauvinism', at the same time its own punitive order encourages lateral co-operation among work sites at the expense of co-operation between successive shifts.

Obstacles to centralization

So far we have argued that adaptation to supply constraints is most effectively accomplished through granting autonomy to operative managers on the shop floor. This becomes even clearer when we examine attempts at centralization.

Computer control

Let us return to the steelmaker at the LD and his assistant who control production at the converter. So far we have talked about how they negotiate relations with other work sites but what happens at the LD itself? They have to decide first how much hot metal and scrap, and then how much fluorspar and lime have to be charged into the converter and finally the quantity of different alloys to be charged into the ladle prior to or during the tapping. They are also responsible for the length of the oxygen blow, that is the volume and the number of blows of oxygen. The converter, like all the other work points in the Combined Steel Works, is equipped with computer-directed operations, so that for any steel on the programme there are instructions as to how the steel should be made.

Given a specific steel to be produced the computer calculates how much scrap and hot metal have to be put into the converter and based on the average composition (in terms of carbon, silicon and manganese) of the last ten heats of hot metal gives up a prescription for the volume of oxygen to be blown in. Where indeed the average composition of the last ten heats of hot metal would predict the composition of the eleventh, and where other factors are held constant the prescription would be an accurate one. In practice this is almost never the case. Often the mixer is nearly empty and so does not perform its homogenizing role, and the hot metal from the blast furnace can be of very uneven quality. This is the first major variation which the computer cannot take into account. The scrap itself is not sorted so that it can vary in content. Then there are a wide range of miscellaneous problems that affect the length of the oxygen blow: the purity of the oxygen, the temperature of the ladle into which the steel is tapped, whether the steel is going to the FAM or to the casting bay, the temperature of the hot metal (pig iron), the size of the tap hole and whether the argon equipment which circulates the steel once it is made is working. The computer cannot take these and other imponderables into account so they have to be assessed by the operator.

The computer is not only unreliable but, in roughly 40 per cent of the heats, fails to give any prescription at all for the oxygen blow. This is usually because the acceptable limits of silicon or of manganese in the hot metal are exceeded, so that their oxidation generates either too much or too little heat. In practice the steelmaker has no such option – not to make a heat when the conditions are not within prescribed limits – so he figures out an appropriate oxygen blow. On one occasion, however, we heard that the production manager had halted the delivery of hot metal from the blast furnace because the silicon level was considerably above that prescribed. Only the top levels of middle management can intervene in such a manner.

That these problems are largely distinctive to a shortage economy was illustrated when the Japanese who installed the computer were recalled because it was not living up to its promise. The programme could not take into account the long stoppages due to malfunctioning of equipment or shortages. At first the Japanese were quite baffled by the problems encountered in the plant. They then tried to reprogramme the system to meet the specific needs of a shortage economy. But it still does not dictate operations and so its use is confined to information processing.

It is not simply a source of information but actually saves a great deal of time by recording the processes of steel production. But even here it is not always accurate. The shortage economy and the incentive system lead to manipulations that the computer does not register and so many of the data are misleading. When one of us asked a manager if we could examine the computer readings on the amount of hot metal in the mixer, he told us we should not bother since they are hopelessly wrong, registering some 2,000 tons! The computer system was originally set up so that operators could not change any of the data on the screen. But this proved incompatible with the exigencies of a shortage economy so that now there is a woman in the production department who is responsible for 'correcting' the data in the computer in accordance with shop-floor manipulations. But anyone who wants to make any changes has to first register that request in a special log book.

The following incident highlights the conflicts that can arise over the proper use of the computer. One Saturday morning, the chief metallurgist came in to inspect the production of a very special steel (because of the high cost of the alloys and the importance of the quality of the product). The problem with this steel is that it requires very low phosphorus and sulphur contents at the same time as a high carbon content. This is difficult to achieve because the conditions for getting rid of phosphorus and sulphur also reduce the carbon level. There is a special de-sulphurizer but this still sometimes leaves the sulphur content too high. To further reduce it requires a very high temperature, but if it is too high the phosphorus which has been eliminated through oxidation and passed into the slag is de-oxidized and returns to the steel. The operation is a delicate one in which, rather than a single blow of oxygen, it is necessary to give two blows keeping the temperature relatively low and pouring in lime and fluorspar to help oxidize the sulphur and phosphorus, thus removing them to the slag. Seeing the operator working to keep the temperature relatively low the chief metallurgist told him he was doing it all wrong and that he should work according to the programme which stipulated a long single oxygen blow. The operator knew that this would not work and took no notice even as the chief metallurgist stood there.

The conclusions are twofold: any attempts to use the computer system as a means of control are doomed to failure because of the uncertainties, mainly from the supply side; and any attempt at the centralization of control in the hands of those who are not attuned to the day-to-day realities of the Combined Steel Works easily leads to the production of scrap. Although middle management does make such attempts at expropriation of control, they accept for the most part the necessity of workshop autonomy.

Quality control

We have shown how shop-floor autonomy helps adjustment to

shortages, particularly in the context of tightly coupled work processes. But it cannot be forgotten that shortages exist only relative to demand constraints, so that as the latter become more severe the former also intensify. This can be seen in the case of quality control.

The second half of the 1970s saw government economic policy for the steel industry turn toward the provision of Hungary's developing manufacturing industry and the expansion of the export of steel to the West. In line with this strategy Red Star proposed that the Combined Steel Works increase and improve the production of its quality and alloy steels. In 1983, two years after the completion of the new complex, it exported 1,500 tons of alloy steel, in 1984 about 50,000 and in 1985 62,000. Most of these steels were produced in the Combined Steel Works but with great scrap costs. Scrap rates have varied from 5 per cent to 40 per cent according to the type of steel. In 1986, for every 1,000 tons of finished steel, 1,400 tons of liquid steel had to be produced.

The difficulties of making quality steels underline the dilemmas of production in a shortage economy. Here the diagnosis and solutions of American experts, brought in to advise the Red Star management but accustomed to problems of a demand-constrained economy, illuminate the distinctive dilemmas of socialist production.[5] The experts attributed increasing rates of scrap to declining effort and a diminishing sense of responsibility. As a solution they proposed the creation of an independent and centralized system of quality control which, through computerization, would trace each heat of steel through its various production processes, pinpointing the source of defective quality, making it possible to correct the problem and immediately halting the continued processing of substandard steel. In theory their proposal was admirable but it did not come to grips with the underlying realities of the uncertain production conditions, be it unreliable machinery or inadequate, or even absent, materials. It was never really implemented.

Frustrated by their apparent powerlessness to affect the quality of production, middle managers in quality control have attempted to follow these plans for centralization.[6] But instead of using surveillance to identify sources of scrap production they have used it to punish those they find culpable of mistakes. This has the unintended effect that inspectors on the shop floor often turn a blind eye to the attempts of operators to push defective steel onto the next work point. They naturally sympathize with the operators' attempts to escape responsibility for what is not of their own doing, whether it be that steel arrives at their work place already defective or working conditions make sub-standard steel unavoidable, that is if it is to be produced at all. The inspectors do not want to be party to punishing workers for mistakes they either did not make or were forced to make. In short, rather than solving the problem the punitive system exacerbates it.

There is, for example, a continual struggle between the primary rolling mill and the Combined Steel Works as to who is responsible for steel that cannot be rolled. The rolling mill blames the steel producers for not turning out steel according to specifications or for uneven surface on the ingots, while the Combined Steel Works blames the rolling mill for mistakes in reheating the ingots or poor rolling practices. Because of antiquated reheating equipment and poor measuring devices and because of the sensitivity of quality steel to rolling practices it is hard to distribute responsibility fairly. The difficulty of discovering the source of the problem is only exacerbated by the application of punitive sanctions, leading each side to cover up its own mistakes and spy on the other. Although the root cause of quality failures lies outside the control of operators, the correction of that which does lie within their control requires immediate co-operation between inspectors and producers. This will only take place in the absence of punitive and arbitrary interventions by middle managers. Centralization of quality control is another exception which proves the rule that technically efficient production depends on autonomous organization at the work place.

Scrap bay

Unaccustomed to the problem of shortages the American experts had nothing to say about attempting to change critical supply conditions, in particular the situation at the scrap yard. Supply uncertainties here are so extreme that no amount of shop-floor autonomy can facilitate adjustment. The history of the scrap bay illustrates well the character and sources of shortage in a socialist economy.

When the Combined Steel Works was being planned the government told the Red Star management that it would provide no more than 10 billion forints to finance the project. The original estimate was 12 billion forints so top management had to decide on cuts. The essential technology had to remain, they argued, and instead reductions should be at the expense of some peripheral part of the plant. Accordingly, in order to reduce the size and therefore the cost of the scrap bay, management inflated figures for the density of scrap they would be receiving. They estimated that the scrap density would be between 1.4 and 1.8 tons per cubic metre whereas the real figure should have been between 0.6 and 0.8 tons. In this way they pushed the responsibility for higher density scrap onto the enterprise which collects and distributes scrap. This higher density, they knew, would only be possible if there were to be capital investment in scrap processing equipment – a very unlikely event. So the scrap bay was built much too small for the voluminous loose scrap and as a result it is impossible to sort the scrap into different grades, as is done in capitalist steel plants. Instead it is simply dumped into one huge disorganized mound. From there the scrap master has to organize deliveries to the UHP and the converter. Both sets of demands are usually urgent, but the cranes are slow in collecting the scrap because they were designed to gather much heavier types. Moreover, when quality steel is being produced it is critical to know the alloy content of the scrap, yet with only a small electronic device at their disposal such a sorting operation is beyond the capability of the work crew.

The consequences are obvious. The scrap master and his work crew have a great deal of autonomy but little control over their work. They are cynical, frustrated and feel the hopelessness of their task. Here autonomy is antithetical to efficient production because the shortages are simply too great in relation to production needs. The original attempt to save on what appeared to be a peripheral operation becomes a major obstacle to the production of quality steel for which the Combined Steel Works was explicitly designed.

Conclusion

We have opposed the common argument that modern technology requires the return of control to the shop-floor. Technology by itself is not determinant: its effective deployment, in particular the most effective work organization, depends on the form of the wider political economy. We highlighted the link between a centralized economy and the character of work organization in a state socialist enterprise using the most up-to-date capitalist techology. More importantly we took issue with another variant of the reskilling argument: the prognosis of Piore and Sabel (1984), that the future of capitalist society heralds increased worker control over production through flexible specialization. They do not argue from technological determinism but give precedence to market factors: the need to cater to a multi-faceted consumer demand. On the basis of what we know about the mini-mills and integrated steel plants in the United States demand pressures lead to centralization and coercive managerial strategies rather than, as Piore and Sabel claim, the resurrection of the craft paradigm (Barnett and Crandall, 1986; Prechel, 1986).

Our own case study suggests that it is in state socialism, where supply constraints are the more significant force shaping development, that some form of shop-floor self-organization holds the greatest potential.[7] Fluctuations in the quality and availability of raw materials, machinery and labour power require some form of autonomous and flexible workshop organization for technical efficiency. We have seen how, on the one hand, there developed dual systems of management and of incentives. In order to adapt to supply constraints in the context of tightly interdependent work sites, shop-floor management had to be given the room to make decisions spontaneously and elaborate a set of plant norms that governed lateral co-ordination. The centrally controlled computer system was mainly useful as a source of information, not as a means of prescription for which it was originally intended. On the other hand, when middle management sought to interfere in the direction of day-to-day operations, crises and work stoppages were a frequent result.

Shop-floor autonomy need not necessarily revolve around a few key figures who direct production. In some situations, such as the machine shop we studied at Banki (Burawoy and Lukács, 1985), workers themselves became the central figures in organizing work. Managers were fewer and acted as the emissaries or agents of workers. At Red Star, on the other hand, the character of the technology and tightly-coupled production involved key leaders at the different work sites, who work out deals among themselves, develop social ties and a sense of joint responsibility. The workers under them undertake a multiplicity of tasks, and in this sense they engage in a form of flexible specialization, but they do not exercise any guiding control over the process of production. Instead they are its agents.[8] This chapter claims that the promotion of technical efficiency, that is the realization of a firm's production possibilities, requires centralization in advanced capitalism and shop-floor autonomy in state socialism. How then do we explain cases of shop-floor autonomy in advanced capitalism and centralization in state socialism?

National economies are constrained not simply by demand or supply, but also by some combination of the two. First, and most simply, within capitalism, shop-floor autonomy springs up precisely where factors of production cannot be controlled, for example in the construction industry or coal mining, just as within state socialism pressures for centralization are most intense where there are stringent demand constraints, for example in military production. Second, supply constraints may become more critical in capitalist societies as profitability becomes less salient. Within a large corporation, divisions may be bound into a political centre much as socialist enterprises are bound to the state, leading to insatiable investment demands and shortages. On the other hand, market competition may develop among divisions within a socialist enterprise so that demand rather than supply becomes the salient constraint.

Third, and even more generally, too categorical a distinction between supply-constrained and demand-constrained economies tends to overlook the mutual determination of supply and demand. That is to say, the more specific and variable the demand the more significant becomes any variation in the quality and availability of factors of production. In as much as the intensification of demand constraints leads to supply problems so shop-floor autonomy may emerge under capitalism. Equally under socialism shortages may so adversely affect the quality of the product that the enterprise will find difficulty selling it and thereby invite centralization.

We can also explain counter-tendencies to our model in terms of worker resistance. In advanced capitalism workers have sometimes successfully resisted the expropriation of skill or centralization of control, just as in state socialism shop-floor operators and workers are often defenceless against the concerted efforts of trade union, party and management to control production. While such economic and social factors explain variations both over time and between places within advanced capitalism and within state socialism, in no way do such variations refute the contention of this chapter that for the survival of these societies the tendencies must be stronger than the counter-tendencies.

Finally we don't want our conclusion to be misunderstood. We are not saying that autonomy on the shop-floor will by itself resolve the dilemmas of socialist economies. Their fate hangs elsewhere, in the hierarchical relations between state and enterprises – relations which create the very problems to which self-organization is one adaptive response.

Notes

Chapter 1   The transformation of work?

1. It is important not to make the mistake of assuming that all writings on flexibility or which emphasize the higher skills and demands resulting from new technologies or managerial concepts are proponents of the flexible specialization thesis. There is also considerable variation amongst writers who accept we are entering a new 'flexible' era. Kern and Schuman, for example, differ from Piore and Sabel (or at least the extreme version of their Second Divide thesis): they do not appear to be so ready to predict an end of assembly work (although they do talk of the end of mass production), but simply of modifications of it, and they stress the extent to which not all workers will gain from the new concepts as there may be increased segmentation in the labour market. Sorge and Streeck (1988), whilst in many ways falling within the broad flexible specialization theory, do give more emphasis to the possible diversity between firms and mediations between technology and outcomes, and prefer the term customized quality production than flexible specialization to denote the new production regime built on reaping increasing returns to scope. For examples of work which focus on flexibility which do not fall in the flexible specialization genre see Jones (1985b, 1986), Libetta (1988), and some of the work dealt with, particularly towards the end, in the overview of German literature by Hoos (1986).

   Whilst there is some variation among both flexible specialization and labour process writers, which complicates definition, in the case of labour process theory there is the added complication that there emerged in the late 1970s what some have called the labour process debate. Initially one of its concerns was the rather deterministic nature of Braverman's deskilling theory, and the importance of worker resistance and negotiation in the work organization. There thus followed a stress by some on the negotiated nature of task structures. Especially in continental Europe this 'negotiated order' approach was increasingly taken to be the labour process approach. Yet others might use it to refer to all parties within the labour process debate, that is assuming they are not hostile to the whole enterprise. The term will be used throughout this book in the more restricted way to more or less equate it with what Lazonick (1983) calls the orthodox Marxist approach to work organization, that is the approach which places workforce control at the centre of the organizational problem and predicts a progressive deskilling as the labour process is increasingly constructed through Taylorist scientific management.

2. For overviews and important contributions to the labour process debate, see Burawoy (1979); Cressey and MacInnes (1980); Edwards (1979); Elger (1982); Kelly and Wood (1984); Littler (1982); Manwaring and Wood (1985); Thompson (1983); Wood (1982).

3. For an excellent summary of Piore and Sabel see Williams, Cutler *et al.* (1987), and for a more general overview of the flexible specialization field see Mahon (1987). For critical appraisals see Block (1985), Hyman (1988), Meegan (1988), Sayer (1989), Williams, Cutler *et al.* (1987), Wood (1988b). For a critical overview of Kern and Schumann see Malsch and Seltz (1987).

4. The debate about the world car and flexible specialization scenarios has been actively encouraged in the MIT study *The Future of the Automobile* (Altshuler *et al.*, 1984). For a more thorough treatment of this see Wood (1986, 1988a).

5. Gerwin and Leung (1986: 166-7) define the various dimensions of flexibility as follows:

Mix flexibility	processing at any one time a mix of different parts which are loosely related to each other in some way, such as belonging to the same family.
Parts flexibility	adding parts to and removing parts from the mix over time.
Routing flexibility	dynamic assignment of machines; that is, re-routing a given part through the system if a machine used in its manufacture is incapacitated.
Design change flexibility	fast implementation of engineering design changes for a particular part.
Volume flexibility	handling shifts in volume for a given part.
Customizing flexibility	processing different mixes of parts on different flexible manufacturing systems in the same company.

Other writers title these types of flexibility differently and, in addition, refer to others, particularly product flexibility, that is the ability to change over to produce a new (set of) product(s) economically (see Adler, 1985b).

6. As Block (1985: 499) has said, 'it is as if they (Piore and Sabel) were writing in 1940 and nobody had yet pointed out that a dramatic shift toward services is taking place'. We could also add that it is as if they had not noticed that the Watertown Arsenal factory (so close to Piore and Sabel's employment) where Taylor tried to implement his ideas is now a shopping mall. Perhaps it is because they are so optimistic about flexible specialization as the saviour of economies that Piore and Sabel do not feel any great need to pay serious attention to the sharp decline in manufacturing employment as a percentage of total employment. Or perhaps they continue to believe (*à la* post-industrial theories) that the service sector is inherently labour intensive and still growing and that it will mop up all excess labour, at least under certain conditions. See Blackburn *et al.* (1985) for a questioning of the assumed low level of labour-saving technology in he service sector. See also Baethge and Oberbeck (1986) for an attempt to deal with the service sector within the context of the flexibility debate.

7. A study of robotics in the German automobile industry by Windolf (1985) not only highlights the existence of losers and negative effects for some, but also questions the extent to which Kern and Schumann's winners' jobs are enriched, or upgraded.

8. It sometimes appears as if writers are leaping to the conclusion that the Japanese are pioneering *the* management system commensurable with a new flexible specialization regime. Reich (1984: 131), to some extent an advocate of flexible specialization as the salvation of the US economy, says that, 'Of all the industrialized countries, Japan's shift from high volume production has been the most rapid'. In effect, he and others often imply Japan is almost there: the recent miracle of Japan is no longer its copying of Western methods, but reflects its leading the way in the ending of Fordism.

    In a paper published after *The Second Industrial Divide* (Katz and Sabel, 1985) Sabel is more cautious about unequivocally associating the Japanese methods with flexible specialization. Talking specifically of alternative fresh strategies for the car industry, Katz and Sabel (1985: 297) distinguish between the Japanese *kanban* method which they treat as 'a variant of mass production', and a second method more akin to the flexible specialization approach in which competition is shifted 'from price to the definition of the product itself'. They do, however, treat the two strategies as 'closely related' and argue that regardless of with which strategy a firm begins its experimentation, it is 'likely to discover the other'. This enables them to continue their exploration of developments in the auto industry in the vein of the flexible specialization thesis. Nothing in the research on Japan points to a decisive reversal in the division of labour. Moreover, Cusuman (1985) shows that much of the increases in flexibility in Japan (and particularly her ability to have more mixed production schedules) took place before the advent of the new technology, and part of Toyota's reluctance to rely on computers was because their management saw them as a possible source of rigidities. This itself runs counter to any simple direct connection between flexibility and new technology.

9. Some of the major inputs to the French regulation school include Aglietta (1979), Boyer (1986), de Vroey (1984), Lipietz (1986, 1987). For a brief overview see Boyer (1987a), and for an attempt to develop analysis which incorporates the service sector see Petit (1986).

10. Kaplinsky (1984: 170-1) makes a distinction between technology and techniques. Technology is the skill, knowledge and procedures for making and using 'useful things'. In contrast techniques are the 'specific, concrete ways of combining people, machines and inputs to produce particular products or services'. For example, micro-electronics is technology – solid-state, binary logic devices – whereas numerically controlled machine tools based on micro-electronics are techniques. The importance of the distinction is that technology even within capitalism may have the potential for more rewarding and flexible work (ibid., 174). But within capitalism, especially because of the industrial-military complex, this is not realized. Instead work continues to be deskilled, with for example machine-pacing in craft areas and the routinization of repair and maintenance work (ibid., 170).

11. Of the 11,500 workers reported by Murray (1985: 30) in 1985 to be involved in producing their clothes, just over 10 per cent were employed directly by Benetton. The core, in-house part of the production process is not defined by the need for functional flexibility or even skill level as

such, but its importance to the quality of the final product. It reflects, that is, the critical 'care' stages.

12. I am greatly indebted to Robin Murray for suggesting this classification.

13. Sabel (1982: 32) for example says he is using 'Fordism as a shorthand term for the organisational and technological principles characteristic of the modern large scale factory'. Melman (1985: 240) notes how throughout *Work and Politics,* Sabel characterizes the conveyerized methods of Fordism in a rather limited and misleading way, as 'moving the work to the men rather than the reverse'.

14. As Linn (1987: 129) says, the assembly line, 'seen as a string of minute labour processes...has become a metaphor for capital's control and degradation of work'. She stresses how it alone does not have a monopoly of rigidity and lack of autonomy. Flow and assembly-line work increased in most countries in discrete stages; for example, it appears to have increased significantly in Britain in three distinct stages: 1890–1910, the 1930s and 1950–60. Yet, it never really covered a majority of even the manufacturing workforce. The application of work study is never likely to have covered more than 50 per cent of this, and its use appears not to have increased since the 1960s, although a survey conducted in the late 1970s noted that just under 50 per cent of firms in manufacturing used work study (Brown, 1981: 112). Even in the car industry, so prominent in discussion, most people do not work on visible assembly lines. In the British car industry in 1981 operators represented 37.2 per cent of all the workforce, whilst the next highest group included inspectors and other indirects whose work was directly related to the line, which constituted 19.9 per cent, and hence at most a total of 58.1 per cent have jobs whose rhythm is directly affected by the line (Marsden, *et al.,* 1985: 69). But even then we cannot assume all are lacking in discretion, routinized and line- or machine-paced. Craftsmen constitute 15.7 per cent of the total workforce, some of whom in the machining areas may have to some extent machine-paced jobs, whilst those connected to maintenance will be strongly affected by the pressure of the line.

Even in the books which stress the possible transformation of work along the lines of Piore and Sabel, work other than manual work is not accorded sufficient significance. Tolliday and Zeitlin's (1986) collection of papers on the development of the auto industry, significantly entitled *The Automobile Industry and Its Workers,* reads as if the industry consists only of white male assembly or skilled workers – there is no mention of designers, white-collar workers, middle managers and supervisors, let alone the issues of gender or racism.

15. Adler (n.d.) suggests that craft satisfaction and autonomy may not combine easily with the 'marvels' of science:

> Think of the modern doctor: the advances of medical science – and not merely of capitalist organization of medicine – have led to a fantastic degree of specialization. No one doctor enjoys 'conscious and purposeful mastery of the labour process'...what do 'autonomy' and 'control' amount to, when the interdependence of multiple specialization makes the individual doctor part of a system of medical care?

16. Allied to the criticism in much of the debate about the inflation of Fordism and Taylorism is the criticism of their characterization in much discussion. Both are open to various interpretations, an issue which extends beyond a simple matter of definition. Taylor was himself acutely aware of the problem of co-operation, as well as of control, for example. The association of Taylorism with control may have led to the related and potentially misleading assumption that the former is inflexible. It also has important consequences for the labour-process reading of history. Taylorism and Fordism at least in practice were concerned with constituting new 'semi-skilled' work forces and not largely, if at all, with the decomposition of skilled ones (Johansson, 1986; Lazonick, 1983).

17. Taylorism is and has been an important backcloth to the Japanese model – as is illustrated, for example, by its early reception in Japan; the labour intensity on a Japanese assembly line (Godel, 1987; Kamata, 1983); the heavy use by Japanese firms in the US and Europe of several essential features of scientific management neglected by many Western firms, such as intensive and scientific employee selection and training (see, for example, my brief account of Nissan in the UK – Wood, 1988b).

18. See, for example, Adler and Borys (1986), Berggren (1980), Burawoy (1979), Clark *et al.* (1988), Cockburn (1983, 1986), Friedman (1977), Jones (1982), Kelly (1985), Lee (1982), Libetta (1988), Littler (1982), More (1982), Nichols and Beynon (1977), Penn (1985), Penn and Scattergood (1985), Rose and Jones (1985), Rumberger (1987), Spenner (1983, 1988), Wood (1988a). Spenner (1988) offers an excellent overview of many of the aggregate studies in the USA and Kelley (1986) of some of the key cases of programmable automation.

19. If the measure is the proportion of men working in occupations which are 90 per cent male then segregation decreased between 1971 and 1981. If, however, it is the proportion of women working in occupations which are more than 70 per cent female then it has increased.

20. A good example of the dangers of making inferences from snapshots at one point in time is the case of a group of researchers who presented in 1987 a study of a new 'greenfield' site which a large food manufacturer had opened in rural Wales in the late 1970s as an example of the new flexible decentralized regime. The problem, however, was that at the very time that they were making this presentation the firm was just completing a £80 million investment on the site of its longstanding British headquarters in the North of England.

Chapter 2 When certainty fails: inside the factory of the future

1. This chapter is based on research funded by the Economic and Social Research Council, and an earlier paper for the conference on *Technology, Innovation and Social Change,* Centre of Canadian Studies, University of Edinburgh, 1984. I wish to thank Stephen Wood for help in revising the contents.

2. For example in David Noble's critical account of the deskilling and dehumanizing logic of computerization in America's metal working industries (Noble, 1984). For the employment implications see the discussion in Francis (1986).

3. For a more detailed analysis of these positions see Jones (1986).
4. The most influential case being Braverman (1974) but see also Conference of Socialist Economists (1980), Edwards (1979), Zimbalist (ed.) (1979).
5. For an overview of the spread of FMS in Britain see Jones (1987) and Scott (1987). I am grateful to Peter Scott for making some of his own findings available to me, as well as for general advice on the contents of this chapter.
6. For a fuller discussion see Jones (1986).
7. B. Jones fieldwork notes, 'Alpha' case-study, May 1984.

Chapter 3   Machinery, labour and location

I would like to thank Michael Burawoy, David Harvey, Bryn Jones, Briggs Nisbet, Andrew Sayer and Stephen Wood for their comments on earlier versions of this paper.

Chapter 4   Multinational corporations and the new international division of labour: a critical appraisal

1. This chapter originally appeared in the *International Regional Science Review*, vol. 11, no. 2 (1988). Permission to reprint is gratefully acknowledged. The author also wishes to thank Shelby Gerking, Norm Glickman, David Harvey, Flavia Martinelli, Frank Moulaert, Stephen Wood and Doug Woodward for their comments and suggestions while relieving them of responsibility for the final outcome.
2. The repeated references to the work of Lipietz in this context merit some explanation as his elaboration of the concept of 'global Fordism' is in many respects a great deal richer than much of the discussion related to the NIDL *per se*. In particular, his argument, along with Aglietta (1979), that the technical and social limits of Fordism have inhibited the expansion of relative surplus value through technological change in production in the core provides a much stronger theoretical underpinning for the necessity of the move offshore in search of lower cost, less militant labour. My own sense is that there is still room for technological and organizational restructuring in production although this may entail a movement away from Fordist principles (see Schoenberger, forthcoming). It remains true that Lipietz's analysis of the geographical patterns associated with global Fordism closely parallels that of the NIDL and, since he is particularly clear in his exposition, it seems worthwhile to rely extensively on it.
3. Low labour costs in themselves do not, of course, guarantee that unit labour costs will be lower, in view of productivity differentials between advanced and developing countries. The development of a free wage labour force with at least some level of industrial experience and discipline remains essential. With that proviso, although aggregate productivity differentials may remain quite large, actual productivity levels achieved in the branch plant of a multinational located in the periphery may be equivalent to counterpart facilities in industrial countries if the production technology is equivalent. Or, if a significant productivity differential still exists, this may be outweighed by a still larger wage gap (Tharakan, 1979).

4. Both Sayer (1985a) and Storper (1985) note the strong parallels between the NIDL and the product cycle model which is particularly explicit about this evolutionary path of production technology. Although the product cycle model will not be directly treated here, it may be noted that while the 'first wave' of foreign investments in the product cycle is expected to be in developed country markets, in the later stages the model assumes increased standardization, price competition and cost pressures, with investment shifting to the periphery. With the gathering weight of maturing products, one would expect to see a rather sizeable shift in the international geography of investment.

5. I will not here devote attention to technological change in the form of product innovation which would be recognized in the NIDL as tending to push production back up the hierarchy to the skill- and knowledge-intensive levels and places. As Sayer (1985a) notes, in the face of growing competition, corporations have a strong incentive to move away from product standardization and homogenization – in short, to replace price competition with product competiton where possible. To the extent that the importance of product innovation and differentiation is under-estimated by the model, this contributes to an excessively cost-driven logic.

Chapter 6   Flexibility and the changing sexual division of labour

1. More recently Beechey has revised her position, no longer considering the reserve army a useful way of conceptualizing changes in women's employment (Beechey and Perkins, 1987).

Chapter 7   The talents of women, the skills of men: flexible specialization and women

1. As usual I am grateful to Greg Albo for suggestions about this chapter. For very useful comments on an earlier draft thanks to Neil Bradford, Fuat Keyman, Alain Lipietz, Rianne Mahon and Stephen Wood.

2. Not all discussions of flexible specialization pay the same attention to the impact on and strategy of the labour movement. Piore and Sabel (1984) grant that question much less importance than do discussions which have arisen in the British context, like Murray (1985) and Gough (1986), the Greater London Council (1985). Mahon (1987) is also particularly concerned with the impact on the labour movement.

3. According to Ritter, 'For obscure reasons, Proudhon says that within the family the only respectful relationships are self-sacrificial ones. It is by offering one another unlimited devotion that members of a family defend pursuit of the distinctive ends sought in love relations and show understanding of them' (1969: 143). For a detailed discussion of Proudhon and the family, see Ritter, 1969: 142-4. At the heart of this vision of the ideal family was Proudhon's assumption that the gender division of labour involved women's devotion to housework and men's to earning a family wage.

4. Even in the versions which do address the consequences of flexible specialization for women, the concept has not been completely thought through, so that 'women' or 'gender effects' are addressed more politically than analytically (see Murray, 1985 and the Greater London Council, 1985).

5. For critiques of gender-blindness in the segmented labour market literature see Milkman (1983: 163-4) and Armstrong (1984: 29ff).

6. Hartmann (1985: 18) cites studies by Bielby and Baron which show 'nearly complete job segregation by sex. In more than half the establishments...job classifications were completely segregated by sex and in only one-fifth were indices of segregation less than 90, meaning that 90 per cent of the women (or men) would have to change jobs to have an occupational distribution identical to that of the men (or women).' Statistics in many countries indicate the same patterns: for France see Bouillaguet-Bernard *et al.* (1981: Part 2); for Canada see Armstrong (1984: Chapter 4); for the United States see Remick (1984: Chapter 1); and for Britain see Hakim (1981), Martin and Roberts (1984).

7. Of course, young people, both women and men, are also popular part-time workers in most countries and are the recipients of temporary contracts. See Armstrong (1984: Chapter 7), Jenson, *et al.* (1988) – especially chapters by Armstrong and Armstrong, Bakker, del Boca, Hagen and Jenson, Humphries and Rubery, and Jenson – and Kergoat (1984).

8. In Germany women and immigrants were hired to fill the unskilled and semi-skilled jobs in what might be called the 'Fordist period' – and the gender and ethnic division has only deepened in the 1980s (Mahon, 1987: 39ff). A similar pattern appears in the French data (Jenson, 1988).

9. Cockburn herself makes this point (1981: 42, 54-6). Beechey also criticizes some recent publications on women and work for the same, virtually exclusive, emphasis on the family and family responsibilities as the major factor explaining women's disadvantaged position in the labour market (1983: 27, 39). For a review of Marxist feminists' stress on the impact of family relations on work, see Milkman (1983: 161ff.). The American literature on 'comparable worth', while less theoretically sophisticated, also stresses that on-going work relations condition the gender division of labour within the firm. See Hartmann (1985: *passim*) and Steinberg (1984), for example.

10. Solinas (1982: 337ff.) shows that even in a highly feminized industry in a traditional 'female' sector – knitwear and ready-to-wear clothing in the Italian province of Modena, Emilia – gender differences within the division of labour abound. In particular, skilled occupations like those of artisan have many more men than do the unskilled positions within factories. Among women, the differences are due to age and location in the family. In this way, the family continues to shape activity in production. See also, for France, Daune-Richard (1988), and Sarsby (1985) for a case study of the gendering of jobs in the British pottery industry.

11. The historical consistency of this observation is great. Often Margaret Mead's observation is cited to support the findings of contemporary studies of the labour process:

    Margaret Mead has said that in all cultures, without any known exception, male activity is seen as achievement. Whatever women do, from seed gathering to skilled crafts, is less valued than when those same tasks are performed by men in a different culture: when men cook, cooking is viewed as an important activity; when women cook it is just a household chore (Shepela and Viviano, 1984: 47).

12. It is interesting to note that North American studies of 'comparable worth' isolate what is termed a 'psychological' factor affecting job evaluation. By this is meant the cognitive content of job evaluation, which defines 'value', and 'skill'; see, for example, Shepela and Viviano (1984). In this chapter, the concept of 'ideology' is used instead to stress that these processes are obviously and importantly social, rather than individual and can be combated successfully only when we understand the practices on which they depend. Sarsby (1985: 68) also emphasizes the ideological content of the sexual division of labour.

13. Milkman (1983: 171ff.) is careful to use this ideological sex-typing as only a partial, although important, explanation. In fact, her study is premised on the observation that the automobile and electrical industries almost equally involve 'hard' and 'light' labour, yet one feminized and the other did not. She turns to strategies of labour control to explain the discrepancy.

14. For an elaboration of this argument with reference to the development of gender identities in Britain and France see Jenson (1988).

Chapter 8: The transformation of training and the transformation of work in Britain

1. Some of the research described in this chapter has been supported by a grant from the Leverhulme Trust which is gratefully acknowledged. I am also obliged to Rebecca Harding and Dennis Harding for their assistance in the early preparation for this chapter; also to Stephen Wood for much patience and sound advice in its later stages.

2. Admittedly, the cheapening of youth labour has also been sought directly, by legislating against unions and against statutory wage restrictions, but to discuss this adequately would go beyond the scope of this chapter (Junankar (ed.), 1987).

3. Renamed the Training Commission, December 1987.

Chapter 9: 'New production concepts' in final assembly – the Swedish experience

1. This chapter is based on three successive research projects on the Swedish automotive industry conducted by the author. The first one, 'Future Production Systems', 1982–3, was a project within the Massachusetts Institute of Technology (MIT)-initiated study of 'The Future of the Automobile'. The main result was an analysis of the state of the art of technology and organization within body and assembly shops. See Appel

and Hilber (1984) for a summary of the projects within the MIT technology sub-programme. In 1984 it was followed by a study of Japanese component manufacturers and sub-contractors in the Aichi prefecture ('Toyota-land') conducted with Toshiko Tsukaguchi. The second project 'Experiences of Development of Work Organization within the Volvo Group' 1984–7, focused on case studies of plants with new design and work organization, comparing them with trad tional operations. Four of these plants, LB, TUN, TC and Vara, figure in this chapter. The project was initiated by the local metalworkers' union. The third project started in 1987 and is a follow-up of the first study.

2.   The evaluation is based on three main types of data:

- interviews with key personnel, specialists, union officers and managers, from first-line foremen to the CEO of Volvo Trucks;
- eighty extensive interviews with assembly workers at the three assembly plants, TC (conventional line), TUN (modified line) and LB; and
- a questionnaire survey of working conditions and participation in the three plants, using basically the same questionnaire.

The composition of the personnel in regard to age, sex and education was approximately the same at each factory. At LB, 85 per cent of the workers answered the questionnaire and at TUN 60 per cent. At TC there was a representative sample of 40 per cent of the workers at Line No. 1 (the day line). In absolute numbers there were 236 respondents at LB, 136 at TUN and 283 at TC, making a total of 655 responses. The study at LB could utilize the fact that over 70 per cent of the workers in the survey had had similar jobs at other Volvo plants.

Chapter 10:   The transfer of Japanese management concepts in the international automobile industry

1.   These interviews were held within the scope of the project on the 'Challenges and Opportunities of the Current Restructuring Measures in the International Automobile Industry for Employees', which was sponsored by the Deutsche Forschungsgemeinschaft and carried out by the author together with Knuth Dohse and Thomas Malsch at the Berlin Science Centre (WZB/AP).

Chapter 11:   Automation, new technology and work content

1.   Translated by Keith Dixon and Alan Marshall. This research is based on work carried out for the PIRTTEM-CNRS (Pluridisciplinary Research Programme on Technology, Work and Employment, the National Centre for Scientific Research) and MRES (the Ministry of Research and Higher Education), France.

2.   In many installations control can be carried out either automatically or manually. In automatic control, the set point is determined by the

operator and the aim is to keep the real value of the parameter as close as possible to the set point by adjusting the valve. In manual regulation, the operator controls the valve directly and automatic control is interrupted.

3. As one operator put it:

> when there is a hitch, I have to elaborate an accurate description of the state and evolution of the chemical reactions. For example, when pressure begins to mount in a steam generator for unknown reasons, I must ask a worker in the installation to check the position of the input valve visually. Yesterday, there was a difference of 15 per cent between the real valve opening and the value indicated on the control panel. To solve such a problem, I have to sift through a great variety of information concerning the state of the regulation loop, the input and output flow rates, the tank level and the real valve opening. Once I have compared these data and drawn my conclusions I can deal progressively with the incidents. However, each time I intervene I must re-check all the parameters.

Chapter 12: Alternative forms of work organization under programmable automation

1. This research was supported by grants from the National Science Foundation (grant no. SES–8520174) and from the Office of Technology Assessment of the US Congress (contract no. 633–2470–0). Neither agency is responsible for the views expressed in this chapter.

Chapter 14: The limits to industrialization: computer software development in a large commercial bank

1. This study focuses on the work of 'applications' programmers who write programmes which use existing computer systems to solve business problems. The bank also has a (smaller) number of 'systems' programmers who create and maintain the software which allows the bank's computers to run.

2. The fact that the organization of programming work is independent of the size of the market for the software being developed seems to contradict Adam Smith's assertion that 'the division of labour is limited by the extent of the market' (Smith, 1979: 121). In systems development, the most widely circulated software may be written by a single person, while programmes developed for a singe application may require the work of a very large team. Smith's aphorism may hold true for reproduction work but it does not hold for development work. In development work, in effect, the size of the batch produced is always one, regardless of the size of the market.

Chapter 15:　Work organization and product change in the service sector: the case of the UK National Health Service

1.　For example, Rajan and Pearson (eds) (1986) forecast a net increase in service industry employment in the UK by 1990, with financial, business, and leisure services (hotels and catering, recreation and cultural services) growing the fastest.

2.　For accounts of the history of the organizational changes and controversies in the National Health Service (NHS) in the 1980s, see Cousins (1986) and Ham (1985).

3.　An account of the NHS's policies for the utilization of information technologies can be found in Scrivens (1985); the take-up of computers in the NHS can be followed in issues of the *British Journal of Healthcare Computing* and in the weekly *Health Service Journal:* see the supplement on 'Health Service Computing' in the issue of 18 June 1987.

4.　The European market for portable (or ambulatory) diagnostic equipment was $31 million in 1984; for blood pressure monitoring devices it was $24 million; see Frost and Sullivan (1985).

5.　The new tests are the product of numerous technological innovations of the past fifteen years. There have been innovations in solid state chemistry which allow the routine production of multiple layers of thin paper and plasticized films impregnated with tiny quantities of reagents and enzymes. These biochemicals are activated when wet with a blood or urine sample and undergo a colour change which can be detected either visually or with an electronic device. These devices have themselves been transformed by micro-electronics and the miniaturization of computer technologies of the past ten years. Diabetics, for example, can now automatically record in a computerized glucose strip-reader the results of over 300 daily tests performed by themselves. The device can present the results in a variety of graphical forms on a colour monitor for interpretation by the diabetic's doctor.

6.　Fischer *et al.* (1984) takes up 300 pages listing the tests that individual doctors in the USA can do in their own 'office laboratories'.

Chapter 16:　What is socialist about socialist production? Autonomy and control in a Hungarian steel mill

1.　This study is based on collaborative field work at Red Star Steel Works where Burawoy worked as a converter furnaceman for six months in 1985, six weeks in 1986 and two months in 1987. Lukács spent several weeks interviewing management during the same periods. As well as workers and managers at Red Star, we should also like to thank Linda Blum, Wlodzimierz Brus, Peter Galasi, Edward Hewett, Pierrette Hondagneu, Michael Liu, Brian Powers, Vicki Smith, Stephen Wood and Rob Wrenn for their comments and Laszlo Cseh-Szombathy for all his help. Burawoy's research was supported by a grant from the National Science Foundation, and a research assistantship from the Institute of Industrial Relations, University of California, Berkeley. Lukács' research was supported by the Institute of Economic Planning, Budapest, the Hungarian Academy of Sciences and the American Council of Learned Societies.

2. It is not surprising, therefore, that capitalist firms facing demand side fluctuations turn to more effective control of supplies, as in the Japanese 'just-in-time' system (Sayer, 1985b; Schonberger, 1982), since these mechanisms establish the conditions under which the greatest centralization of control can occur.

3. Here we have been influenced greatly by the work of Szelenyi (1982) on the character of central appropriation, by the work of Bauer (1978) on plan bargaining and by the work of Kornai (1980) on the shortage economy. While we accept Kornai's criticism of equilibrium theory and his description of capitalism and socialism, as respectively, suction and shortage economies, we find his explanation of the differences inadequate. Focusing on hard and soft budget constraints obscures precisely the contributions of Szelenyi and Bauer, namely the importance of the logics of appropriation and distribution in the two systems.

4. Originally the scrap yard was fitted out with a computer system which would automatically register the amount of both heavy and light scrap charged. The idea was that the front end of the car that delivers the scrap would be filled with light scrap to cushion the impact of the heavy scrap at the rear when both hit the converter walls. In this way the converter would have a longer life. But shortage of scrap and of time, particularly due to programme changes when the amount of scrap would be changed abruptly, made this sorting out process infeasible. So the computer control system does not work, all scrap is registered manually and therefore easily subject to manipulation. Similar manipulations take place in the case of the hot metal. The crane driver is responsible for registering the amount of hot metal. He can turn his counter to zero after there are already a few tons of hot metal in the ladle.

5. These experts came from a consulting firm linked to one of the biggest United States steel corporations. They had been sent to Red Star at the insistence of the Ministry of Industry as part of the World Bank's loan conditions.

6. The careful following of heats from the point of steel production to their departure from the factory as finished steel is still not possible. We found it impossible to trace what happened to a given heat after it left the Combined Steel Works. Part of the problem is that because there are so many different steels being produced, parts of the same heat may end up in different places. Another problem, we were told, is that the storage yard contains so many types of steel that it would be virtually impossible to locate a particular heat. And then there does not seem to be a careful recording of steel that is scrapped and returned to production.

7. Of course, there is the important proviso that self-organization is ineffective and perhaps counter-productive in the context of intense shortages, most likely to occur in peripheral sectors of state socialist economies or in the early period of taut planning in the Soviet Union (Andrle, 1985). But as state socialism develops and the problem of shortages, while remaining, becomes less severe so self-organization becomes a possible solution to increase technical efficiency.

8.   Here one might also refer to the emergence of worker collectives which are essentially internal subcontracting systems made up of self-selected, self-organized groups of workers and managers paid for the completion of specific tasks. Collectives can be found at Red Star but in declining numbers. In a fascinating article Stark (1986) underlines their simulation of rudimentary markets adapted to uncertainties generated in bureaucratic environments whereas we regard them as signifying the requirements of self-organization on the shop-floor.

Bibliography

Abercrombie, N. and Urry, J. (1983), *Capital, Labour and the Middle Classes*, London: Allen & Unwin

Abernathy, W. J. (1978), *The Productivity Dilemma*, Baltimore: John Hopkins University Press

Abernathy, W. J., Clark, K. B. and Kantrow, A. M. (1983), 'The New Industrial Competiton' in A. M. Kantrow (ed.) *Survival Strategies in American Industry*, New York: Harvard Business Review Executive Book Series, pp. 72–95

Abernathy, W. J., Clark, K. B. and Kantrow, A. H. (1984), *Industrial Renaissance: Producing a Competitive Future for America*, New York: Basic Books

ACARD (Advisory Committee on Research and Development) (1986), *Medical Equipment*, London: HMSO

Adler, P. (1985a), 'Technology and Us', *Socialist Review*, vol. 85, pp. 67–98

Adler, P. (1985b), 'Managing Flexibility: A Selective Review of the Challenges of Managing the New Technologies – Potential for Flexibility, a report to the Organization for Economic Co-operation and Development, mimeo, Stanford: Stanford University, Department of Industrial Engineering and Engineering Management

Adler, P. (n.d.), *Beyond Deskilling: The Forgotten Dimensions of Work*, mimeo, Stanford: Stanford University

Adler, P. and Borys, B. (1986), *Automation and Work: Lessons from the Machine Tool Case*, mimeo, Stanford: Stanford University

Aglietta, M. (1979), *A Theory of Capitalist Regulation*, London: New Left Books

Aglietta, M. (1984), 'Long-term Trends in the American Economy and Possible Future' in L. Lindberg, A. Lejins, and K. Engberg (eds) *American Futures, Conference Papers 4*, Stockholm: The Swedish Institute of International Affairs, pp. 17–29

Agurén, R. (1985), *Volvo Kalmar Revisited: Ten Years of Experience*, Stockholm: Efficiency and Participation Development Council

Albin, P. S. (1985), 'Job Design, Control Technology, and Technical Change', *Journal of Economic Issues*, **17**, no. 3, pp. 703–30.

Altmann, N., Deiss, M., Doehl, V. and Sauer, D. E. (1986), '"Neuer Rationalisierungstyp" – Neue Anforderungen an die Industriesoziologie', *Soziale Welt*, vol. 37, no. 2/3, pp. 197–207

Altshuler, A., Anderson, M., Jones, D., Roos, D. and Womack, J. (1984), *The Future of the Automobile*, Cambridge, Mass./London: MIT Press/Allen and Unwin

Amin, S. (1979), 'The Third World Today and the International Division of Labor', *Japan-Asia Quarterly Review*, vol. 11, no. 1, series no. 39

Andrle, V. (1985), 'The Management of Labour in Soviet Industry: Objectives, Methods and Conflicts in the 1930s, mimeo, York University (England): Sociology Department

Appel, H. and Hilber, K. (1984), *Product and Production Technology of Future Automobiles*, Berlin: Technische Universität

Appelbaum, E. (1984), 'The Impact of Technology on Skill Requirements and Occupational Structure in the Insurance Industry', mimeo, Philadelphia, Pa: Temple University

Appelbaum, E. (1988), 'Technology and the Redesign of Work in the Insurance Industry' in B. Wright (ed.) *Women, Work and Technology: Transformations*, Ann Arbor, Michigan: University of Michigan Press, pp. 182–201

Appelbaum, E. (1989) 'The Growth in the US Contingent Labor Force', in R. Orago and R. Pereleman (eds.), *Microeconomic Issues in Labour Economics: New Approaches*, Sussex: Wheatsheaf, in press

Appelbaum, E., Albin, P.S. and Koppel, R.J. (1988) 'Implications of Workplace Information Technology: Control, Organization of Work and the Occupational Structure', in I.H. Simpson and R.R. Simpson (eds) *Research in the Sociology of Work*, Vol. 4; Greenwich, Conn.: JAI Press, pp, 125–52.

Armstrong, P. (1984), *Labour Pains: Women's Work in Crisis*, Toronto: Women's Press

Armstrong, P. (1988) 'Labour and Monopoly Capitalism' in R. Hyman and W. Streeck (eds) *New Technology and Industrial Relations*, Oxford: Blackwell, pp. 143–59

Ascher, K. (1987), *The Politics of Privatisation*, Basingstoke: Macmillan

Ashton, D. and Maguire, M. (1986), *Young Adults in the Labour Market*, Research Paper no. 55, London: Department of Employment

Ashton, D., Maguire, M. and Garland, V. (1986), *Youth in the Labour Market*, London: Youthaid

Atkinson, J. (1985), 'Flexibility: Planning for an Uncertain Future', *Manpower Policy and Practice*, vol 1, Summer, pp. 26–9

Atkinson, J. (1988), 'Recent Changes in the Internal Labour Market Structure in the UK' in W. Buitelaar (ed.) *Technology and Work: Labour Studies in England, Germany and the Netherlands*, Aldershot: Avebury, pp. 133–49

Babbage, C. (1832), *On the Economy of Machinery*, London: C. Knight

Baethge, M. and Oberbeck, H. (1986), *Die Zukunft der Angestellten. Neue Technologien und berufliche Perspektiven in Buro und Verwaltung*, Frankfurt: Campus Verlag

Bagguley, P. and Walby, S. (1987), *Women and Local Labour Markets: A Comparative Analysis of Five Localities*, Lancaster Regionalism Group Working Paper

Bagnasco, A. (1977), *Tre Italie*, Bologna: Mulino

Bakker, I. (1988), 'Women's Employment in Perspective' in J. Jenson, E. Hagen and C. Reddy (eds) *Feminization of the Labor Force: Paradoxes and Promises*, Cambridge: Polity, pp. 17–44

Baran, B. (1985), 'Office Automation and Women's Work: The Technological Transformation of the Insurance Industry' in M Castells (ed.) *High Technology, Space and Society*, Beverly Hills: Sage Publications, pp. 153–71

Baran, B. (1987), 'The Technological Transformation of White Collar Work: A Case Study of the Insurance Industry' in H. I. Hartmann (ed.) *Computer*

Chips and Paper Clips: Technology and Women's Employment, vol. II, Washington, DC: National Academy Press, pp. 25–62

Barnett, D. and Crandall, R. (1986), *Up From the Ashes*, Washington, DC: The Brookings Institute

Bauer, T. (1978), 'Investment Cycles in Planned Economies, *Acta Oeconomica*, vol. 21, no. 3, pp. 243–60

Beaumont, P. B. (1987), *The Decline of Trade Union Organization*, London: Croom Helm

Beavis, S. (1988), 'Ford Aims to Build Car for all the World', *The Guardian*, Monday, 7 March, p. 20

Beechey, V. (1977), 'Some Notes on Female Wage Labour in the Capitalist Mode of Production', *Capital and Class*, no. 3, pp. 45–66

Beechey, V. (1978), 'Women and Production: A Critical Analysis of Some Sociological Theories of Women's Work' in A. Kuhn and A. M. Wolpe (eds) *Feminism and Materialism: Women and Modes of Production*, London: Routledge & Kegan Paul, pp. 154–97

Beechey, V. (1982), 'The Sexual Division of Labour and the Labour Process: A Critical Assessment of Braverman' in S. Wood (ed.) *The Degradation of Work?* London: Hutchinson, pp. 54–73

Beechey, V. (1983), 'What's so Special about Women's Employment? A Review of Some Recent Studies of Women's Paid Work', *Feminist Review*, no. 15, pp. 23–45

Beechey, V. and Perkins, T. (1987), *A Matter of Hours: Women, Part-Time Work and the Labour Market*, Cambridge: Polity Press

Bell, D. (1974), *The Coming of Post-Industrial Society*, London: Heinemann

Bell, R. (1972), *Changing Technology and Manpower Requirements in the Engineering Industry*, Watford: Sussex University Press & Engineering Training Board, for Science Policy Research Unit

Berger, S. and Piore, M. (1980), *Dualism and Discontinuity in Industrial Societies*, Cambridge: Cambridge University Press

Berggren, C. (1980), 'Changes in the Rationalization Pattern and Organization of Work within the Swedish Engineering Industry' *Acta Sociologica*, vol. 21, no. 4, pp. 239–60

Bernoux, P., Cavestro, W., Lamotte, B. and Troussier, J-F. (1987), *Technologies nouvelles, nouveau travail*, Paris: Fédération de l'Education nationale Ed

Berry, M. (1985), 'Des robots au concret. Les réalités cachées derrière les mythes', *Annales des Mines*, no. 8, pp. 7–9

Bessant, J. (1985), 'Flexible Manufacturing Systems – An Overview', mimeo, Brighton: Department of Business Management, Brighton Polytechnic,

Bessant, J., Lamming, R. and Senker, P. (1985), 'The Challenge of Computer-Integrated Manufacturing', *Technovation*, vol. 3, no. 4, pp. 283–95

Beynon, H. (1984), *Working for Ford*, Harmondsworth: Penguin

Bisseret, A. (1981), 'Application of Signal Detection Theory to Decision Making in Supervisory Control', *Ergonomics*, vol. 24, no. 2, pp. 81–94

Blackburn, P., Coombs, R. and Green, K. (1985), *Technology, Economic Growth and the Labour Process*, London: Macmillan

Blackhurst, C. and Inman, B. (1987), 'Industry Wakes to a Drugs Nightmare', *Business*, February, pp. 61–3

Block, F. (1985), 'Economy and Nostalgia', *Dissent*, Fall, pp. 498–50

Bluestone, B. and Harrison (1982) *The De-industrialization of America: Plant Closings, Community Abandonment and the Dismantling of Basic Industry*, New York: Basic Books

Blumberg, M. and Gerwin, D. (1981), *Coping with Advanced Manufacturing Technology*, discussion paper IIM/LMP 81–12, Berlin: Wissenschaftszentrum

Bonnafos, G. de, Chanaron, J. J. and Mautort, L. de (1983), *L'industrie automobile*, Paris: La Découverte/Maspero

Bouillaguet-Bernard, P., Gauvin-Ayel, A. and Outin, J.L. (1981), *Femmes au travail: prospérité et crise*, Paris: Economica

Boyer, R. (ed.) (1986), *La flexibilité du travail en Europe*, Paris: Editions La Découverte

Boyer, R. (1987a), 'Regulation' in J. Eatwell, M. Milgrate and P. Newman (eds) *The New Palgrave: A Dictionary of Economics*, London: Macmillan, pp. 126–8

Boyer, R. (1987b), 'Labour Flexibilities: Many Forms, Uncertain Effects', *Labor and Society*, vol. 12, no. 1, January, pp. 107–129

Bowles, S., Gordon, D. and Weisskopf, T. (1983), *Beyond the Wasteland*, New York: Basic Books

Braverman, H. (1974), *Labor and Monopoly Capital: The Degradation of Work in the Twentieth Century*, New York and London: Monthly Review Press

Brenner, R. (1977), 'The Origins of Capitalist Development: A Critique of Neo-Smithian Marxism', *New Left Review*, vol. 104, pp. 25–92

Breugel, I. (1979), 'Women as a Reserve Army of Labour: A Note on Recent British Experience', *Feminist Review*, no. 3, pp. 12–23

Bright, J. (1958), *Automation and Management*, Boston, Mass.: Harvard University Press

Brodie, J., and Jenson, J. (1988), *Crisis, Challenge and Change: Party and Class in Canada*, Toronto: Methuen

Brodner, P. (1985) *Fabrik 2000. Alternative Entwicklungspfade in die Zukunft der Fabrik*, Berlin: Sigma-Verlag

Brooks, F. P. jr. (1975), *The Mythical Man-Month*, Reading, Mass.: Addison-Wesley Publishing Company

Brown, W. (ed.) (1981), *The Changing Contours of British Industrial Relations*, Oxford: Basil Blackwell

Browning, D., Cowell, D., Kilshaw, D., Knowles, D., Randall, J. and Singer, R. (1984), 'Clinical Chemistry Equipment Outside the Laboratory', *Medical Laboratory Science*, vol. 41, no. 1, pp. 99–107

Brusco, S. (1982), 'The Emilian Model: Productive Decentralisation and Social Integration', *Cambridge Journal of Economics*, vol. 6, no. 2, pp. 167–84

Brusco, S. and Sabel, C. (1983), 'Artisan Production and Economic Growth' in F. Wilkinson (ed.) *The Dynamics of Labour Market Segmentation*, London: Academic Press, pp. 99–113

Buckley, P. J. and Casson, M. C. (1976), *The Future of the Multinational Enterprise*, New York: Holmes & Meier

Burawoy, M. (1979), *Manufacturing Consent*, Chicago: University of Chicago Press

Burawoy, M. (1985), *The Politics of Production*, London: Verso

Burawoy, M. and Lukács, J. (1985), 'Mythologies of Work: A Comparison of Firms in State Socialism and Advanced Captalism', *American Sociological*

Review, vol. 50, no. 6, pp. 723–37

Burns, A. (1934), *Production Trends in the United States Since 1870*, New York: National Bureau of Economic Research

Burns, T. and Stalker, G. (1961), *The Management of Innovation*, London: Tavistock Press

Business Week (1986), 'High Tech to the Rescue', *Special Report*, 16 June, pp. 100–8

Business Week (1987a), 'General Motors: What Went Wrong', *Special Report*, 16 March, pp. 102–10

Business Week (1987b), 'The Push for Quality', *Special Report*, 8 June, pp. 130–53

Butcher, J. (1983), 'FMS Offering a Way to Remain Competitive', in K. Rathmill (ed.) *Proceedings of the Second International Conference on Flexible Manufacturing Systems*, Bedford and Oxford: IFS (Conferences) Ltd North Holland Publishing, pp. xi–xii

Carney, J., Hudson, R. and Lewis, J. (eds) (1980), *Regions in Crisis: New Perspectives in European Regional Theory*, London: Croom Helm

Casey, B. (1986), 'The Dual Apprenticeship System and the Recruitment and Retention of Young Apprentices in West Germany', *British Journal of Industrial Relations*, vol. 24, no. 1, pp. 63–81

Casey, B. (1988), *Temporary Employment: Practices and Policies in Britain*, PSI Report no. 669, London: Policy Studies Institute

Castells, M. (1985), 'High Technology, Economic Restructuring and the Urban-Regional Process in the United States' in M. Castells (ed.) *High Technology, Space and Society*, Beverly Hills: Sage Publications, pp. 11–40

Caves, R. E. (1971), 'International Corporations: The Industrial Economics of Foreign Investment', *Economica*, vol. 38, no. 149, pp. 1–27

Caves, R. E. (1974), 'Industrial Organization' in J. H. Dunning (ed.) *Economic Analysis of the Multinational Enterprise*, New York: Praeger, pp. 115–46

Caves, R. E. (1982), *Multinational Enterprises and Economic Analysis*, Cambridge: Cambridge University Press

Cavestro, W. (1984a), 'Automatisation, organisation du travail et qualification dans les PME', *Sociologie du travail*, vol. 26, no. 4, pp. 434–46

Cavestro, W. (1984b), *L'automatisation dans les industries de biens d'équipment*, vol. 2, Paris: Centre d'Etudes et de Recherches sur les Qualifications.

Cavestro, W. (1984c), 'Automation, evolution of skills in small and medium sized firms', in T. Martin (ed.) *Design of Work in Automated Manufacturing Systems*, International Federation of Automatic Control, Oxford: Pergamon, pp. 1–5

Cavestro, W. (1986a), Automation, Work Organization and Skills: The Case of Numerical Control, *Automatica*, vol. 22, no. 6, pp. 739–43

Cavestro, W. (1986b), 'Automation and the evolution of the division of labour and skills, the case of sheet metal industry' in P. Brödner (ed.) *Skill Based Automated Manufacturing*, International Federation of Automatic Control Workshop, preprints, pp. 115–18

Cavestro, W. (1987a), 'Nouveaux outils, nouveau travail' in P. Bernoux *et al.*, (eds) *Technologies nouvelles, nouveau travail*, Paris: Fédération de l'Education Nationale Ed.

Cavestro, W. (1987b), 'Travail et nouvelles formes de coopération dans les

PME', Annales des Mines, no. 8, pp. 40-3

Cavestro, W. (1988a), 'Automatisation, organisation et contenu du travail' in Stankiewicz, F. (ed.) *Les stratégies d'enterprises face aux ressources humaines. L'après Taylorisme*, Paris: Economica, pp. 56–66

Cavestro, W. (1988b), 'Automation, new man-machine system and skills', *International Journal of Robotics and Automation*, vol. 3, no. 1, pp. 50-4

Cavestro, W. (1988c), 'Automation, skills and the content of work', *International Journal of Systems Science*, vol. 19, no. 8, pp. 1407–18

Chapman, P. and Tooze, M. (1987), *The Youth Training Scheme in the United Kingdom*, Aldershot: Avebury

Charles, N. (1983), 'Women and Trade Unions in the Workplace', *Feminist Review*, no. 15, pp. 3–22

Christopherson, S. and Storper, M. (1989), 'The Effects of Flexible Specialization on Industrial Politics and the Labour Market: The Motion Picture Industry', *Industrial and Labor Relations Review*, vol. 42, no. 3, pp. 331ff

Clark, J., McLoughlin, I., Rose, H. and King, P. (1988), *The Process of Technological Change*, Cambridge: Cambridge University Press

Clark, R. (1979), *The Japanese Company*, New Haven and London: Yale University Press

Cockburn, C. (1981), 'The Material of Male Power', *Feminist Review*, no. 9, pp. 41–58

Cockburn, C. (1983), *Brothers: Male Dominance and Technological Change*, London: Pluto Press

Cockburn, C. (1986), 'Women and Technology: Opportunity is Not Enough' in K. Purcell, S. Wood, A. Waton and S. Allen (eds) *The Changing Experience of Employment*, London: Macmillan, pp. 173–87

Cockburn, C. (1987), *Two Track Training*, Basingstoke: Macmillan

Cohen, R. (1981), 'The New International Division of Labor, Multinational Corporations and Urban Hierarchy' in M. Dear and A. Scott (eds) *Urbanization and Urban Planning in Capitalist Society*, New York: Methuen, pp. 287-315

Cohen, R. (1987), *The New Helots: Migrants in the International Division of Labour*, Aldershot: Gower

Cohen, S. (1987), 'A Labour Process to Nowhere', *New Left Review*, vol. 165, pp. 34–50

Cole, R. E. (1971), *Japanese Blue Collar*, Berkeley: University of California Press

Cole, R. E. (1979), *Work Mobility and Participation – A Comparative Study of American and Japanese Industry*, Berkeley, Los Angeles, London: University of California Press

Collins, H. M. (1985), 'Where's the Expertise: Expert Systems as a Medium of Knowledge Transfer', in M. Merry (ed.) *Expert Systems '85*, Cambridge: Cambridge University Press, pp. 323–34

Collinson, D. and Knights, D. (1986), '"Men Only": Theories and Practices of Job Segregation in Insurance' in D. Knights and H. Wilmott (eds) *Gender and the Labour Process*, Aldershot: Gower, pp. 140-78

Commoner, B. (1976), *The Poverty of Power*, New York: Knopf/Bantam

Conference of Socialist Economists, Micro-Electronics Group (1980), *New Technology and The Working Class*, London: CSE Books

Cooke, P. (1983), *Theories of Planning and Spatial Development*, London: Hutchinson

Cool, K. O. and Lengnick-Hall, C. A. (1985), 'Second Thoughts on the Transferability of the Japanese Management Style', *Organization Studies*, vol. 6, no. 1, pp. 1–22

Coombs, R. (1985), 'Automation, Management Strategies and Labour-Process Change' in D. Knights, H. Willmott and D. Collins (eds) *Job Redesign: Critical Perspectives on the Labour Process*, Aldershot: Gower, p. 142

Coombs, R. (1987), 'Accounting for the Control of Doctors: Management Information Systems in Swedish Hospitals', *Accounting, Organisations and Society*, vol. 12, no. 4, pp. 389–407

Coombs, R. and Jones, B. (1988), 'Alternative Successors to Fordism', paper presented at the conference on Society, Information and Space, Swiss Federal Institute of Technology, Zurich 21–2 January 1988, mimeo, Manchester and Bath: UMIST and Bath University

Coriat, B. (1983), *La Robotique*, Paris: La Découverte/Maspero

Cousins, C. (1986), 'The Labour Process in the State Welfare Sector' in D. Knights and H. Willmott (eds) *Managing the Labour Process*, Aldershot: Gower, pp. 85–108

Cousins, C. (1988), 'The Restructuring of Welfare Work', *Work, Employment and Society*, vol. 2, no. 2, June, pp. 210–28

Cowan, R. S. (1983), *More Work For Mother: The Ironies of Household Technology from the Open Hearth to the Microwave*, New York: Basic Books

Cressey, P. and MacInnes, J. (1980), 'Voting for Ford: Industrial Democracy and the Control of Labor', *Capital and Class*, no. 11, pp. 5–33

Crompton, R. and Jones, G. (1984), *White-Collar Proletariat: Deskilling and Gender in the Clerical Labour Process*, London: Macmillan

Crompton, R. and Reid, S. (1982), 'The Deskilling of Clerical Work' in S. Wood (ed.) *The Degradation of Work?*, London: Hutchinson, pp. 163–78

Cross, M. (1985), *Towards the Flexible Craftsman*, London: Technical Change Centre

Cummings, B. (1984), 'The Origins and Developments of the Northeast Asian Political Economy', *International Organization*, vol. 38, no. 1, pp. 1–40

Cunnison, S. (1986), 'Gender, Consent and Exploitation amongst Sheltered-Housing Wardens' in K. Purcell, S. Wood, A. Waton and S. Allen (eds) *The Changing Experience of Employment*, London: Macmillan, pp. 188–205

Curson, C. (ed.) (1986), *Flexible Patterns of Work*, London: Institute of Personnel Management

Cusumano, M. (1985), *The Japanese Automobile Industry*, Cambridge, Mass.: Cambridge University Press

Dale, A. and Bamford, C. (1988), 'Temporary Workers: Cause for Concern or Complacency', *Work, Employment and Society*, vol. 2, no. 2, pp. 210–28

Daniels, P. W. (1985), *Service Industries*, London: Methuen

Dankbaar, B. (1984), 'Maturity and Relocation in the Car Industry', *Development and Change*, vol. 15, no. 2, 223–50

Dankbaar, B. (1988), 'New Production Concepts, Management Strategies and the Quality of Work', *Work, Employment and Society*, vol. 2, no. 1, pp. 25–50

Daune-Richard, A. M. (1988), 'Gender Relations and Female Labour' in J. Jenson, E. Hagen and C. Reddy (eds) *Promises and Paradoxes: The Feminization of the Labor Force*, Polity/Cambridge, pp. 260–75

Deakin, B. and Pratten, C. (1987), 'Economic Effects of YTS', *Employment Gazette*, vol. 95, no. 10, pp. 491–7

De Kadt, M. (1979), 'Insurance: A Clerical Work Factory' in A. Zimbalist (ed.) *Case Studies in the Labor Process*, New York: Monthly Review Press, pp. 242–56

De Vroey (1984), 'A Regulation Approach to and Interpretation of the Comtemporary Crisis', *Capital and Class*, no. 23, pp. 45–66

Demes, H. (1989), 'Beförderung und Entlohnung in einem japanischen Automobilunternehmen', West Berlin: Science Center, Berlin

Dempsey, F. E. (1983), 'New Corporate Perspectives in FMS' in K. Rathmill (ed.) *Proceedings of the Second International Conference on Flexible Manufacturing Systems*, Bedford and Oxford: IFS (Conferences) Ltd/North Holland Publishing, pp. 3–17

Department of Education and Science (1987), 'Education and Economic Activity of Young People Aged 16 to 18', *Statistical Bulletin no. 2/87*, London: DES

Department of Employment (1987), '1984 Census of Employment and Revised Employment Estimates', *Employment Gazette*, vol. 95, no. 1, January pp. 31–53

Dex, S. (1985), *The Sexual Division of Work*, Brighton: Wheatsheaf

Dex, S. (1987), *Women's Occupational Mobility: A Lifetime Perspective*, London: Macmillan

Dex, S. and Shaw, L. (1986), *British and American Women at Work: Do Equal Opportunities Policies Matter?*, London: Macmillan

Doeringer, P. and Piore, M. (1971), *Internal Labour Markets and Manpower Analysis*, Lexington, Mass.: Lexington Books

Dohse, K., Jürgens, U. and Malsch, T. (1985), 'From "Fordism" to "Toyotism"? The Social Organization of the Labor Process in the Japanese Automobile Industry', *Politics and Society*, vol. 14, no. 2, pp. 115–46

Dore, R. (1973), *British Factory – Japanese Factory*, Berkeley: University of California Press

Dore, R. (1986), *Flexible Rigidities*, London: Athlone Press

Driscoll, J. (1984), 'The Use of Flexible Manufacturing Systems', mimeo, Liverpool: Department of Industrial Studies, Liverpool University

Dull, K. (1985), 'The Analysis of New Forms of Work Organization – Results of Case Studies from the Federal Republic of Germany, France and Italy' in P. Grootings, B. Gustavsen, L. Hethy (eds) *New Forms of Work Organization and their Social and Economic Environment*, Budapest: Vienna Centre and Institute of Labour Research Budapest, pp. 197–230

Dunlop, J. (1958), *Industrial Relations Systems*. New York: Holt, Rinehart and Winston

Dunning, J. H. (1971), *The Multinational Enterprise*, London: Allen & Unwin

Dunning, J. H. (ed.) (1974), *Economic Analysis and the Multinational Enterprise*, New York: Praeger

Dunning, J. H. (1981), *International Production and the Multinational Enterprise*, London: George Allen & Unwin

Durand, J-P., Lojkine, J., Mahieu, C. and Durand, J. (1984), *Formation et informatisation de la production: le cas de l'automobile*, Vitry: Centre d'Etudes Sociales sur l'Informatisation de la Production

Du Roy, O., Hunault, J. C. and Tubiana, J. (1985), *Réussir l'investissement productif*, Paris: Les Editions d'Organisation

Dutton, P. A. (1987), *The Impact of YTS on Engineering Apprenticeship – local labour market study*, Engineering Industry Training Board and Institute of Employment Research, Coventry: University of Warwick

Edwards, R. (1979), *Contested Terrain: The Transformation of the Workplace in the Twentieth Century*, New York and London: Basic Books and Heinemann

Edwards, R., Gordon, D. and Reich, M. (1975), *Labour Market Segmentation*, Lexington, Mass. Lexington Books

Elger, T. (1982), 'Braverman, Capital Accumulation and Deskilling' in S. Wood (ed.) *The Degradation of Work?*, London: Hutchinson, pp. 23–53

Equal Opportunities Commission (EOC) (1985a), *Research Bulletin*

Equal Opportunities Commission (EOC) (1985b), *Women and Men in Britain: A Statistical Profile*, Manchester: EOC

Equal Opportunities Commission (EOC) (1987), *Women and Men in Britain: A Statistical Profile, 1986*, Manchester: EOC

Eversley, J. (1986), 'Trade Union Responses to the MSC' in C. Benn, and J. Fairley (eds) *Challenging the MSC*, London: Pluto Press, pp. 201–26

Fevre, R. (1986), 'Contract Work in the Recession' in K. Purcell, S. Wood, A. Waton and S. Allen (eds) *The Changing Experience of Employment*, London: Macmillan, pp. 18–34

Fineberg, H. V. (1979), 'Clinical Chemistries: The High Cost of Low Cost Diagnostic Tests' in S. H. Altman and R. Blendon (eds) *Medical Technology: The Culprit behind Health Care Costs*, Washington, DC: US Department of Health, Education and Welfare, pp. 144–65

Finn, D. (1987), *Training Without Jobs*, Basingstoke: Macmillan

Fischer, P., Addison, L.A., Curtis, P. and Mitchell, J. M. (1984), *The Office Laboratory*, Norwalk, Conn.: Appleton-Century-Crofts

Flamm, K. (1985), 'The Internationalization of Semiconductors' in J. Grunwald and K. Flamm (eds) *The Global Factory: Foreign Assembly in International Trade*, Washington, DC: The Brookings Institute, pp. 38–136

Foster, D. (1963), *Modern Automation*, London: Pitman

Francis, A. (1986), *New Technology at Work*, Oxford: Oxford University Press

Franko, L. (1983), *The Threat of the Japanese Multinational*, New York: John Wiley & Sons

Freeman, C. (1982), *The Economics of Industrial Innovation*, London: Frances Pinter, 2nd edn

Freeman, C., Clark, J. and Soete, L. (1983), *Unemployment and Technical Innovation*, Westport, Conn.: Greenwood

Freyssenet, M. (1979), *Division du travail et mobilisation quotidienne de la main-d'oeuvre*, Paris: Centre de Sociologie Urbaine

Friedman, A. L. (1977), *Industry and Labour: Class Struggle at Work and Monopoly Capitalism*, London: Macmillan

Friedmann, G. (1963), *Où va le travail humain?*, Paris: Gallimard

Froebel, F., Heinrichs, J. and Kreye, O. (1980), *The New Industrial Division of Labour: Structural Unemployment in Industrialized Countries and Industrialization in Developing Countries*, Cambridge: Cambridge University Press

Frost and Sullivan (1985), *Home Health Monitoring Market in Europe*, London: Frost & Sullivan

Galjaard, J. H. (1982), *A Technology Based Nation*, Delft: Inter-university Institute of Management

Garnsey, E. (1981), 'The Rediscovery of the Division of Labour', *Theory and Society*, vol. 10, pp. 337–58

Gershuny, J. (1983), *Social Innovation and the Division of Labour*, Oxford: Oxford University Press

Gershuny, J. and Miles, I. (1983), *The New Service Economy: The Transformation of Employment in Industrial Societies*, London: Frances Pinter

Gerwin, D. and Leung, T. K. (1986), 'The Organizational Impacts of Flexible Manufacturing Systems', *Human Systems Management*, vol. 1, pp. 237–46

Gibson, K., Graham, J., Shakow, D. and Ross, R. (1984), 'A Theoretical Approach to Capital and Labour Restructuring' in P. O'Keefe (ed.) *Regional Restructuring Under Advanced Capitalism*, London: Croom Helm, pp. 39–64

Glen, E. N. and Feldberg, R. L. (1979), 'Proletarianizing Clerical Work: Technology and Organizational Control in the Office' in A. Zimbalist (ed.) *Case Studies on the Labor Process*, New York: Monthly Review, Press, pp. 51–72

Glickman, N. and Petras, E. (1981), 'International Capital and International Labor Flows: Implications for Public Policy', working papers in Regional Science and Transportation, mimeo, Philadelphia: University of Pennsylvania, Working Paper no. 53

Godel, M. (1987), 'The Unfashionable and Controversial Findings of Japan', *Futures*, vol. 19, no. 4, pp. 371–84

Gold, B. (1964), 'Industry Growth Patterns: Theory and Empirical Results', *Journal of Industrial Economics*, vol. 13, no. 1, pp. 53–73

Goldthorpe, J. (1980), *Social Mobility and the Class Structure in Modern Britain*, Oxford: Clarendon Press

Goldthorpe, J. (1984), 'The End of Convergence: Corporatist and Dualist Tendencies in Modern Western Societies' in J. Goldthorpe (ed.) *Order and Conflict in Contemporary Capitalism*, Oxford: Clarendon Press, pp. 315–43

Goldthorpe, J. (1985), 'Employment, Class and Mobility: A Critique of Liberal and Marxist Theories of Long-term Change', mimeo, Oxford: Nuffield College, Oxford University

Gough, J. (1986), 'Industrial Policy and Socialist Strategy: Restructuring and the Unity of the Working Class', *Capital and Class*, no. 29, pp. 58–81

Gray, D. and King, S. (1986), *The Youth Training Scheme: The First Three Years*, YTS Evaluation Series no. 1, Sheffield: Manpower Services Commission

Greater London Council (1985), *London Industrial Strategy*, London: GLC

Green, A. (1986), 'The MSC and the Three-Tier Structure of Further Education' in C. Benn and J. Fairley (eds) *Challenging the MSC*, London: Pluto Press, pp. 99–122

Greenbaum, J. (1979), *In the Name of Efficiency: Management Theory and Shopfloor Practice in Data-processing Work*, Philadelphia: Temple University Press

Griffiths Report (1983), *Report of the NHS Management Enquiry*, London: DHSS

Guest, R. and Walker, C. (1952), *Man on the Assembly Line*, Cambridge, Mass.: Harvard University Press

Haas, V. (1983), 'Team-konzept – Mitarbeiter planen und betreiben ihr Arbeitssystem', in H.-J. Bullinger and H. J. Warnecke (eds.) *Wettbewerbsfähige Arbeitssysteme, Problem-lösungen für die Praxis, Vorträge der 2.* Stuttgart: Verein zur Förderung produktions-technischer Forschung e. v. pp. 129–89

Hagen, E. and Jenson, J. (1988), 'Paradoxes and Promises: Work and Politics in the Postwar years' in J. Jenson, E. Hagen and C. Reddy (eds) *Feminization of the Labour Force: Paradoxes and Promises*, Cambridge Polity, pp. 3–16

Hakim, C. (1979), *Occupational Segregation: A Comparative Study of the Degree and Pattern of the Differentiation Between Men and Women's Work in Britain, the United States and other Countries*, Department of Employment Research Report no. 9, London: HMSO

Hakim, C. (1981), 'Job Segregation: Trends in the 1970s', *Employment Gazette*, vol. 89, no. 12, December, pp. 521–9

Hakim, C. (1987a), 'Homeworking in Britain: Key Findings from the National Survey of Home-based Workers', *Employment Gazette*, vol. 95, no. 2, February, pp. 92–104

Hakim, C. (1987b), 'Trends in the Flexible Workforce', *Employee Gazette*, vol. 95, no. 11, November, pp. 549–60

Hall, P. and Markusen, A. (eds) (1985), *Silicon Landscapes*, Boston: Allen & Unwin

Ham, C. (1985), *Health Policy in Britain*, London: Macmillan

Hansen, N. (1979), 'The New International Division of Labor and Manufacturing Decentralization in the United States', *Review of Regional Studies*, vol. 9, no. 1, pp. 1–11

Harris, C. (1987), *Redundancy and Recession*, Oxford: Basil Blackwell

Harrison, B. and Bluestone, B. (1988), *The Great U-Turn*, New York: Basic Books

Hartley, J. (1984), *FMS at Work*, Bedford: IFS Publications

Hartmann, G., Nicholas, I., Sorge, A. and Warner, M. (1983), 'Computerised Machine Tools, Manpower Consequences and Skill Utilization: A Study of British and West German Manufacturing Firms', *British Journal of Industrial Relations*, vol. 21, no. 2, pp. 221–31

Hartmann, H. (1985), *Comparable Worth: New Directions for Research*, Washington, DC: National Academy Press

Harvey, D. (1977), 'The Geography of Capitalist Accumulation: A Reconstruction of Marxian Theory' in R. Peet (ed.) *Radical Geography*, Chicago: Maaroufa, pp. 263–92

Harvey, D. (1982), *The Limits to Capital*, Oxford: Basil Blackwell

Harvey, D. (1985), 'Paris, 1850–1870', D. Harvey (ed.) *Consciousness and the Urban Experience*, Baltimore: Johns Hopkins University Press, pp. 63–220

Hayashi, M. (1982), *The Japanese Style of Small-Group QC Circle Activity*, Tokyo: Chuo University

Health Service Journal (1987), supplement on 'Health Service Computing', 18 June, vol. 97, no. 5055

Hendry, C. and Pettigrew, A. (1988), 'Multiskilling in the Round', *Personnel Management*, April, pp. 36–43

Herold, M. W. and Kozlov, N. (1987), 'A New International Division of Labor? The Caribbean Case' in M. Davis (ed.) *The Year Left 2*, London: Verso, pp. 218–41

Hirschhorn, L. (1984), *Beyond Mechanization: Work and Technology in a Post-industrial Age*, Cambridge, Mass.: MIT Press

Holmes. J. (1985), 'Industrial Change in the Canadian Automotive Products Industry, 1973–1984: The Impact of Technical Change in the Organization and Locational Structure of Automobile Production', paper presented to the IGU Commission on Industrial Change Conference on Technology and

Industrial Change, Nijmegen, The Netherlands, 19–24 August, and to the IBG/CAG Industrial Geography Symposium on Technical Change in Industry, University College, Swansea, Wales, 22–6 August, mimeo, Kingston, Ontario: Department of Geography, Queens University

Holmes, J. (1986), 'The Organization and Locational Structure of Production Subcontracting' in A. Scott and M. Storper (eds) *Production, Work, Territory: The Geographical Anatomy of Industrial Capitalism*, Boston: George Allen & Unwin, 80–106

Holusha, J. (1986), 'A New Way to Build Cars', *The New York Times*, 13 March

Hoos, D. (1986), 'Technology and Work in the Two Germanies' in P. Grootings (ed.) *Technology and Work; East–West Comparison*, London: Croom Helm, pp. 231–72

Hounshell, D. (1984), *From the American System to Mass Production, 1800-1932*, Baltimore: Johns Hopkins University Press

Huws, U. (1985), 'Challenging Commoditisation – Producing Usefulness Outside the Factory' in Collective Design/Projects (eds) *Very Nice Work if You Can Get It: The Socially Useful Production Debate*, Nottingham: Spokesman

Hyman, R. (1988), 'Flexible Specialization: Miracle or Myth?' in R. Hyman and W. Streeck (eds) *New Technology and Industrial Relations*, Oxford: Basil Blackwell, pp. 48–60

Hymer, S. (1972), 'The Multinational Corporation and the Law of Uneven Development', in J. Bhagwati (ed.), *Economics and World Order*, London: Collier Macmillan, pp. 113–40

Hymer, S. (1976), *The International Operations of National Firms: A Study of Direct Foreign Investment*, Cambridge: MIT Press

Inagami, T. (1984), 'Employment Adjustments in Japan', *Japan Labor Bulletin*, vol. 23, no. 8, pp. 5–8

Incomes Data Services (1982), *Part-time Workers*, Study 267, London: Incomes Data Services, 5

Incomes Data Services (1983), *Temporary Workers*, Study 295, London: Incomes Data Services

Incomes Data Services (1984), *Craft Flexibility*, Study 322, London: Incomes Data Services

Institute of Production Engineers (UK), Technical Policy Board (1988), *The Way Ahead: Current and Future Trends of Man Management and Technology in the United Kingdom*, London: Institute of Production Engineers

Iwao, Y. etal. (1979), *Tenkankinō Kigyō-kōdō* (Enterprise Behaviours in the Period of Transformation), Tokyo: Token

Jackson, M. (1986), 'A Seat at the Table?' in C. Benn and J. Fairley (eds) *Challenging the MSC*, London: Pluto Press, pp. 26–39

Jaikumar, R. (1984), *Flexible Manufacturing Systems: A Managerial Perspective*, working paper 1–74–078. Cambridge, Mass.: Division of Research, Harvard Business School

Jenkins, R. (1984), 'Divisions over the International Division of Labor', *Capital and Class*, no. 22, pp. 28–57

Jenson, J. (1988), 'The Limits of "And The" Discourse: State Policies and Women in France' in J. Jenson, E. Hagen and C. Reddy (eds) *Feminization of the Labour Force, Paradoxes and Promises*, Cambridge: Polity pp. 155–72

Jenson, J., Hagen, E. and Reddy, C. (eds) *Feminization of the Labour Force: Paradoxes and Promises*, Cambridge: Polity

Jessop, B., Bonnett, K., Bromley, S. and Ling, T. (1988), 'Popular Capitalism, Flexible Accumulation and Left Strategy', *New Left Review*, vol. 165, pp. 104–24

Johansson, A. (1986), 'The Labour Movement and the Emergence of Taylorism', *Economic and Industrial Democracy*, vol. 7, no. 4, November, pp. 449–85

Johnson, C. (1982), *MITI and the Japanese Miracle*, Stanford: Stanford University Press

Jones, B. (1982), 'Destruction or Redistribution of Engineering Skills? The Case of Numerical Control' in S. Wood (ed.) *The Degradation of Work?* London: Hutchinson, pp. 179–200

Jones, B. (1983), 'Technical, Social and Political Constraints on Operator Programming of NC Machine Tools' in U. Briefs, C. Ciborra and L. Schneider (eds) *Systems Design For, With and By the Users*, London/ Amsterdam: North Holland Publishing

Jones, B. (1984a), 'Computer Integrated Manufacturing: Two Faces of Control?', paper presented at the Table Ronde Sur L'Information de la Production dans les Industries, Aix-en-Provence, France, mimeo, Bath: Bath University

Jones, B. (1984b), 'Divisions of Labour and Distribution of Tacit Knowledge in the Automation of Small Batch Machining' in T. Martin (ed.) *Design of Work in Automated Manufacturing Systems*, Oxford: Pergamon Press, pp. 19–22

Jones, B. (1985a), 'Controlling Production on the Shopfloor. The Role of State Administration and Regulation in the British and American Aerospace Industries' in S. Tolliday and J. Zeitlin (eds) *Shopfloor Bargaining and the State*, Cambridge: Cambridge University Press, pp. 219–55

Jones, B. (1985b), 'Flexible Technologies and Inflexible Jobs: Impossible Dreams and Missed Opportunities', mimeo, Bath: Bath University

Jones, B. (1986), 'Factories of the Future: Conflicts from the Past' in B. Elliott (ed.) *Technology, Innovation and Social Change*, University of Edinburgh: Centre of Canadian Studies, pp. 81–94

Jones, B. (1987), 'Social Problems of Flexible Automation: The British Case', paper to the Vienna Centre Conference on the Social Problems of Flexible Automation, Turin, Italy, mimeo, Bath: Bath University

Jones, B. (1989), 'Flexible Automation and Factory Politics: Britain in Contemporary Perspective' in P. Hirst and J. Zeitlin *et al.* (eds) *Reversing Industrial Decline*, Leamington Spa: The Berg Press, pp. 95–121

Jones, B. and Scott, P. J. (1985), *FMS in Britain*, mimeo, Bath: University of Bath

Jones, B. and Scott, P. J. (1987), 'Working the System: The Management of Work Roles in British and American Flexible Manufacturing Systems', *New Technology, Work and Employment*, vol. 1, no. 2, pp. 27–36

Jones, B. and Wood, S. (1984), 'Qualifications tacites, division du travail et nouvelles technologies', (Tacit Skills, Division of Labour and New Technology), *Sociologie du Travail*, vol. 26, no. 4, pp. 407–21

Jones, R. (1983), 'How to Clear the Justification Hurdle', *FMS Magazine*, vol. 1, no. 2

Junankar, P. (ed.) (1987), *From School to Unemployment?*, Basingstoke: Macmillan

Jürgens, U. and Stroemel, H-P. (1987), 'The Communication Structure between Management and Shop Floor – A Comparison of a Japanese and a German Plant' in H. Trevor (ed.) *The Futernationalization of Japanese Business Europlan and Japanese Perspectives*, Frankfurt: Campus Verlag, pp. 92–110

Jürgens, U., Dohse, K. and Malsch, T. (1986), 'New Production Concepts in West German Car Plants' in S. Tolliday and J. Zeitlin (1986) *The Automobile Industry and Its Workers*, Cambridge: Polity Press, pp. 258–81

Jürgens, U., Malsch, T., Dohse, K. (1988), Moderne Zeiten in der Automobilfabrik. Berlin/New York: Springer-Verlag.

Kamata, S. (1979), *Jidōsha-zetsubō-kōjō* (Car Factory of Despair). Tokyo: Gendaishi-shuppankai.

Kamata, S. (1983), *Japan in the Passing Lane*, London: George Allen & Unwin

Kaplinsky, R. (1984), *Automation*, Harlow: Longman

Katz, H. (1985), *Changing Gears*, Cambridge, Mass.: MIT Press

Katz, H. and Sabel, C. (1985), 'Industrial Relations and Industrial Adjustment in the Car Industry', *Industrial Relations Journal*, vol. 24, no. 3, pp. 295–315

Keep, E. (1986), *Designing the Stable Door: A Study of How the Youth Training Scheme was Planned*, Warwick Papers in Industrial Relations no. 8, Warwick: University of Warwick Industrial Relations Research Unit

Kelley, M. R. (1984), 'Tasks and Tools: An Inquiry into the Relationship Between Tasks, Skills and Technology with Application to the Machining Labor Process', Ph.D dissertation, Cambridge, Mass.: Sloan School of Management, Massachusetts Institute of Technology

Kelley, M. R. (1985), 'Implications of Programmable Machines: The U.S. Experience', *Advance Technology Alert System Bulletin: Microelectronics-Based Automation Technologies and Development*, United Nations Centre for Science and Technology for Development, vol. 2, pp. 95–9

Kelley, M. R. (1986), 'Programmed Automation and the Skill Question: A Reinterpretation of the Cross-National Evidence', *Human Systems Management*, vol. 6, pp. 223–41

Kelley, M. R. (1988), 'Skill dimensionality and specialization: a conceptual model for the analysis of automation, job skills and internal labor market structures', mimeo, Pittsburgh (Pa): School of Urban and Public Affairs, Carnegie Mellon University

Kelley, M. R. and Brooks, H. (1988), *The State of Computerized Automation in US Manufacturing*, Cambridge, Mass.: Center for Business and Government, John F. Kennedy School of Government, Harvard University

Kelley, M. R. (1989) 'Unionization and Job Design under Programmable Automation in US Manufacturing', *Industrial Relations*, in press

Kelly, J. (1982), *Scientific Management, Job Redesign and Work Performance*, London: Academic Press

Kelly, J. (1985), 'Management's Redesign of Work: Labour Process, Labour Markets and Product Markets' in D. Knights, H. Wilmott and D. Collinson (eds) *Job Redesign: Critical Perspectives on the Labour Process*, Aldershot: Gower, pp. 171–96

Kelly, J. and Wood, S. (1984), 'Le Taylorisme en Grande Bretagne' in M. de Montmollin and O. Pastré (eds) *Le Taylorisme*, Paris: Editions la Découverte, pp. 257–72

Kendrick, J. (1961), *Productivity Trends in the United States*, Princeton: Princeton University Press for NBER

Kergoat, D. (1984), *Les femmes et le travail à temps partiel*, Paris: La Documentation Française

Kern, H. and Schumann, M. (1977), *Industriearbeit und Arbeiterbewusstsein*, Frankfurt am Main: Suhrkamp Verlag

Kern, H. and Schumann, M. (1984), *Das Ende der Arbeitsteilung? Rationalisierung in der industriellen produktion*, Munchen: G.H. Beck

Kern, H. and Schumann, M. (1987), 'Limits of the Division of Labour', *Economic and Industrial Democracy*, vol. 8, no. 2, pp. 151–70

Kern, H. and Schumann, M. (1989), 'New Concepts of Production in German Plants' in P. Katzenstein (ed.) *Industry and Politics in West Germany: Towards the Third Republic*, Ithaca, NY: Cornell University Press, in press

Keyser, V. de (1987) 'De l'évolution des métiers' in C. Levy Leboyer and J-C. Sperandio (eds) *Traité de psychologie du travail*, Paris: Presses Universitaires de France, pp. 177–95

Killeen, J. with Robertson, E. (1988), *Technological Change and the Work of Women in Industry: Case Studies in the Sexual Segregation of Production Work*, Hertford: NICEC, Hatfield Polytechnic

Kindleberger, C. P. (1970), *The International Corporation*, Cambridge: MIT Press

Kindleberger, C. P. and Audretsch, D. B. (1983), *The Multinational Corporation in the 1980s*, Cambridge: MIT Press

Kinnucan, P. (1983), 'Flexible Systems Invade the Factory', *High Technology*, July, pp. 32–42

Klingender, F. (1935), *The Condition of Clerical Labour in Britain*, London: Martin Lawrence

Kochan, A. (1984), 'FMS: An International Overview of Applications', *FMS Magazine*, vol. 2, no. 3, pp. 153–6

Kochan, T., Katz, H. and McKersie, W. (1986), *The Transformation of American Industrial Relations*, New York: Basic Books

Koike, K. (1983), 'Internal Labour Markets: Workers in Large Firms' in R. Shirai (ed.) *Contemporary Industrial Relations in Japan*, Madison, Wis.: University of Wisconsin Press, pp. 29–61

Koike, K. (1987), 'Human Resource Development and Labor-Management Relations' in K. Yamamura and Y. Yasuba (eds) *Political Economy of Japan, Volume 1, The Domestic Transformation*, Stanford: Stanford University Press, pp. 289–330

Kornai, J. (1980), *The Economics of Shortage*, 2 vols, Amsterdam: North Holland Publishing Company

Koshiro, K. (1983), *Nihon no Rōshi Kankei* (Labour Relations in Japan), Tokyo: Yûhikaku

Kraft, P. (1977), *Programmers and Managers: The Routinization of Computer Programming in the United States*, New York: Springer-Verlag

Kusterer, K. (1978), *Know-How on the Job: The Important Working Knowledge of 'Unskilled' Workers*, Boulder, Colo: Westview Press

Kuznets, S. (1930), *Secular Movements in Production and Prices*, Boston: Houghton Mifflin

Lane, C. (1988), 'Industrial Change in Europe: The Pursuit of Flexible Specialisation in Britain and West Germany', *Work, Employment and Society*, vol. 2, no. 2, pp. 141–68

Langrish, J., Gibbons, M., Evans, W. G. and Jevons, F. (1972), *Wealth from*

Knowledge: Studies of Innovation in Industry, London: Macmillan

Lash, S. and Bagguley, P. (1987), 'Labour Flexibility and Disorganized Capitalism', mimeo, Lancaster: University of Lancaster, Department of Sociology

Lazonick, W. H. (1983), 'Technological Change and the Control of Work: The Development of Capital–Labour Relations in US Manufacturing Industry', in H. F. Gospel and C. R. Littler (eds) *Managerial Strategies and Industrial Relations,* London: Heinemann, pp. 111–36

Leadbetter, C. (1987), MSC Criticises Standard of Youth Training, *Financial Times,* 13 May, p. 1

Lee, D. J. (1982), 'Beyond Deskilling: Skill, Craft and Class' in S. Wood (ed.) *The Degradation of Work?,* London: Hutchinson, pp. 146–62

Lee, D. J., Marsden, D., Hardey, M. and Rickman, P. (1986), *Education Guardian,* 19 September, p. 10

Lee, D. J., Marsden, D. and Rickman, P. (1987), 'Youth Training, Life Chances and Orientations to Work' in P. Brown and D. Ashton (eds) *Education, Unemployment and Labour Markets,* Lewes: Falmer Press, pp. 138–59

Leontief, W. (1983), 'Technological Advance, Economic Growth and the Distribution of Income', *Population and Development Review,* vol. 9, no. 3, pp. 403–10

Leplat, J. and Cuny, X. (1984), *Introduction à la psychologie du travail,* Paris: Presses Universitaires de France

Libetta, L. (1987), 'New Technology and Tacit Skills', mimeo, Bath: Bath University, School of Humanities and Social Sciences

Libetta, L. (1988), 'Computerising Skill: New Technology and Tacit Skills', paper presented to PICT/ESRC workshop on Work and Information and Communication Technology, mimeo, Bath: Bath University, School of Social Sciences

Liff, S. (1987), 'Women's Experience of Technical Change', paper presented to the BSA Annual Conference, mimeo, Loughborough: Loughborough University

Lindley, R. M. (1983), 'Active Manpower Policy' in G. S. Bain (ed.) *Industrial Relations in Great Britain,* Oxford: Basil Blackwell, pp. 339–60

Linn, P. (1987), 'Gender Stereotypes, Technical Stereotypes' in M. McNeil (ed.) *Gender and Expertise,* London: Free Association Books, pp. 127–51

Lipietz, A. (1982), 'Towards Global Fordism?', *New Left Review,* no. 132, March-April, pp. 33–47

Lipietz, A. (1985), 'Fordisme, Fordisme périphérique et métropolisation', working paper no. 8514 (March), Paris: CEPREMAP

Lipietz, A. (1986), 'New Tendencies in the International Division of Labor: Regimes of Accumulation and Modes of Regulation' in A. Scott and M. Storper (eds) *Production, Work, Territory: The Geographical Anatomy of Industrial Capitalism,* Boston: George Allen & Unwin, pp. 16–40

Lipietz, A. (1987), *Mirages and Miracles,* London: Verso

Littek, W. (1986), 'Rationalisation, Technical Change and Employee Reactions' in K. Purcell, S. Wood, A. Waton and S. Allen (eds) *The Changing Experience of Employment: Restructuring and Recession,* London: The Macmillan Press, pp. 156–72

Littler, C. (1982), *The Development of the Labour Process in Capitalist Societies,* London: Heinemann Educational Books

Littler, C. (1985), 'Taylorism, Fordism and Job Design' in D. Knights, H. Wilmott, D. Collinson (eds) *Job Redesign: Critical Perspectives on the Labour Process*, Aldershot: Gower, pp. 10–29

Lund, B. and Hansen, J. A. (1983), *Connected Machines, Disconnected Jobs. Technology and Work in the Next Decade*, Cambridge, Mass.: Centre for Policy Alternatives, Massachusetts Institute of Technology

MacInnes, J. (1987), *Thatcherism at Work: Industrial Relations and Economic Change*, Milton Keynes: Open University Press

MacLennan, C. and Walker, R. (1980), 'Crisis and Change in U.S. Agriculture: An Overview' in R. Burbach and P. Flynn (eds) *Agribusiness in the Americas*, New York: Monthly Review Press, pp. 20–40

Mahon, R. (1987) 'From Fordism to …?: New Technology, Labour Markets and Unions', *Economic and Industrial Democracy*, vol. 8, no. 1, pp. 5–60

Malsch, T., Dohse, K. and Jürgens, U. (1984), 'Industrial Robots in the Automobile Industry, A Leap Towards "Automated Fordism"?', Discussion Paper IIVG/dp 84–222, West Berlin: Wissenschaftszentrum

Malsch, T. and Seltz, R. (eds) (1987), *Die neuen produktionskonzepte auf dem Prufstand*, Berlin: Edition Sigma

Manwaring, T. and Wood, S. (1985), 'The Ghost in the Labour Process', in D. Knights, H. Wilmott, D. Collinson (eds) *Job Redesign: Critical Perspectives on the Labour Process*, Aldershot: Gower, pp. 171–96

Marginson, P., Edwards, P.K., Martin, R., Purcell, J. and Sisson, K. (1988), *Beyond the Workplace*, Oxford: Basil Blackwell

Marglin, S. (1974), 'What do Bosses do?', *Review of Radical Political Economy*, vol. 6, no. 2, pp. 60–92

Marks, V. and Alberti, K. G. M. M. (eds) (1985), *Clinical Biochemistry Nearer the Patient*, Edinburgh: Churchill Livingston

Marks, V. and Alberti, K. G. M. M. (eds) (1986), *Clinical Biochemistry Nearer the Patient II*, London: Bailliere Tindall

Marsden, D. (1986), *The End of Economic Man: Custom and Competition in Labour Markets*, Brighton: Wheatsheaf Books

Marsden, D., Morris, T., Willman, P. and Wood, S. (1985), *The Car Industry*, London: Tavistock

Marsden, D. and Ryan, P. (1986), 'Where do Young Workers Work? Employment by Industry in Various European Economies', *British Journal of Industrial Relations*, vol. 24, no. 1, pp. 83–102

Marsh, P. (1980), 'Towards the Unmanned Factory', *New Scientist*, vol. 87, no. 1212, 31 July, pp. 373–77

Marsh, S. (1986), 'Women and the MSC', in C. Benn and J. Fairley (eds.), *Challenging the MSC*, London: Pluto Press, pp. 152–75

Marsland, S. and Beer, M. (1983), 'The Evolution of Japanese Management: Lessons for U.S. Managers', *Organizational Dynamics*, vol. 11, no. 3, pp. 49–67

Martin, J. and Roberts, C. (1984), *Women and Employment: A Lifetime Perspective*, London: HMSO

Marx, K. (1967 edn), *Capital*, New York: International Publishers

Marx, K. and Engels, F. (1952 edn), *Manifesto of the Communist Party*, Moscow: Progress Publishers

Massey, D. (1978), 'Capital and Locational Change: The UK Electrical Engineering Industry', *Review of Radical Political Economics*, vol. 10, no. 3, pp. 39–54

Massey, D. (1984), *Spatial Divisions of Labour: Social Structures and the Geography of Production*, London and New York: Macmillan/Methuen

Massey, D. and Meegan, R. (1982), *The Anatomy of Job Loss*, London: Methuen

Maurice, M. (1986), *Flexible Technologies and Variability of the Forms of the Division of Labour in France and Japan*, paper given at the International Workshop on New Technology and New Forms of Work Organisation, Berlin (GDR), Vienna Centre and Nationalkomitee fur Soziologische Forschung, mimeo, Aix-en-Provence: Laboratoire d'Economie et du Sociologie du Travail

Maurice, M., Eyraud, F., d'Iribarne, A. and Rychener, F. (1986), 'Des enterprises en mutation dans la crise', rapport de recherche, Aix-en-Provence: Laboratoire d'Economie et de Sociologie du Travail

Maurice, M., Sorge, A. and Warner, M. (1980), 'Societal Differences in Organising Manufacturing Units', *Organisational Studies*, vol. 1, no. 1, pp. 59–86

Mayo, E. (1933), *The Human Problems of an Industrial Civilisation*, New York: Macmillan

McElroy, J. (1985), 'No More Business as Usual: Ford's Production Philosophy', *Chilton's Automotive Industries*, vol. 165, no. 4, pp. 42–4

McIntosh, M. and Weir, A. (1982), 'Towards a Wages Strategy for Women', *Feminist Review*, no. 10, Spring, pp. 5–20

McNally, F. (1979), *Women for Hire: A Study of the Female Office Worker*, London: Macmillan

Meegan, R. (1988), 'A Crisis of Mass Production?' in J. Allen and D. Massey (eds), *The Economy in Question*, London: Sage Publications in association with The Open University, pp. 136–83

Mehler, M. (1985), 'CIM is No Passing Fad in Semiconductor Fab', *Electronics Business*, February 15, pp. 148–53

Meissner, M. (1970), *Technology and the Worker: Technical Demands and Social Processes in Industry*, San Francisco: Chandler

Melman, S. (1985), 'Review of C. Sabel's Work and Politics: The Division of Labor in Industry', *Work and Occupations*, vol. 12, pp. 234–41

Metcalf, D. (1986), 'Labour Market Flexibility and Jobs: A Survey of Evidence from OECD Countries with Special Reference to Great Britain and Europe', Centre for Labour Economics, LSE, discussion paper no. 254, London: Centre for Labour Economics, LSE

Miles, I. (1988), *Information Technology and Information Society: Options for the Future*, PICT Policy Research Papers, no. 2, London: Economic and Social Research Council

Milkman, R. (1976), 'Women's Work and the Economic Crisis: Some Lessons of the Great Depression', *Review of Radical Political Economy*, vol. 8, no. 1, pp. 73–97

Milkman, R. (1983), 'Female Factory Labor and Industrial Structure: Control and Conflict over "Women's Place" in Auto and Electrical Manufacturing', *Politics and Society*, vol. 9, no. 3, pp. 379–407

Mills, J. (1979), 'The San Francisco Waterfront: The Social Consequences of Industrial Modernization', in A. Zimbalist (ed.), *Case Studies on the Labor Process*, New York: Monthly Review Press, pp. 127–58

Mincer, J. (1962), 'Labor Force Participation of Married Women: A Study of Labor Supply' in National Bureau of Economic Research, *Aspects of Labour*

Economics: A Conference of the Universities-National Bureau Committee for Economic Research, Princeton: Princeton University Press

Mincer, J. (1966), 'Labor-Force Participation and Unemployment: A Review of Recent Evidence' in R. Gordon and M. Gordon (eds) *Prosperity and Unemployment,* New York: John Wiley & Sons, pp. 73–112

Mitter, S. (1986), 'Industrial Restructuring and Manufacturing Homework', *Capital and Class,* vol. 27, pp. 37–80

Monden, Y. (1981), 'What Makes the Toyota Production System Really Tick', *Industrial Engineering,* January, pp. 37–44

Monden, Y. (1983), *Toyota Production System,* Atlanta: Industrial Engineering and Management Press

Monjardet, D. (1987), 'In Search of the Founders: The Traités of the Sociology of Work' in M. Rose (ed.) *Industrial Sociology: Work in the French Tradition,* London: Sage, pp. 112–19

Montmollin, M. (de) (1984), *L'intelligence de la tâche,* Berne: Peter Lang

Montmollin, M. (de) and Pastre, O. (1984), *Le Taylorisme,* Paris: Éditions La Découverte

More, C. (1982), 'Skill and the Survival of Apprenticeship' in S. Wood (ed.) *The Degradation of Work?,* Hutchinson: London, pp. 109–21

Moss, B. (1976), *The Origins of the French Labor Movement 1830–1914: The Socialism of Skilled Workers,* Berkeley, University of California Press

Moulaert, F. and Salinas, P. W. (eds) (1983), *Regional Analysis and the New International Division of Labor,* Boston: Kluwer Nijhoff

Murray, F. (1983), 'The Decentralization of Production: The Decline of the Mass Collective Worker', *Capital and Class,* no. 19, pp. 74–99

Murray, R. (1985), 'Benetton Britain', *Marxism Today,* November, pp. 7–13

Murray, R. (1987), 'Ownership, Control and the Market', *New Left Review,* 164, July–August, pp. 87–112

Nakane, C. (1973), *Japanese Society,* Harmondsworth: Penguin Books

National Economic Development Office (NEDO) (1986), *Changing Working Patterns: How Companies Achieve Flexibility to Meet New Needs,* London: National Economic Development Office

National Labour Movement (1987), *National Labour Movement Inquiry into Youth Unemployment and Training,* seven parts, Birmingham: Trade Union Research Centre

Naville, P. (1961), *L'automation et le travail humain,* rapport, CNRS

Naville, P. (1963), *Vers l'automatisme social?,* Paris: Gallimard

Nelson, K. (1984), 'Back Offices and Female Labor Markets: Office Suburbanization in the San Francisco Bay Area, 1965–1980', Ph.D dissertation, Berkeley: University of California

Nichols, T. and Beynon, H. (1977), *Living with Capitalism,* London: Routledge & Kegan Paul

Noble, D. (1977), *America by Design,* New York: Alfred Knopf

Noble, D. (1979), 'Social Choice in Machine Design: The Case of Automatically Controlled Machine Tools' in A. Zimbalist, (ed.) *Case Studies on the Labor Process,* New York: Monthly Review Press, pp. 18–50

Noble, D. (1984), *Forces of Production: A Social History of Industrial Automation,* New York: Alfred Knopf

Nohara, H. (1987), 'Technological Innovation, Industrial Dynamics and the Transformation of Work: The Case of the Japanese Machine-Tool

Industry', paper presented to the Conference: High Tech and Society in Japan and the Federal Republic of Germany, mimeo, West Berlin: Wissenschaftszentrum

Nomura, M. (1985), '"Model Japan"? Characteristics of Industrial Relations in the Japanese Automobile Industry', West Berlin: Wissenschaftszentrum IIVG85–207

Noyelle, T. (1983), 'The Implications of Industry Restructuring for Spatial Organization in the United States' in F. Moulaert and P. W. Salinas (eds) *Regional Analysis and the New International Division of Labor*, Boston: Kluwer Nijhoff, pp. 113–33

Odaka, K. (1984), *Nihon-teki keiei* (Japanese-style Management), Tokyo: Chū-ō-kōronsha

Ohno, T. (1984), 'How the Toyota Production System was Created' in K. Sato and Y. Hoshino (eds) *The Anatomy of Japanese Business*, Armonk, NY and London: M. E. Sharpe, Inc. and Croom Helm

Okayama, R. (1986), 'Industrial Relations in the Japanese Automobile Industry 1945–70: The Case of Toyota' in S. Tolliday and J. Zeitlin (eds) *The Automobile Industry and its Workers*, Cambridge: Polity, pp. 168–89

Okimoto, D., Sugano, T. and Weinstein, F. (1984), *Competitive Edge*, Stanford: Stanford University Press

Okuda, K. (1972), *Rōmu kanri no Nihon-teki Tenkai* (Developments in Japanese Labour Management), Tokyo: Nihon Seisan-sei Honbu

Organization for Economic Co-operation and Development (1986), *Labour Market Flexibility*, Paris: Organization for Economic Co-operation and Development

Palloix, C. (1976), 'The Labour Process: From Fordism to Neo-Fordism' in CSE Pamphlet, *The Labour Process and Class Strategies, Stage 1*, London: Conference for Socialist Economists, pp. 46–67

Papadimitriou, Z. (1986), 'Changing Skill Requirements and Trade Union Bargaining' in O. Jacobi, B. Jessop, H. Kastendiek and M. Regini (eds) *Technical Change, Rationalisation and Industrial Relations*, London: Croom Helm, pp. 35–49

Penn, R. (1985), *Skilled Workers in the Class Structure*, Cambridge: Cambridge University Press

Penn, R. and Scattergood, H. (1985), 'Deskilling or Enskilling?: An Empirical Investigation of Recent Theories of the Labour Process', *British Journal of Sociology*, vol. 36, no. 4, pp. 611–30

Perrons, D. C. (1981), 'The Role of Ireland in the New International Division of Labor: A Proposed Framework for Regional Analysis', *Regional Studies*, vol. 15, no. 2, pp. 81–100

Perry, P. (1976), *The Evolution of British Manpower Policy*, London: British Association for Commercial and Industrial Education

Petit, P. (1986), *Slow Growth and the Service Economy*, London: Frances Pinter

Pfeffer, R. (1979), *Working for Capitalism*, New York: Columbia University Press

Pfeffer, J. and Baron, J. (1988), 'Taking the Workers Back Out: Recent Trends in the Structuring of Employment' in B. Staw and L. Cummings (eds) *Research in Organizational Behavior*, vol. 10, Greenwich, Conn.: JAI Press, pp. 257–303

Phillips, A. (1983), 'Review of Brothers', *Feminist Review*, no. 15, pp. 101–4

Phillips, A. and Taylor, B. (1980), 'Sex and Skill: Notes Towards a Feminist Economics', *Feminist Review*, no. 6, pp. 79–88

Piore, M. (1968), 'The Impact of the Labour Market Upon the Design and Selection of Productive Techniques Within the Manufacturing Plant', *Quarterly Journal of Economics*, vol. 82, no. 4, pp. 435–49

Piore, M. (1984), 'Technology, Flexibility and Work Structure', paper presented at the American Economic Association Meeting, December 1984, mimeo, Cambridge, Mass.: MIT

Piore, M. (1986) 'Perspectives on Labor Market Flexibility', *Industrial Relations*, vol. 25, no. 2, pp. 146–66

Piore, M. and Sabel, C. (1984), *The Second Industrial Divide: Possibilities for Prosperity*, New York: Basic Books

Pollert, A. (1987), '"The Flexible Firm": A Model in Search of Reality (or a Policy in Search of a Practice?)', *Warwick Papers in Industrial Relations*, no. 19, Coventry: Warwick University

Pollert, A. (1988), 'Dismantling Flexibility', *Capital and Class*, no. 34, pp. 42–75

Pollock, F. (1957), *L'automation, ses conséquences économiques et sociales*, Paris: Editions de Minuit

Prechel, H. (1986), 'Capital Accumulation and Corporate Rationality. Organizational Change in an American Steel Corporation', doctoral dissertation, Lawrence: University of Kansas

Pred, A. (1977), *City Systems in Advanced Economies*, London: Hutchinson

Przeworski, A. (1985), *Capitalism and Social Democracy*, Cambridge: Cambridge University Press

Raffe, D. (1984a), 'YOP and the Future of YTS' in D. McCrone (ed.) *Scottish Government Year Book 1984*, Edinburgh: University of Edinburgh Unit for the Study of Government in Scotland, pp. 194–213

Raffe, D. (1984b), *Youth Employment and the MSC, 1977–83*, Centre for Educational Sociology, Edinburgh: University of Edinburgh

Raffe, D. and Smith, P. (1986), *Young Peoples' Attitudes to YTS: The First Two Years*, Centre for Educational Sociology, Edinburgh: University of Edinburgh

Rajan, A. (1987), *Services – The Second Industrial Revolution?*, London: Butterworth

Rajan, A. and Pearson, R. (eds) (1986), *UK Occupation and Employment Trends to 1990*, London: Butterworth

Ranson, S. (1985), 'Towards a Tertiary Tripartism: New Codes of Social Control and the 17+' in P. Broadfoot (ed.) *Selection, Certification and Control*, Lewes: Falmer Press, pp. 221–46

Rasmussen, J. (1981), *Human Systems Design Criteria*, Amsterdam: North Holland Publishing

Rathmill, K. (ed.) (1983), *Proceedings of the Second International Conference on Flexible Manufacturing Systems*, Bedford and Oxford: IFS (Conferences) Ltd/North Holland Publishing

Reich, R. (1984), *The Next American Frontier*, Harmondsworth: Penguin

Remick, H. (1984), *Comparable Worth and Wage Discrimination: Technical Possibilities and Political Realities*, Philadelphia, Pa: Temple University Press

Richardson, R. and Vood, S. (1989), 'The Coal Industry and the New

Industrial Relations', *British Journal of Industrial Relations,* vol. 27, no. 1, pp. 33–55

Rickman, P., Marsden, D. and Lee, D. (1986), *Training for What?,* paper to BSA Youth Study Group, mimeo, Colchester: University of Essex Sociology Department

Ritter, A. (1969), *The Political Thought of Pierre-Joseph Proudhon,* Princeton: Princeton University Press

Roberts, B., Okamoto, H. and Lodge, G. (1979), *Collective Bargaining and Employee Participation in Western Europe, North America and Japan,* New York: The Trilateral Commission

Roberts, K., Dench, S. and Richardson, D. (1986), 'Youth Labour Markets in the Eighties', *Employment Gazette,* vol. 94, no. 6, pp. 241–6

Roberts, M. (1983), 'The Impact of Technology on Union Organizing and Collective Bargaining' in D. Kennedy, C. Craypo and M. Lehman (eds) *Labor and Technology: Union Response to Changing Environment,* Department of Labor Studies, Pennsylvania State University

Robinson, O. (1988), 'The Changing Labour Market: Growth of Part-time Employment and Labour Market Segmentation in Britain', in S. Walby (ed.) *Gender Segregation at Work,* Milton Keynes: Open University Press, pp. 114–35

Robinson, O. and Wallace, J. (1984), *Part-time Employment and Sex Discrimination Legislation in Great Britain: A study of the Demand for Part-time Labour and of Sex Discrimination in Selected Organizations and Establishments,* Department of Employment Research Paper no. 43, London: HMSO

Rose, M. and Jones, B. (1985), 'Managerial Strategy and Trade Union Responses in Work Reorganization Schemes at Establishment Level' in D. Knights, H. Willmott and D. Collinson (eds), *Job Redesign: Critical Perspectives on the Labour Process,* Aldershot: Gower, pp. 81–106

Rosenberg, N. (1976), *Perspectives on Technology,* Cambridge: Cambridge University Press

Rothwell, R. and Zegveld, W. (1982), *Industrial Innovation and the Small and Medium Sized Enterprise: Their Role in Employment and Economic Change,* London: Frances Pinter

Rowand, R. (1984), 'Buick-City Job 1 Nears', *Automotive News,* 31 December, p. 18

Rubenowitz, S. (1980), 'Experience of Autonomous Working Groups in a Swedish Car Factory', in H. Jain (ed.) *Worker Participation,* New York: Praeger Publishers, pp. 224–32

Rumberger, R. (1987), 'The Potential Impact of Technology on the Skill Requirements of Future Jobs', in G. Burke and R. Rumberger (eds.), *The Future Impact of Technology on Work and Eduation,* Philadelphia, The Falmer Press, pp. 74–95

Ryan, P. (1986), *Apprenticeship and Industrial Relations in British Engineering: The Early Interwar Period,* workshop on Child Labour and Apprenticeship, mimeo, Cambridge: Kings College, Cambridge

Ryan, P. (1987), 'Youth Special Employment Measures: Substitution Effects and Trade Union Policy, mimeo, Cambridge: Kings College, Cambridge

Sabel, C. (1982) *Work and Politics: The Division of Labour in Industry,* Cambridge: Cambridge University Press

Sabel, C. (1984), 'Industrial Reorganization and Social Democracy in Austria', *Industrial Relations,* vol. 23, no. 3, pp. 344–61

Sabel, C. (1989), 'The Reemergence of Regional Economies', in P. Hirst and J. Zeitlin (eds) *Reversing Industrial Decline?*, Leamington Spa: The Berg Press, pp. 17–70

Sackett, P. J. (1983), 'Flexible Manufacturing Systems in Small High-Technology Companies – an Alternative Approach' in K. Rathmill (ed.) *Proceedings of the Second International Conference on Flexible Manufacturing Systems*, Bedford and Oxford: IFS (Conferences) Ltd/North Holland Publishing, pp. 577–84

Sackett, J. P. and Rathmill, K. (1982), 'Manufacturing Plant for 1985 – Developments and Justification', *Proceedings of the Institute of Mechanical Engineers*, vol. 196, September, pp. 265–80

Sako, M. and Dore, R. (1986), 'How the YTS Helps Employers', *Employment Gazette*, vol. 94, no. 6, pp. 195–204

Samuel, R. (1977), 'Workshop of the World: Steam Power and Hand Technology in Mid-Victorian Britain', *History Workshop Journal*, no. 3, Spring, pp. 6–72

Sarsby, J. (1985), 'Sexual Segregation in the Pottery Industry', *Feminist Review*, no. 21, pp. 67–93

Sayer, A. (1985a), 'Industry and Space: A Sympathetic Critique of Radical Research', *Society and Space*, vol. 3, no. 1, pp. 3–29

Sayer, A. (1985b), 'New Developments in Manufacturing and their Spatial Implications', Working Paper, Urban and Regional Studies, Brighton (Sussex): University of Sussex

Sayer, A. (1986a), 'Industrial Location on a World Scale: The Case of the Semiconductor Industry' in A. J. Scott and M. Storper (eds) *Production, Work, Territory: The Geographical Anatomy of Industrial Capitalism*, Boston: Allen & Unwin, pp. 107–24

Sayer, A. (1986b), 'New Developments in Manufacturing: The Just-in-time System', *Capital and Class*, vol. 30, pp. 43–71

Sayer, A. (1989), 'Fordism in Question', *International Journal of Urban and Regional Research*, vol. 13

Schoenberger, E. (1985), 'Foreign Manufacturing Investment in the United States: Competitive Strategies and International Location', *Economic Geography*, vol. 61, no. 3, July, pp. 241–59

Schoenberger, E. (1986), 'Competition, Competitive Strategy, and Industrial Change: The Case of Electronic Components', *Economic Geography*, vol. 62, no. 4, October, pp. 321–33

Schoenberger, E. (1987a), 'Americans in Europe: Aspects of US Investment Strategies in the European Market', paper presented at the annual meeting of the Regional Science Association, Baltimore, November, mimeo, Baltimore: Johns Hopkins University

Schoenberger, E. (1987b), 'Technological and Organizational Change in Automobile Production: Spatial Implications', *Regional Studies*, vol. 21, no. 3, pp. 199–214

Schonberger, R. (1982), *Japanese Manufacturing Techniques*, New York: The Free Press

Schumpeter, J. (1939), *Business Cycles*, New York: McGraw-Hill

Scott, A. (1983), 'Industrial Organization and the Logic of Intra-Metropolitan Location I: Theoretical Considerations', *Economic Geography*, vol. 59, no. 3, pp. 233–50

Scott, A. and Storper, M. (1988), 'The Geographical Foundations and Social Regulation of Flexible Production Complexes' in J. Wolch and M. Dear (eds) *Territory and Social Reproduction*, Boston: Allen & Unwin, in press

Scott, P. J. (1987), *Craft Skills in Flexible Manufacturing Systems*, Ph.D. dissertation, Bath: University of Bath, School of Humanities and Social Sciences

Scrivens, E. (1985), *Policy, Power and Information Technology in the National Health Service*, Bath: Centre for Analysis of Social Policy, University of Bath

Seale, C. (1984), 'FEU and MSC: Two Curricular Philosophies and Their Implications for the Youth Training Scheme', *The Vocational Aspect of Education*, Vol. 36, no. 1, pp. 3–9

Senker, P. and Beesley, M. (1986), 'The Need for Skills in the Factory of the Future', *New Technology, Work and Employment*, vol. 1, no. 1, pp. 9–17

Serrin, W. (1985), 'Saturn Labor Pact Assailed by a U.A.W. Founder', *New York Times*, 26 October, A13

Shackleton, J. (1985), 'Is the UK Labor Market Inflexible?', *Royal Bank of Scotland Review*, no. 147, September, pp. 27–41

Shaiken, H. (1984), *Work Transformed: Automation and Labor in the Computer Age*, New York: Holt, Reinhart & Winston

Shaiken, H., Herzenberg, S. and Kuhn, S. (1986), 'The Work Process Under More Flexible Production', *Industrial Relations*, vol. 25, no. 2, pp. 167–83

Shaiken, H., Kuhn, S. and Herzenberg, S. (1984), 'Case Studies on the Introduction of Programmable Automation in Manufacturing', vol. II, part A, *Computerized Manufacturing Automation: Employment, Education and the Workplace*, Washington, DC: US Government Printing Office

Sheard, P. (1983), 'Auto Production Systems in Japan: Organizational and Locational Features', *Australian Geographical Studies*, vol. 21, April, pp. 49–68

Sheldrake, J. and Vickerstaff, S. (1987), *The History of Industrial Training in Great Britain*, Aldershot: Avebury

Shepela, S. and Viviano, A. (1984), 'Some Psychological Factors Affecting Job Segregation and Wages' in H. Remick (ed.) *Comparable Worth: Technical Possibilities and Political Realities*, Philadelphia, Pa: Temple University Press, pp. 43–57

Shingo, S. (1981), *The Toyota Production System*, Tokyo: Japan Management Association

Shirai, T. (1968), *Kigyō-betsuKumiai*(Enterprise-wideUnionism),Tokyo:Chū-ō-kōronsha

Shimizu, T. (1979), 'Wirtschaftliche und humane Aspekte eines Systems zur Produktionssteuerung in der Japanischen Automobilindustrie' in R. Wunderer (ed.) *Humane Personal – und Organisationsentwicklung*, S. West Berlin: Dunker und Humblot, pp. 321–43

Simonyi, A., Ladó, M. and Tóth, F. (1985) 'From Taylorism to the New Forms of Work Organization – The Ways of Adjustment' in P. Grootings, B. Gustavsen, and L. Hethy (eds) *New Forms of Work Organization and Their Social and Economic Environment*, Budapest: Vienna Centre and Institute of Labour Research, pp. 31–50

Sims, C. (1986), 'Boom in Drug Tests Expected', *New York Times*, Monday 8 September, ps D1 and D22

Smith, A. (1979), *The Wealth of Nations*, New York: Penguin Books (first published 1776)

Snell, M. (1979), 'The Equal Pay and Sex Discrimination Acts: their impact in the workplace', *Feminist Review*, no. 1, pp. 37–57

Snell, M., Glucklich, P. and Povall, M. (1981), *Equal Pay and Opportunities: A study of the implementation and effects of the Equal Pay and Sex Discrimination Acts in 26 Organizations*. Department of Employment Research Paper, no. 20. London: HMSO

Solinas, G. (1982), "Labour market segmentation and workers' careers: the case of the Italian knitwear industry", *Cambridge Journal of Economics*, vol. 6, no. 3, pp. 331–52

Sorge, A. and Streeck, W. (1988), 'Industrial Relations and Technical Change: The Case for an Extended Perspective', in R. Hyman and W. Streeck (eds.), *New Technology and Industrial Relations*, Oxford: Blackwell, pp. 19–47

Sorge, A. and Warner, M. (1986), *Comparative Factory Organisation*, Aldershot: Gower

Spenner, K. (1983), 'Deciphering Prometheus: Temporal Change in the Skill Level of Work', *American Sociological Review*, vol. 48, no.6, pp. 824–37

Spenner, K. (1988), 'Technological Change, Skill Requirements and Education: The Case of Uncertainty', in R. Cyert and D. Mowery (eds), *The Economic and Employment Effects of Technological Change*, New York: Ballinger Publishing Co., pp. 131–84

Stanworth, M. (1984), 'Women and class analysis: a reply to John Goldthorpe', *Sociology*, vol. 18, no. 2, pp. 159–70

Stark, D. (1986), 'Rethinking Internal Labour Markets: New Insights from a Comparative Perspective', *American Sociological Review*, vol. 51, no. 4, pp. 492–504

Steering Committee on Future Health Scenarios (1987), *Anticipating and Assessing Health Care Technology*, vol. 1, Dordrecht: Martinus Nijhoff

Steinberg, R. (1984), "'A Want of Harmony": Perspectives on Wage Discrimination and Comparable Worth' in H. Remick (ed.) *Comparable Worth and Wage Discrimination: Technical Possibilities and Political Realities*, Philadelphia, Pa: Temple University Press, pp. 20–37

Stewart, A., Prandy, K. and Blackburn, R. M. (1980), *Social Stratification and Occupations*, London: Macmillan

Storey, J. (1986), 'The Phoney War? New Office Technology: Organisation and Control' in D. Knights, and H. Wilmott, (eds) *Managing the Labour Process*, Aldershot: Gower, pp. 44–66

Storper, M. (1982), 'The Spatial Division of Labor: Technology, the Labor Process and the Location of Industries', Ph.D. dissertation, Berkeley: University of California

Storper, M. (1985), 'Oligopoly and the Product Cycle: Essentialism in Economic Geography', *Economic Geography*, vol. 61, no. 3, July, pp. 260–82

Storper, M. and Christopherson, S. (1987) 'Flexible Specialization and Regional Industrial Agglomerations', *Annals of the Association of American Geographers*, vol. 77, no.1, pp. 104–17.

Storper, M. and Walker, R. (1983), 'The Theory of Labour and the Theory of Location', *International Journal of Urban and Regional Research*, vol, 7, no. 1, pp. 1–41

Storper, M. and Walker, R. (1989), *Capitalist Imperative: Territory Technology and Industries Growth*, Oxford: Basil Blackwell

356   *The Transformation of Work?*

Streeck, W. (1987), 'The Uncertainties of Management in the Management of Uncertainty: Employers, Labor Relations and Industrial Adjustment', *Work, Employment and Society*, vol. 1, no. 3, pp. 281–308

Streeck, W. and Hoff, A. (1983), 'Manpower Management and Industrial Relations in the Restructuring of the World Automobile Industry', Discussion Paper IIM/LMP 83–35, Wissenschaftszentrum, West Berlin: Wissenschaftszentrum

Stute, G. (1981), '"State-of-the-Art" in FMS', *The Management of Innovation*, British Management Data Foundation

Sugimori, Y., Kusunoki, F., Cho, F. and Uchikawa, S. (1977), 'Toyota Production System and Kanban System: Materialization of Just-in-Time and Respect-for-Human System', *International Journal of Production Research*, vol. 15, no. 6, pp. 553–64

Sumiya, M. (ed.) (1985), *Gijutsu-kakushin to Rōshi-kankei* (Technological Innovation and Labour Relations), Tokyo: Nihon Rōdō Kyōkai

Summerfield, P. (1984), *Women Workers in the Second World War*, London: Croom Helm

Susman, P. (1984), 'Capital Restructuring and the Changing Regional Environment' in P. O'Keefe (ed.) *Regional Restructuring Under Advanced Capitalism*, London: Croom Helm, pp. 91–107

Szelenyi, I. (1982), 'The Intelligentsia in the Class Structure of State Socialist Societies' in M. Burawoy and T. Skocpol (eds) *Marxist Inquiries: Studies of Labor, Class and States*, Chicago: University of Chicago Press, pp. 287–326

Taylor, B. (1979), 'The Men are as Bad as Their Masters: Socialism, Feminism and Sexual Antagonism in the London Tailoring Trade in the Early 1830s', *Feminist Studies*, vol. 8, no. 1, pp. 7–40

Taylor, F. W. (1967), *The Principles of Scientific Management*, New York: W. W. Norton & Co. (first published 1911)

Taylor, M. and Thrift, N. (1982), 'Introduction' in M. Taylor and N. Thrift (eds) *The Geography of Multinationals*, London: Croom Helm, pp. 1–13

Teece, D. (1981), 'The Multinational Enterprise: Market Failure and Market Power Considerations', *Sloan Management Review*, vol. 22, no. 3, Spring, pp. 3–17

Terssac, G. de and Coriat, B. (1984), 'Micro-électronique et travail ouvrier dans les industries de process', *Sociologie du Travail*, vol. 26, no. 4, pp. 384–97

Tharakan, P. (ed.) (1979), *La division internationale du travail et les entreprises multinationales*, Paris: Presses Universitaires de France

Thompson, P. (1983), *The Nature of Work*. London: Macmillan

Thompson, P. (1989), 'Crawling from the Wreckage. The Labour Process and the Politics of Production' in D. Knights and H. Wilmott (eds), Labour Process Theory, London: Macmillan, in press

Tolliday, S. and Zeitlin, J. (eds) (1985), *Shopfloor Bargaining and the State*, Cambridge: Cambridge University Press

Tolliday, S. and Zeitlin, J. (1986), 'Introduction: Between Fordism and Flexibility' in S. Tolliday and J. Zeitlin (eds) *Between Fordism and Flexibility*, Oxford: Basil Blackwell, pp. 1–25

Touraine, A. (1962), 'L'organisation professionnelle de l'entreprise' in G. Friedmann and P. Naville (eds) *Traité de sociologie du travail*, Paris: A. Colin

Treiman, D. and Hartmann, H. (eds) (1981), *Women, Work and Wages: Equal Pay for Jobs of Equal Value*, Committee on Occupational Classification and

Analysis, Assembly of Behavioural and Social Sciences, National Research Council, Washington, DC: National Academy Press

Troussier, J-F. (1987), 'Considerations on the Collective Dimension of Work', *New Technology, Work and Employment*, vol. 2, no. 1, pp. 37–46

Tsuda, M. (1987), 'Shin nijū kōzōjidai wa tōrai suruka?' (Is the Dual Structure Being Renewed?), *Nihon Rōdō Kyōkai Zasshi* (Monthly Organ of the Japan Institute of Labor), January issue, 1987, pp. 33–43

Turbin, J. (1988), 'State Intervention into the Labour Market for Youth: The Implementation of the Youth Training Scheme in Three Local Labour Markets', Ph.D., Leicester: University of Leicester

Uchiyama, T. (1982), *Sengo Nihon no Rōdōkatei* (Labour Process in Post-War Japan), Tokyo: San-ichi-schobō

Unterweger, P. (1983), *Work, Automation and the Economy*, paper given at the American Association for the Advancement of Science Annual Meeting, 27 May 1983, mimeo, Detroit: Michigan United Auto Workers, Research Department

Ure, A. (1858), *Philosophy of Manufacture*, London: C. Knight

US Congress, Office of Technology Assessment (1987), *International Competition in Services*, OTA-ITE-328, July 1987, pp. 228–9

US Department of Commerce (1976), *Foreign Direct Investment in the United States*, 9 vols, Washington, DC: Government Printing Office

US Department of Commerce, (1982), *Selected Data on U.S. Direct Investment Abroad, 1950–1976*, Washington, DC: Government Printing Office

Vanek, J. (1980), 'Time Spent in Housework' in A. Amsden (ed.) *The Economics of Women and Work*, Harmondsworth: Penguin, pp. 82–90

Varaiya, P. (1987), 'Productivity in Manufacturing and the Division of Mental Labor', paper presented to Symposium on Research and Development, Industrial Change and Economic Policy, University of Karlstad, 20–6 June, mimeo, Berkeley, Calif.: Department of Electricity Engineering and Computer Sciences, University of California, Berkeley

Vernon, R. (1960), *Metropolis 1985: An Interpretation of the Findings of the New York Metropolitan Region Study*, Cambridge, Mass.: Harvard University Press

Vernon, R. (1966), 'International Investment and International Trade in the Product Cycle', *Quarterly Journal of Economics*, vol. 53, no. 2, pp. 190–207

Vernon, R. (1974), 'The Location of Economic Activity' in J. H. Dunning (ed.) *Economic Analysis and the Multinational Enterprise*, New York: Praeger, pp. 89–114

Vernon, R. (1979), 'The Product Cycle Hypothesis in a New International Environment', *Oxford Bulletin of Economics and Statistics*, vol. 41, no. 4, pp. 255–67

Vinnicombe, S. (1980), *Secretaries, Management and Organizations*, London: Heinemann

Vonnegut, K. jnr (1952), *Player Piano*, New York: Dell Publishing

Vuskovic, P. (1980), 'Latin America and the Changing World Economy', *NACLA Report on the Americas*, vol. 14, no. 1, January–February

Walby, S. (1985), 'Spatial and Historical Variations in Women's Unemployment' in Lancaster Regionalism Group, *Localities, Class and Gender*, London: Pion

Walby, S. (1986), *Patriarchy at Work: Patriarchal and Capitalist Relations in Employment*, Cambridge: Polity

Walker, C. and Guest, R. (1976), *The Man on the Assembly Line*, Cambridge, Mass.: Harvard University Press

Walker, R. (1985a), 'Is There a Service Economy? The Changing Capitalist Division of Labor', *Science and Society*, vol. 49, pp. 42–83

Walker, R. (1985b), 'Technological Determination and Determinism in Industrial Growth and Location' in Manuel Castells (ed.), *High Technology, Space and Society*, Beverly Hills: Sage Publications, pp. 226–64

Walker, R. (1985c), 'Class, Division of Labor and Employment in Space' in D. Gregory and J. Urry (eds) *Social Structure and Spatial Relations*, London: Macmillan, pp. 164–89

Walker, R. (1988a), 'The Dynamics of Value, Price and Profit', *Capital and Class*, no. 35, pp. 146–81

Walker, R. (1988b), 'The Geographical Organization of Production Systems', *Society and Space (Environment and Planning D)*, forthcoming

Walker, R. and Storper, M. (1981), 'Capital and Industrial Location', *Progress in Human Geography*, vol. 5, pp. 473–509

Walton, R. (1985) 'From "Control" to "Commitment" in the Workplace', *Harvard Business Review*, vol. 63, no. 2, pp. 77–84

West, J. (1978), 'Women, Sex and Class' in A. Kuhn and A-M. Wolpe (eds) *Feminism and Materialism: Women and Modes of Production*, London: Routledge & Kegan Paul, pp. 220–53

Whitaker, A. (1986), 'Managerial Strategy and Industrial Relations: A Case Study of Plant Relocation', *Journal of Management Studies*, vol. 23, no. 6, pp. 657–78

Wickens, P. (1987), *The Road to Nissan*, London: Macmillan

Wild, R. (1975a), *Work Organization*, Bristol: John Wiley & Sons

Wild, R. (1975b), 'On the Selection of Mass Production Systems', *International Journal of Production Research*, vol. 13, no. 5, pp. 443–61

Wilkinson, B. (1983), *The Shopfloor Politics of New Technology*, London: Heinemann Educational Books

Williams, K., Cutler, T., Williams J. and Haslam, C. (1987), 'The End of Mass Production?', *Economy and Society*, vol. 16, no. 3, August, pp. 405–39

Williams, K., Williams, J. and Haslam, C. (1987), *The Breakdown of Austin Rover*, Leamington Spa: Berg

Williams, K., Williams, J., and Thomas, D. (1983), *Why are the British Bad at Manufacturing?*, London: Routledge & Kegan Paul

Williams, R. (1986), 'Negotiating the Introduction of New Manufacturing Technologies: Union and Management Strategies and Initiatives' in *Proceedings of The Third International Conference on Human Factors in Manufacturing*, Kempston: IFS Publications

Willman, P. and Winch, G. (1985), *Innovation and Management Control: Labour Relations at BL Cars*, Cambridge: Cambridge University Press

Windolf, P. (1985), 'Industrial Robots in the West German Automobile Industry', *Politics and Society*, vol. 14, no. 4, pp. 459–95

Wood, S. (1982), 'Introduction' in S. Wood (ed.), *The Degradation of Work?* London: Hutchinson, pp. 11–22

Wood, S. (1986), 'The Co-operative Labour Strategy in the US Auto Industry', *Economic and Industrial Democracy*, vol. 7, no.4, pp. 415–47

Wood, S. (1987), 'The Deskilling Debate: New Technology and Work Organization', *Acta Sociologica*, vol. 30, no. 1, pp. 3–24

Wood, S. (1988a), 'Between Fordism and Flexibility? The Case of the U.S. Car Industry' in R. Hyman and W. Streeck (eds) *Trade Unions, Technology and Industrial Democracy*, Oxford: Basil Blackwell, pp. 101–27

Wood, S. (1988b), 'From Braverman to Cyberman' in W. Buitelaar (ed.) *Technology and Work: Debates from England, Germany and Holland*, Aldershot: Avebury, pp. 24–42

Wood, S. (1988c), 'Some Observations on Industrial Relations in the British Car Industry 1985–87', in B. Dankbaar, U. Jürgens and T. Malsch (eds) *Die Zukunft der Arbeit in der Automobilindustrie*, West Berlin: Edition Sigma, pp. 229–48

Wood, S. (1989), 'The Japanese Management Model', *Work and Occupations*

Wood, S. and Kelly, J. (1982), 'Taylorism, Responsible Autonomy and Management Strategy' in S. Wood (ed.) *The Degradation of Work?*, London: Hutchinson, pp. 74–89

Yahata, S. (1987), 'Gegenwartiger Stand und Entwicklungsperspektiven von Kleingruppenaktivitaten in japanischen Automobilunternehmen', Ein Forschungsbericht des National Institute of Employment and Vocational Research; West Berlin: Wissenschaftszentrum (IIVf/re 87–206)

Yamamoto, K. (1980), 'Labour–Management Relations at Nissan Motor Co. Ltd', *Annals of the Institute of Social Science*, no. 21, University of Tokyo

Zeitlin, J. (1985), 'Engineers and Compositors: A Comparison' in R. Harrison and J. Zeitlin (eds) *Divisions of Labour: Skilled Workers and Technological Change in Nineteenth Century England*, Sussex: Harvester Press, pp. 185–250

Zimbalist, A. (1979), 'Technology and the Labor Process in the Printing Industry', in A. Zimbalist, (ed.) *Case Studies on the Labor Process*, New York: Monthly Review Press, pp. 103–26

Zimbalist, A. (ed.) (1979), *Case Studies on the Labor Process*, New York: Monthly Review Press,

Zussman, Y. E. (1983), 'Learning from the Japanese: Management in a Resource-Scarce World', *Organizational Dynamics*, vol. 11, no. 3, pp. 68–80

Index